Becoming Ottomans

Becoming Ottomans

Sephardi Jews and Imperial Citizenship in the Modern Era

JULIA PHILLIPS COHEN

OXFORD
UNIVERSITY PRESS

OXFORD
UNIVERSITY PRESS

Oxford University Press is a department of the University of Oxford.
It furthers the University's objective of excellence in research, scholarship,
and education by publishing worldwide.

Oxford   New York
Auckland   Cape Town   Dar es Salaam   Hong Kong   Karachi
Kuala Lumpur   Madrid   Melbourne   Mexico City   Nairobi
New Delhi   Shanghai   Taipei   Toronto

With offices in
Argentina   Austria   Brazil   Chile   Czech Republic   France   Greece
Guatemala   Hungary   Italy   Japan   Poland   Portugal   Singapore
South Korea   Switzerland   Thailand   Turkey   Ukraine   Vietnam

Oxford is a registered trade mark of Oxford University Press
in the UK and certain other countries.

Published in the United States of America by
Oxford University Press
198 Madison Avenue, New York, NY 10016

© Oxford University Press 2014

First issued as an Oxford University Press paperback, 2017

A portion of Chapter 2 is adapted from "Conceptions rivales du patriotism ottoman: les célébrations juives de
1892," in Esther Benbassa, ed., *Itinéraires sépharades: Complexité et diversité des identités* (Paris: Presses de
l'Université Paris-Sorbonne, 2010), 109–125, and is reprinted here with the permission of the Presses
universitaires de Paris-Sorbonne. Different sections of Chapter 3 appear in slightly altered form as "'Zeal and
Noise': Jewish Imperial Allegiance and the Greco-Ottoman War of 1897," in Michael Laskier and Yaacov Lev,
eds., *The Divergence of Judaism and Islam: Jews and Muslims in a Changing World* (Gainesville: University Press
of Florida, 2011), 29–50, reprinted with the permission of the University Press of Florida, and "Between
Civic and Islamic Ottomanism: Jewish Imperial Citizenship in the Hamidian Era," *International Journal of
Middle East Studies* 44, no. 2 (2012): 237–255, reprinted with the permission of Cambridge University Press.

Library of Congress Cataloging-in-Publication Data
Cohen, Julia Phillips, author.
Becoming Ottomans : Sephardi Jews and imperial citizenship in the modern era / Julia Phillips Cohen.
p.   cm.
Includes bibliographical references and index.
ISBN 978-0-19-934040-8 (hardcover); 978-0-19-061070-8 (paperback)
1. Jews—Turkey—History—19th century. 2. Jews—Turkey—Identity. 3. Jews—Cultural assimilation—
Turkey. 4. Sephardim—Turkey—History. 5. Jews—Turkey—Identity. 6. Turkey—Politics
and government. 7. Turkey—Ethnic relations. I. Title.
DS135.T8C64 2014
305.892'405609034—dc23   2013023272

To my parents and to Ben

CONTENTS

LIST OF ILLUSTRATIONS

PREFACE

In *The Souls of Black Folk*, published in 1903, W. E. B. Du Bois attempted to capture the experience of living as a black man in a racist society by asking "How does it feel to be a problem?"[1] Although Du Bois posed the question with the racial inequalities of the early twentieth-century United States in mind, it is also an apt point of departure for studies of Jews in modern Europe and beyond.[2] Indeed, by the nineteenth century, most states with significant Jewish populations—including a few with hardly any Jews—had developed their own version of a Jewish Question. Long before the rise of Nazism, European politicians, intellectuals, and activists alike debated how the problem Jews posed to their countries could be solved. Yet, for a variety of reasons that I seek to elucidate in the pages that follow, in the context of late Ottoman politics, Jews were rarely singled out as a "problem" community. Indeed, according to various nineteenth-century commentators, there was no Jewish Question in the Ottoman Empire.[3]

The approach I take here is therefore closer to the question Vijay Prashad has formulated about the experience of South Asians in the United States. Turning Du Bois's question on its head, Prashad asks "How does it feel to be a solution?"[4] The suggestion that South Asian Americans are both hardworking and pliant appears to offer the ultimate proof of the viability of the American dream, Prashad argues. "Successful" immigrant communities become the poster children for the country's multicultural claims, yet the proposal that certain groups have succeeded often carries with it an indictment of other groups who have not yet arrived. Assuming model status—becoming a solution, as Prashad puts it—makes sense only in relation to others who don't measure up.[5]

Rather than inquiring how it feels to be a solution, this book asks, "How does a community become a solution?" It seeks to reveal what the process of becoming a model community in the multi-lingual, multi-religious Ottoman

Empire entailed during its final half century of existence. What kind of work, alliances, compromises, and sacrifices did the process involve? How did Ottoman Jews find themselves in a position to claim "model minority" status?[6]

Becoming Ottomans is the first book to tell the unparalleled story of Jewish political integration into a modern Islamic empire. It begins with the process set in motion by the imperial state reforms known as the Tanzimat, which spanned the years 1839–1876 and legally emancipated the non-Muslims of the empire. Throughout this period, Jews remained little more than an afterthought in imperial politics. Even Abdülmecid's famous 1856 Reform Decree failed to mention them explicitly, referring instead only to "Christians and other non-Muslim communities" of the empire.[7] Four decades later the situation was difficult to recognize. By the close of the nineteenth century, Ottoman Muslims and Jews alike regularly referred to Jews as a model community, or *millet*—as a group whose leaders and members knew how to serve their state and were deeply engaged in Ottoman politics. This book charts this dramatic reversal, following the changing position of Jews in the empire over the course of half a century.

In presenting this story, *Becoming Ottomans* speaks to the emerging scholarship on modern forms of imperial citizenship. Until very recently, work on the late Ottoman Empire—much like studies of the other land-based empires that disappeared after the First World War—has portrayed the state's attempts to turn its subjects into imperial citizens as a failed project.[8] To support this position scholars cite the state's inability to conscript non-Muslims into the imperial army for over half a century after emancipating them.[9] Others point to the limited reach of the new imperial courts and schools, which continued to compete with parallel institutions run by different non-Muslim communities and foreign powers during the final century of Ottoman rule.[10] Yet, as this book shows, even in the absence of universal state education, courts, or military conscription—all institutions assumed to be crucial in producing citizens—Ottoman Jews collectively took it upon themselves to learn and teach each other how to become citizens of their empire.[11]

By exploring the kinds of negotiations imperial citizenship involved, this book joins a number of works that have begun to bridge the fields of Citizenship and Empire Studies. Although these fields have not always overlapped—due to citizenship scholars' tendency to focus on the nation-state and empire scholars' tendency to speak of subjects rather than citizens—this has recently begun to change: new work on areas ranging from French Mandate Syria to late Ottoman Palestine and the British Raj all reveal local citizenship discourses and practices where they were once ignored or thought impossible.[12] This book contributes to this literature by showing that the aspiration to imperial citizenship emerged much earlier than even these studies—which deal almost exclusively with the twentieth century—suggest. Indeed, already by the mid-nineteenth century, Ottoman Jews as well as other Ottomans across the empire had begun to attempt to understand, debate, and perform their newly acquired roles of imperial citizens.

Even in places where top-down imperial initiatives for political integration did not reach, I argue, Ottoman Jews—together with other Ottomans—fashioned their own form of patriotism from below.[13] The book therefore trains its focus away from formal state institutions to various other locales—ranging from Jewish communal newspapers, schools, synagogues, and social clubs to sites of inter-communal sociability, such as libraries, coffeehouses, and dance halls—in order to identify emerging forms of imperial citizenship that have escaped the attention of scholarship focused on the state's role in effecting change. Rather than treat these spaces as sites of resistance to, or apart from, the state, the book furthers recent lines of inquiry that investigate the porous boundaries between state and society in modern Middle Eastern contexts.[14] My approach has been inspired in particular by Elizabeth Thompson's concept of the civic order, which she defines as "the arena where state policy and political power are negotiated among soldiers, politicians, bureaucrats, and various social groups."[15] Understanding imperial citizenship as a series of negotiations between different parties, *Becoming Ottomans* traces the different strategies Ottoman Jewish communal leaders employed in order to promote their new patriotic project within an emerging imperial civic order, while also exploring how different audiences received the lessons in patriotism Jewish elites had to offer. It shows that Ottoman Jews created a mediated form of citizenship that has gone unrecognized by scholars of Ottoman history, who have left untapped a wealth of sources produced by Ottoman Jews during the final half century of the empire's existence.

Ultimately, the process of becoming a model *millet* was fraught with contradictions: as Ottoman Jews attempted to teach other Ottoman Jews how to become imperial citizens, they instilled in them the values of love of homeland, serving the greater good, and brotherhood (or less frequently, sisterhood) among Ottomans of all faiths. Yet, as they sought to prove to the authorities and to the Muslims of the empire that they were a model community with a special relationship to the state, they simultaneously competed with other groups for the attention of their government. Gaining visibility brought new complications. On the one hand, moving into the spotlight meant more scrutiny and thus, more pressure to live up to the new expectations of imperial citizenship. On the other hand, succeeding in earning the praise of imperial officials could also put new strains on Ottoman Jews' relations with other groups in the empire. Being a solution brought with it its own problems.

ACKNOWLEDGMENTS

Writing this book would not have been possible without the support of numerous people in various countries over the course of many years. At Stanford, Zachary Baker and Heidi Lerner guided my library searches and generously offered their time and expertise, while Vered Shemtov went above and beyond her role as Hebrew teacher to read and speak the language with me. There are not enough hot chocolates in the world to repay her. In Philadelphia, David and Deborah Sheby opened up their home to me, allowing me to explore the great wealth of *soletreo* postcards David has collected over the years. Bob Bedford of the Foundation for the Advancement of Sephardic Studies and Culture also shared his publications and unending enthusiasm for Sephardi history with me since we met many years ago. Anne-Sophie Cras of the Centre des Archives Diplomatiques in Nantes helped me to locate important documents, as did Gerhard Keiper of the Auswärtiges Amt, Politisches Archiv in Berlin. Beatrice Schmidt and Manuela Cimeli in Basel gave me access to hard-to-come-by materials from the Viennese Sephardi community, for which I am grateful.

In Paris, Esther Benbassa invited me into her home and offered advice about my project during its earliest stages. Rose Levyne and Jean-Claude Kuperminc guided my research in the archives of the Alliance Israélite Universelle on various occasions. I am indebted to Gaëlle Collin for finding, and helping me find, countless books and documents, as well as for her generosity and friendship over the past decade. Pandelis Mavrogiannis has proved a lively interlocuter on the various occasions we have had to meet in his adopted city. More recently, Marie-Christine Varol shared her research and personal archives with me and regaled me with stories, songs, and jokes culled from her many decades of fieldwork with Ladino speakers in the Balat District of Istanbul and beyond.

In Salonica, Angelos Chotzidis guided me through the collections of the Museum for the Macedonian Struggle, as did Erika Perahia Zemour in the city's Jewish Museum. Yannis Megas also generously shared with me various citations and rare Jewish periodicals from Salonica that make up part of his private collection. Rena Molho provided advice and insights into Salonican Jewish history. Paris Papamichos Chronakis offered me personalized tours of his country, city, and bookshelves in search of forgotten Sephardi pasts, making my trip to Greece both invaluable and unforgettable. Although I met him in the United States, Isaac Nehama has also opened various Greek pasts for me, not least by translating a number of Greek-language documents that were relevant to this project, but also through the many stories he shared of his own early years in Athens and as a partisan in Thessaly during the Second World War.

My many trips to Turkey over the course of a decade have also been enriched by the support and friendship of numerous people. In Izmir, the Hazan family offered me copies of original newspapers published by their relative Aron de Yosef Hazan over a century ago. In Istanbul, Karen Sarhon at the Research Center for Ottoman-Turkish Sephardic Culture provided assistance early on. My first summers spent in Istanbul were made particularly special by visits to the home of Rıfat Birmizrahi and his late wife, who opened up their home and cooked traditional Sephardi meals for me while permitting me to sift through the Hebrew and Ladino library of Rıfat's father. Rıfat Bali has guided my research over the course of many years, offering his unmatched bibliographic expertise on modern Turkish Jewish history, providing me with books old and new, and, along with his wife Beti, also becoming a dear friend. More recently, Selcuk Aydın of Atatürk Kitaplığı, Ümit Sevgi of the IFEA library, and Fuad Bey of the Başbakanlık Osmanlı Arşivi all facilitated my work in a number of ways. I am extremely grateful to Abdullah Uğur for his many years as my research assistant, Ottoman tutor, tour guide, and friend. Thanks are also due to Sevim Yılmaz Önder, Elif Özcan, and Esra Derya Dilek for guiding me through the long and often arduous journey of Ottoman paleography and, more recently, to Esra for research assistance as well. Making the acquaintance of Ceyda Arslan and Vangelis Kechriotis while studying Turkish at Boğaziçi University was fortuitious and has led to many fruitful exchanges. I am also grateful to Vangelis for introducing me to Noémi Lévy, whose work on the Greco-Ottoman War of 1897 in Salonica inspired one of the present chapters of this book. Mukaram Hhana, Catalina Hunt, and Alan Mikhail all graciously provided me with archival and bibliographic material from Istanbul when I could not make the journey myself. Thanks are also due to Alan for providing invaluable advice over the years and for inspiring me to cross the bridge from Stanford to U.C. Berkeley many years ago for a graduate seminar with Leslie Peirce—who encouraged and supported me during my early forays into Ottoman history.

In Israel, Shmuel Rafael and the staff at the Naime & Yehoshua Salti Center for Ladino Studies at Bar-Ilan University always offered a warm welcome. In Jerusalem, I spent many months at the Central Archives for the History of the Jewish People, the Jewish National University Library and—most of all—immersed in Ladino materials at the Ben-Zvi Institute. To all of the staff at these institutions I would like to express my gratitude, but especially to Eli Ben-Yosef, who has the amazing capacity to make a trip to the archives feel like a reunion of old friends, to Dov Cohen, who knows more about Ladino books than anyone I am ever likely to meet, and to Esther Guggenheim, who probably learned more about Ladino materials during my year in the city than she ever would have planned. I would also like to extend my thanks to Avner Perez, who provided me with materials from his collection. I was lucky enough to meet David Ashkenazi, who sat and read through numerous letters contained in the collections of Istanbul's chief rabbinate with me. Thanks are also due to Professor Yaron Harel, for generously giving me permission to peruse his research team's catalogued version of this collection. Yaron Ben-Naeh graciously welcomed me into his classroom at the Hebrew University and exposed me to a new world of plurilingual Sephardi texts. I am also grateful for having met Eliezer Papo, a vivacious person and a veritable walking repository of linguistic and cultural knowledge about the Balkan Sephardi world he knows so intimately.

During the many years I pursued this project, I have benefited from the insights and questions of participants in various workshops and conferences. These include the "Bridging the Worlds of Judaism and Islam" conference convened by Michael Laskier and Yaacov Lev at Bar-Ilan University; a Ladino Studies Program talk at the Hebrew University organized by David Bunis; the workshop "Late Ottoman Port Cities and their Inhabitants" at the 8th Mediterranean Research Meeting of the European University Institute organized by Vangelis Kechriotis and Malte Fuhrmann; the Group for the Study of the History of the Jews of Greece, convened by Giorgos Antoniou, Rika Benveniste, Tony Molho, and Paris Papamichos Chronakis in Salonica; the Jewish Studies Series with ME/SA at the University of California, Davis; the Works in Progress Workshop at the Association for Jewish Studies, run by Claire Sufrin and Adam Shear; the "Itinéraires Sépharades" Conference at the Sorbonne convened by Esther Benbassa and Aron Rodrigue; the Jewish Studies Program at the University of South Carolina; an Ottoman-Sephardic workshop at Georgetown University organized by Sylvia Önder; the "Jews and Empire" Symposium convened by Sarah Abrevaya Stein at UCLA; the Charles Phelps Taft Research Center at the University of Cincinnati; the University of Chicago's Symposium on Modern Jewish and Israeli History, coordinated by

Orit Bashkin and Leora Auslander; an "Ottoman Citizenships" panel at Florida State University organized by Will Hanley; the "Jews and Empire" Lavy Colloquium at Johns Hopkins University convened by Marina Rustow and Kenneth Moss; and the "Sefarad an der Donau" Symposium in Vienna, organized by Michael Studemund-Halévy. I am especially indebted to Michael for bringing me to Vienna and introducing me to the world of Sephardi Studies in Europe.

I am grateful to my many, wonderful colleagues at Vanderbilt, who have offered me their support and invaluable advice since I joined the faculty in the fall of 2008. Special thanks are due to Allison Schachter and Catherine Molineux for invaluable input and to Leah Marcus, Shaul Kelner, Liz Lunbeck, and Jim Epstein, my chairs in the Program in Jewish Studies and the Department of History. Jim Toplon and the entire Interlibrary Loan staff at Vanderbilt have been tremendously helpful in aiding me in searches that often spanned the globe. Tamesha Derico and Nick Schaser provided research assistance and spent long hours in front of microfilm machines. Lindsey Bunt helped catch errors at the eleventh hour.

For their generous support of this project, I am thankful to the Taube Center at Stanford University, the National Foundation for Jewish Culture, the Memorial Foundation for Jewish Culture, the Stanford Humanities Center and Mellon Foundation, the Tauber Institute for the Study of European Jewry at Brandeis University, the Institute for Turkish Studies, the American Research Institute in Turkey, a Foreign Language and Area Studies grant for Turkish study at Boğaziçi University, a UCLA Maurice Amado Program Faculty Incentive Grant, and Vanderbilt's RSG summer and fellowship funding.

It was a tremendous privilege to have the chance to work with a number of wonderful mentors during the formative stages of this project. Aron Rodrigue has remained a dedicated teacher and inspiring interlocutor for over a decade, and I owe him my sincerest thanks for his time, insights, and continued encouragement and support. Steve Zipperstein has trained me not only to be a Jewish historian, but also to search for ways to bring creativity and the beneficial influences of other disciplines into the writing of history. Together, he and Aron have been a wonderful team and a source of incessant support to me. Toward the end of my graduate career, serendipity brought me a third advisor, Elizabeth Frierson, who, like Aron and Steve before her, I count as a lifelong mentor. Elizabeth's incisive and careful readings of my work have pushed me in new directions and forced me to ask new questions and will, no doubt, continue to do so in the future.

I am also indebted to Sebouh Aslanian, Olga Borovaya, David Bunis, Michelle Campos, Paris Papamichos Chronakis, Paula Daccarett, Michal Friedman, Emily Greble, Esther Juhasz, Matthias Lehmann, Amalia Skarlatou

Levi, Lital Levy, Nazan Maksudyan, Vivian Mann, Bedross Der Matossian, Kenneth Moss, Devin Naar, Derek Penslar, Sarah Abrevaya Stein, Darin Stephanov, and Claire Sufrin, as well as two anonymous readers, all of whom have provided me with countless references, suggestions, and questions during different stages of this project. Olga in particular has been there from the earliest stages—although we still can't settle on the exact date—first as a teacher and mentor, more recently also as a co-author, and always as a cherished friend. During the final stages of this project, I also had the great pleasure of working with Susan Ferber. I could not have asked for a more engaged or insightful editor and I am deeply indebted to her for her careful readings and guidance throughout the publication processs. Max Richman and Smita Gupta were instrumental in shepherding the book through production. I am grateful to both of them for their input and help preparing my manuscript. My mother, Margaret Phillips, has offered detailed readings of much of my work, and has been a source of constant support, as has my father, Ronald Cohen, and the rest of my family and friends. For enriching my life in ways I cannot even begin to enumerate, I extend my sincerest gratitude to all of them. Finally, I would like to thank Ari Joskowicz, who joined my life partway into this project but whose role in helping me advance it has been tremendous. For your intellectual companionship, thoughtful questions, and so much more, thank you.

NOTES ON TRANSLITERATION

For over four centuries, Jews in Ottoman southeastern Europe and the Levant spoke and wrote in an Ibero-Romance language grammatically akin to fifteenth-century Castilian but encompassing loan words from various other languages, including Italian, Portuguese, French, Hebrew, and Turkish. Traditionally printed in the Rashi Hebrew script and penned in the *soletreo* handwriting style, it has been known by different names, including Judeo-Spanish, Judezmo, and Ladino. I employ the term Ladino here, as has become common practice in English-language works on the subject. I have chosen the Aki Yerushalayim transcription system, which reflects Ladino pronunciation—with the exception of names that commonly appear in scholarly works in other forms (e.g., Fresco rather than Fresko). In transliterating Ottoman Turkish sources, I use a simplified version of the system of the *International Journal of Middle East Studies*. For Hebrew and Greek, I use the Library of Congress system, but without diacritics and applying phonetic guidelines.

Where relevant, place names have been rendered according to their modern Turkish variants but in the English alphabet (e.g., Istanbul rather than Constantinople; Izmir rather than Smyrna) or according to commonly accepted English versions of place names (e.g., Salonica instead of Thessaloniki). In cases where Ottoman words are widely used in English, I have opted for the English version (e.g. Pasha rather than Paşa).

Unless otherwise noted, all dates are in the Gregorian calendar. Those dates that appear in either the Hebrew, Islamic, or Ottoman fiscal calendrical systems are followed by their Gregorian equivalents in brackets.

Becoming Ottomans

Introduction

Becoming a Model Millet

In the spring of 1992, a foundation headed by Turkish Jewish and Muslim entrepreneurs organized various public events and sponsored a host of publications, lectures, and travel itineraries marking five hundred years of Turkish-Jewish "friendship."[1] Calling their new organization the Quincentennial Foundation, its members suggested that their aim was to "broadcast as fully as possible, both at home and abroad, the humane approach the Turkish nation [displayed] in opening its arms" to the Jews who fled the Spanish expulsion in 1492 and who "chose to make their new homeland on Turkish soil."[2] In the words of one of the Quincentennial Foundation's publications, the Jews of Turkey felt profound gratitude to the Turkish state because its Ottoman predecessor had "extended the hand of friendship to a persecuted minority of faith and culture different from its own."[3]

Jews and others have been telling different versions of this story of Ottoman-Jewish relations for a very long time. In a sense, it is recognizable even beyond its specific Ottoman context, as Jewish expressions of attachment to the empire's sultans over the ages offer an example of the royal alliance scenario so familiar to Jewish history.[4] More concretely, the narrative of a special Ottoman-Jewish relationship dates to the early modern era, when different Jewish chroniclers praised the empire for receiving Jewish refugees when no one else would have them.[5] For these authors, the idea of a special Ottoman-Jewish relationship forged in the wake of the Spanish expulsion was a story of redemption meant to console those who had lived through the trauma. Starting in the nineteenth century, the same narrative became central to Ottoman Jews' attempts to turn their coreligionists into model Ottoman patriots during a period of dizzying change. In an era marked by the social and political reordering of Ottoman society, territorial losses, and the empire's increasing incorporation into the global economy, the idea of the unbreakable bond Ottomans and Jews had forged in the wake of 1492 was particularly appealing to Ottoman

Jewish elites, who sought to smooth over the ruptures their relationship with the state had suffered in the interim. Today, once again, political tensions and opportunities in modern Turkey and beyond have made it opportune to speak of the long continuities of Turkish Jews' love for their state.

For all its changing uses, the narrative of Ottoman-Jewish (and later Turkish-Jewish) friendship is built upon a set of common tropes, the most important of which is the image of the Ottoman Empire as a safe haven for Jewish refugees and a place of unprecedented tolerance where Jews and Muslims formed a special bond during centuries of coexistence. Through their frequent repetition, these tropes of Ottoman-Jewish history have not only taken on the aura of unquestionable truth, they have also concealed other stories that have not served the agendas of different authors throughout the ages. The historian Yosef Hacker has made this point forcefully by demonstrating that Ottoman and Jewish historians' continued reliance on the writings of a small number of early modern Jewish chroniclers who were sympathetic to the Ottoman state has obscured Jews' negative experiences of Ottoman rule during the empire's earliest centuries. Having uncovered forgotten accounts of Jews who lamented their treatment at the hands of Ottoman authorities—including those who suffered from the state's attempts to repopulate newly conquered areas through forced relocation policies—Hacker suggests that later authors silenced such stories because they seemed less threatening than the challenges facing their community during their own lifetime. Subsequent depictions of the Ottoman Empire as a place of refuge were always simultaneously a denunciation of the Christian kingdoms that had chased Jews out of their realms. Portraying the Ottomans as a foil to the persecutory regimes of Europe left little room for nuance.[6]

As a result, most histories of the Ottoman-Jewish encounter have focused on the Jews who arrived in the empire as refugees from Iberia rather than the Jewish communities who lived in the region prior to Ottoman rule. This selective approach to Ottoman Jewish history has reinforced the impression that the empire served as a haven for Jews—a country they encountered by choice rather than by conquest. This narrative also largely effaced the history of the Jewish communities that had lived in the area before the Ottomans arrived on the scene—such as the Greek-speaking Romaniot Jews of the eastern Mediterranean basin and the Arabic-speaking communities spread across the empire—as well as those who found their way to the empire for reasons entirely unrelated to the Iberian expulsion. It also allowed the Judeo-Spanish communities of the empire's European and Anatolian provinces to stand in for Ottoman Jewry as a whole, permitting authors who spoke of a special *Jewish* relationship to the Ottoman Empire to conjure visions of an imagined special *Sephardi* relationship to the empire, and vice versa.

By the second half of the nineteenth century, Jewish scholars and communal elites from the predominantly Sephardi centers of Istanbul, Izmir, and Salonica drew upon this small repertoire of historical narratives in order to convince their coreligionists of their longstanding special relationship to the Ottoman state. This chain of transmission—from early modern chroniclers to modern Ottoman Jewish scholars and constituencies—created the illusion of a static story. It conveniently placed Jews at the center of an unchanging alliance with their state, masking what was in fact a complex, multi-layered, and constantly changing dynamic between the Ottoman authorities and Jewish communities over the many centuries of the empire's existence.

Contrary to the statements modern Ottoman Jews pronounced time and again—and to the impression that has remained largely undisturbed until this day—there were moments when the bonds Jews had with the Ottoman government were by no means guaranteed. This was certainly the case during the reign of Bayezid II from 1481 to 1512—the very same sultan who welcomed Iberian Jewish refugees "with open arms," as so many versions would have it. Bayezid II not only encouraged Jewish refugees to settle in his domains, but also spearheaded campaigns directed against newly opened synagogues and applied significant pressures on Jews to convert to Islam.[7]

The messianic fervor that surrounded Shabbatay Sevi in the seventeenth century offers yet another example of uneasy relations between the Ottoman state and its Jewish population. It was not simply the hubris of the messianic pretender that so disturbed Sultan Mehmed IV, but also the fact that his numerous Jewish followers—the sultan's own subjects—had taken to calling Sevi their king and to disregarding the laws of the land.[8] The messianic hopes surrounding Sevi reportedly led Jews to expect the imminent fall of not only "all of the crowns of Christendom" but also "of the Crescent."[9] Indeed, historian Marc Baer has suggested that Shabbatay Sevi's appearance "could not have come at a worse time for the Jewish elite in Istanbul" since it "confirmed for the Ottomans that Jews were untrustworthy and helped convince them to turn to the Jews' rivals, Orthodox Christians, as the two groups struggled for positions of power and influence."[10] The precariousness of Ottoman Jews' position in the midst of the Sabbatean upheaval was not lost on them. Some began to suggest that they faced an impending massacre unless they turned their new leader over to the authorities. Although "sundry miracles and celestial warning" saved them from this gruesome fate, even by their own accounts, Jews' positions in the empire had clearly been compromised in the process.[11] Taken together, these examples make clear that Ottoman-Jewish relations were more complex—and at times significantly more troubled—than the most popular versions of their history have made them out to be.[12]

Put simply, the story of the special Ottoman-Jewish relationship is a myth. By labeling it thus, I do not mean to suggest that those who penned the myriad documents or gave the countless speeches testifying to the special nature of Ottoman-Jewish relations were insincere. Rare glimpses into the private lives of late Ottoman Jews indicate the extent to which they internalized their identification with the empire. Ritual objects featuring the crescent and star of the empire and stylized representations of the sultan's calligraphic Arabic signature, or *tuğra*, bear witness to this trend (Figures 0.1–0.4).[13]

Yet the aim of the book is to present the story of Jewish allegiance to the Ottoman state not as the history of a sentiment, but rather as the history of a process and a project. That project was born in the nineteenth century in response to a complex set of new socio-political and legal realities, even as it borrowed from earlier narratives of Ottoman-Jewish history. Indeed, even the habit of integrating crescents and *tuğras* into the design of Jewish ceremonial art appears to have been a modern phenomenon sparked by the new expectations and promises of imperial citizenship; no examples of this style are known to date before the nineteenth century. Neither the historical narratives nor the material culture that Ottoman Jews left behind offer evidence of their uninterrupted love affair with the Ottoman state. Patriotism had to be taught and learned, and, later, maintained and managed.

In order to explore the ways that different Jewish elites—including lay and religious leaders, journalists, schoolteachers, merchants, and charitable women—crafted an ideal image of their communities in response to their new patriotic project, *Becoming Ottomans* analyzes a series of historical moments (two wars, an invented holiday, a world's fair, and a sultan's tour) that provide important clues about the worlds of late Ottoman Sephardi communities. It sets out to understand how Jews in Salonica, Izmir, and Istanbul—the three largest Judeo-Spanish population centers of the empire—chose to represent themselves in print and in public at various moments, and the messages they sent about their place within their empire as they did so.[14]

The book also examines how these Jewish leaders were received by Jewish audiences of different cities, ages, classes, genders, and political persuasions, as well as by non-Jews within the empire and abroad. Drawing upon such a wide array of perspectives and sources allows for an analysis of what anthropologist James Scott has called the "public transcripts" of the different events under study as well as the "hidden transcripts" that inevitably accompany them.[15] The various political performances explored in the book provide rich examples of the public image different historical actors crafted and labored to uphold while also offering hints about what happened offstage. Imperial citizenship, as it emerges in the pages that follow, was not merely a legal category, but also a process of continual individual and collective self-invention. The forces that

Figure 0.1 Jewish marriage contract (*ketubah*) from Haifa, 1893—Ben-Zvi Institute, *ketubah* no. 815b.

Figure 0.2 Prayer shawl (*talit*) from Istanbul, 5658 (1897/1898)—Courtesy of the Quincentennial Foundation Museum of Turkish Jews.

Figure 0.3 Silver spice tower, Turkey, nineteenth or twentieth century—Courtesy of the Jewish Museum London.

Figure 0.4 Jewish marriage contract (*ketubah*) from Rodosto (Tekirdağ), 5676 (1915/1916)—Courtesy of the Quincentennial Foundation Museum of Turkish Jews.

set this process in motion converged in the early nineteenth century, as the Ottoman government began the dramatic reorganization of its state administration and as Jewish leaders in the empire sought new means of raising the public profile of their community.

From Rupture to Rapprochement

By the eighteenth century, Ottoman Jews had begun to lose hold of many of the economic niches they had filled during earlier centuries, including their once important role in textile production, international commerce, and at court.[16] Various accounts also suggest that in the hierarchy of Ottoman religious communities, Jews often ranked at the bottom.[17] The demographic situation of Ottoman Jews no doubt contributed to their relative invisibility to imperial state administrators. Compared to the Greek Orthodox and Armenian communities, composed of some 2,000,000 and 2,400,000 souls, respectively, in the mid-nineteenth century, the number of Jews in the empire never reached above 500,000.[18] Smaller than other non-Muslim communities, impoverished, and lacking foreign protectors, Ottoman Jews do not seem to have garnered either the particular favor or the special concern of the Sublime Porte during this period.[19] Indeed, various contemporary anecdotes reinforce the impression that, by the early nineteenth century, Jews were often little more than an afterthought in imperial politics.[20]

There were exceptions to the Porte's benign neglect of the Jews, however. In the 1820s, Istanbul's Jewish community saw a number of leading Jewish businessmen murdered at the behest of the sultan, Mahmud II.[21] The first of these was Yehezkel Gabbay, Mahmud II's chief moneychanger, who was an ally of the increasingly unwieldy Janissary Corps. His connections with the Janissaries, together with his ongoing rivalry with the lessee of the royal mint, an Armenian Ottoman subject named Kazaz Artin led to his demise. In 1823 Gabbay was exiled to the Ottoman city of Antalya, where he was killed.[22] Then, in 1826, as Sultan Mahmud II took steps to streamline the Ottoman military, he purged the infamous Janissary Corps and had two other Jewish communal leaders who were financially attached to the institution executed.[23] For a community already struggling economically, this spelled disaster.[24] Thousands of Jews who had in one way or another been tied to a Janissary-based economy were left without a livelihood, while the Jewish community lost its most prominent leaders almost overnight.[25]

There may have been more to the murder of the Jewish leaders than their connection to the Janissary Corps. Certain scholars indicate that the Ottoman government did away with the Jewish bankers in order to transfer their substantial wealth to the coffers of the imperial treasury.[26] Others have attributed the murders to ongoing competition between influential members of different Ottoman religious communities, noting that Armenian bankers moved in to fill the positions of the executed Jews.[27] Yet it is difficult to know if the Jews of the Ottoman capital who tried to grasp the events that unfolded before their eyes were privy to the inner-palace intrigues or the treasury concerns of the state.

The evidence Ottoman Jews left behind suggests that they considered the death of their leaders at the hands of the government inexplicable and unjust. This interpretation can be seen in a dirge Ottoman Jews produced in the wake of the murder of the Jewish bankers. In the capital's synagogues, the reading of the dirge on *Tisha B'Av*, a somber day of mourning in the Hebrew calendar, became an annual ritual. "We have been orphaned," it proclaims, noting that Chelebi Behor Carmona (one of the three executed men) "was famous throughout the world, and the crown of the Jews. Adjiman [yet another of those executed] came second only to him." The elegy continues, "You were not ill, my precious Behoradji / you left . . . so quickly, for no sin of your own, you were not guilty." The tradition treated the betrayal of the leaders as entirely senseless. So, the dirge explained, Ottoman Jews turned "to the Heavens, asking for justice." However subtle, there was something potentially subversive in this last line. Calling upon a higher authority, the lamentation asks that justice might be meted out. But to whom? The state? Or to some of its representatives? Another verse conveyed just how powerful and lasting the events of 1826 appeared to the Jews of the Ottoman capital who composed the poem: "We cry and lament, the evil that befell us," it read, "Even if we live 1,000 years, we will not forget this."[28]

The memory of these events clearly persisted well beyond the generation that lived through them. The dirge was reportedly still circulating around the city's synagogues when the Ottoman Jewish scholar and schoolteacher Moïse Franco recorded it in the late nineteenth century. Those who visited the Jewish cemetery in the Kuzguncuk district of Istanbul could similarly find reference to the trauma Mahmud II had inflicted upon Ottoman Jews during his purges. Making reference to Psalms 94:1 and 79:10, the tombstone of the murdered Yehezkel Gabbay called for revenge: "Wreak your vengeance, O God! / Avenge the blood of Your servant, which has been spilt," it read. His son Nissim's grave also points to the continuing disquiet felt by the Jewish community after the unnatural deaths of so many of their leaders, bearing the words: "Blessed be He who decrees, God who knows [all] / But I shall investigate the cause of these tribulations that have befallen us / Why the light of my sun no longer shines."[29] Meanwhile, across the city, in the Jewish cemetery of Balat, local Jews maintained a special plot said to hold the bodies of "those murdered by the sultan."[30]

The execution of their leaders served as a cautionary tale to Jews in the empire. The historian Salomon Rosanes, writing in the early part of the twentieth century, explained Ottoman Jews' response to the 1826 trauma thus: "From that time on, the Jews, in their fear [of the authorities], excused themselves from assuming dangerous responsibilities for the government. . . . Many days passed without one Jew in the service of the state."[31] The rupture of 1826 clearly left a scar on the leadership of the Jewish community and also damaged its standing vis-à-vis the Ottoman government.[32] Later attempts to forge ties with the Sublime Porte and at the same time to claim their unbroken nature were thus attempts at rapprochement with the state dressed up in the guise of continuity.

Nineteenth-Century Reforms and New Ottoman Jewish Realities

Legend has it that sometime in the early nineteenth century the Ottoman sultan Mahmud II (r. 1808–1839) announced his vision for the future of his empire with the words "Muslims in the mosque, Christians in the church, and Jews in the synagogue," implying that the public differences between the Ottoman communities were destined to recede with time, as the spirit of a new era overtook his realm.[33] Although scholars differ as to exactly when (and whether) Mahmud II pronounced these words, their vision of a shared imperial identity did make its way into a sumptuary law Mahmud II promulgated in 1829.[34] The law dictated that all civil servants should from that point on wear a fez, frock coat, and tailored pants as a new, official uniform designed for men across the empire.

The new dress code promised to make the differences between different Ottoman groups invisible in public.[35] By attempting to erase the visual distinctions that had once separated imperial subjects according to religion, class, and profession, the law offered new possibilities to non-Muslim men, many of whom reportedly adopted the fez with great enthusiasm.[36] Not all imperial subjects were so eager to change their sartorial patterns; many resisted the new measure, from the lower and working classes, who often retained their professional or religious headgear, to the upper classes, who preferred to flaunt the latest fashions from Europe.[37] Although the effects of the decree remained limited, the concept of equality and the impulse to erase difference reflected in Mahmud II's clothing laws represented a radical departure from previous imperial policies.

Within a decade, in 1839, Mahmud II's successor Sultan Abdülmecid promulgated the Hatt-ı Şerif of Gülhane, or the Noble Rescript of the Rose Chamber, inaugurating the Tanzimat ("Reordering") period of reforms.[38] Drafted by the influential Ottoman reformer and bureaucrat Mustafa Reşid Pasha, the decree guaranteed the life, honor, and property of all Ottoman subjects regardless of religion. It also boasted a new vocabulary of patriotism and imperial citizenship, signaling the state's concern with assuring its subjects' attachment to "state and nation," and to fostering within them "a growing zeal" and "rising affection" for their fatherland.[39] Although this language pointed to the Ottoman authorities' interest in widening the imperial body politic to include non-Muslims, certain passages in the edict remained ambiguous, leaving open the question of whether the "nation" to which subjects owed their loyalty was a newly imagined Ottoman community or their particular religious group.[40] Later bureaucratic and administrative reforms of the Tanzimat period would never completely resolve this tension, as they often reinforced rather than unraveled the corporate existence of the non-Muslim *millets*, even as they asked their members to announce their allegiance to the state as individuals. Such tensions notwithstanding, Abdülmecid's decree offered new possibilities for thinking about equality and imperial belonging for all groups in the empire.[41]

In 1856, Abdülmecid introduced a second Reform Decree, the Islahat Fermanı (also known as the Hatt-ı Hümayun), which was significantly more wide ranging and radical in the changes it announced for Ottoman society. Appearing in the final stages of the Crimean War, the decree took shape in part due to internal pressure for reform at the Porte and in part due to the pressures the Ottomans' French and British allies exerted on the empire in exchange for their support in the empire's fight against Russia. Written in the form of an address by Sultan Abdülmecid to his Grand Vizier Mehmed Emin Ali Pasha, the edict bore the imprint of European statesmen who hoped to obtain new rights for Ottoman Christians.[42] Fearing that their coreligionists in Ottoman realms might be left out of the process, European Jewish leaders interceded to ensure that any new measures taken on behalf of Christians would include Jews as well.[43]

The resulting edict not only proclaimed all Ottoman subjects to be "united . . . by the cordial ties of patriotism" and equal in the sultan's eyes, it also offered practical solutions for how equality might be measured and regulated.[44] Among these was its announcement that any "distinction or appellation tending to render any class whatsoever . . . inferior to another class because of religion, language, or race, shall be forever erased from administrative protocol."[45] The decree similarly declared government schools and service open to all Ottoman subjects, regardless of religion, "providing they otherwise satisfy the conditions of age and examination requirements," including knowledge of the language of the state. In the midst of the reforms, non-Muslims also gained the right to serve in the Ottoman army on a voluntary basis.[46] New legal definitions of Ottoman citizenship emerged soon after, first in select Ottoman provinces and later as an empire-wide measure with the 1869 Citizenship Law, which declared all those born in the empire Ottoman citizens unless they offered proof to the contrary.[47] That same year the Regulation of General Education outlined a new civil school system open to all Ottomans.[48]

All of these developments laid the foundation for the creation of an equal Ottoman citizenry undifferentiated by religion. In their wake, inhabitants of the empire found themselves confronted with a new framework for understanding their world. This framework—often referred to as Ottomanism—was based on the assumption that all of the various religious and ethnic communities of the empire would unite in support of their homeland.

Although the new legal reforms applied equally to all non-Muslims in the empire, the situation of Ottoman Jews was unique in one important respect. The pressures Ottoman Jews felt from the state coincided with other forces that encouraged them to consider serving their country in new ways. Unlike their Greek Orthodox, Armenian, or Bulgarian neighbors, Ottoman Jews' contacts with foreign coreligionists who appeared in the empire as "interested outsiders" did not introduce the ideals of irredentism or separatist nationalism. Although scholars have suggested that the vast network of Franco-Jewish Alliance Israélite Universelle schools established across the empire ultimately alienated their pupils from their local surroundings by instilling in them a love of France and French culture, the organization's official aim was to create good, active, and loyal Jewish citizens wherever it found them. Later, when foreign Zionists arrived on the scene, they declared their commitment to preserving the territorial integrity of the empire, suggesting that their goal was nothing other than the creation of an autonomous Jewish center in Ottoman Palestine. For Ottoman Jews, the messages the Ottoman state and their foreign brethren sent were one and the same. Ottoman Jewry had no counternarrative to empire.[49]

Indeed, ever since the Porte made gestures toward emancipating its non-Muslim populations, European Jews had begun to actively involve themselves in the lives of their Ottoman coreligionists in the hopes of making them useful imperial citizens worthy of their recently gained equality. By the time the Alliance Israélite Universelle introduced its first school in the empire in 1865, Ottoman Jewry was embarking on a steady course of transformation.[50] Soon, much of the Ottoman Jewish elite identified with European bourgeois standards of behavior. Imagining that French-Jewish models of integration into the French nation-state could be applied to Jews of the empire, the directors and instructors of the new Alliance schools were convinced that it was their duty to teach their Eastern brethren how to become modern, civilized, upright members of their society. Confronting novel vocabularies and practices of patriotism and citizenship, Ottoman Jews began to propagate new discourses of belonging as they attempted to work out what a shared imperial identity might entail.

The process was not seamless. The western modes French Jews hoped would take root among imperial Jewish communities were superimposed onto very different foundations. In the end, Ottoman Jewish leaders came to shape their patriotic project according to ideas of personal obligation and belonging to a nation-state, while at the same time imbuing these notions with uniquely Ottoman characteristics: As they spoke of the new responsibilities Ottoman citizenship required of them as individuals, Ottoman Jewish leaders attempted to effect this change from within the framework of their particular religious community, or *millet*. Their vision—in short—was meant to bring about a radical reorientation of Jews' loyalties to their state and fellow citizens while at the same time leaving the Jewish community intact.

Meanwhile, the Ottoman statesmen who attempted to advance much of the Tanzimat legislation met with resistance from various realms.[51] The new laws were applied unevenly for some time, and plans to organize universal conscription and education did not materialize.[52] State schools ultimately attracted an overwhelmingly Muslim student body, while communal and missionary schools continued to serve principally non-Muslim pupils. Statistics from the late Ottoman period also indicate that even those non-Muslims who attended imperial schools or secured government employment were less likely than Muslims to climb the ranks of the bureaucracy.[53] Even more than other non-Muslim groups, Jews faced obstacles to entering state service, as few among them were proficient in Ottoman, the language of imperial officialdom.[54] Indeed, throughout the nineteenth century, Jewish observers decried the absence of Jewish individuals in state institutions, from the imperial School of Medicine to the Senate.[55] Despite the efforts of Jewish communal leaders, activists, teachers, and journalists to propagate the Ottoman language among their coreligionists, their efforts had limited effect.[56]

Although the vast majority of Ottoman Jews in the nineteenth century encountered state patriotism in mediated form—through their newspapers, communal schools, charitable societies, and synagogues—a small but select group began to enter state-run schools during the second half of the nineteenth century, thereby preparing themselves to join the ranks of a newly emerging class of government employees.[57] Among these were graduates from the Medical School, where twenty-four Jewish pupils were in attendance by 1847.[58] Under the reign of Abdülmecid, the school set up a kosher kitchen and special place of prayer that would accommodate Jewish students.[59] After 1856, military schools also opened to non-Muslims, allowing their entrance into the empire's military and naval academies for the first time.[60]

The movement of Jews into civil and military positions—however insignificant in number—helped Ottoman Jews forge new ties with the Porte.[61] Jewish civil servants attended communal events dressed in their imperial uniforms, while lists of Jews decorated by the sultan, as well as those who found government employment or graduated from state schools, appeared in the Ottoman Jewish press on a regular basis. Such demonstrations and announcements helped reinforce the myth of the Jews' special connection to the Ottoman government. They also seem to have helped erase the unpleasant memories of a not-so-distant past when not one Jew was in the service of the state.[62]

Becoming Imperial Citizens

While Ottoman Jews had few public venues or media of their own during the mid-nineteenth century, there is evidence that they learned to speak the language of the new Tanzimat regime from its earliest moments. In 1840, just a year after Abdülmecid announced his first reform decree, Jews from Rhodes invoked the reforms when they called for justice for members of their community who remained under siege after accusations of ritual murder had turned violent on the island. Proclaiming their innocence in patriotic language, they protested: "We would be unworthy of being God's children if now, after the Hatt-ı Şerif of Gülhane . . . bestowed its benefits upon us, we would cause the government the smallest unpleasantness by our behavior."[63] Within a few years, the first Ladino newspaper of the empire appeared bearing a similar message.[64] Writing from Izmir in 1846, its editor, Rafael Uziel, urged readers to understand their relationship to their state and society anew as a result of the recent reforms. Going forward, religious difference pertained only to matters of conscience, he explained, and would not interfere with their "rights as citizens."[65] Mixing concepts familiar and new, Uziel referred to his compatriots both as "subjects of the same sovereign" and "sons of the same fatherland," explaining that the sultan hoped members of all the different religious communities within his empire would learn to love one another and to consider each other brothers.[66] Even the Sephardi rabbi Yehudah Alkalai of Belgrade— who in 1840 issued a call for the resettlement of Jews to the Land of Israel in anticipation of the coming of the messiah—found reason to praise Abdülmecid's latest reforms. To Alkalai they represented a "renewal of the kingdom" that offered proof of the dawning of a new age.[67]

Ottoman Jews also engaged in subaltern readings of the new reforms. When a group defining itself as the "Jewish poor" came together in Izmir in 1847 to oppose Jewish communal elites in their city, its members invoked the political changes the reforming Ottoman regime had set in motion.[68] Writing that they once abided being "dishonored and abused" by local Jewish notables upon whom they depended for financial support, the anonymous signatories of the 1847 pamphlet explained that they would do so no longer. They had "realized that as a result of the Tanzimat-ı Hayriye [Beneficial Reforms], which our merciful king has applied to all of his reign, there are no longer any additional taxes or fines apart from the poll tax, and the profit tax which each person must pay individually."[69] The latest reforms had set them free, in other words, both from the burdensome taxes they had once considered their lot and—no less important—from the arbitrary abuses of their own communal leaders. Like peasants and commoners across the empire at the mid-century, Izmir's rebellious Jewish poor clearly "viewed the Tanzimat as a mandate for social . . . as well as religious liberation."[70]

Using the language of the Tanzimat regime to assert their new freedoms was one thing, but taking on the new duties citizenship entailed was another. According to Ludwig August Frankl, an Austrian Jewish traveler who passed through the Ottoman capital shortly after Abdülmecid announced his Reform Decree in 1856, his coreligionists in the empire saw in the new edict not only the promise of equality but also an unprecedented burden. "We are no longer the oppressed and despised ones of the earth," the Ottoman chief rabbi reportedly informed his guest, since it was the sultan's "desire that we should be civilized. He has ordered schools to be established, and we will prove our gratitude by obedience." Yet, as he continued his ambivalence about the new laws became increasingly clear:

> I have learned that you, in the West, understand better what is meant by exemption from slavery, and the equality of all men, without distinction of religion. The Jews of the East must first learn this, and then begin to extend their knowledge. When the great law was passed, believers rejoiced that the stigma was removed from the servants of the true and only God; and unbelievers rejoiced, because all restraint was withdrawn, and they were left to the freedom of their own wills. But there are many who believe that the holy ordinances of religion are endangered by it, and fear that it may sink into decay, and lose its force, as among the Franks [Europeans]. But the chief ground of their apprehension arises from the Jews being now obliged to serve in the army. The descendants of the heroes of God, and of the Maccabees, are not afraid to meet death on the battlefield; but they know that, as soldiers, they must violate many of the precepts of our holy faith.[71]

The decree, it would seem, promised to benefit the faithful as well as those who hoped to cast off religion entirely. Worse still, it threatened to challenge Jewish observance by requiring that Jews break their Sabbath and dietary laws for the good of their country. If the Ottoman chief rabbi put it mildly, others expressed their concern in bolder terms. During his visit to Istanbul, Frankl encountered a group of indigent Jews who had taken refuge in an abandoned building—a Jewish squatter's colony in the heart of the Ottoman capital. Having entered the residence of a family of musicians, he asked the father of seven to sing to him. What the man chose to perform for his foreign guest reveals a great deal about the hidden transcripts of Ottoman Jews at this moment, as it offers a rare glimpse into the words they spoke when the state was not listening. The song the man sang was "the production of some unknown poet," Frankl explained, and had been inspired by the latest reform decree. It told of how the Jews of the empire had "violated all that is old and highly-prized . . . cast aside their piety and their reverence for the Supreme Being, and been rendered apostate and Godless by the Tanzimat and Hatt-ı Hümayun."[72] Even as the author of these words went unnamed, the Jewish musician who performed them sent a defiant message of his own about the dangers the reforms posed to the faithful.

Jews' resistance to the new measures also appeared in other guises. During the Crimean War, European Jewish observers complained that their Ottoman coreligionists remained indifferent to pleas that they volunteer for military service.[73] Others suggested that Ottoman Jewish religious leaders were doing everything in their power to ensure that members of their community avoid conscription.[74] Although certain local Jewish notables supported plans to form a Jewish legion in the Ottoman army, they remained skeptical about the prospect that their coreligionists would enlist if they were not obliged to do so.[75] Indeed, while scores of foreign Jews came to the empire to aid the Ottomans in their war against Russia, Ottoman Jews apparently preferred to support their empire by offering donations to the imperial cause.[76] They were not alone. Although the state officially signaled its readiness to allow non-Muslims into the imperial army, various Christian representatives also resisted the new measure, preferring to pay a military exemption tax—the bedel-i askeri—rather than serve.[77]

While most Ottoman Jews did not experience the conflict from the battlefields, the period of the Crimean War pushed their patriotic project forward in other ways. A short-lived Ladino newspaper entitled Or Israel, which appeared in Istanbul between 1853 and 1855, offered its readers instructions in appropriate conduct during wartime. Foremost among them was its advice not to spread rumors about the course the war was taking.[78] Later issues of the paper spoke of the justness of the Ottoman cause and the depravity of its enemy, Russian "Tsar Nicholas, who strove to deceive the entire world and, above all, the Greeks," with talk of a Byzantine restoration slated to begin in the Ottoman capital. There was no more bitter a deception than the Greeks' when they found that the tsar would not be restoring them to their erstwhile glory, the paper continued. "God willing, they will learn from this bitter lesson."[79] Or *Israel*'s readers no doubt found lessons of their own in its pages, which spoke of the value of circumspection and steadfast allegiance to their empire.

The subsequent chapters follow Ottoman Jews' patriotic project forward from this moment, over the course of the final half century of Ottoman rule in Salonica, Istanbul, Izmir, and beyond. The book proceeds chronologically, with each chapter also introducing the new political options that appeared to Ottoman Jews during the late imperial era. Chapter 1 discusses the emergence of civic models of Ottoman citizenship; chapter 2 introduces the option of "Easternism"; chapter 3 treats Jews' engagement with politicized forms of Islam in the empire; and chapter 4 introduces both Zionism and socialism (as well as anti-Zionism) as new forms of Jewish attachment to the empire after 1908. Exposing the different options Jews debated over the course of many decades helps challenge the assumption still prevalent in the scholarship that Ottoman Sephardi elites "were consistently and unfailingly committed to a civic model of Ottoman political identity predicated on an idealized vision of Westernization."[80] It also demonstrates that patriotism was never simply a fact on the ground—the proverbial unstinting gratitude passed down through the generations—but rather an ongoing, contested, and evolving project.

In its earliest stages, Ottoman Jewish elites attempted to further this project by teaching their coreligionists how to become proper Ottomans and by seeking to gain visibility for their community in the eyes of their state. For various Ottoman Jewish leaders, this meant finding a way to make Jews count in imperial politics and to allow them to "catch up" with other Ottoman *millets*—namely, the Armenian and Greek Orthodox communities they considered to be more advanced than their own. Chapter 1, "Lessons in Imperial Citizenship," examines these developments as they culminated in a moment of radical political and territorial reconfiguration in the empire. The chapter opens with the proclamation of the Ottoman constitution of 1876 and concludes with the Ottomans' dramatic defeat in the Russo-Ottoman War of 1877–1878. The empire's successive wars with Serbia, Montenegro, and Russia during these years brought Ottoman non-Muslims one of the first opportunities to put their newfound citizenship into practice. In contrast to the positions they had taken during the Crimean War, Jewish leaders now did everything in their power to have their flock contribute to the empire's war effort—not solely by the traditional means of prayers and donations—but also by encouraging young, able-bodied Jewish men to sign up for the army and telling men and women alike to subordinate their personal needs to those of the state.[81] Putting both the interests and the laws of their country above all else, Jewish community leaders initiated a process that—taken to an extreme—had the potential to diminish their hold on the audience they addressed and attempted to lead.[82]

Chapter 2, "On the Streets and in the Synagogue: Celebrating 1892 as Ottomans," analyzes the participation of Ottoman Jews in two different commemorations of the year 1492. In the first case, Jews decided to treat the four-hundredth anniversary of their ancestors' expulsion from Spain as a cause for patriotic celebration, transforming it into a holiday marking their arrival in Ottoman lands. The chapter explores the genesis of this invented holiday in the political context of its time, noting that it emerged just as the Ottoman government was deciding whether to allow large numbers of Jews fleeing Russia, Romania, and Corfu to settle within its borders. The celebration thus served a dual purpose. Its architects hoped to persuade the sultan to offer safe haven to Jews fleeing persecution and to encourage Ottoman Jews to honor their state in new ways. The second commemorative event featured in this chapter honored a journey to different shores in 1492. This was the 1893 World's Columbian Exposition, which offered Ottoman Jews a number of opportunities to assert their Ottomanness in a foreign land. As Jewish merchants crossed the Atlantic to represent their state in Chicago, Ottoman Jewish journalists sought to instill in their readers a sense of pride in their coreligionists' activities abroad and to reflect on what it meant to call their empire home.

With time, communal elites moved from trying to teach their coreligionists how to become modern Ottomans to realizing the potentially unsettling consequences patriotism could entail. Chapter 3, "Battling Neighbors: Imperial Allegiance and Politicized Violence," examines this process by exploring Ottoman Jews' responses to two moments of heightened tension and politicized violence in the empire—massacres of Armenians in Istanbul in 1896 and the Greco-Ottoman War of 1897. The strategies of self-representation that Jewish elites employed during these moments attest to their willingness to work within a framework of politicized Islam in response to the changing political climate in the empire. Their claims of Jews' special affinity with Muslims during this period helped solidify Jews' image as a model *millet* precisely as the relationship between the Sublime Porte and its Armenian and Greek Orthodox citizens became increasingly strained. Yet Jewish elites' choice to publicly "side" with their Muslims neighbors, and thus with the state, during both moments also resulted in a number of more troubling developments. Across the empire, Jews participated in violent and spontaneous manifestations of patriotism that their communal leaders considered beyond the pale of acceptable identification with their country's cause. The increasing polarization of the period also prompted new rifts between Ottoman Jews and their Christian neighbors, some of which would prove long-lasting.

The final chapter, "Contest and Conflict: Jewish Ottomanism in a Constitutional Regime," analyzes Jews' responses to the visit of the newly instated Sultan Mehmed V to Salonica during his tour of Ottoman Macedonia in the summer of 1911. By this time, the empire had witnessed an explosion of new political parties and ideologies following the Young Turk Revolution of 1908. In this context, Zionist, "assimilationist," and socialist Jewish groups competed for the attentions of their sovereign and state as well as the support of various constituencies. Although they continued to speak of their community's special relationship to the state, under the new government, Ottoman Jewish leaders found it increasingly difficult to speak in one voice. Indeed, while under the reign of Abdülhamid II (1876–1909) Jewish elites had often attempted to distance themselves and their communities from groups imperial authorities had deemed "suspect," various Jewish activists and authors now sought to distance themselves from members of their own community whose politics they rejected. Despite the fierce competition among different Jewish parties during the sultan's visit, no clear victor emerged. New and divergent definitions of Jewish Ottomanism coexisted on an expanded political stage.

The analysis offered in these chapters relies on printed and archival materials—ranging from newspapers to letters, consular reports, photographs, and postcards—to explore the developments Jewish elites sought to highlight and those they hoped would remain hidden from view as they told polished stories of Ottoman Jewish loyalty to themselves and the world. The pages that follow illuminate the opportunities, frictions, and negotiations the process of becoming imperial citizens involved. Conflicts, plans rejected, and those silenced in the process may not have made the headlines but are part of the larger story of Ottoman Jewish citizenship. They speak to the struggles of different Jewish individuals and groups to define the public face of their communities, and thus help shape their future. Unlike the routine acts of everyday life, the public events featured in this book constituted clear signposts in the lives of Jewish individuals and communities. Placing them under the public scrutiny of all eyes—both Ottoman and foreign, Jewish and non-Jewish—such moments of heightened visibility forced them to continually reconsider their place in imperial, as well as local, political configurations.

Exploring the opportunities and limitations Ottoman Jewish leaders encountered as they tried to mold Jews into imperial citizens during this period often presents a paradoxical picture. During the course of the nineteenth century, and well into the twentieth, they seem, on the one hand, to have been performing a tenuous tightrope act and, on the other, to have succeeded, sometimes well beyond their own expectations, in reinforcing and propagating the myth of their special connection to the Ottoman Empire. Both perspectives are important parts of the story of Ottoman Jewish patriotism in this period. Taken together, they reveal the ways that leaders of a particular group attempted to make Ottoman patriotism merge with their own values and visions for their cities and communities. They did so while facing a considerable array of constraints and—despite their constant claims of undisturbed allegiance and links with the state—with an unmistakable anxiety they attempted to keep far from the public eye. More broadly, *Becoming Ottomans* highlights the paradoxes and tensions embedded in the project of grafting models of patriotism and new forms of belonging onto expansive and diverse imperial landscapes, what Benedict Anderson has called "stretching the short tight skin of the nation over the gigantic body of the empire."[83] In doing so, this book explores how Ottoman Jewish leaders both confronted and embodied many of the contradictions their project involved.

1

Lessons in Imperial Citizenship

On March 12, 1878—nearly eleven months after war had erupted between Russia and the Ottoman Empire—Eliyahu Abraham Rosenblit drafted a letter to the Ottoman sultan, Abdülhamid II. Rosenblit did not live in the empire, nor did he have any known link to its government. At the time of his writing, he was a resident of San Francisco, California. It was not the first time Rosenblit had addressed the Ottoman sovereign. After having written to the Porte the year before, he complained, "I have yet to receive word from the sultan. I do not know why."[1]

What Rosenblit offered "could save the entire Kingdom of Togarma," he insisted—using a biblical term commonly employed in Hebrew to refer to the Ottoman Empire—while also ensuring "the salvation of the House of Israel."[2] Determined, he tried again. This time he addressed the acting chief rabbi of the empire, Moshe Halevi, asking that he deliver the message personally "to the sultan or to his servants." Rosenblit's letter went on to describe a novel and seemingly miraculous gun he had recently developed. It could shoot up to one thousand times per minute and its fire reached great distances. This new invention was the secret weapon that would help the Ottoman Empire win its war against Russia, Rosenblit ventured. He concluded by explaining that he would do everything in his power to provide the empire with these weapons "at the lowest price possible" should the sultan decide to take him up on his offer.

Today, Rosenblit's correspondence sits in the archives of the chief rabbinate of Istanbul. Whether it ever reached its intended audience remains unclear, but it is certain that its author's hopes were dashed in another regard at least. Not only did his miracle weapon remain unknown to the empire, at the moment that he penned his last missive to the Porte, the Ottoman Empire had already lost the war. Nine days before Rosenblit composed his letter, Ottoman representatives had signed the Treaty of San Stefano in a village on the outskirts of Istanbul, cementing the empire's defeat with the loss of large amounts of territory, primarily in its European provinces. Casualties on both sides were great, but Russia and its allies emerged as the war's undisputed victors.

For the Ottomans, the experience of the war pushed the state further into economic crisis and sent hundreds of thousands of refugees searching for new homes within the empire.[3] Although Muslims made up the majority of the displaced, among the refugees were many thousands of Jews.[4] Russia had hardly been undone, as Rosenblit had hoped. Rather, in the wake of the conflict, its strength appeared redoubled.

Rosenblit was not alone in depicting Russia as an enemy of both the Jews and the Ottomans throughout this period.[5] On countless occasions during the war, Ottoman Jewish leaders sent the same message. The assertion resonated differently when articulated from within the empire, however, where Russia assumed the guise of a "double enemy" of Ottoman Jewry. This was because Rosenblit had presented himself as an *ally* of the Ottomans but a *member* of the Jewish people, whereas Ottoman Jewish leaders had begun to fashion themselves and their coreligionists as both Ottomans *and* Jews during this period.[6]

The proclamation of the First Ottoman Constitution in December of 1876 had reinforced their resolution in this regard. It guaranteed new freedoms to the inhabitants of the empire while simultaneously declaring that they should begin to consider themselves Ottomans regardless of faith or background.[7] This move represented an innovation, since the term Ottoman (*osmanlı* in Ottoman Turkish) had originally referred to members of the ruling dynasty of the empire and had for some time been reserved for an important class of Muslim officials employed by the state.[8] Although attempts to create unity among the empire's residents were not new, the constitution was arguably the clearest and most forceful articulation of this platform to date.[9] It also led, within a year, to the opening of the first Ottoman Parliament, which drew delegates from the diverse regions and communities of the empire and offered imperial citizens their first glimpse of representative government on an imperial scale.

These changes, coupled with the empire's consecutive wars with Serbia and Montenegro in 1876 and Russia in 1877, dramatically propelled the Ottoman Jewish patriotic project. Throughout these years, the reality of war was inescapable even for those who remained far from the fronts. This was also true for Jews. Violence engulfed a number of cities and towns throughout Ottoman southeastern Europe where Jews resided, while waves of refugees poured into cities with large Jewish populations, such as Istanbul, Salonica, and Izmir. By the end of the Russo-Ottoman War in 1878, Russian forces were stationed in a suburb of the imperial capital, and—according to the redrawn map of southeastern Europe that was proposed at San Stefano—Salonica was destined to become a border town.[10]

Caught up in these events, one Ottoman Jewish journalist reminded his audience that such times of crisis gave "true friends" of the empire the opportunity to prove themselves. "This is the hour to show your philanthropy and your patriotism," he exhorted his readers.[11] Both attributes—philanthropy and patriotism—were integral to the nascent vision of citizenship that reformist Jewish leaders attempted to instill in their coreligionists during this period. Both required activism and self-sacrifice to an entity larger than the religious community alone. The "greater good" that Ottoman Jewish leaders began to describe in the process appeared sometimes in the form of an imagined Ottoman community and, at others, in the form of the cause of "civilization" or humanity at large. Crafting their new ideal against the foil of those they imagined as the passive subjects of the past, Ottoman Jewish leaders called on their fellow Jews to become active citizens and to treat their country of residence as a sacred homeland.

Yet, even as Ottoman Jewish leaders attempted to imbue their coreligionists with the novel values of individual citizenship and expansive new allegiances, they were convinced that this transformation would come primarily in mediated form. In many respects, this was a logical conclusion. Like members of other non-Muslim *millets* of the empire at the time, Jews were primarily educated in institutions run by members of their own religious community. Ottoman Jews were also at a particular disadvantage when it came to participating in state institutions, since few among them read or wrote the language of the state well enough to enroll in imperial schools or secure government employment. Jewish and non-Jewish observers alike agreed that Jews lagged behind their Armenian and Greek Orthodox neighbors in this and practically every respect during these years.[12]

It was precisely the perception of their own community's backwardness vis-à-vis the other non-Muslim *millets* of the empire that led various Jewish individuals to propose the radical transformation of Ottoman Jewry with such urgency. Responding to the new exigencies of wartime, Jewish journalists, teachers, and rabbis implored their fellow Jews to show their patriotism by giving everything they could to their country and to prove their humanity through a wide range of philanthropic initiatives. Since the refugees who fled the formerly Ottoman territories of southeastern Europe had done so in order to escape the empire's enemy, their flight seemed to confirm the confluence of Jews' interests with those of the Ottoman government.[13] Serving the poor as well as the *patria* swiftly became political acts of allegiance to the state and its people. In this climate, Ottoman Jewish reformers found that they might construe any self-sacrificing initiative as part of the fight against Russia, their "double enemy."

All of this worked on the rhetorical level, at least. In practice, Ottoman Jewish leaders had to find ways to encourage their coreligionists to activism on both the home and battlefronts. As they asked their coreligionists to make sacrifices on an unprecedented scale, they often paired indications of the ruptures this process would require with talk of continuities. Their references to Jewish traditions of charity and loyalty to the ruler were presumably meant to make the new values of patriotic and philanthropic citizenship more palatable and familiar to the Ottoman Jewish masses. In the process, Ottoman Jewish leaders attempted to help their communities adjust to radically new social and political programs by recasting them in a traditional mold. Not surprisingly, things did not always turn out to be as simple as they seemed at first glance: the enemy was not necessarily so easily defined, nor were the interests of the empire and the Jewish community always as indistinguishable as communal leaders suggested they should be.

This chapter explores the means through which various Jewish communal leaders from Salonica, Izmir, Istanbul, and beyond attempted to mobilize their coreligionists to patriotic and philanthropic ends during this time of unprecedented political reform as well as crisis in the empire. The goals Jewish elites set for themselves during this period were threefold: they considered it their mandate to foster a sense of brotherhood among Ottomans of all faiths, yet they also sought to raise their own community out of obscurity, poverty, and "backwardness" in the hopes of ensuring that Ottoman Jews would finally be "counted and esteemed," as various other non-Muslim communities in the empire were. No less important, they hoped to prove that Ottoman Jews, as a collective, were true friends of the empire, dedicated to their country's cause and willing to sacrifice all to support it. The different sections of this chapter trace these various efforts—beginning with Jewish communal leaders' attempts to create new bonds between Jews and their Christian and Muslim neighbors throughout the 1870s, and moving to their efforts to gain visibility in the eyes of government representatives before concluding with an analysis of Jews' responses to a series of wars that put both their patriotism and their empire as a whole to the test. Ottoman Jewish communal leaders were ready with advice at each turn. Yet, as the responses of different Ottoman Jews to the changing circumstances in the empire make clear, their patriotic project was still in its earliest stages. There were many lessons still to be learned.

New Visions of Civic Ottomanism

In the years leading up to the proclamation of the constitution of 1876, Jewish leaders had begun to add their voices to those who urged the empire's inhabitants to regard their neighbors as brothers and to work toward the greater good of their country. Writing in 1874 the Ottoman Jewish banker and philanthropist Abraham Behor de Camondo explained: "We cannot recommend enough, dear friends, that you live harmoniously with your brothers of all faiths. . . . Let us banish all rancor and regrettable memories of the past. Tolerance, charity, fraternity should be our course."[14] Speaking of the new civil society Jews would create alongside Ottoman Christians and Muslims, Camondo urged his coreligionists to forge new relationships with their neighbors, invest in education, and donate their time and money to interconfessional causes.

Many Jewish elites sought to effect this transformation through the press. Local news stories regularly offered warnings about the type of behavior that would earn readers public censure in the new Ottoman society Jewish reformers envisioned. When Aron de Yosef Hazan, the editor-in-chief of Izmir's Ladino newspaper, *La Esperansa*, told his readers of the approximately one thousand indigent Jewish poor who wandered his city's main plaza every Tuesday and Friday begging for money, for example, this was not news. His readers had presumably witnessed the same scenes themselves. Rather, he introduced the story into his columns in order to ask fellow Jews to do something about the situation.[15] Not only were the poor in need of help, they were entering the shops of Christians, where they incurred insults and brought shame to the entire Jewish community. In a city with only twenty thousand Jews, it was a dishonor to allow one thousand of their coreligionists to roam the streets begging and making a mockery of their community, Hazan explained.[16] Something had to be done.

While Jewish journalists regularly used the pages of their papers to demand the intervention of their communal leaders, they often targeted those they considered trouble makers more directly, calling them out by name and warning readers to avoid their indiscretions. "And so it was," read one such article in *La Esperansa* of Izmir,

> that last Saturday a certain Moshe ben Ezra, formerly a member of the [Jewish] community administration . . . forgot that we no longer live in a time when Jews holding religious positions could rule over the whole community. Apparently under the impression that the government had given him the streets as a present, and finding himself in Irgat Bazaar[17] where a Turk was selling ice cream, the man ordered the Turk to leave the premises so that the Jews of the neighborhood would not be tempted to his ice cream after having recently eaten meat . . . . The Turk met the orders with indignation, and was about to respond when some Jews who were nearby—realizing the great harm their coreligionist might cause their whole community—had him taken away at once.[18]

In case the message had not been clear enough, the author of the report spelled it out for his readers, recalling the words of the Jewish men who had observed the disturbing scene: "Not even the authorities have the right to stop a man from pursuing his occupation," they had reportedly chided, "nor a Turk from selling his ice cream!"[19] The streets belonged to everyone, readers learned. When outdoors, they would be expected to exercise discretion and not to impose their own private laws on others.[20]

The same imperatives applied to Jews' neighbors. When others broke this rule, Jewish journalists expressed their indignation. The spring of 1877 brought one such instance into the columns of Salonica's Ladino weekly. The piece in *La Epoka* explained that during Carnival a number of local Christians celebrating the holiday had entered one of the city's cafés in costume. Much to the consternation of those who documented the affair, two of the masked men were dressed as Jewish beggars. The worst offense came when the pair began to impersonate the Jews, portraying their "nation" with all of the "worst possible qualities."[21] The report suggested that Jews stop frequenting the café, whose owners were said to have condoned the offensive behavior of their patrons.[22]

These different reports had in common their portrayal of Ottoman Jews as poor and backwards. In one case, a Jew who had "forgotten which century he lived in" had not known how to behave properly toward a Muslim compatriot in public. Other articles told of the scores of Jewish beggers who earned the scorn of the Christian shop owners they approached for support. These developments gave cause for concern among Jewish elites not only because they had to decide how to care for the impoverished among them but also because their coreligionists' public behavior was affecting how members of other Ottoman communities saw them. Indeed, the image of the destitute Jew had apparently become a common enough sight so as to lend itself to mockery and reproduction in the form of a Carnival costume.

Journalists, religious leaders, and other self-appointed Ottoman Jewish reformers sought to eradicate the image of the poor and backwards Jew roaming the streets with outstretched hand, replacing it with that of an enlightened and philanthropic citizen, someone who was an Ottoman as well as a Jew. If these local news stories served as foils to the ideal type journalists were eager to portray, they appeared alongside a different type of story that provided a model for respectable behavior.

Examples of positive models often appeared in the form of announcements of philanthropic donations made by members of one Ottoman religious community to another. Such reports lent weight to the burgeoning project of civic Ottomanism, which was founded on expectations of cooperation among Ottomans of all confessions. Thus, when the Armenian and Greek Orthodox communities of Izmir planned charitable balls, they were announced in the

Ladino press.[23] Jewish journalists encouraged their readers to attend these events, whose proceeds went to a worthy cause. Sharing social spaces such as dance halls with Ottomans of other faiths was considered a great act of progress, "tolerance," and imperial brotherhood.

Although they encouraged their coreligionists to attend these gatherings, members of *La Esperansa*'s editorial staff also expressed concern that their readers might be unprepared for such high-class affairs. When the Jewish community decided to host its own ball to raise funds for the recently opened Alliance Israélite Universelle school in the city, *La Esperansa* issued a warning. Individuals from the large Greek Orthodox community of Izmir had already joined the board of organizers and had begun to purchase tickets for the event. The Jews in town were advised not to fall behind. Anticipating possible objections from a community with little experience in such matters, the paper announced that it was "not enough for the four or five Jewish families who own the proper attire for a ball to buy tickets." The notice made clear that it was "also the responsibility of those among our coreligionists who are not accustomed to going to balls but who have the means to purchase tickets" to take part.[24] As the occasion drew nearer, another advertisement graced *La Esperansa*'s pages. If the paper's editor was correct to assume that only a small handful of Jewish individuals from the city counted gala-worthy suits and ball gowns among their possessions, the advertisement must have been an uncomfortable one for the rest of his readers. The notice asked those who planned to attend the event to come dressed in the proper attire. These instructions were not to be taken lightly. In order to preserve the honor of the city's Jews in the eyes of their non-Jewish compatriots, anyone judged to have arrived in an inappropriate outfit would be turned away at the door.[25] The experience of becoming Ottomans, it would seem, promised to be a complicated and costly affair.

The search for new kinds of shared spaces went beyond the dance halls, to other institutions that bound Jews to their non-Jewish neighbors.[26] During the same period, members of the Greek Orthodox community of Izmir approached two influential Jewish merchants of that city, asking them to donate to a public library recently opened by a Greek Orthodox initiative.[27] The reformist Jewish elite seized upon the moment. Aron de Yosef Hazan dedicated a front-page article in *La Esperansa* to the topic, with the aim of winning his audience over to the cause.[28] "The century in which we live is full of curious contrasts," he wrote: in London, one could find the richest but also the poorest people in the world. Paris, that great center of civilization, also housed a great number of ignorant people. So it was in Izmir. True, their city was known for its religious intolerance, he admitted; true too that only a few years before the Jews in that place had suffered from ritual murder accusations, as had so often been their lot.[29] Yet, he assured his readers that it was only Christians from the lowest classes who participated in such scandalous attacks. The Greek society of Izmir had made great strides in recent years, as was evidenced by the recent establishment of this Hellenic library, funded entirely by private donations. The aim of that institution was not only to make its approximately twelve thousand books available to those without the means to buy their own; its founders also intended to help root out the religious intolerance that continued to plague the city by enlightening its inhabitants.[30]

Hazan called upon the Jews of Izmir to donate to the new Hellenic library collection in their city, suggesting that local rabbis might offer some of their own works as a gift. He also invited his coreligionists to take advantage of the center by dedicating a few hours a week to reading there. "This way," he concluded, "we will prove to our compatriots . . . that we do not deserve the label of ignorant folk they so often ascribe to us and which we have hardly done enough to combat." In subsequent issues, Hazan published news of the donations Jewish individuals and organizations had made to the library in response to his appeal.[31] The results were impressive: the committee of the Alliance Israélite Universelle had managed to collect some ninety-eight Hebrew volumes from a variety of famous Jewish personalities in Europe as well as a number of local Jewish contributors.[32] Despite his optimism, Hazan continued to remind the city's chief rabbi, Abraham Palache, that the Hellenic library awaited his donation as well. Izmir's Jews depended on their spiritual leader to raise their community in the eyes of their neighbors, Hazan wrote. This would not be the last time that Jewish lay elites attempted to enlist religious leaders to their cause.

Making Jews Count in Imperial Politics

As much as Ottoman Jewish leaders hoped to earn the respect of their non-Jewish neighbors, they were also concerned with garnering the attention of their state. Ottoman Jews were some "twenty to thirty years behind" the other non-Muslim communities of their country, a writer for Istanbul's *El Tiempo* lamented, and their backwardness was the reason they were scarcely represented in the offices of government.[33] If, like the members of other *millets*, Jews could become better educated and learn the language of their country, the same author suggested, they would surely come to play a more significant role in state affairs.

From Izmir, Aron de Yosef Hazan advised readers and communal leaders alike how Ottoman Jews ("*nozotros djudios turkinos*," in his words) "could arrive at the level of our Christian compatriots." He suggested that they had every chance to advance in society and needed only to seize the opportunities available to them. Even in "liberal" Russia, Hazan wrote—mocking that country's declaration of its intent to protect the Christian Orthodox populations of the Ottoman Empire from the sultan's tyranny—"the subjects of Alexander [II], and our coreligionists in particular, do not enjoy such liberties as we do under . . . His Majesty the Sultan."[34]

Their proclamations of gratitude notwithstanding, Ottoman Jewish leaders also expressed their unease about their role in their government's administration. This discomfort came to light early in 1876 after Sultan Abdülaziz convened a council meeting designed to implement the terms of a recent firman reinforcing equality in the empire. Although the wording of the document had given space to both Muslim and non-Muslim populations—and although various Ottoman Christians were represented in the council—no Jew had been included.[35]

Rather than blame the Porte for the situation, Hazan admonished his coreligionists for failing to make sufficient efforts to pursue an education in state schools or find gainful employment in government administration. The three or four Jews who could be found in high posts in the capital could not hold more than one position at a time, he reasoned and, as such, were unsuitable candidates for appointment to the sultan's council. "We can no longer cover our eyes and remain in a state of ignorance," he continued, "announcing that we do not want to teach our children Turkish or French or any other language because they have to learn our holy tongue." Attachment to Jewish tradition was not sufficient reason to shut themselves off from the world.[36] Learning the language of their state and studying secular subjects would offer Ottoman Jews a gateway to modern living as well as the respect of their compatriots and their government. In short, he promised, it would allow them to be "counted and esteemed" as the Jews of Europe were in their own countries and as members of other non-Muslim *millets* were in the empire.

When the new sultan Abdülhamid II failed to appoint a Jewish representative to the reorganized Council of State after his ascension to the throne in August 1876, *La Epoka*'s reaction was less timid.[37] Rather than blaming the elision on the backwardness of his own religious community, the Salonican author's response was one of indignation. The recently configured council had sixty-two members, he protested, "half Muslims, half Christians . . . and the Jews? It is as if [our] nation did not exist." The article went on to report that the European journals in the capital had protested on the Jews' behalf, but to no avail. "We never figure into any of the calculations concerning 'non-Muslims' in the imperial firmans," *La Epoka*'s author announced, "because *we count for nothing in the Ottoman Empire*."[38]

The same author objected that this neglect was unjustified and that Ottoman Jews were numerous enough to deserve inclusion in government affairs.

Departing from the opinions so often expressed by his contemporaries, the Salonican Jewish writer ventured that the Jews of the empire were no less capable than their Muslim or Christian compatriots in their knowledge of "finances, commerce, industry, or anything else that would help to build the wealth of a country." Competent, intelligent, progressive, enlightened Jews who knew the Ottoman language were not so rare as to render the authorities incapable of appointing even one Jew to the Council of State, he contended. Anticipating the suggestion that the omission might have been driven by Muslim "fanaticism" or anti-Jewish prejudice, however, the Salonican author provided his readers with an already familiar formula: the Jews had never faced discrimination throughout their long history in the empire. There was no reason to believe that this had suddenly changed.

The only possible explanation was that it had been a simple oversight.[39] The Jews in Ottoman domains had never done their government any harm, *La Epoka*'s contributor ventured, "something other communities in the empire are unable to declare." It was a bold claim. The author's words shed light not only on the ways Ottoman Jewish leaders attempted to argue for their special relationship with the Porte by bringing the loyalty of other communities into question. They also illuminate the particular challenges Ottoman Jews faced during this period. *Not* harming one's government was not entirely different from being absent from its councils. Both were predicated on what Ottoman Jews did not do, rather than what they might offer. The widespread conviction that the Jews of the empire were poor and backwards threatened to render them invisible to their government. As such, they remained part of an undifferentiated mass—subjects, not citizens.

The Ottoman-language press soon caught wind of these debates. From Istanbul, the newspaper *Sabah* reported—somewhat disingenuously, it would seem—that its Salonican Jewish colleague had been mistaken in believing that Jews would be excluded from the council.[40] After British Jewish representatives submitted queries about the situation to the Porte, the Ottoman-language paper *İttihad* printed the reassurances of London's Ottoman Ambassador Musurus Pasha that Jews, Christians, and Muslims alike would soon be included.[41] Responding to the widespread attention the issue had raised in the press of the empire and abroad, the government soon appointed Behor Efendi Ashkenazi, a Jewish notable who had already served on the council under Abdülaziz, to Abdülhamid II's newly constituted committee.[42]

Yet the fact that Jews had been left out of one important political institution after another prompted Jewish communal elites to undertake new efforts to facilitate Jews' integration in the empire. In Izmir, Hazan did his part to try to rectify the situation. In addition to running *La Esperansa*, he offered Ottoman language lessons to the Jewish schoolchildren of the city and also founded a society for the propagation of Turkish among the Jews.[43] David Fresco, editor-in-chief of the Ladino periodical *El Nasional* of Istanbul, also backed a new initiative meant to help his coreligionists learn Ottoman Turkish.[44] In an article entitled "The Language of our Country," Fresco offered his audience an introduction to what he called "the science of politics." "Highest among the duties of a citizen," he declared, "is knowledge of the language of the country. The great lessons of history prove that in order to foster ties between members of a state, and to ensure that all of the subjects of a government enjoy the rights of citizens, it is necessary to have ... an official language known by all." It was only natural, then, that those who did not know this language could not hold a position in any state body.[45]

Confusing the "science of politics" with myth, Fresco turned to a description of Jews' special relationship with the Ottoman state, which—in the context of his recent declaration of their glaring absence from government offices—took the form of a supplication to his readers. What better way to convince them that they should become model citizens of their state, after all, than to tell them that—in a certain sense—they had always been just that? "The Ottoman government has always been good to our nation [the Jews]," Fresco exclaimed. "It has always allowed us to enjoy our freedom and all the rights of citizens, *even more than the other peoples who have found shelter in this vast empire.*"[46]

Fresco's claim that Jews had "even more" reasons to be thankful to the Ottoman state than other communities remained a foundational part of the story that he and other Jewish leaders told about their relationship with their government throughout this period and in the decades to follow. The myth of the special Jewish relationship with Ottoman authorities was, in the words of its Jewish proponents, predicated on the idea of the double debt modern Ottoman Jews owed their country. According to this interpretation, Jews were indebted to their government not only because it granted them religious freedom—a privilege enjoyed by all members of the empire—but also because it had given their ancestors shelter from persecution many centuries before. By suggesting as much, Ottoman Jewish authors implied not merely that they were a loyal *millet*, but that they were, in fact, the most loyal *millet* of all.

Trying his hand at history once again, Fresco ventured that the Jews "of the Orient" who had held high posts in the Ottoman administration in centuries past did so due to their knowledge of the Ottoman language. He concluded with no small dose of dramatic effect: "Unfortunately, today our brethren have forgotten this language to such an extent that if we were to estimate the number of Jews who read and write [Ottoman] Turkish from among the 500,000 who reside in the empire, the figure would not go beyond three digits."[47] Even if the source of Fresco's calculations remained obscure, his point was clear. The number of individuals from the other Ottoman religious communities who knew the language of the state and found employment there dwarfed that of the Jews.[48] Armenian and Greek Orthodox subjects filled government departments, "enjoying honor and influence," while the Jews remained "behind, suffering in misery, dishonor, and disgrace."[49]

Determined to change the role his community played in the empire, Fresco announced that the printing press of his newspaper, *El Nasional*, was preparing an Ottoman-Ladino dictionary. In order to make the product more affordable, his press planned to offer the work in serialized form, composed of sixteen-page installments.[50] Fresco offered readers an example from the dictionary. It consisted of a short Turkish phrase in Arabic script, a transliterated version in Rashi Hebrew script, and—finally—its Ladino translation. Fresco's choice of expressions was a puzzling one. It read: "He who wants a friend without faults remains without a friend" (Figure 1.1).[51] Yet in a sense, the choice was telling. Fresco and his contemporaries often spoke of the Jews as the "true friends" of the empire. Although they would have preferred to present their community as one without faults, their coreligionists rarely lived up to their expectations, especially in the early years of the transformative project they undertook to turn their fellow Jews into imperial citizens.

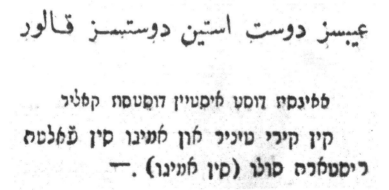

Figure 1.1 Sample phrase from David Fresco's Ottoman-Ladino dictionary, *El Nasional*, 1877.

Defending the Empire, Defending the Nation

In the summer of 1876, as the empire was embroiled in its conflict with Serbia and Montenegro, it appeared as if the Jews of the empire were going to be left out of yet another important imperial organization. News of a volunteer unit that had formed in Istanbul pointed to the participation of

Ottoman Muslims and Christians, but there was no mention of Jews. All the more frustrating for the Jews desirous of earning the praise of their government, the new company of men marched through the streets of the imperial capital in uniform and garnered a great deal of attention. Historian Kemal Karpat has suggested that, with the Porte's prodding, the Ottoman press gave the story of the mixed unit pride of place within its columns with an eye to dramatizing the new unity of all Ottomans.[52] The group even had its own flag, which boasted the star and crescent of the empire on one side and a cross on the other, thus crystallizing the Jews' absence from this new formation in symbolic form.[53]

The imbalance was not destined to last long, however. By August, *La Epoka* proudly announced that the recent action of two hundred young men from Salonica was setting an example for the rest of the empire. Among these individuals were a small number of Jewish men "from good families" who had begun earning praise from all corners after choosing to take up arms in defense of their city. At first, there were only four Jewish volunteers, but the author of *La Epoka*'s report was optimistic. "There will be others," he forecast, adding that "learning how to use a weapon is a useful thing" and that it would be "a great way to honor our government."[54] It was not long before Jewish volunteers had their turn to parade around their city's streets in uniform, accompanied by government officials and a marching band.[55] *La Epoka* advised interested parties that they would be expected to train three times a week. Although the civil guard units were designed to protect the city and were not expected to prepare for the battlefront, this did not lessen the impact of the story, which quickly spread across the empire and beyond.[56]

The movement of Jews into the volunteer unit continued apace. By the next week, the number of Jewish volunteers spiked to thirty. By early September, it rose to forty.[57] Announcing their hope that the Jewish members of the new guard would "stand out for their good behavior," *La Epoka*'s editorial staff promised to publicize the young men's successes at every turn. A suitable example soon came from unexpected quarters: among the recruits was the son of *La Epoka*'s editor-in-chief, Sa'adi Halevi.[58] Both the young Halevi and another Jewish man named Isaac de Boton earned special mention in the newspaper's reports, as they were quickly promoted to the rank of corporal.[59] From Izmir, a writer for *La Esperansa* lauded the young Jewish men who had volunteered for the civil guard, suggesting that their actions offered evidence of the close collaboration between Jews and their Muslim compatriots in Salonica, and expressing the hope that a similar group might form in his city.[60]

The Salonican unit, with its Jewish volunteers and two corporals, quickly came to represent the apotheosis of Ottoman Jewish patriotism; its members became patriotism embodied. This was, at least, the opinion of *La Esperansa*'s correspondent in the imperial capital, who complained that his coreligionists in Istanbul had so far proven indifferent to similar calls, as was their custom. "But the Jews of Salonica deserve our praise and . . . gratitude," he exclaimed, since they had set an example that Jews elsewhere in the empire could follow. The same author suggested boldly that in this instance the Jews of the empire might even set a standard for Ottoman Christian activism.[61]

Like the mixed Christian-Muslim unit half a year earlier, Salonica's multi-confessional civil guard quickly captured the attention of observers across the empire. In the fall of 1876, members of the city's special unit began preparing a trip to the imperial capital to meet the sultan.[62] By January, newspapers in diverse locales announced the group's arrival in Istanbul.[63] Meanwhile, in Salonica, *La Epoka* interrupted its publication due to the departure of the volunteers, who counted the paper's chief printer among them. Apparently taking for granted the presence of Muslims among the city's volunteer force, *La Epoka* reported only that, "in addition to a number of Christians," as many as sixty Jews formed part of the company that had made its way to the capital.[64] Factoring in the members of a second company that had stayed behind, reports now set the total number of Jews enrolled in the civil guard of Salonica at over a hundred.[65]

Despite their enthusiasm about Jews' newfound visibility at this moment, *La Epoka*'s editors soon began to express their discomfort with these developments. Not long after the Salonican company arrived in Istanbul, a disturbing story about the group's Jewish members had appeared in the local press, the paper explained. "It is well known that the Jews of the Orient remain faithful to their religious commandments," its report began. Among these was the obligation not to consume food that had not been prepared according to Jewish dietary requirements. Taking Jews' kosher laws into account, the military officials in charge of the touring company had planned to prepare a separate kitchen and eating area for the Jewish volunteers in their company.

Rumor had it that these plans had failed because the young Jewish members of the company had declined the offer of their superiors. Reports told of how "the brave Jewish volunteers had refused to remain apart, and asked for the favor of eating . . . alongside their companions." Writing in the wake of the recently announced Ottoman constitution, the author of the report attributed the young men's gesture of brotherhood to the latest reforms. Yet, he explained, those at *La Epoka*'s offices were compelled to reproach the Jewish volunteers for their decision, however well-intentioned. "The true sign of civilization and progress the world over is the freedom of religion," he counseled, "meaning that each person should be free to keep his religion." Clearly, the non-Jewish officers who had given the young Jewish volunteers in their company the chance to eat kosher food had understood this principle of civilization, the same author opined. But for reasons he could not under-stand, the young recruits had failed "to appreciate or even understand" this lesson. In Europe, Jewish leaders regularly made a point of requesting that their followers be allowed to observe their religious commandments, he added. If the Jewish volunteers had believed they were acting like modern Jews by breaking the laws of their faith for the sake of their compatriots and country, they had missed the point. The article, sardonically entitled "The Fruits of the Constitution," made sure they could not miss it again. "We realize that they did all of this without understanding their error and to make things easier on the government, but we must repeat again what we have said before: it is absolutely necessary to maintain the commandments of our faith on all occasions, whatever the circumstances."[66]

La Epoka's editors did not have the last say on the matter. The following issue included the letter of one of the Jewish volunteers who had traveled with the company to Istanbul. Seeking to bring "the truth to light," the young man scolded the paper's editorial staff for so rashly jumping to conclusions. It was true, he explained, that—in order not to be a burden on the others—a large number of the Jewish volunteers had left the company during breaks in search of food. Only a few had remained behind in the Süleymaniye barracks with the rest of their unit. On one occasion, when everyone had been required to remain at the barracks in preparation for a ceremony slated for early the next morning, the Jewish volunteer soldiers had sent for kosher food from the res-taurant of Moshe Tiano and Haim Menashe, in the neighborhood of Çorapçı Han.[67] "We repeat once again that we were motivated merely by the desire not to disturb our government unnecessarily with the needs of a small number of Jews during such a short period. We hardly thought that the editors of your journal would be so quick to judge us without verifying these reports." The young volunteer did not end his message there. Suggesting that they should not have broached the topic at all, he offered *La Epoka*'s editors a lesson of his own. "The first duty of a political journalist is not to discuss issues pertaining to religion," he advised. Purporting to write on behalf of all of the Jews who had traveled with the volunteer company to the capital, the young man signed only as "a volunteer in the civil guard."

Responding to the volunteer's correspondence, a final note from the edi-tors clarified their position. While they were pleased to learn that their coreli-gionists had in fact made efforts to observe Jewish dietary practices while away, they were not in the position to apologize for having suggested otherwise. The indication that the young men had broken their religious laws while touring with their company had appeared in a French-language journal of the capi-tal. As such, the responsibility lay with the accused to disabuse the public of any possible misinformation. *La Epoka*'s article closed by claiming that, far from straying from its duty the paper had met one of its principal objectives—the defense of Judaism.[68] Despite its apparently happy resolution, the example of Salonica's Jewish volunteers for the civil guard offered unsettling hints of the tensions that could arise as Ottoman Jews searched for ways to put the needs of their state first while also staying true to their faith.

A Double Enemy

By the spring of 1877, a more menacing threat to the empire loomed on the horizon: although the fighting with Serbia and Montenegro had ceased, by April Russia declared war on the Ottoman state.[69] Ottoman Jews responded to the news with public demonstrations of patriotism and a new sense of urgency. Within a matter of weeks, Jews in the Ottoman capital filed into the Ahrida Synagogue, located in Balat on the southern shore of the Golden Horn. They gathered to pray for the victory of the Ottoman army. According to various reports, all of Istanbul's Jewish notables were in attendance. An impressive number of civil and military representatives also figured among the guests. In addition to official personalities, synagogue-goers—reportedly numbering in the thousands—arrived to participate in the important event. Their numbers were so great that crowds of expectant onlookers spilled over into the surrounding courtyard and streets.[70]

Those who never made it inside due to the overflow missed an impressive sight. At least one artist or photographer must have attended the event, as etchings of the scene were later printed in English, French, and German-language publications (Figures 1.2 and 1.3).[71] According to these images, various Ottoman Jewish rabbis donning robes and turbans officiated, while state representatives, dressed in their official uniform of frock coat and fez, lined the sides of the Jewish house of prayer. Graced with the seat of honor, Istanbul's chief of police sat in a lone chair placed upon a small floor rug in the center of the synagogue. As various high-ranking figures of the imperial capital filled the building, those present needed only look around to believe that the Jewish community was no longer going unnoticed.

Even more striking than the impressive cast of characters attending the prayer service was the presence of two enormous Ottoman flags on either side of the Torah ark, their crescent and stars present both on the flags' fabrics and in the form of carved finials atop the flag poles. Whether these symbols had entered the Jewish house of worship specifically for the occasion or were already part of its permanent décor, their presence in this Istanbul synagogue in 1877 suggests that the distinction between being

Figure 1.2 Prayers for the Ottoman army at the Ahrida Synagogue, Istanbul, *L'Illustration*, 1877.

a Jew in the synagogue and an Ottoman on the street had already begun to blur.[72]

Seeking to balance the novelty of the moment with a sermon that invoked traditional images and familiar tropes, the acting chief rabbi, Moshe Halevi, reminded the Jews in attendance that their holy law commanded them to pray for the peace and prosperity of their ruler. Was this not especially true for Ottoman Jews, Halevi asked, since that country had awarded equality to all its subjects? It was the Ottoman Empire that had sheltered Jews "since the moment when our people was attacked and persecuted like criminals in Spain," he continued, "at a time when barbarism covered the face of the earth . . . when no one would take us in, and we were killed, drowned, and made . . . to wander from city to city. It was at this moment that the Ottoman government took us in and saved us from . . . death." He pleaded: "Now our homeland needs us . . . the empire is in danger, its enemies want to weaken its power; they want to destroy its cities and resume the persecutions of Israel.

Figure 1.3 Prayers for the Ottoman army at the Ahrida Synagogue, Istanbul, *The Illustrated London News*, 1877.

Our great mother sheds tears of blood, but not for herself. She does so for us, [as our enemies] want to take us into captivity once more."[73]

Halevi's sermon rendered Russia a perpetual biblical Egypt, a place where Jews were persecuted and from which they would always need to flee. This approach strengthened the image of the Ottoman Empire as a foil, a promised land of refuge from the Spanish expulsion and a bulwark against Russia, which he portrayed as a modern-day pharaonic Egypt. That great power, the "Colossus of the North," had its eye not only on Ottoman territories, but also on its Jews, he suggested.[74] The idea that Ottoman realms represented sacred terrain for the Jews also appeared in Halevi's suggestion that Jews around the globe felt a special connection with the empire and prayed for its preservation. The fate of world Jewry hung in the balance, he concluded, much as Eliyahu Abraham Rosenblit had done, writing from his home in San Francisco.

With Halevi's Manichean predictions came his appeal to the congregants. Praying for an Ottoman victory was not enough, Halevi warned. Only those whose age or health barred them from activism could be satisfied with prayer alone. For others, the looming struggle might entail sacrificing everything, even their lives. Yet, just as the Ottoman government had "always done for our forefathers and for us," he explained, the Jews of the empire were obliged to help their country through "its darkest hours."

With this last exhortation, Halevi hinted at what was novel in his message. Having commenced his sermon with traditional visions that couched present sufferings in a biblical past, he now spoke to his congregants of the new duties he envisioned for them. Ostensibly gathering his audience there to pray, Halevi in fact sought to push the Ottoman Jewish patriotic project in new directions.[75] As it turns out, he had already declared the Jews' willingness to die for their country many months earlier in an announcement that had rippled through the Ottoman-language press of the empire.[76] Halevi now called upon his listeners to live up to the promise he had made on their behalf.

In the days following the ceremony, Jewish journalists across the empire accelerated their attempts to mobilize their readers in support of the war effort. At a moment when the Ottoman government had reopened the question of allowing non-Muslims into the regular army, *La Esperansa* endorsed the idea unconditionally.[77] In a front-page article entitled "Jewish Soldiers," Aron de Yosef Hazan added his voice to those of other Ottomans who spoke in favor of non-Muslim military service during the war, from the Ottoman parliament in Istanbul to the Arabic-language press of Aleppo.[78] Anticipating the terror a call to arms was bound to stir in the hearts of Jewish parents, he explained that they were obliged to let their sons go, since their first duty as Jews was to defend the homeland and come to its aid at all costs. Although he wrote that the love of a parent for a child was "a very sacred thing indeed," Hazan pressed on undeterred. "The departure of a Jewish soldier, while saddening his parents, will serve the greater good of our nation, and we must remember that the good of the nation ranks above that of the individual."[79]

Hazan turned next to the thorny issue of religious observance in the army, addressing fears that the demands of service might undermine the Judaism of new recruits. "Many among you will say that this demand is destined to weaken our faith, and make us lose something of our Judaism," he wrote. Yet here too he counseled his coreligionists not to allow their fear to prevent them from offering their sons up as soldiers: readers needed only to turn to the case of "the great Sanhedrin" called together by Napoleon to learn that an authoritative body had declared that Jewish soldiers did not compromise their Judaism by doing things during their time of service that they would not do when they were free. While the notion that Jews might suspend their regular religious observance on the battlefield did not belong to Napoleon's Sanhedrin alone, it is not surprising that the author drew upon this example.[80] Given the growing influence of the Paris-based Alliance Israélite Universelle in Ottoman Jewish communities during this period, the idea that the empire's Jews should learn to become modern citizens of their state by following French Jews' lead was a familiar one.

More surprising was Hazan's decision to reference a second Jewish community as a potential source of inspiration for Ottoman Jewish audiences. "Recently, we have even seen hundreds of Jewish societies form in Russia with the scope of getting kosher food to Russian soldiers," he wrote. Portraying Russian Jews as actively engaged in a struggle to preserve their own Judaism while fighting for their country complicated the image Moshe Halevi had conjured in his sermon just days before, when Russia had appeared as "the great enemy of Jews." *La Esperansa*'s article suggested instead that Russian Jews had rights as well as duties and that they were undertaking initiatives worthy of imitation. Although he avoided addressing the point directly, Hazan asked his readers to take as their model the very same Russian Jewish soldiers against whom he invited them to fight.

This was not the only issue the article avoided. In an attempt to win his readers over to the cause of bearing arms for their country, Hazan spoke of the duties and benefits of war without addressing its most gruesome and irrevocable realities. Expressing a naïve approach to the battlefield and a persevering faith in progress, he urged parents not to despair as they watched their sons march off to the front. "War does not last forever," he explained, "whereas the advantages their acts can bring us are eternal. We are convinced that all of our young coreligionists who are lucky enough to become soldiers will return happily to their families with the satisfaction of having completed a sacred duty, and of having earned the respect of their government and their compatriots, too." Surely Hazan, as well as the concerned parents he addressed, were aware that their sons might not all return from battle. Although the article skirted the possibility that certain volunteers might become martyrs rather than celebrated veterans, elsewhere discussions of the value of spilling one's blood for the empire became commonplace among non-Muslim communal leaders during the war.[81] The acting chief rabbi Moshe Halevi had joined these conversations as he announced the Jews' willingness to sacrifice their lives for their land.[82]

In the days and months that followed these appeals, reports emerged of young Jewish men from across the empire who had announced their intention to enlist and fight.[83] By June, large numbers of young Jewish men were preparing a special Jewish company in Izmir.[84] Following the example set by their Russian coreligionists, a committee had formed to provide the group with kosher provisions. The unit also boasted a special flag. On one side, it bore the Hebrew prayer *Shema' Yisrael*, on the other, the star and crescent of the Ottoman state.[85] The fact that the Jews of the empire now had their own double-sided flag, like the mixed Christian-Muslim unit had the year before, signaled to Jewish observers that their community was no longer being left behind. Fighting beneath that flag meant the defense of their empire and their religion at the same time, a concept that matched the claims of various Jewish leaders that their community faced a "double enemy" during the war.

Even after Muslims began to speak of the war with Russia as a jihad, or holy war for Islam, Ottoman Jews did not desist from claiming the cause as their own.[86] Instead, Jewish journalists introduced their audiences to the terms and concepts involved. Reminding their readers that Abdülhamid II was not only the sultan of the Ottomans but also the caliph of Muslims the world over, they told of the donations that poured in for the Ottoman war effort from Muslims in India and of the rebellion of Muslims under the Tsar.[87] They also explained the significance of the standard of the prophet, which was to be unfurled when a holy war was declared, of the figure of the *şehid*, or religious martyr, and of the concept of the *gazi*, or warrior for the faith—a title Sultan Abdülhamid II acquired during the war with Russia.[88] Both of these figures, the *şehid* and the *gazi*, fought in the name of their religion and their homeland, the Ladino reading public learned.[89] The formula should have struck them as familiar, since Ottoman Jewish leaders had employed the same causes—of country and religion—to describe the conflict with Russia from an Ottoman Jewish perspective. Russia was not only the "enemy of Islam," after all, as a Muslim author suggested in the pages of the Ottoman-language journal *Basiret* of Istanbul in the midst of the war, but also the enemy of the Jews.[90]

This message was reinforced by a remarkable call to arms that appeared in a Ladino periodical of Vienna not long after war was announced. The serial, *El Koreo de Viena*, was the organ of a small community of Sephardi Jews who had lived in the Habsburg capital as Ottoman subjects since the late eighteenth century.[91] Its intended reach, as described on the paper's masthead, was "the entire Orient," defined as "Turkey, Serbia, and Romania."[92] In the midst of the Russo-Ottoman War, *El Koreo*'s editors printed a manifesto on their front page entitled "Brothers, Ottoman Subjects!" The piece explained that as Ottomans, its readers were obliged to help their country. As Jews, they owed the empire a double debt of gratitude, for only their "brother Ishmael" had taken Jews in from Spain at a time when no one else would have them. Now Russia claimed to fight for "the culture of the Orient," but it was a ruse. Russia was the Amalek of their fatherland, the Ottoman Empire, and their religion commanded them to help erase its name from under heaven.[93] "Therefore," those behind the call addressed their audience, "let us join forces, each of us, to help expel Amalek from our homeland."[94] Using the biblical trope implied that Russia, as Amalek's modern-day stand-in, was guilty of an unprovoked attack on innocent civilian populations.[95] Strikingly, it also raised the conflict in question to the level of a holy war, "validated by divine command."[96]

The article made ripples in the press, both Ottoman and foreign. The *Neue Freie Presse* of Vienna commended its colleagues for aligning themselves with the Ottoman Empire, a position it judged to be both prudent and dutiful.[97] The German *Allgemeine Zeitung des Judenthums* offered similar words of encouragement, noting that the "Jews of the Orient" whom *El Koreo* counted among its readers appeared to have understood its message, since they had been undertaking great acts of patriotism.[98] Ottoman-language journals also picked up the story, praising the Jewish authors behind the patriotic program, while *La Esperansa* reported that the circulation of the story in Izmir had been fortuitous and had earned the Jews in that place the public sympathy of their Muslim neighbors.[99] The entire text of *El Koreo*'s patriotic declaration even made its way to Ottoman governmental offices, where it was translated and filed away among the empire's records.[100]

Such extreme descriptions of Russia as the enemy of both the empire and the Jews—couched as they were in biblical imagery through references either to the Pharaoh's Egypt or the figure of Amalek—were also meant to conjure the war in a very concrete manner. Articles in the Ladino press reported regularly on the suffering of the Jews in the territories occupied by Russian troops or their allies during the conflict, noting that many had become victims of massacre, rape, and pillage.[101] Many thousands who had managed to escape had fled to areas still under Ottoman control but arrived with little more than the clothes on their backs and remained in great need of assistance. Ottoman Jewish leaders and journalists thus attempted to facilitate collection campaigns for their coreligionists, who continued to follow the retreating imperial forces as well as the hundreds of thousands of Muslim refugees who began heading south and east both during and after the hostilities.

The plight of the Jewish refugees received extensive coverage in various newspapers of the empire and beyond and became part of the propaganda war waged between those sympathetic or antipathetic to the Ottoman cause throughout the conflict.[102] An etching of one such group of Jewish refugees printed in the pages of *The Graphic* of London thus became "news" in the Ottoman Jewish press, which regularly searched for outside verification of Russian cruelty and "barbarism" toward the Jews and Muslims of the war zone (Figure 1.4).[103] Reporting on atrocities committed against Jews by Russians, Bulgarians, or Romanians could serve both to rouse Ottoman Jews to action on behalf of their less fortunate coreligionists and to strengthen Ottoman claims of enemy brutality. Doing so advanced the larger project of Ottoman image management, which sought to draw attention to atrocities committed by Russians and Bulgarians against Ottoman civilians as a counter-measure to the anti-Ottoman literature that had accompanied reports of the massacres of Bulgarians at the hands of Ottoman irregulars in 1876. None other than the former British Prime Minister William Gladstone

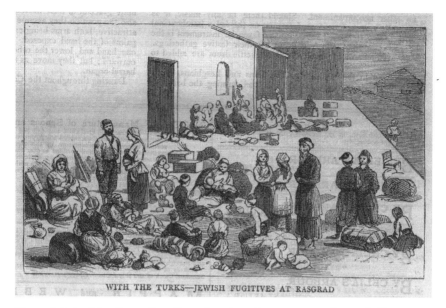

WITH THE TURKS—JEWISH FUGITIVES AT RASGRAD

Figure 1.4 Jewish refugees from Rusçuk at the railway station in Razgrad, *The Graphic*, 1877.

had famously responded to these massacres by concluding that the "Turks," were "the one great anti-human specimen of humanity."[104]

Various Ottoman authors consequently expended great effort trying to prove their own humanity while "exposing" the inhumanity of the enemy camp, thus effectively inverting the claims made against their state. As a writer for the Ladino paper *La Epoka* of Salonica put it: "Turkey, that country which the Christian nations of Europe consider a 'barbaric nation,' has now proven itself to be the most merciful [power] of the civilized world."[105] It was no coincidence that myriad periodicals of the empire, Ladino serials included, called upon their readers to support the refugees pouring into the capital and other cities of the empire not only out of patriotism but also as a gesture of humanitarianism.[106] Ottoman citizens were busy proving their humanity to the "civilized" world at the same time that they sought to prove their patriotism to their state.

Conclusion

As the conflict wore on, the Ottoman Jewish leaders who had issued calls designed to induce their coreligionists to patriotic activism had reasons to be optimistic. In Salonica, a number of Jewish notables joined the local committee of the

Red Crescent Society, a Jewish merchant offered a small steamship to the
government for the transport of soldiers, and rabbinic authorities ruled that
the Jewish longshoremen in that city were allowed to unload arms for the war
effort during the Sabbath.[107] Reports also told of Ottoman Jewish ladies who
had formed a society for the purpose of nursing sick and wounded soldiers in
the capital and of young Jewish students who planned to give the proceeds of
their theater performance to the imperial army.[108] In Izmir, the chief rabbi and
the Jewish notable Alexander Sidi went door to door, visiting the houses of
their coreligionists and asking for donations for the war wounded.[109] Word also
spread of two volunteer companies composed entirely of Jewish students, merchants, and "sons of bankers" making their way from Jerusalem to the Balkans
to fight for the Ottoman Empire. The group reportedly had a uniform not unlike
those of other Ottoman soldiers, as well as its own cantor, and had arranged to
have food prepared "according to the law of Moses."[110]

This flurry of patriotic activity had its limits, however. Although Jewish
donors in various cities had been giving generously to the imperial war fund,
whether with money, clothes, blankets, medical supplies, or cigarettes, the financial situation in the empire was worsening and—as a result—they had less
and less to offer.[111] Motivated by the desire to prove their patriotism but aware
that they were not in a financial position to contribute as other communities
were, Jews in the capital decided to ask their religious leaders to donate some
of the ornamental silver objects they kept in the numerous synagogues of the
city. "What good are they doing locked up?" David Fresco demanded through
the pages of *El Nasional*. Hoping to inspire a movement with his words, and
anticipating the possible immensity of such an undertaking, he wrote that the
project was sure to set an example for Jews across the empire as well as for
members of the other *millets*.[112]

Although Fresco's "silver" campaign gained momentum daily among Jews
in the capital, according to his own reports, rumors had begun to spread that
certain Jewish communal leaders were working to stall the project. What
shame this would bring upon Ottoman Jews, Fresco warned, asking publicly
that the heads of the community execute the will of the people by pushing the
plan forward.[113] The reports that followed suggested progress. The chief rabbi
and Jewish council had met to discuss the idea and promised to pursue it.[114]
Ottoman and French-language periodicals in Istanbul also began to praise
the Jewish community for its philanthropic and patriotic proposal. Yet, as
Fresco's paper made clear, those who threatened to block the initiative had not
given up.[115] As weeks passed more support poured in, yet the plan did not materialize.[116] Fresco asked for answers, but none came.[117] Having stirred great
excitement among the Jewish population, the initiative was blocked from
above. Nothing more was heard on the matter, but Fresco and other supporters

of the silver campaign no doubt felt that their community had failed their government on this score.

Despite the efforts of various journalists and communal leaders to suggest that Ottoman Jews' interests coincided completely with those of their state, certain events hint at early cracks in this narrative. An unnerving series of developments that took place in the fall of 1877 brought this tension into clear relief. At that time, large numbers of Ottoman Jews working at the imperial gunpowder factory near Istanbul went on strike.[118] It was hardly a prudent thing to do in the midst of a war and for a community trying to prove itself, but they had their reasons. Reportedly, the strike was a response to a great fever that had spread in the area of the factory, leaving the workers afraid to go near the place.[119] The government responded by sending guards to bring these people to work by force. From Istanbul, David Fresco was up in arms. He spoke scathingly of Jewish leaders who had pointed out the factory workers to the authorities and watched as the police dragged them to their former workplace against their will.

"Thus it is that in recent days," Fresco's report read, "that all we hear among the Jewish masses are the cries of mothers, fathers, the elderly, and children." They "wailed in the streets and threw themselves at the feet" of the Jewish communal leaders who forced them back to the fever-ridden factory grounds. Deriding the Jewish men who had stood by as their community suffered, Fresco wrote of their "expensive uniforms" and of the "spotless fabric" they used to wrap around their fezzes. Their mustaches even shined "as brightly as a mirror," he noted with disgust. They were wealthy, in other words, and the Jewish workers they compelled to work at the gunpowder factory were poor.

At first glance it would seem that Fresco avoided critiquing the government directly by transferring the blame to the Jewish communal leaders involved, but disentangling the relationship between the authorities and the Jewish elites who had done their bidding was not an easy task. Were the Jewish men he lambasted not in government employ or, at the very least, its self-selected allies? "The imperial government is in great need of workers, it is true," Fresco conceded, and in the case of the gunpowder factory, he explained that this meant "only Jews," although he did not explain why members of his community alone were expected to perform this job.[120] Unwilling to let that be the last word, Fresco proposed that the Jewish community devise a new means of selecting individuals to work at the gunpowder factory, rather than dragging grown men away from families that depended on them. Even after the fever passed, forcing the Jewish strikers to work at the complex was a source of disgrace for the entire Jewish community, he wrote. Worst of all, it gave the impression that the Jews did not want to perform their duty to the government.[121]

In light of the reports suggesting that Ottoman authorities had singled Jews out to do this work during the war, Jews' claims of their "special relationship" with the state took on new meaning. For those among Fresco's readers who recalled the first Ottoman language lesson he had offered them in the pages of his paper ("He who wants a friend without faults remains without a friend"), it turned out that the saying went two ways. The Jews of the empire were not perfect when it came to what they offered their government; this they knew well. But the state too was not without its faults. If the Jews were going to attempt to be the most "intimate" friends of their empire—as many Ottoman Jewish leaders hoped they would—it was a good thing they had learned this important lesson concerning the true nature of friendship early on.[122]

2

On the Streets and in the Synagogue

Celebrating 1892 as Ottomans

In the early 1890s, the Ottoman Jewish press ran a campaign focused on changing the burial practices of the Jews of Salonica. Much to the chagrin of the journalists who reported on the issue, Salonican Jews were holding their funerals at night. As the nocturnal processions made their way through the streets to the cemetery, they passed through a largely Greek Orthodox neighborhood of the city, awakening their neighbors with their mournful cries. What was worse, the reports added, the *hazans* who led the Jews in their prayers seemed intent upon competing with one another. Each wailed louder than the last, one journalist explained, creating such an "extraordinary charivari, that instead of a dirge" their cries "give the impression that there is a brawl underway between large numbers of people."[1] A Salonican correspondent of the Istanbul paper *El Tiempo* complained that the nighttime funerals were getting so out of hand that recently two gravediggers charged with carrying the body of a deceased baby girl had failed to notice that the poor child's body had fallen from her casket as they hurried to bury her at such a late hour. The night was pitch black and the two men, apparently, were drunk. Only after arriving at the tomb did they become aware that they had lost the girl, and had then gone in search of her body.[2]

It was not just the reports of a rare and upsetting event such as this one that made the custom objectionable to its critics. Rushing to lay their dead to rest, the mourners were keeping the city's inhabitants awake and frightening the more susceptible among them with their nightly announcements of death. The papers called on Salonica's chief rabbi to forbid all processions after sunset.[3] They further requested that all interments be conducted "quietly . . . and without great tumult" and that the mourners wait until arriving at the cemetery to recite their prayers for the dead.[4] Although the authors of the articles did not address directly the more unpleasant troubles that might ensue from their coreligionists' unseemly habits, they did complain that "no other people" observed such a custom.[5] This meant that their non-Jewish neighbors suffered from the misfortune of living in the path of the Jewish mourners' processions, which tested their patience, the editorials continued. Their message was clear: the current state of affairs interfered with the cause of the city's elite to maintain good relations between all religious groups in Salonica. As far as the Ottoman Jewish journalists were concerned, such disagreeable habits could be left behind in the century that was swiftly coming to a close.[6]

Theirs was an era of a different sort of public procession, meant to exhibit the civic responsibility, patriotism, and propriety of their celebrants. The din that plagued Salonica in the form of late-night mourners' parades met none of these criteria. Those who traipsed through the streets making a public display of their private sorrows neglected the well-being of their fellow citizens, behaved in an undignified manner, and—equally important—had no greater cause to call their own.[7] The Ottoman Jewish journalists who objected so vehemently to the practices of their coreligionists did so because they clashed with their own project of modeling new ways to behave on their cities' streets. It was this impulse—the search for respectable and patriotic ways of being in public—that drove Ottoman Jews' participation in two events, both celebrations of the year 1892.

Taking as their reference the national holidays and international expositions that had become so popular by the late nineteenth century, Ottoman Jews commemorated the year 1492 in ways that they hoped would mark them as both modern and Ottoman. Their desire to do so dovetailed with larger trends within their empire, whose official representatives sought to manage their country's image in the world through public display and international diplomacy.[8] Moreover, Jewish communities abroad had long been making a point to participate in the patriotic parades and world's fairs of the period, most often as representatives and adherents of the countries to which they belonged.[9] It was the general abundance of frenzied performances of advancement and national pride that Eric Hobsbawn has described as constituting a "centenarian revolution" during precisely this moment.[10]

Attempting to find a place in the triumphant celebrations of the nineteenth century, Jews from various countries searched for their own approach to the patriotic ceremonies of their time. This was the case in 1891, when the Jews in France marked the centenary of their emancipation, after having already observed the 1889 anniversary of the revolution itself in synagogues across the country.[11] Caught up in the celebratory spirit of the moment, Zadoc Kahn, the Chief Rabbi of France, spoke of the anniversary of the French Revolution as the French Jews' "Exodus from Egypt . . . our modern Passover."[12] Jewish journalists also provided their readers with formulas for the appropriate ways to celebrate a centenary. Writing in 1892 for the German Orthodox periodical

Der Israelit, one author noted how Poles had chosen to commemorate the loss of their independence with a sense of dignity he found admirable. He hoped that his coreligionists would observe the anniversary of their expulsion from Spain in 1492 with a similar sense of pride and self-restraint, he explained.[13] Commemorations of any sort were meant to reflect well upon their celebrants. Even if the year 1892 occasioned painful memories among Jews, there was no more place for their public mourning of the event than there was for the disturbing night funerals undertaken by the Jews of Salonica. Public events worked best when triumphant. If joyous celebration was not possible, a commemoration should at least signal the progress and self-respect of its participants.

By 1892, lessons to this effect seemed to emerge from all quarters: people and countries from across the globe were preparing to celebrate the year as the four-hundred-year anniversary of Christopher Columbus' discovery of a "new world." Slated to take place in Chicago in 1892 (and later, by 1893, due to delays), the World's Columbian Exposition honored Spain for the explorer it had commissioned some four centuries before, as well as the continent he had encountered quite by accident. State representatives, merchants, and visitors from all parts of the world scrambled to join the festivities.

It was within this context that Aron de Yosef Hazan, a journalist, schoolteacher, philanthropist, Jewish communal council member, and Ottoman translator at the Italian consulate in his native city of Izmir, decided to invent a holiday of his own. It was to be called "the four-hundredth anniversary of the arrival of the Spanish Jews in Ottoman lands." Announcing his plan within the pages of his Ladino serial *La Buena Esperansa,* Hazan suggested that the new holiday was worthy of the age in which he lived as well as the patriotic project he hoped to further among his Ottoman coreligionists. No less important, it allowed him an official venue through which to plead with Ottoman authorities to welcome Jewish refugees fleeing persecution and expulsion elsewhere in the world during his own day. In response to Hazan's proposal, Jewish journalists and occasional contributors from different parts of the empire produced a flurry of articles declaring their support for the plan.

This chapter begins by analyzing the planning and eventual execution of this Ottoman Jewish holiday in 1892. The discussions that surrounded this event, as well as the final form it took, reveal a great deal about the political aspirations of Ottoman Jews during this period as well as the various challenges they faced as they attempted to dream up a holiday worthy of their community, their state, and their age. Later, the chapter turns to an exploration of the ways Ottoman Jews participated in the other four-hundredth anniversary celebration of the time—the Columbian World's Fair of 1893—as representatives of their empire in Chicago. In both cases, Ottoman Jews found that the centenary offered them a means through which they could seek to reinforce their relationship to their state and fashion themselves anew as members of the civilized world and as citizens of their Eastern empire.

Rewriting 1492 from the East

The holiday that came to be known as the "four-hundredth anniversary of the arrival of Spanish Jews in Ottoman lands" had no precedent. There were no 1792, 1692, or 1592 celebrations.[14] In a reflection of the official nature of the sources that have been used to interpret the moment, scholars who have mentioned the occasion have fixed their attention squarely on the Jewish press of Istanbul, on the acting chief rabbi of the time, and on the holiday itself, as it took place in synagogues across the empire. As a result, the holiday has acquired an aura of timelessness—of forming part of a tradition of Jewish allegiance to the Ottoman dynasty dating back centuries. Interpreters of the moment have similarly assumed that its execution served to bolster the position of Ottoman Jews vis-à-vis their government in tangible ways.[15] Yet, the 1892 centenary celebrations were exceedingly more complex than the official sources produced at the moment of the celebration indicate. What is more, the holiday was not born within the headquarters of the Chief Rabbinate, in the pages of the Jewish press of Istanbul, or anywhere else in the imperial capital, for that matter.

Although he did not make the comparison explicit as he announced the idea in the summer of 1891, Aron de Yosef Hazan may well have drawn inspiration for his plan to mark the fourth centenary of Jews' "redemption" by the Ottomans from the centenary celebration French Jews observed during the same year.[16] The Ladino press of the empire—Hazan's *La Buena Esperansa* included—had certainly dedicated a great deal of space to the historic anniversary of French Jews' emancipation in 1791 during the months leading up to Hazan's proposal.[17] At the same time, the historical parallels between the flight of Iberian Jews in the late fifteenth century and the flight of so many thousands of Jews into Ottoman lands from Russia and Romania four hundred years later could hardly have been far from his mind. These Jewish refugees, who poured into different Ottoman cities in the thousands throughout the early 1890s, were joined by the Jews of Corfu, who fled that island *en masse* after a blood libel led to a massive pogrom in 1891.[18]

That Ottoman Jews were expected to liken the plight of their ancestors and the trials of these refugees was made explicit in their papers throughout this period. As one writer put it, if his readers had any difficulties imagining the great suffering their forebears had endured upon their expulsion from Iberia, they hardly needed to search within the pages of medieval chronicles. They could simply open their newspapers to find the regular reports of the misery of Russian Jews or look to their own city streets to see the hundreds of new immigrants who crowded the courtyards of their synagogues in search of shelter.[19] Drawing this historical parallel in the context of the proposed 1892 celebrations had obvious political significance, as another Ottoman Jewish contributor made clear. While Russia offered modern examples of intolerance, he wrote, Abdülhamid II followed the precedent set by his ancestor Sultan Bayezid II, "of blessed memory," by opening his realms to the expelled Jews.[20] An Izmir correspondent for *El Tiempo* sang the praises of Islamic societies such as the Ottoman Empire. "Muslims," he explained, were "inspired by a monotheistic religion of charity and humanity" and their representatives, the Ottoman sultans, were "the blessed angels of God on earth." The same rulers who had opened their territories to the Jews in 1492 did so again, he enthused, for "our brothers from Russia and Greece today."[21]

The image of the tolerant Muslim ruler and of European intolerance continued to appear in these discussions of Jewish expulsion and redemption. Echoing the assertions of various Ottoman intellectuals and public figures of the period, Ottoman Jews described their empire as having preceded all of the so-called civilized nations in its tolerance of religious difference.[22] To drive this point home, one author reminded his readers that none of the great powers of their day (in his words, "free America, civilized England, France, that great lover of humanity, and Germany, with all of its great thinkers") had existed four centuries before when only "Torquemadas and Popes had ruled despotically in all of Christian Europe." The Ottoman government alone had remained unseduced by the religious fanaticism of the time and opened its arms to the Jews of Iberia, he proclaimed.[23] Taking the concept of the Ottoman invention of tolerance to its logical conclusion, Jewish writers not only painted their government as the most tolerant power on earth, but also went so far as to suggest that it had been the first to emancipate its Jews.[24] As one contributor to *El Tiempo* put it, the Jews fleeing persecution and expulsion in 1492 had found that they "were permitted to settle wherever they pleased, and that *all the rights of citizens were accorded to them.*"[25] It was this same dynasty that had given Jews refuge from "the tyranny of the Spanish government and European barbarism"—now for a second time—that deserved the total dedication of its Jewish population.[26] Ottoman Jewish journalists repeatedly informed their coreligionists that while anyone who lived within the realms of their empire was indebted to their sultan for the moral and material advancement he had secured for them, the Jews of his domain were obliged to offer special displays of gratitude, even more than other populations of the empire.[27]

Aron de Yosef Hazan's vision for an 1892 celebration was not a straightforward gesture of gratitude, however; it was also a plea. As it turned out, the situation of the Jews fleeing into Ottoman territories throughout the early 1890s did not match the vision projected by the proponents of the new holiday as closely as they suggested. While the empire had begun to permit large numbers of these Jewish refugees to settle within its domains, it also prevented numerous others from doing so. Those who could prove Ottoman nationality were sent at the government's expense to the provinces of Salonica Aydın. Yet, as a general rule, foreign Jews were expected to leave the country.[28] Large numbers of these recent Jewish refugees carried Ottoman passports that state officials judged to be forgeries, and were thus vulnerable to expulsion.[29] In the wake of the constant influx of Jewish migrants arriving in the empire during this period, the Sublime Porte announced its intent to avoid the spread of disease by assuring that large numbers of these immigrants not settle in any single location. They also sought to curb further Jewish settlement in Palestine in particular.[30] At times, the authorities issued orders to close their ports to the Jewish refugees, hundreds of whom were turned back on ships hailing from Odessa.[31] Intimations of these policies made their way into the Ottoman Jewish press, albeit in the form of telegraphic reports, while local charitable organizations emerged to ameliorate the situation of those immigrants who remained in the empire.[32] In this context, the constant conflation of 1492 and 1892 in Ottoman Jewish papers took on the function of a request to the Ottoman government that it live up to the image Jews had created of it.

Ottoman Jewish supporters of the proposed holiday also hoped that the festivities would improve their community's image in the eyes of their rulers as well as the Muslim population. As he announced his plan, Aron de Yosef Hazan described his conviction that celebrating the historic date would offer the Ottoman government the ultimate proof of the gratitude the Jews felt toward their state: the spectacle of loyalty he envisioned was certain to "bring about great satisfaction at the imperial court and among the Ottoman nation," he assured his readers. Although he did not define what he meant by "Ottoman nation," that it was primarily meant to reference Ottoman Turkish-speaking Muslims is indicated by the general Ottoman Jewish discourse of Muslim tolerance at the time, as well as the way that other proponents of the holiday came to use the terms "Turkish nation" and "Muslim nation" as synonyms for Hazan's "Ottoman nation" on other occasions.[33]

Hazan left other things unsaid as well. Nowhere did he acknowledge that not all Ottoman Jews were Sephardim and that celebrating the four-hundredth anniversary of the Jews' arrival in Ottoman lands necessarily effaced the story of those Jewish communities whose ancestors were indigenous to the regions the Ottomans had eventually conquered. Yet his conflation of Ottoman Jewry with Sephardi Jewry served a clear purpose. Not only did he announce the project within the Judeo-Spanish culture sphere of the empire, his attempts to paint all Ottoman Jews as a collective that had become Ottoman by choice rather than by conquest also helped reinforce his patriotic plan.

Within days of his call for Ottoman Jews to turn 1892 into an empire-wide fête, Hazan began receiving enthusiastic responses from his readers, who inquired how they might go about preparing for such a holiday. He was ready with prescriptions: each community should form a committee and raise funds in support of the endeavor, so as to ensure that the celebration would be designed to impress. He also insisted that the committees report on their preparations at every stage so as to keep the general public involved.[34] Offering to take the initiative to form one such group in his native Izmir, he encouraged others to do the same. According to Hazan's vision, the commemoration promised to be a holiday "of the people," democratically decided and universally celebrated. Even "the smallest citizen" would have a chance to join the efforts and express his patriotism by contributing what he could, other newspapers ventured; those without the means of donating funds could volunteer their time and further the project by contributing to open debates in the press. As one author writing from Salonica assured his readers, weighing a number of different options would allow them to collectively decide on the best possible plan. "Debate brings advancement," he concluded.[35]

Before long things appeared to be proceeding along precisely the lines the partisans of the project imagined. Journalists and contributors to newspapers across the empire began to discuss their plans for the event with a sense of urgency. Just a few weeks after Hazan announced the idea, one observer even claimed that Ottoman Jews spoke of nothing other than the upcoming fourth centenary celebration of their ancestors' arrival in the empire.[36] Still, they had no formula, let alone blueprint, for the festivities. With little consensus about what the patriotic commemorations would look like, or when or where they would take place, a number of different individuals ventured their visions for the holiday they had just decided to invent.

Some proposed that in order to create a lasting memory of the commemoration, Ottoman Jewish communities should establish or endow institutions for the public good, such as hospitals or shelters for the poor.[37] "What kind of enduring impression, what memory of all festivities will remain unless we can create a permanent tribute to this day in each province?" a correspondent writing for *La Epoka* inquired. The entrance to each foundation created in honor of the holiday could be emblazoned with the words "project founded in honor of the memory of the great hospitality the empire of Osman bestowed upon our ancestors who fled Spain."[38] This vision, while meant to serve as a durable testament to the Jews' special relationship to the Ottoman state, also had its undeniably practical side: Jewish communities across the empire were in dire need of improved public institutions, a proponent of this plan explained. In one city, a hospital might be sorely lacking; in another, a synagogue or Jewish religious school. Elsewhere, a Jewish community might need to arrange the affairs of a charity organization that cared for the sick through house visits and the distribution of medicine, food, and blankets.[39]

There were also those who interpreted the vision of a lasting monument to Ottoman tolerance more literally still. Some were convinced that the best way to make the memory of the holiday endure was to build a public monument that told the story of Jews' arrival in 1492. This impulse led one author to propose that Ottoman Jews erect a sculpture portraying the Sultan Bayezid II with his arms outstretched to the Spanish exiles. A famous artist "from Europe" could be hired for that purpose, he suggested, apparently undisturbed by the irony of bringing a European sculptor to depict Ottoman Muslim tolerance (and, according to the same logic, European intolerance). When completed, the monument might be placed near Abdülhamid II's Yıldız Palace, the same author suggested. Sculptures were "catching on in Turkey," he wrote, adding that placing one in a public spot in the imperial capital would help to further develop the Ottoman public's appreciation for the art form. A related proposal suggested that the same scene might be depicted in a painting that could be housed at an important location.[40]

Whatever the idea, those writing in with recommendations imagined a grand affair. Some believed that the holiday deserved to be celebrated with a procession composed of various Jewish notables from the provinces as well as Jewish bankers, merchants, doctors, civil servants, and schoolteachers resident in the capital. They suggested that delegates be elected locally and sent from "every city of Turkey" to Istanbul.[41] According to this version of the plan, the participants would begin in a central location of the city and make their way to the Yıldız Palace, bearing banners, playing music, and escorted by a detachment of Ottoman soldiers.[42] Arriving at their destination, they would be greeted by the acting chief rabbi, Moshe Halevi, while a selected few among them could give speeches "on behalf of the Jews of the Levant" before bestowing a gift upon the Sultan.[43]

Different contributors to the Ottoman Jewish press also forwarded their own calculations as to exactly when the day of the centenary celebration should be set.[44] Capturing the festive spirit of the holiday, some sources began to refer to it as a new Purim for Ottoman Jews.[45] Would the celebrations then be made to coincide with the Hebrew calendar? Some hoped so.[46] Yet, an Ottoman Jewish writer writing in Istanbul's French-language paper *Stamboul* proposed that Jews search in the annals of Ottoman history instead, for it was within Ottoman chronicles that they would be able to find the precise day on which Sultan Beyazıd II promulgated the edict authorizing the Jews to settle in his realms.[47] No such document surfaced, however, and the date of the centenary remained to be decided.

By late July 1891, just a few weeks after Hazan had published the first call for Ottoman Jews to turn 1892 into a patriotic holiday, a committee of thirteen members formed in Izmir and convened its first meeting.[48] By the time the group was announced in the press, its members had already begun to elaborate a program for the festivities, which they forwarded to the chief rabbi in the capital for approval. Hazan reiterated his hope that all communities of the empire would celebrate this event with great pomp and splendor and urged the "large Ottoman Jewish communities" such as Istanbul, Salonica, and Edirne to begin forming their own committees as well. In fact, he explained, they had little choice but to do so. Nearly all of the Ottoman-language journals of the capital had already begun writing with great interest of the event Ottoman Jews were planning, he wrote: "Now that our project is so widely known, we can hardly wait any longer to come to an agreement as to how we should proceed."[49]

Hazan registered the receipt of letters from the chief rabbis of Crete, Alexandria, and Cairo, all of whom showed their support for the initiative.[50] Representatives from Salonica and Edirne had not yet contacted him, he explained, but he remained hopeful that they would soon join the efforts. After having assured his readers that everything was set to fall into place, Hazan issued a warning: "Not associating oneself with this holiday would be—God forbid—to show a lack of patriotism." Although he went on to claim that "such sentiments have never existed among our coreligionists," Hazan was evidently concerned about the solidity of that which he declared to be fact.[51] The patriotism of Ottoman Jews was not a given, he hinted. In this case, it could not be proven without the help of the chief rabbi.

Writing just a few days later, *La Epoka* of Salonica announced that members of Izmir's planning committee had reconvened and decided to draft a letter to Chief Rabbi Halevi. They planned to send circulars to all of the large Jewish communities of the empire containing a detailed list of recommended measures to be taken in preparation for the upcoming celebration. They now simply awaited the approval of their spiritual leader. Meanwhile, a group of "Jewish youths from Istanbul" publicly addressed a letter to David Fresco, editor of *El Tiempo*, and—indirectly—to the chief rabbi as well. Suggesting that it was impossible to move their patriotic project forward without his support, they inquired as to his intentions: was "the Chief Rabbinate of Istanbul going to take the initiative or not?" The movement in support of the proposed holiday was creating such a stir that leaving the population without answers or guidance could have regrettable consequences, the anonymous authors intimated.[52]

In its next issue, *El Tiempo* acted as the intermediary for the silent Chief Rabbi, who offered an indirect response through the medium of the newspaper:

Halevi looked very favorably upon the initiative—Fresco wrote—but for reasons he did not disclose "his eminence was waiting for certain Jewish communities of the empire to forward their requests to him directly before taking the necessary steps to obtain authorization," presumably from the sultan.[53] The language of this communication gave no further details about which communities had failed to send official requests to the capital. The chief rabbi's alternating silence and evasive pronouncements remained a hallmark of his response to the discussions of the 1892 celebrations.

Undeterred, Hazan continued to push his plans forward. His committee now met on a regular basis—despite the delays from the offices of the Istanbul Chief Rabbinate. He also managed to secure the support of the chief rabbi of Izmir, Abraham Palache, who accepted the position of honorary president of the city's 1892 planning committee.[54] El Nuvelista of Izmir soon entered the discussion, requesting that plans for the event be accelerated.[55] By late August, a committee formed in Salonica.[56] The editors of La Epoka limned the activities of its members with pride and called upon the Jewish youth of the city to join the preparations for the holiday, which it suggested was bound "to give every Jew an opportunity to demonstrate the sentiments of recognition and gratitude we profess towards our magnanimous sultan and country."[57]

Whether that opportunity would come, however, was still far from certain. After the Berlin-based Hebrew periodical Ha-Magid added its voice to the discussions, the Ottoman Jewish press offered new warnings to the silent chief rabbi. Referencing the Jewish correspondents who had begun broadcasting news of Ottoman Jews' planned holiday across Europe, from Tatar Pazardjik to Paris, and from Marseille to Vienna, Aron de Yosef Hazan voiced new reasons why the Jews of the empire were obliged to carry through with their plans: "Not only will doing so offer absolute proof of the profound gratitude we feel towards the Ottoman government, it will also constitute a direct response to those antisemites who accuse us [the Jews] of being ingrates and who claim that we are not true patriots."[58]

Such warnings did little good. There was still no word from the chief rabbi. Different newspapers explained that a great movement was building among Ottoman Jews, but no definitive action had been taken on account of the delay from their spiritual head. El Tiempo published a long article on the subject of the 1892 anniversary plans as well as a public letter addressed directly to Chief Rabbi Halevi.[59] La Buena Esperansa, La Epoka, and El Tiempo all began referring to the proposed celebration as a "sacred holiday," somewhat ironically perhaps, since it did not yet have the blessing of their religious leader.[60] Suggesting that he was not beyond resorting to insubordination, Hazan threatened that Jews in Izmir would not be dissuaded from celebrating the holiday—even if they had "to stand alone."[61]

La Buena Esperansa repeated this defiant message in articles that followed. Hazan's open rebellion against the official leaders of Ottoman Jewry—and his expression of provincial independence—came through clearly in his new editorials. Refusing defeat in the face of the inaction of the chief rabbi in Istanbul, Hazan claimed an alternative source of power as he announced his plans to lead the Jews of his province in their celebration without Halevi's support. If he could not spur the commemoration of 1892 among all Jews in the empire, he was determined—at the very least—to see that those in his city and region did so and to put himself at the vanguard of this movement. Yet, by late fall, it appeared that Hazan's alternative plans of provincial defiance might not be necessary after all. The chief rabbi had finally deigned to respond. On September 28, *La Buena Esperansa* announced that Moshe Halevi had publicly expressed his favorable opinion of the patriotic plans and promised to contact the sultan in order to request authorization to proceed with the festivities.[62]

Although the announcement suggested that plans for the holiday were moving forward, it appears to have simply bought Halevi time. After his initial promise to bring the matter to the sultan, no word was heard from his offices for the rest of 1891. As the year came to a close, *La Epoka* issued a warning: "Readers! Beginning on the first of January, there will be only eighty-nine days left until those Ottoman Jews descended from the Jews of Spain will commemorate four hundred years since their arrival in Turkey."[63] The article continued, warning again that falling short on their promise to fashion a memorable holiday in 1892 would bring shame to their community. Hazan soon employed the same tactic, issuing his own countdown warning on the last day of December by claiming that the memory project he had initiated was crumbling before his eyes. He continued: "What will the non-Jews say? One can only imagine that they will claim that Jews celebrate with their words but not with their deeds, and sadly they will be right."[64] The date of March 31, was swiftly approaching, he warned. From Salonica, *La Epoka* warned that each province should be prepared to celebrate the holiday on its own.[65]

Despite both authors' insistence that they faced a looming deadline, this was, in fact, the first time they had mentioned their chosen date in print. Although no specific timeline had surfaced in the early stages of the planning of the holiday, some six months after having broached the topic the Ladino press discussed the date as if it were a settled matter. No one ventured an explanation for why this was. Although Hazan had promised that the committees would publish all of their deliberations in the press, Moshe Halevi's inaction on the matter had apparently prevented them from doing so. It remains clear nonetheless that those who had taken over the organization of the event in private committee meetings had chosen March 31 because it was the day that

the edict of the expulsion of the Jews of Spain had been signed some four centuries earlier.[66] They could hardly have believed that Iberian Jews arrived in
the empire on the very day their expulsion had been decreed. Yet, since Ottoman records offered no record of the date on which Sultan Bayezid II admitted the expelled Spanish Jews into the empire, the architects of the 1892
celebrations had instead chosen a different symbolic day famous in the history
of their Iberian forefathers. Moreover, of the various dates they might have
chosen—including the announcement of the expulsion edict on May 1, or July
31, the final date Jews were permitted to remain on Iberian soil—March 31
was the soonest. By pushing for the earliest possible date, Jewish journalists
from Salonica to Izmir were able to put further pressure on the chief rabbi to
act quickly and lend the Ottoman Jewish centenary his stamp of approval.

These efforts to persuade the chief rabbi of the urgency of the situation did
not have the desired effect. Moshe Halevi was apparently unmoved by the
warnings that Jewish patriotism was on trial. He remained silent until finally,
in late February 1892, he announced that he had lodged a request with the
sultan concerning the proposed festivities. Now it was the sultan's turn to
remain silent, it seemed. In response to the new situation, Hazan proposed an
alternative to the chief rabbi, in case he believed imperial permission would be
difficult to ensure.[67]

The new plan that Hazan offered was a clear compromise. At the very least,
he suggested, the holiday should be celebrated in the synagogues of the empire,
"without much noise." The Jews could "decorate the balconies and interiors of
their places of worship and send telegrams to the Porte in recognition of their
gratitude to the government," he explained. Strikingly, this time Hazan's recommendations did not go unheeded. The final celebration of the "four-hundredth
anniversary of the Spanish Jews arrival in Ottoman lands" ended up going
almost exactly as he had suggested. Yet it followed his second, compromise
proposal. In late February, the chief rabbi announced that the holiday would
be celebrated quietly, in the empire's synagogues, and that he would compose a
special prayer on the occasion. This had been the sultan's wish, he explained.[68]
The Jewish journalists, occasional contributors, and planning committee
members who had advocated a loud and imposing spectacle suddenly found
themselves facing the precise formula journalists had offered the late-night
Jewish mourners of Salonica during the same period, as they were forced to
turn their celebration into a more private affair destined to take place "quietly
. . . and without great tumult."[69] The holiday had been domesticated and made
official. Jewish representatives from communities beyond Ottoman territories wishing to "join in the loyal manifestations evoked through celebration
by the Jews of Turkey" sent formal letters of congratulations to the sultan on
the occasion of holiday, just as Hazan suggested they might in his second, less

ambitious proposal. Such letters arrived from Jewish communities in Calafat, Romania (through the Ottoman Embassy in Bucharest), London, and Paris (Figure 2.1).[70] Without much fanfare, the Ottoman and French-language press of the empire issued brief reports on the special prayers that different Ottoman Jewish communities held in synagogues across the empire on the appointed day.[71]

Signs of provincial defiance did not die off with these official pronouncements, however. In early March of 1892, Salonica's *La Epoka* responded to the recent announcement that the commemoration of the Jews' arrival in Ottoman lands would coincide with Passover services in synagogues across the empire and that Moshe Halevi would compose a special prayer to honor the fourth centennial holiday. "We ask one thing in this case," wrote one of its correspondents. "Let us not read the prayer that will be composed for the occasion immediately after regular prayers, since during each holiday we always read Ha-Noten [a prayer in honor of a non-Jewish ruler]. Instead, let us designate two or three vast open spaces in each province where—long after the services have finished—we can congregate to recite a prayer of a less religious character than the first."[72] The article then proposed that after this "less religious" prayer, a handful of speakers offer the population uplifting sermons exhorting their listeners to "walk a straight path" in life, to be united among themselves, and to support their neighbors. "In short, sermons with morals," the piece concluded. Nowhere did the author of the article acknowledge that the very idea of a "less religious" prayer might be unsettling to the spiritual leadership of Ottoman Jewry. Nor did he mention that what he proposed went directly against orders the Ottoman Jewish public had just received from the acting chief rabbi and—through him—from the sultan.

It is well-known that Sultan Abdülhamid II was suspicious of large gatherings and regularly forbade them.[73] Yet Ottoman Jewish papers and various leaders from Izmir to Salonica had nonetheless proceeded with their plans as if they believed their patriotic project would be immune from such a policy. Ultimately, Ottoman Jews' visions of a democratic process, communal ownership of the holiday, and a public ceremony with mass participation did not materialize, but the whole affair was so bizarre, contested, and prolonged that it raises a number of questions. Why had the chief rabbi guarded his silence concerning the proposed patriotic holiday for so many months throughout the course of 1891 and the early months of 1892? Was it only according to Abdülhamid II's wish that the dreams of the various Ottoman Jews who debated and planned the event were dashed? Why had Halevi taken months to announce that he would agree to bring the matter before the sultan? Was it a matter of crowd control perhaps? If so, then Abdülhamid II was not alone in this concern.

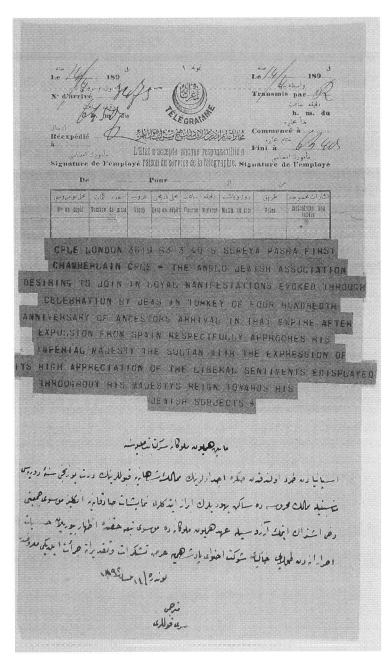

Figure 2.1 Telegraph sent by the Anglo-Jewish Association of London to the Sublime Porte on the occasion of the 400th anniversary of the Spanish Jews' arrival in Ottoman lands, 1892—Courtesy of the Başbakanlık Osmanlı Arşivi.

Although Halevi followed Hazan's second set of recommendations nearly to the last detail, he made one notable alteration. Rather than celebrating the Ottoman Jewish holiday of 1892 on March 31 as the previous partisans of the plan had proposed, Moshe Halevi discovered that the same date (according to the Julian calendar used by the Spanish Monarchs who had expelled the Jews) coincided serendipitously that year with the first day of Passover.[74] A brilliant tactical move, given the symbolic valence the day carried and the positive image of redemption it sent to the state, there was something else at stake in this shift of emphasis as well. Moving the day of the celebration to a date from the Hebrew calendar, Chief Rabbi Halevi had found a way of domesticating the event and making it his own. By celebrating an Ottoman Jewish holiday on Passover, he had managed to merge Ottoman Jewish patriotism with Judaism and—in the process—also reinforced his central role for the Ottoman Jewish community. Hazan's proposal to celebrate the holiday on the streets on March 31 and the calls of the editorial staff of *La Epoka* to hold the event in a "large open space" separate from the religious services in the synagogue were calls to move Ottoman Jews further into secular time and the public domain. Both of these suggestions represented a threat to Moshe Halevi's basis of power and— as such—remained unacceptable to him.

Hazan and the others who had been involved in planning the holiday in its earliest stages had been concerned with finding new ways to turn their coreligionists into modern Ottoman patriots. References to the role Judaism itself would play in the process were as absent as the chief rabbi was silent on the matter of the holiday. Ultimately, the various Ottoman Jewish leaders who participated in the event's planning and execution were engaged in a battle over who would be allowed to run the Ottoman patriotic project, as well as the form it would take. Although the centenary celebration he invented did eventually come to pass, Aron de Yosef Hazan made no secret of his discontent over the outcome. In a report he published after Jews across the empire celebrated the holiday quietly in their synagogues in the spring of 1892, he wrote that the moment was not without its merits, "even though it had not been celebrated as many had hoped."[75] Indeed, a thorough examination of the frustrated efforts and closed doors that accompanied the celebration of the four-hundredth anniversary of Jews' arrival in Ottoman lands belies the notion that this moment represented a simple success story of Ottoman Jewish patriotism.

After the newly invented holiday had come and gone, *El Tiempo* published a special commemorative issue in honor of the centenary. In this way, the Ladino paper offered a creative alternative to the debate that had raged in the Ottoman Jewish press for nearly ten months over whether the holiday would be celebrated on the streets or in the synagogues—that is, over who could lay claim to it and who would serve as its architects. Publishing a sixteen-page special edition of the newspaper, David Fresco sidestepped the debate by making his own newspaper the final site of the celebration of the "four-hundredth anniversary" of Ottoman Jews. Fresco's special issue dealt with the history of the Jews of Iberia, their flight to Ottoman lands, and their development since that time. Bearing two imperial coats of arms with Abdül-hamid II's signature (*tuğra*), the crescent and star of the empire, and titles in both Ottoman and Ladino, the cover made the patriotic message of its contents clear even to those to non-Jews who were unable to read its contents (Figure 2.2). Yet even in his special commemorative edition, Fresco apparently

Figure 2.2 Special edition of *El Tiempo* in honor of Ottoman Jews' Fourth Centenary Celebration, 1892—Courtesy of the Ben-Zvi Institute.

felt compelled to dedicate the last lines to a different story—the story of how the holiday had been born, co-opted, and transformed. The final words of the issue read "On this page, which will someday be considered of great historical value, we should mention the name of Mr. Aron de Yosef Hazan, director and editor of *La Buena Esperansa* . . . which was the first of all of the Ottoman Jewish papers to propose the celebration of this fourth centenary." And then, on the final line: "His eminence the *Kaymakam* Efendi Moshe Halevi took this project under his supervision and put it into execution."[76]

What had happened in the intervening ten months—between proposal and execution, and between the different Jewish and non-Jewish, Ottoman and foreign papers that had weighed in on the plans—had been an experiment in unofficial patriotism. Although attempts to design the holiday from the provinces and beyond official centers of power were eventually appropriated, moved to the capital, and directed by Jewish individuals employed by the state, the debates that ensued offer evidence that a large number of Ottoman Jews had considered it possible to orchestrate public manifestations of their own version of patriotism from below. That their government and its representatives might not have looked favorably on their project went largely unacknowledged in the Ottoman Jewish press. For nearly eight months, supporters of the 1892 centenary continued to challenge the chief rabbi to accept the plans they had dreamt up.

Ironically, although Hazan and the various other proponents of a public 1892 celebration envisioned an event that would allow them to praise their state and to strengthen Ottoman Jews' ties to the Porte, their plans posed a challenge to the authorities on numerous levels. Indeed, their calls for democratic process might have struck Abdülhamid II—who had closed the first Ottoman parliament in 1878 after less than a year of its existence—as a veiled threat to the very basis of his rule. The fact that opponents of the regime operating both within the empire and from abroad drew upon a discourse of democracy made these discussions all the more disconcerting.[77] This was also true for Moshe Halevi, whose rule similarly depended on the established hierarchies of the state's bureaucracy. Ottoman Jews' public suggestions that the Porte give succor to the tens of thousands of Jewish refugees entering the empire from Russia, Romania, and Corfu during the period also pushed against the government's concern with limiting the number of indigent immigrants in its care, preventing the outbreak of disease, and avoiding the concentration of Jewish settlers in Palestine.[78] Still, censors had not prevented enthusiasts of the 1892 holiday from entertaining lengthy debates in the press of the empire or from undertaking various activities to advance their plans. As the Ottoman historian Nadir Özbek has shown in another context, the Hamidian regime quelled public activism only selectively. On various occasions, it attempted instead "to mold . . . 'bottom-up' initiatives to serve its own political concerns."[79] Assuring that the synagogue won out over the streets as the site of Ottoman Jews' celebrations of 1892, Abdülhamid II and Moshe Halevi together managed to promote the patriotism and voluntary initiatives of their subjects while simultaneously limiting and controlling them.[80]

Meanwhile, during the same period, the second, more famous centenary celebration of 1492 offered Ottoman Jews new avenues for public celebration as well as greater flexibility in their self-representation. As plans for the Chicago's World's Fair of 1893 coalesced, a separate group of unofficial Ottoman Jewish individuals found that their government had approved their request to create a very different type of patriotic display, this time half a world away. There, they would find—on the shores of Lake Michigan if not along the Bosphorus—they could announce themselves as Ottomans in daily displays on the "streets of Constantinople."

Ottomans Abroad: Visiting the Chicago Exposition of 1893

After the 1892 holiday had come and gone, Ottoman Jews began to turn their attention toward Chicago. After months of delays, the Columbian Exposition was finally scheduled to open in the Windy City in May 1893.[81] Yet, on May 8, instead of news of the exposition, Ottoman Jewish readers encountered a lengthy front page article framed by the characteristic bold font of the death notice of a very important individual. Elia Souhami, one of the leading philanthropists and merchants of the Jewish community of Istanbul, had died.[82] The obituary published in *El Tiempo* mentioned the tragic irony of the timing of Souhami's death on May 1, the very day that the World's Fair had opened in Chicago. Although the company bearing Souhami's name had been granted the Ottoman concession at the fair that year, Elia Souhami, dead at 53, was never able to see the fruits of his life's labor culminate in the momentous event.[83]

According to the obituary published in *The Levant Herald and Eastern Express* of Istanbul, Souhami's burial drew the largest number of mourners of any Jewish funeral in the Ottoman capital since the death of the local banking mogul Count Abraham de Camondo two decades earlier.[84] *El Tiempo* also described the event as a grand affair with as many as five thousand people in attendance. Those who arrived to pay their respects to Elia Souhami's memory included members of the Jewish community of Istanbul, local policemen, municipal council members, foreign consular representatives, Armenian clergymen and communal leaders, and various Persian merchants. Signaling the good relations Souhami had nurtured with local Armenian notables through his mercantile and philanthropic pursuits, *El Tiempo* reported that his "enormous funeral retinue was met with the doleful sounding of church bells as it passed by the Armenian Church" in the neighborhood of Yenimahalle.[85]

Elia Souhami's funeral could not have been further removed from the nocturnal burials that had earned the wrath of the Ottoman Jewish press just a year earlier. While certain Salonican Jews' habit of holding raucous late night funerals appeared to Jewish reformers in the empire as examples of uncritically inherited traditions, Souhami's last rites appeared to them as their mirror opposite—as conscientious modern practice. Following the dictates of the age, it was a celebration: even as its participants grieved, they celebrated the life of an exemplary Ottoman Jewish patriot, leader, and philanthropist.

Uniting Muslims, Christians, and Jews, imperial and foreign citizens, and much of the high society of the Ottoman capital, Souhami's funeral offered Ottoman Jewish reformers a model for proper behavior in the civic sphere. While the parade of mourners drew crowds in the thousands, local Jewish papers described only its enviable orderliness. The Jews in attendance had little reason to be concerned about disturbing their non-Jewish neighbors as they made their way to the cemetery: their neighbors were among the mourners. Indeed, Souhami had evidently maintained good relations with members of various faiths and national communities. Many of the Persian and Armenian merchants present were likely one-time business associates of the firm he ran with his Ottoman Muslim business partner Sadullah Bey.[86] At the same time, the presence of various Jewish charitable societies at the funeral announced Souhami's towering status as a philanthropist of the first order.[87] Since the Porte had entrusted his company, which specialized in Oriental carpets, tapestries, and other "Eastern" items, with the task of representing the empire to the world at the Columbian Exposition in Chicago that year, Souhami's private commercial enterprise had similarly been transformed into an official, patriotic venture.

Souhami's transformation from private entrepreneur to Ottoman patriot had crystalized in the years and months leading up to the opening of the Chicago exhibition, as various members of his firm had set sail across the Atlantic in order to begin work on the Ottoman display. As early as the fall of 1891, Robert Levy, a representative of Elia Souhami Sadullah & Co., had helped to erect the first foreign flag on the fairgrounds during a ceremony in which the crescent and star of the empire were raised alongside the stars and stripes of the host country on the future site of the Ottoman exhibit.[88] That the empire eventually found itself in a desirable position near the displays of various European powers on the fair's Midway Plaisance was largely the result of these early efforts of members of Elia Souhami's company.[89] Not only had the imperial government given its seal of approval to this grand international display—as it had refused to do in the case of the Paris Exposition of 1889—Ottoman Jews were now foremost among those representing the empire during the festivities.[90]

The role that Ottoman Jews came to play in this broader imperial venture did not escape the attention of the Ottoman press.[91] Reporting on the arrival of imperial representatives at the fairgrounds in the fall of 1891, the Otto-man-language paper *Sabah* announced triumphantly that some six hundred Ottomans—"Muslims, Jews, and Armenians"—were in Chicago laying the foundations for what would become the imperial displays at the fair.[92] Soon, as the exhibit began to take shape, the editors of the Ottoman-language periodi-cal *Servet-i Fünun* boasted that Levy's Turkish Village on the Midway—which housed a replica mosque, obelisk, and bazaar modeled after major monuments in the imperial capital—gave imperial citizens reason to be proud.[93]

Once the Ottoman government officially conferred the contract for the im-perial exhibit to Elia Souhami Sadullah & Co., newspapers from the empire began to prepare their readers for the upcoming fair.[94] *El Tiempo* of Istanbul instructed its audience that those interested in displaying their merchandise in Chicago should make arrangements directly with representatives of that company, while a following issue announced that Souhami Sadullah & Co. would secure passports for anyone hoping to attend the exposition.[95] The French-language *Le Moniteur oriental* and *El Tiempo* informed their readers that the company had begun exhibiting at its headquarters "an Oriental-style bedroom" that was slated to be included in the Ottoman section at Chicago.[96] The general public of Istanbul thus had the opportunity to experience the em-pire's displays in their own city before the Ottoman exhibit traveled overseas.

Meanwhile, as he supervised the construction of his company's replica Turkish Village on the Midway, Robert Levy began to introduce American audiences to an Ottoman's perspectives on global politics. In an article de-scribing a gathering of fair organizers at the Palmer House Hotel in that city, a journalist for the *Chicago Daily Tribune* introduced Levy as an "enthusiastic Turk" who was so "thoroughly patriotic" that he declared he "would lose his last drop of blood . . . in defense of his country."[97] As evidence of this asser-tion, the author of the article described Levy's discussion with the American officials in charge of the exposition. The conversation had become heated as they broached the topic of the Dardanelles. Levy was quick to warn his au-dience that if England and Germany supported the passage of Russian war-ships through the Straits a worldwide conflagration would ensue. He had told as much to the "Honorable" William E. Gladstone fifteen years earlier, he continued—though without noting how it was that he had come to speak to Britain's prime minister.[98]

According to the American journalist who captured the moment on paper, Levy continued his appeal in a "most excitable manner," asking what harm the

Ottoman Empire had ever done to the nations of Europe "that they should always be doing us an injustice and great injury?" His country was free to everyone, he added, and European merchants of different nations traveled and traded there without any hassle. "But treaties are made with us and then broken; promises are made but are never carried out," he added.[99] With these words, Levy was perhaps the first among a number of Ottomans who "spoke back" to the Americans they encountered in Chicago in 1893 by suggesting that they were not the atavistic, passive subjects that Orientalists imagined.[100] Doing so apparently earned him the respect of his interlocutors, who considered an articulate defense of one's country among the most supreme values one could hold and thus a sure sign of progress.

Levy appears to have made a habit of speaking publicly of his home country while in the United States. During an "International Bazaar" organized in Chicago to raise funds for the Columbian World's Exposition, he directed a "Turkish booth," where—in addition to selling everything from coffee pots to carpets—he reportedly told stories to captive crowds of "the land of the sultan" from which he hailed.[101] On another occasion, while entertaining an American journalist in his office, Levy sipped coffee while overlooking the Turkish Village he had helped erect. Watching the Ottoman men and women who lived on a back street of the model neighborhood of Istanbul on the Midway—complete with a mosque, the famous obelisk of Sultan Ahmet Square, an Ottoman-style restaurant, concert-café, Turkish theater, and various other displays—Levy reportedly grew nostalgic. "There was something in the touch of the Chicago spring," the American journalist surmised, "which made Effendi Levy dream of his old home in the Orient, and he began talking about his country."[102]

As Levy recounted stories of his empire to the Americans he met in Chicago, Ottoman Jewish newspapers began to offer imperial citizens updates about the exposition taking place across the ocean. *El Tiempo* reported that the Ottoman section was capturing the attention of the myriad visitors who had arrived there.[103] "Turkey is in fashion in the land of dollars," that paper announced. "American women in particular are constantly trying to keep up with everything concerning the Orient."[104] An author writing for the Ladino serial *El Telegrafo* of Istanbul boasted that the Ottoman section had been one of the favorites of the fair, in large part thanks to the "honorable Elia Souhami Sadullah & Co, which did not attempt to cut corners in any way, and which gave an unlimited account to Mr. Robert Levy so that he could construct a section worthy of our empire." The care with which these imperial representatives had designed their site was not lost on the Americans, the same report boasted. "It earned us a very flattering compliment from the President of the United States, Mr. Cleveland, who remarked during his visit to the Ottoman exhibit that 'one has to be Turkish to be so exact.'"[105] Here, as elsewhere, Ottoman

222222

1111111

111111

1

Jewish journalists made no mention of the negative stereotypes Ottoman subjects encountered on a regular basis during the Exposition.[106] Aiming to encourage a sense of patriotism among their audiences, they handpicked the choicest examples of accolades the empire's exhibit had engendered for reproduction within the columns of their papers.

As they recreated the version of their empire that had recently been constructed in Chicago, these reports encouraged readers to reflect upon the symbolism and uses of what was supposed to represent a small piece of their homeland near the shores of Lake Michigan.[107] Addressing an audience more familiar with the intended referents of the exhibit than the throngs of various nationalities who visited the site daily, Ladino papers also offered specific details: the bazaars on Chicago's Midway were meant to recall those of the *Yeni Cami* (or New Mosque) and of the Tuesday Market of the imperial capital.[108] The wooden houses with protruding balconies were meant to reproduce a typical street scene from the Istanbul neighborhood of Üsküdar, *El Telegrafo* explained.[109] Ladino readers who wanted to put an image to such descriptions found one published in *El Telegrafo* in 1894 (Figure 2.3).[110]

Various Ottoman observers also applauded the "Oriental" decorations of the imperial exhibit, suggesting that such decorative choices were well suited to the Ottoman national character. Describing the interior of the imperial commissioner's residence in Chicago, the Ottoman-language *Servet-i Fünun* wrote approvingly that it had been designed in "Eastern style" (*şark usulü*), with carpets, tapestries, upholstered cushions on benches lining the wall and elaborately carved low wooden tables at the center.[111] *Sabah* and *El Tiempo* similarly described the Eastern setting of the imperial exhibit in enthusiastic terms. Having been prepared "in the Oriental style," the furnishings of the rooms, the clothing of the employees, the food and drink, all were authentic, familiar and good, Ottoman readers learned.[112]

The same language continued to appear in articles published by the Ottoman and Ladino-language press well after the Chicago fair closed in late 1893. By January 1894, Albert Souhami, one of Elia Souhami's sons who had traveled to Chicago and sold Oriental items at the company's shop at the Turkish Bazaar erected there, packed up many of the Ottoman exhibit's attractions and brought them west to San Francisco, where a Midwinter Fair had opened. (See Figure 2.4 for Sadullah Souhami & Company's Shop in the Turkish Bazaar in Chicago).[113] While Robert Levy remained in Chicago to tie up loose ends, Albert Souhami took over the business of running the new Ottoman exhibit held in Golden Gate Park. The report of the Ottoman-language paper *Sabah* on this second fair described how the young Souhami had faithfully employed an "Eastern style of architecture" for the Turkish Bazaar he built there, composed of some fifty stores boasting "minaret-style towers." The same author

Figure 2.3 Ottoman section on Chicago's Midway (front right), *El Telegrafo*, 1894—
Courtesy of Rıfat Birmizrahi.

was careful to add the approximately 350–400 Ottomans who staffed this exhibit "all dressed in Ottoman-style outfits," a choice that earned them the admiration of American onlookers.[114] In the hands of the editor of the Ladino *El Tiempo* of Istanbul, who translated the Ottoman-language report for his readers, the minaret-style towers of Souhami's Turkish Bazaar in San Francisco, as

IN THE TURKISH BAZAAR.

Figure 2.4 Shop of Elia Souhami Sadullah & Co. at the "Turkish Bazaar" on
the Midway—H. D. Higinbotham and C. D. Arnold, *Official Views of the World's
Columbian Exposition* (Chicago: Press Chicago Photo-Gravure Co., 1893).

well as the Ottoman-style clothes of the exhibit's employees, became simply
"Oriental" towers and attire.[115] Although each writer employed different terms
to describe Souhami's exhibit, their messages converged: Ottoman style was in
fact Eastern style and vice versa. In this sense, Albert Souhami announced his
love of country not only by erecting a banner reading "Long Live my Sultan"
(*padişahım çok yaşa*) above his temporary bazaar in Golden Gate Park, but also
by dressing his staff and arranging his displays in the style of his empire.[116]

Ottoman press reports on the exposition also sought to reinforce their readers' sense of identification with their empire by dramatizing their difference
from members of other nations. Although they studiously avoided any mention of Americans' critiques of their own country or compatriots, Ottoman
journalists did not shy away from painting the Americans they encountered in
a less than flattering light.[117] Describing the nargileh craze that had overtaken
the local population during the exposition, *El Tiempo* reprinted an article
from the Ottoman-language *Sabah* explaining that American visitors to the

fairgrounds had picked up the bad habit of breaking the Eastern-style water pipes, consequently finding themselves obliged to pay for the damages. "It is a true curiosity to see the manner in which these Americans attempt to smoke the nargileh," the report continued. "Despite the instructions offered by those serving them, many of the Americans who come to enjoy the nargilehs blow into their tubes, pushing the water out of the pipe and wasting the whole thing. Others, on the contrary, breathe in so much smoke that they end up leaving in a drunken stupor."[118] As they read these amusing reports, Ottoman readers were meant to understand that the stuff and styles of their empire—however popular they were abroad—ultimately belonged only to them, as they best understood how to use and appreciate the objects of their country.

While such reports suggested that Americans were ultimately out of place on that section of the Chicago Midway where hundreds of Ottomans lived and worked, others suggested that the imperial citizens who left their home in order to travel to the fair were similarly disoriented by their experiences with a foreign culture and people. This was the message of a thirteen-part series run by *El Telegrafo* in 1894 on the subject of the Chicago Exposition. That series brought its readers on a journey from the docks of the Ottoman capital, to a port in Le Havre, France, to New York, to Washington D.C., and finally to the banks of Lake Michigan.[119]

Written in the form of an Ottoman man's travelogue of America, the articles highlighted their protagonist's sense of estrangement from the "natives" he encountered.[120] The first installment noted that the travel package cost a "mere" 1,900 to 2,360 francs, depending on the seating one selected for the transatlantic journey. No doubt, this sum was well beyond the reach of the vast majority of the newspaper's readers. Yet, the paper suggested, the trip had become a collective one, which its audience could experience vicariously in the process of reading. A second essay in the series entitled "Let's Go to Chicago!" reinforced this idea, as it prepared its audience for the journey. "As you will soon see as you travel with us, we will be home in just thirty-eight days," it began.[121]

Once the Ottoman sojourner leaves the ship for the shore, the mood of anticipation turns to awe. This shift in tone becomes apparent with a subsequent installment, which describes the protagonist's arrival in the great American metropolis of New York via steamer on a Sunday afternoon. After disembarking, he finds that all of the stores are closed and people are out in hordes. "Women are in the majority," the traveler's report explains, and although "modestly dressed," they are "free to show the fresh color on their cheeks: they do not wear a veil. Everyone has a happy disposition . . . the places of worship fill up and empty in turns, as their prayers do not last long. Their sermons, songs, everything is done in a hurry. The otherwise animated crowds are quiet, calm, and attentive during their prayers. The women are able to go out on the streets,

at any hour, without being afraid of a sideways glance, an insult, or of being followed."[122] Quite unlike their embarrassing behavior in the cafes of Chicago's
Turkish Village, in other words, Americans' habits could also be exemplary,
as various references in this passage made clear. Indeed, expanding women's
rights, restricting the veil, and behaving with decorum in public and during
prayer were values held by different Ottoman reformers during this period.[123]

Even as they heaped praise upon the society they described, such reports
were also intended to remind readers of the chasm that separated them from
members of a foreign nation. This technique was facilitated by lending the observations of American manners and customs an anthropological tone, as is
clear in the following passage: "It is notable that in this city, women greet men
first," or in another: "Americans eat four times a day. They have many drink-
ing places for the consumption of alcoholic beverages, and they drink these
standing up. Even though such establishments are frequented on a regular
basis, they are not looked upon kindly, and thus have discrete doors at each
entrance."[124]

After replicating an overwhelming and tiring journey in a strange land
amidst strange people, El Telegrafo offered its readers the final essay of its series
on the fair. This installment was entirely dedicated to the Ottoman exhibit.
Praising Robert Levy for his displays of energy and imagination, the author of
the article concluded that Levy's "careful attention to the thousands of details
of the Exposition" had given the Ottoman section a "local color so rich that
the inhabitants of Istanbul who found themselves on its premises in Chicago
had believed themselves transported back to their beloved homeland ("sus
kerida patria"), where they could return once again to an Oriental life ("la
vida oriental")."[125] The article suggested to its audience that the experience of
traveling to Chicago as a visitor that year might be considered a patriotic act.
That is, it was not only the partners of Elia Souhami Sadullah & Co.—charged
with representing their empire for the world in 1893—who had been put in
the position of becoming "more Ottoman" and more patriotic as a result of
the contract they had been given by their government. Those who read about
the experience and relived it in the pages of their newspapers were also taught
new patriotic lessons on the love of their land, which was meant to endure and
affect them wherever they went in the world.

In fact, those who read about the exposition in Chicago, as well as those who
actually traveled there that year, soon saw that everything at the fair had been
organized according to a national logic. There was something of a consensus
among the participants that pride in one's country was a requisite for membership in any community of modern citizens. That the international expositions of the period were envisioned as tributes to the progress of humankind
in general in no way contradicted their uses in the process of nation-building;

the two were intimately linked.[126] Simply put, the experience of the fair drove home the sense that one could not be a modern citizen of the world without being a citizen of a particular state as well. The Ottoman Jewish newspaper reports on the exposition followed this logic and were designed to further transform their readers into Ottoman patriots. Having invited readers along for the ride to Chicago, they did not fail to remind them where home really was and which lifestyle (the "Oriental life") they were to consider their own.

Conclusion

In the summer of 1891, a letter sent to the French-language periodical *Stamboul* of the Ottoman capital explained that while people from around the globe planned to celebrate the fourth centenary of 1492 in Chicago, another 1892 centenary was being dreamt up in Istanbul. "This anniversary does not interest all of humanity as the other does," the author of the editorial had announced, "that much is clear; it pertains only to the Jews and, most particularly, to the Jews of the Ottoman Empire."[127] Although this brief comment may appear harmless enough at first glance, it hints at something that otherwise went unspoken during the entire period: the holiday Ottoman Jews invented to mark the "four-hundredth anniversary of the Spanish Jews' arrival in Ottoman lands" was a fraught project from the outset. In addition to posing a challenge to the chief rabbi's authority and potentially disturbing the political sensibilities of Abdülhamid II, who was suspicious of large gatherings, it also left a more deeply unsettling message.

The myth upon which the 1892 celebration was founded, and the myth it helped to develop—that of the special relationship of Ottoman Jews to their state—was not one shared by all Ottomans.[128] The underlying story of Jewish rescue at the hands of past sultans and the image of the empire as a place of sanctuary were not likely to have been entirely comfortable for the Jews' Greek Orthodox or Armenian compatriots, for example, even those most deeply committed to their empire. Being part of communities that identified as indigenous to the lands in which they resided meant that their version of a narrative of first contact with the Ottomans was necessarily one of conquest rather than refuge. That there were Jewish communities in the empire whose ancestors had not arrived in the empire as refugees went largely unacknowledged throughout the period.

The gulf that existed between the narrative Sephardi Jews constructed of their welcome in the empire and those circulating about other non-Muslim communities' first encounters with the Ottomans is not difficult to surmise in sources from the period. In August 1890, during a period of rising tensions between

Ottoman Armenians and the imperial government, the Ottoman-language paper *Mizan* referred overtly to the Armenians as a conquered nation. David Fresco's Ladino serial *El Tiempo* soon reproduced the article for its Jewish readers. Strikingly, the Ottoman author of the article suggested that he intended to persuade Armenian readers not to go the way of national separatism by reminding them that their country had not existed for nearly a millenium and that the Ottomans who had captured their land had simply been the last in a long chain of conquerors in the region.[129] *El Tiempo*'s translation of *Mizan*'s address to the empire's Armenians would have only served to highlight for Ladino readers the difference in the two groups' historical experiences. Focusing on the story of one particular community's imagined "first encounter" with the Ottomans, as the Jews' 1892 festivities did, was not a likely path to fostering a sense of shared imperial belonging. Even claims such as the one issued by the Ottoman statesman İbrahim Hakkı Bey that "Turkey has always distinguished itself by its religious tolerance and mild treatment of conquered nations" emphasized that certain Ottomans identified with the conquerers, while others continued to identify, or be identified, as the conquered.[130] Indeed, early during his reign, Abdülhamid II prohibited the public celebration of the anniversary of the 1453 Ottoman conquest of Istanbul for fear that it would be interpreted as a holiday for Ottoman Muslims alone, and that it could provoke resentment among Greek Orthodox observers who identified with the Ottomans' Byzantine predecessors.[131]

Ultimately, the holiday discussed and celebrated by Ottoman Jews in 1892 was not unlike the idea of marking the Ottoman capture of Istanbul in 1453. The special anniversary commemorations of Jews' arrival in Ottoman lands in 1492 raised the interest and discussion of a number of parties, but it was—and could only be—celebrated by the empire's Jews. As such, the early proposals for the event had troubling implications for the Ottoman state, and for Ottomanism as well. Following the logic of that vision, parading one's difference—even in patriotic guise—went against the idea of forging a united Ottoman citizenry. Only shared imperial fêtes could have a place in that project (or, at least, a public one). Attempts to confine the celebration of the Jews' 1892 holiday to the synagogues of the empire may have helped to limit some of its more uncomfortable political implications. Had its original architects succeeded in securing the state's permission to celebrate their holiday on the empire's streets, the message sent to other non-Muslim communities in the empire would not have been a pleasant one.

At the same time, the proposal to celebrate the holiday generated nearly unanimous support in the Ottoman-language press. In this sense, it helped strengthen the perceived ties between Ottoman Jews and Muslims during this period. Ottoman Jews constructed the holiday as a tribute to Muslim tolerance after all, suggesting that the Ottoman sultans of the early empire had blazed the path of civilization at a time when the "so-called civilized countries" were mired in backwardness. Ultimately, the experience of the 1892 celebrations offered Jews a trade-off: building up the myth of a special relationship to the state and to its Muslim population served the Jews well in a number of respects, but it could also potentially strain their relations with members of the other *millets*. This would not be the last time that Ottoman Jews were torn between their attempts to forge ties with their fellow Ottomans of all faiths and an approach to patriotism that favored their connections to Muslims and to Islam and advanced the idea of a Muslim-Jewish alliance. The fact that the new holiday never took on the proportions its supporters had hoped may well have prevented overt conflicts over the message it sent about Jews' privileged place in the empire.

Press reports on Ottoman Jews' participation in the World's Columbian Exposition, by contrast, painted their efforts as contributions to a common imperial venture. That Jews formed part of a shared effort between Ottomans of all faiths presented a fundamentally different model than did the Ottoman Jewish celebrations of 1892 being planned (and thwarted) at the very same time. While Jews had been foremost among the empire's representatives at the fair, they had ultimately gone to Chicago as Ottomans. That they were sometimes mistaken for Muslims or understood to be "Turks" by the fair-going public and that they used Orientalist images of the Ottoman Empire in order to represent their country at the exposition stemmed as much from their sense that doing so was part of a patriotic project as it did from the expectations of local fairgoers who sought to find evidence of an imagined and unchanging East in their Ottoman interlocutors.[132]

In fact, Ottoman Jews also searched for that which was specific and "authentic" about themselves and their empire during this period: identifying what was particular about who they were and where they came from promised them entry into a modern universal community that barred membership to those with no land or cause. This point was brought home to Ottoman Jews most poignantly as they journeyed abroad in 1893, read about the travels of their coreligionists in the pages of their papers, and visited on their own city streets the imperial displays bound for America. In this context, being Oriental in Chicago was not to be confused with uncritically inherited traditions: it was part of conscientious modern practice.

3

Battling Neighbors

Imperial Allegiance and Politicized Violence

In the archival collections of the Alliance Israélite Universelle in Paris sits a letter written by a certain V. Gerson. In the fall of 1896, Gerson addressed the president of the French Jewish organization with a report on the political situation of Jews in Istanbul. By the time of his writing, the Central Committee of the Alliance in Paris had come to expect regular reports from its employees and affiliates not only about the progress of their pupils but also their views on the general state of affairs in the cities and regions where they resided. In this sense, Gerson's correspondence was hardly extraordinary. Yet, its contents dealt with a particularly sensitive subject. Gerson wrote to discuss his recommendations concerning the appropriate response of Jews to violence recently perpetrated against their Armenian fellow citizens in Istanbul. He was concerned that Jewish notables in Istanbul intended to circulate a statement to European newspapers in response to rumors that Jews had been involved in the violent scenes. The aim of such a statement, he explained, was to prove "that the Jews of our capital behaved bravely and honestly during the recent massacres undertaken by Kurds and Lazzes against the poor Armenians of Hasköy." Although he believed the intentions of the statement's authors to be entirely noble, he wrote: "The most basic caution should counsel the Jews of the empire not to say or publish anywhere the fact that they lent their services to the Armenians, people the Ottomans consider, perhaps with some justification, to be traitors, ingrates and anarchists."[1]

Despite his clear ambivalence toward his Armenian compatriots—whom he described as both unfortunate and unruly in turn—the position Gerson advocated could not have been clearer: whatever Jews had done to aid the Armenians of the city that summer, announcing those efforts would compromise the position of his coreligionists in the empire. "Aiding traitors," he warned, "is not the work of a patriot." He followed with foreboding: if the Jews of the capital had such statements published—even if they did so far

74

beyond the reaches of Ottoman territory—the news was bound to upset "the Ottomans" and possibly even spur them to take revenge. Who could know what might befall the Jews should a new massacre occur?[2]

Just a month before Gerson wrote these ominous words, in August 1896, Armenians in the capital had fallen prey to large-scale massacres. The immediate trigger of these events was an action by members of the Armenian Revolutionary Federation (the Hai Heghapokhakan Dashnaktsutiun) who placed bombs throughout Istanbul and held up the Ottoman Bank in an effort to make their demands for Armenian rights known to the world, killing and wounding dozens in the process. Within hours, large mobs armed with clubs, iron bars, and knives beset the city, murdering Armenian residents and pillaging their property. Although official bulletins published in the wake of the violence called on Ottomans of all classes and religions to get along, warned against vigilantism, and threatened to punish anyone who dared to disobey, the massacres lasted two days before the authorities intervened and put an end to the killing.[3]

Contemporary commentators and historians have attributed the attacks on Istanbul's Armenian population alternately to "angry mobs from the lower classes of the capital," "Kurds and Lazzes," or "*softas* [Islamic theology students] and Mussulman roughs."[4] While some scholars insist that the mobs were "disorganized and excitable Muslim . . . rowdies" and "religious extremists," the suggestion of different sources that the attackers carried uniform clubs has led others to surmise police involvement.[5] Although government estimates set the Armenian death toll at just over one thousand, most foreign accounts suggest that many thousands of Armenians were killed over the two-day period.[6] Among the areas with the most victims was the neighborhood of Hasköy, also home to large numbers of the city's Jews, including many of its poorest.

Almost immediately, competing claims arose concerning the role Istanbul's Jews had played in the violence.[7] The version of events suggesting that Jews had aided their Armenian neighbors—the version Gerson hoped to suppress—is corroborated by various eyewitness accounts. Two separate sources tell of Jews in Istanbul who offered their *tefilin* (phylacteries, or leather boxes worn on the arm and head during prayers) to their Armenian neighbors in order to disguise them as Jews amidst the violence.[8] Another source spoke of a "patriarchal old Jew" of Hasköy who hid thirty-one Armenians in his house while "valiantly refusing admittance to hordes of infuriated Turks."[9] A Jewish man by the name of Aboab reported from Cairo that the owners of various Jewish-run department stores in the Ottoman capital had helped their Armenian employees escape on ships bound for Port Said.[10] Still others suggested that hundreds of Jewish families had come to the rescue of the persecuted Armenians during the massacres and that Jewish individuals donated large sums to the ravaged Armenian community after the violence subsided.[11]

Other sources suggest that there were also Jews who helped the attackers find their victims and then joined in the pillaging of Armenian homes.[12] A report lodged by the Armenian Patriarch to the Ottoman government requested state funds to repair Armenian homes pilfered by Jews following the massacres.[13] This version of events made its way not only to Ottoman authorities but also to the *New York Times*, which suggested that in the aftermath of the attacks in Hasköy, "much of the plunder was found in Jewish houses."[14] It also appeared in the account of a Jewish woman who lived in Istanbul's Peri Paşa neighborhood during the massacres and who recalled that "two lower class" Jews from her quarter had taken part in the looting, adding that they were subsequently "ostracized by their neighbors" and that "no good ever came to them because they were cursed by the stolen goods."[15] The stories of Jewish looters who took part in the pillaging of Armenian property in the Ottoman capital also surfaced in an editorial issued by *El Amigo del Puevlo*, a Ladino serial of Sofia. Unburdened by the pressures of censorship within the empire—which prohibited Ottoman journalists from discussing the massacres in any detail— the Bulgarian Jewish author critiqued David Fresco, *El Tiempo*'s director in Istanbul, writing that when "some derelict Jews threw themselves upon the poor Armenians of Istanbul, plundering from them at the hour when they were being hunted down, [the director] . . . did not open his mouth to condemn this act of barbarism."[16]

It was precisely this type of public condemnation that Jewish leaders in the Ottoman capital hoped to combat by circulating a refutation in the foreign press of any Jewish involvement in the 1896 attacks on Armenians. Some did so by focusing exclusively on the stories of the Jews who had sheltered Armenians in their homes and schools amidst the attacks, while also trying to explain away any reports of Jewish wrongdoing by suggesting that those Jews who had joined in the plundering of Armenian homes were impoverished porters forced to carry the goods by the mobs who invaded their neighborhoods.[17] Others took a third position. Suggesting that Jews neither aided the Armenians of the city nor joined the attackers, one letter sent to London's *Jewish Chronicle* denied Jewish involvement in the events altogether. According to the author of this piece, in Istanbul's Halıcıoğlu district not a single Jew ventured out onto the streets during the massacres. Any claims to the contrary, the author asserted baldly, were mere rumors dreamt up by Armenian revolutionaries.[18]

Against such attempts to create the impression of Jews' neutrality, more than one observer explained Jewish involvement in the massacres as overtly political acts. They had "sided with the Turks against the Christians," according to a British source.[19] The antisemitic press of Germany, which picked up—and embellished—the story of Jewish involvement in the violence with no small dose of satisfaction, claimed that the Jews who carted off the possessions of the victims had done so partly because of their hatred of Armenians, with whom they were in economic competition, but most of all because they had "wanted to make a good impression on the Turks."[20] Even some of those who sought to discredit the rumors spoke in similar terms as they attempted to deny the Jews' "supposed support of the Turks against the Armenians."[21]

While publicly Jews met with and refuted claims that they had been on the "side" of Ottoman Muslims—and thus also of the government—privately Gerson suggested that the opposite interpretation was also possible: having sheltered Armenian Ottomans against the wrath of the massacring mobs, Jews might be judged to have placed themselves on the wrong side of the line that increasingly separated "true" Ottomans from the rest.[22] Responding to what he believed to be the expectations of Ottoman patriotism at this moment, Gerson counseled silence. Even if Jewish communal leaders could not control how their coreligionists had acted during the August massacres, they could more carefully craft their position after the fact.

It did not take long until Jewish communal leaders reverted to positions more in line with the civic model of Ottomanism, founded on expectations of cooperation among Ottomans of all faiths. By late October, Moshe Halevi, the acting chief rabbi of the empire, announced publicly that many hundreds of "persecuted Armenians" had found refuge in Jewish houses in the midst of the violence. Although he conceded that items pillaged from Armenian homes had made their way into the homes of some of his coreligionists, he insisted that they had purchased them unknowingly. His announcement further informed readers that all involved parties had returned the stolen goods through his person to the Armenian community after learning of their provenance.[23] Equally notable was the fact that the Jews who donated to the Armenians of the capital in the wake of the massacres chose to do so publicly, ensuring that Jewish names would hold an important place on the lists of donors. The Jewish-run Allatini firm of Salonica was prominent among them.[24]

In early 1897—just half a year after the massacres of Armenians in the Ottoman capital—*El Tiempo* reported that Jewish communal figures had gone to greet the newly appointed Armenian Patriarch during his trip to an Armenian orphanage in the neighborhood of Hasköy.[25] The paper took this opportunity, as it often did on the occasion of an official visit by leaders of one Ottoman community to another, to declare the meeting proof of the excellent relations that existed between Armenians and Jews. The visit was clearly an attempt to repair relations between the two communities. Given the meeting's location in the neighborhood of Hasköy, such an interpretation would not have been lost on readers.[26] Istanbul's Jewish press gave few hints of this possibility, however, instead selecting and publishing stories that could help reinforce a sense of shared Ottoman civic identity among their readership now that the "troubles" were over.[27]

Stories of harmonious interactions between Ottomans of different faiths offered Jewish readers coded instructions about how to strive for peaceful relations with their neighbors. Doing so would make them both model imperial citizens and good Jews who served their community and their state simultaneously. The gala events introduced into cities of the empire in previous decades continued to rank among journalists' favored means of reinforcing civic Ottomanism. Each year, Jewish newspapers from Istanbul to Izmir to Salonica announced balls where Ottoman Christians, Jews, and Muslims alike brushed shoulders and even danced together.[28] It was the kind of social mixing in high society that led to rare marriages between members of the different religious communities in the empire.[29] Ottoman Jewish elites could enact their visions of an integrating Ottoman citizenry as they participated in these formal affairs. Reporting on such events, Jewish journalists hoped to offer the same lesson to broader classes of Jews, who came to read about this form of upper- and middle-class mixing through their pages.[30]

Still, like other inhabitants of the empire, Jews lived with the fear that politicized violence might engulf their neighborhoods, as it had in Istanbul during the summer of 1896.[31] This left them attempting a precarious balancing act. Over-identification with the state held the prospect of worsening their relations with their Christian neighbors and undermining the civic-Ottomanist work their communal leaders had undertaken for decades in an attempt to forge ties of solidarity with imperial citizens of other faiths. At the same time, evidence of alliances with groups deemed suspect by the Ottoman government meant potentially alienating themselves from the authorities or from the city's Muslim population, thus jeopardizing their attempts to make a place for themselves within the Islamic Ottomanist politics of their time. Jewish communal leaders responded to this dilemma with ambivalence, both reacting to and propagating competing definitions of Ottomanism.

The new force shaping Ottoman Jewish politics was Islamic Ottomanism, an imperial ideology that produced what one scholar has called the "slow whittling down of multiethnic, multi-confessional variants of Ottoman patriotism to the narrower scope of Ottoman Muslim patriotism."[32] Gaining momentum following the Russo-Ottoman War of 1877–1878—which ended not only in Ottoman defeat but also resulted in the loss of most of the empire's European territories and a significant portion of its Christian subjects—Abdülhamid II's Islamic politics focused on the Muslims who remained and now constituted approximately three-quarters of the imperial population.[33] The Hamidian regime increasingly chose to emphasize the sultan's role as caliph, or spiritual leader of Muslims worldwide—including those in territories recently lost to the empire—while also seeking to prevent separatist nationalism among Ottoman Muslims.[34]

Abdülhamid II's growing concern over the threat imperialist powers and separatist movements posed to Ottoman territorial integrity was a driving factor behind his decidedly Islamic statecraft, which he intended to resist foreign encroachments into Ottoman affairs.[35] As different non-Muslim communities came to be associated with the expansion of irredentist movements or rival imperial powers, increasing numbers of Ottoman authors and bureaucrats began to regard them with suspicion, as "metaphorical foreigners."[36] It was in this climate that negative portrayals of non-Muslims, especially Armenian and Greek Orthodox Ottomans, made their way into the Ottoman-language press.[37] Seen in this light, Islamic Ottomanism was not only a positive effort to forge ties with Muslims in the empire and beyond, but also an attempt to separate out the internal outsiders from the rest of the imperial population.

Islamic Ottomanism thus offered a potentially disturbing option for Ottoman Jews as well. Civic Ottomanism, the all-encompassing multi-religious form of imperial identification developed during the early reforms of the Tanzimat era, promised Jews a clear place in the social fabric. If the tide continued to turn toward increasingly Islamic definitions of Ottoman belonging, exactly what would the place of Ottoman Jews be? Though the prospect of such a future raised uncomfortable questions, by the time of the 1897 war with Greece, Ottoman Jews were already working out an answer.[38]

Different sources of this period indicate that Jews from Izmir to Istanbul to Salonica continued to search for ways to place themselves at the center of definitions of an ideal Ottoman community, even as these definitions were shifting. Responding to the growing politicization of Islam in the empire, on the one hand, and to long-standing frictions and competition with Ottoman Christian groups on the other, Jews across the empire came to express their identification with Ottoman Muslims, and even with Islam, throughout the period. This trend only intensified as hostilities with Greece erupted in the spring of 1897. The fact that Ottoman Jews viewed their Muslim neighbors as a hegemonic group meant that forging horizontal alliances with them went hand-in-hand with strengthening their vertical alliances with the state.

As much as different Ottoman Jews attempted to prove their loyalty and to adapt themselves to the changing political landscape of the empire during the late Ottoman era, it was no simple task. Jews across the empire faced the challenge of proving they were not internal outsiders at the very moment when thousands of Jewish pupils were attending foreign schools in the empire, particularly those of the Alliance Israélite Universelle (hereafter Alliance).[39] Ottoman Jewish leaders also sought to show that they held no aspirations for national separation as the Zionist movement prepared to make its international debut with the first international Zionist Congress scheduled for the summer of 1897.[40] In their efforts to navigate these tensions, Ottoman Jewish elites searched for ways to continue their public endorsement of an all-inclusive civic Ottomanism while also attempting to keep "suspect" groups at arm's length so as to bind their fortunes with those of Ottoman Muslims and with the state.

Serving the "Greater Good": Reporting on the War from Istanbul

In the spring of 1897, war erupted between the Ottoman Empire and the Kingdom of Greece over the status of Crete, where Greeks from the mainland had joined local Christian islanders in revolt against Ottoman rule. It was not the first time that revolts had challenged Ottoman sovereignty over the island. However, this time public opinion in Greece reached a fever pitch in favor of war.[41] After local Muslims attacked Christian islanders in reprisal for the revolts, the Greek government sent naval ships to Crete to protect them. After a few months of unsuccessful attempts at international intervention, the Ottoman Empire declared war on the Hellenic kingdom on April 18, 1897.[42]

Reports of clashes on the island appeared in Ottoman Jewish newspapers in the capital and beyond, driving home a point that would not have appeared as news to their readers: despite Ottoman Jewish elites' efforts to foster harmonious inter-communal relations, tensions between different religious groups continued to exist and resurfaced in this time of trouble. Violent confrontations between Christians and Muslims were recorded in cities across the empire, from Scutari to Ankara to Izmir.[43] Some of these clashes manifested explicitly as religious conflicts, such as in Scutari, where rumors spread that Christians had defamed a local mosque, or in Salonica, where Muslims allegedly ripped off the armbands of Red Cross personnel because of the cross they bore.[44] Participants in these scuffles appeared to be reenacting on their own streets the war between the Greek and Ottoman armies on the battlefield.

As the conflict escalated, Ottoman suspicions turned toward the empire's Greek Orthodox population.[45] Imperial officials expressed concerns that Greek insurgents across the border would arm Ottoman Christian populations and provoke them to rise up against their state.[46] Although various Greek Orthodox communities and individuals publicly pledged their support for the Ottoman war effort, hundreds of Greek Orthodox young men—Hellenic and Ottoman citizens among them—were reported to be leaving the empire's shores in order to volunteer for the Greek army.[47] The Porte took measures to prevent its nationals from decamping to Greece, while ordering those holding

Greek citizenship to either leave Ottoman realms or renounce their legal status as Hellenes.[48] The measure affected as many as twenty-five thousand Greek citizens residing in the city of Izmir alone.[49] The ecumenical version of Ottoman belonging was thus put to the test once again: officially, the Hamidian regime continued to differentiate between its own Greek Orthodox citizens, whom it suggested remained loyal, and citizens of the Kingdom of Greece, whom it considered as hostiles throughout the duration of the war. Yet various communications from the time suggest that this distinction was not always so clear.[50] In this context, fraternizing with Greek Orthodox Ottomans—an act that would have appeared as an expression of civic Ottomanism just a few months earlier—now threatened to make the position of Jews suspect.

During the war, Jewish journalists and communal leaders in Istanbul began to speak less often of harmonious relations and more of the hardening line between those they portrayed as the friends and enemies of the empire. Editorials marked the rebels of Crete as "Christian brigands" who deserved to be treated like "bandits," while the Muslims who fought against the Christians of the island became noble defenders of the Ottoman cause.[51] In other instances, both the Muslim and Jewish inhabitants of the island appeared as victims in the pages of the empire's Ladino press. As had been the case during the Russo-Ottoman War of 1877–1878, these reports portrayed Ottoman Muslims and Jews as refugees fleeing the violence of the battle zones and retreating into the Ottoman interior together.[52]

Ottoman Jewish journalists pointed their readers toward the confluence of their own interests and experiences and those of Ottoman Muslims. Without making the comparisons explicit, Jewish journalists wrote of how Muslims around the world found new opportunities to unite around the figure of the sultan as caliph, while noting that Jews outside of Ottoman territory honored the sultan in remarkably similar ways. Both during and after the war, Ladino papers reported that Muslims in India and Sephardi Jews in Vienna held public prayers for the Ottoman state, sending first their donations from afar and then their congratulations to the imperial army as it emerged victorious from the conflict in late May.[53] They also told of Bosnian Muslims who had crossed into Ottoman territory to fight for the cause of the Islamic empire just as they ran articles on Jews of Ottoman origin who had found their way to the front from Paris and Vienna.[54]

In some accounts, Jews and Muslims came to stand in for the whole of Ottoman society. A report sent to Istanbul's *El Tiempo* by a Jewish correspondent from Izmir offers a striking example. Opening with the subtitle "Among the Jews," the article described the various patriotic activities the city's Jewish population had undertaken during the conflict, then turned to a description of Ottoman Muslims' patriotism subtitled "Among the Muslims," before coming to an abrupt end. "In short," it concluded, "all of the different communities of our city are proving that they are at the height of their patriotic devotion."[55] Despite his assertion that he spoke of "all of the different communities" of Izmir, the author of the article left out, among others, the local Greek Orthodox population, which by many accounts represented the single largest religious community in the city.[56]

The author's discursive erasure of Christians conferred Jews a special symbolic place at the side of their Muslim compatriots, but to the exclusion of other communities. *El Tiempo*'s contributor was hardly alone in this approach. Although Ottoman Jewish leaders and journalists had long expressed their desire for the camaraderie of all Ottoman religious communities, in wartime they spoke more frequently—sometimes exclusively—of Jews and Muslims when discussing Ottoman patriotism. They also increasingly referred to their "Muslim brothers" when discussing their compatriots, thus effecting the discursive erasure not only of Ottoman Christians but also of women.[57]

Both during and after the war, Ladino publications of the empire actively employed the language of Islamic Ottomanism. *El Tiempo* ran a story on "The Death of a Brave Man," which honored the life of an Albanian Muslim religious martyr, using the Ottoman term of Arabic origin, *şehid*. The man had died fighting the Greeks at Domokos, Jewish readers learned, thus sacrificing his life "for his religion and country" in the final battle of the war.[58] The paper also issued an article entitled "The Caliphate," which explained to its Jewish audience that the Qur'an obligated Muslim allegiance to the sultan-caliph. The Ottoman state was the only remaining Muslim power in the world, the article continued. Because it was the seat of the Caliphate, the vitality of the Islamic faith depended on the empire's continued existence.[59]

During the same period, the Ladino press of the capital invented a new rubric entitled "The Patriotism of the Jews," which began to appear immediately after the empire declared war.[60] These sections told of donations arriving from Jews from all corners of the empire and beyond, of the efforts of young schoolgirls and women who sewed uniforms and visited the sick, of continued pledges to the military subscription fund, of fundraisers for the displaced Muslims of Crete, and of young Jewish volunteers to the army from across the empire.[61]

The new category soon boasted an account from the war that almost immediately bore the makings of a legend. Correspondents from the German and British Jewish press first broke the story.[62] Ottoman and Ladino-language newspapers soon followed.[63] The tale also made its way back to Paris through a letter of an Alliance representative in the capital.[64] These reports spoke of an elderly Jewish man who had risked his life to warn an Ottoman regiment entering the town of Larissa that the bridge they planned to cross was packed

with dynamite. After saving hundreds of Ottoman soldiers, this brave man had
died at the hands of vengeful Greeks.

That was how the story went the first time around at least. It had something of an afterlife, however, and appeared a few weeks later in some of the
same newspapers in a more legendary guise.[65] By this point, the old man had a
name—Nahum. The new account quoted an Ottoman notable of Larissa, who
recalled the old man's last words: "Pasha, do not pass this way!" Nahum reportedly cried. Halting their approach to the mine-laden bridge, he had thus saved
scores of Ottoman lives and allowed imperial forces to successfully capture the
city of Larissa.

Some days later, *El Tiempo* published an official version of the story sent
from the Jewish communal council of the city of Larissa. Having convened at
the behest of the sultan, the authors of this report sought to identify the man
by name so as to bestow a pension in perpetuity upon his family. Although
reports had until this point referred to the Jewish hero of Larissa as Nahum, he
was now identified as a seventy-year-old greengrocer by the name of Salomon
Beja. His son (Joseph Beja), a petty trader, and a friend (Isaac Abraham), a
water carrier, were reportedly with him at the time.[66] After having called out
to warn the regiment of the trap, they were discovered by some Greek "revolutionaries" who shot and killed the old man's son and seriously wounded his
friend. Ironically, little mention is made of the fate of the old man Beja himself
in this version, only that the old man lived.[67] The official reports that made
their way to the Ottoman archives match the later version of the story, suggesting that Salomon and his wife, Esther, were the ones who received government
compensation for the death of their son.[68]

In the end, the precise details of the episode mattered less to those recount-
ing it than the fact that Ottoman Jewry had its own wartime martyr. The tale
became a favorite of the Jewish press during the war and earned the Jews praise
in Ottoman and European circles alike.[69] Elsewhere, the story's popularity had
more adverse effects. It appears to have been the source of the accusations by
the Greek press that Larissa's Jews were engaged in espionage.[70] The historian
Abraham Galante has even claimed that the memory of the incident contributed to the mass flight of Jews from Thessaly after Greek forces retook the
region the following year.[71]

Meanwhile, as Jews in the Ottoman capital read of Jewish wartime heroes
out on the battlefields, the war intruded on their lives in other, subtler ways.
They began replacing the functions and high-class balls boasting guests of all
backgrounds with patriotic events in a more narrow sense. Reports on these
new gatherings tended to mention only that Muslims had been in attendance.[72]
Another change came as the Ottoman Jewish community of the capital began
to shift the focus of its sponsored activities from Jewish charity to efforts

dedicated to the "general good." Given the Hamidian regime's endorsement of Islamic definitions of Ottoman identity, coupled with the new strains of the war with Greece, it is perhaps not entirely surprising that their visions of the general good became increasingly entangled with those of Ottoman Muslims.

This was the case with Ottoman Jews' campaigns to assist the Muslim refugees of Crete, a cause that also garnered a great deal of attention in Ottoman Muslim circles.[73] Although Jews fled the island during the conflict as well, the Ottoman Jewish press did not announce any parallel program to come to their aid.[74] The task of providing for the Cretan Jewish refugees arriving in different cities of the empire was covered mostly by the Alliance, while Ottoman Jews appear to have focused their energies on the "common cause" of aiding Muslim refugees from the island.[75] That Jews were shifting their philanthropic patterns away from Jewish charity during the war was suggested obliquely in several notices published in the Ladino press, which lamented the sorry state of Jewish institutions and their lack of funds at the same time that Jews organized communal efforts toward aiding Muslims from Crete.[76] Although the capital's Jewish press offered no explicit discussion of what these choices meant, its pages often brought the potential slippage between the terms "Ottoman" and "Muslim" into relief.[77]

Just how entangled religious and imperial categories could become is demonstrated by a series of press reports on an Ottoman women's organization formed in Istanbul to provide for soldiers wounded during the war.[78] Though articles appearing in *El Tiempo* encouraged Jewish women across the empire to support the new endeavor, they initially referred to the organization as a "Committee of Muslim Ladies . . . composed of women from the highest ranks of Muslim society."[79] The Ladino press was hardly alone in identifying the society as a Muslim one: the Ottoman-language women's periodical *Hanımlara Mahsus Gazete* similarly introduced the organization as an Islamic Ladies' Society during the same period.[80] The fact that these reports used the term "Muslim" in the committee's title did not stop *El Tiempo* from calling on its female readers to join the group or from praising the efforts of those who did. The newspaper issued various reports about the activities of Madame Elias Pasha, the wife of the Jewish military doctor and Sultan Abdülhamid II's private opthalmologist, who figured prominently among the committee's members; other Ottoman, French, and Ladino papers of the empire similarly recorded the donations she secured for the organization from celebrated foreign philanthropists.[81] There is ample evidence that scores of Ottoman Jewish women contributed directly to the society; both during and after the war, their names regularly appeared among the lists of donors to the committee printed in the Ladino, Ottoman, French, and English press of the imperial capital.[82]

While the designation of the organization as "Muslim" likely served as a marker of the actual religious identity of the majority of the committee's founding members, in the pages *of El Tiempo* it also became a flexible and symbolic term that did not bar Jews' belonging. Remarkably, Ladino reports continued to refer to the society as Muslim even after articles in the empire's Ottoman and French-language press as well as official reports sent to the Porte about the group's activities all came to define the committee in more ecumenical terms, as an Ottoman women's organization.[83] Still, the title of "Muslim" may not have been an entirely comfortable one for Jewish journalists or their reading publics; after some time, *El Tiempo* experimented with calling the charitable organization by other names.[84] It briefly selected the rather bulky label of "The Society Established by Madame Şükrü Bey, Daughter of the Grand Vizier."[85] By late June, the paper finally exchanged the term "Muslim" for "Ottoman," referring to the group as the "Committee of Ottoman Ladies for the Wounded," while also noting the presence of Ottoman Christian women in the society for the first time.[86]

It would be easy enough to conclude that these changes show how Jewish journalists reporting on the society had recognized the incongruity of calling the organization—in which Jews and Christians had played an active role—a Muslim society and that they had finally solved the problem. Easy enough, perhaps, but not wholly accurate: a few weeks after apparently having settled on designating the group as Ottoman, as various other press reports from the empire had done, *El Tiempo* reverted to the original appellation marking the society as Muslim.[87] The terms, as well as the concepts they represented, remained in flux. Ottoman Jews, like other Ottomans, simply lived with the tension.

The war heightened such tensions and made different individuals' and communities' attempts to prove their patriotism more pressing. It was a time to be "on guard," according to the words of a circular issued by Istanbul's Chief Rabbinate to all Ottoman Jewish communities after the war began.[88] During the course of the month-long war, the Jewish community of Istanbul managed the task with relatively few problems and no apparent disasters. A few weeks after the outbreak of hostilities on the Greek-Ottoman frontier, however, Jews of the Ottoman capital found a disconcerting notice in the press that threatened to mar their community's patriotic record.

Troubles surfaced when a number of Jewish notables began to grumble that they had heard nothing after sending donations for the military campaign to the offices of the Chief Rabbinate. They issued a query to the editor of *El Tiempo*: why were their donations not being acknowledged in the Ottoman press as promised? Had the chief rabbi failed to pass them on to the appropriate authorities?[89] A response sent from the Chief Rabbinate's office explained that the Jews as a collective had not yet reached their announced

86 BECOMING OTTOMANS

goal and that notice of individual contributors was being withheld until they
did so.[90] This was not an entirely pleasant message to receive. It hinted that
certain authorities—whether those at the Chief Rabbinate or the responsible
Ottoman officials—had opted to refrain from acknowledging contributors in
the hopes of pressuring them to add more to the imperial coffers. Worse still,
it implied that the Jewish community of Istanbul had fallen short of its patriotic duty on this score. Blame fell first upon the Chief Rabbinate, who rapidly shifted responsibility to the city's local Jewish administrators for having
bungled the matter.[91]

Yet, overall, Istanbul's Jewish community survived the war relatively un-
scathed. Some of its most prominent members even garnered special attention
from the Porte, such as Madame Navon, the Alliance girls' school teacher who
had her pupils sew soldiers' uniforms during the conflict, and Madame Elias
Pasha, the leading member of the "Ottoman" Ladies' Committee in the city.[92]
Elias Pasha, who had long served the imperial army as a Division General in
his capacity as a doctor, was awarded a Greco-Ottoman war medal.[93] Quite
to the contrary of Gerson's forebodings, the Jews of the capital had not been
caught up in the kind of violence perpetrated against Armenians on the streets
of Istanbul in 1896. It was in other Jewish communities of the empire—namely
Salonica and Izmir—that the Greco-Ottoman War of 1897 would truly come
home, in profound and unexpected ways.

From "Zeal and Noise" to Strategies of Silence: Confronting the War in Salonica

In late April 1897, journalists marveled that the recently announced war between the Ottoman Empire and Greece had not led to any disturbances in
the nearby Ottoman port city of Salonica, despite its proximity to the theater
of war.[94] Although it housed the depot for soldiers departing for and returning from the front on a daily basis, Salonica reportedly gave the impression
that it was free from the violence besetting the nearby countryside. One article published by the Jewish-run *Journal de Salonique* just a few days after the
outbreak of hostilities explained the situation by noting that: "The incidents
occurring on the [Greek-Ottoman] border have not damaged in any respect
the excellent relations maintained . . . between all of the different [religious]
communities."[95] That general order had been maintained in a city of Jews,
Muslims, Greek Orthodox, and other Christian groups was indeed impressive,
especially in light of the spontaneous, urban conflicts between members of
different religious communities recorded elsewhere during the conflict. Something was apparently working to ensure the cooperation of all of the city's

residents, despite the fact that as many as nine Greek ships cruised the Gulf of Salonica at the height of hostilities, threatening the city with bombardment.[96]

Salonican Jews' response to the crisis appeared to match perfectly Jewish communal leaders' vision of patriotism in the public sphere. Throughout the war, the city's Jewish journalists announced the various ways Ottoman Jews—and Jews in their city in particular—were proving their unflagging loyalty to the state by outdoing their usual shows of allegiance to the empire.[97] The patriotic campaigns they announced were organized, orderly acts that met with the approval of all authorities and thus rendered an active service to the empire without targeting local scapegoats as associates of the enemy or disturbing relations between different Ottoman communites in the process.

One of the first such stories of Jewish patriotism appeared in the pages of *La Epoka*, which told of two Salonican Jewish youths from "honorable" families who—upon learning of the declaration of war—immediately expressed their desire to take part in the "battle the empire waged to preserve its honor." The article suggested that the two young men had since spurred an "extraordinary movement now spreading among the Jewish youth of the city," over fifty of whom had already applied from every social class to volunteer as Ottoman soldiers. The article also predicted that approximately 150 young Jewish men from Salonica would soon enlist, though it did not explain where this number came from.[98] By early May, the Ottoman periodical *Asır* of Salonica reported that nearly one hundred young Jewish men from the city had volunteered for the army. From the capital, the Ottoman-language newspaper *İkdam* echoed reports of the young men's patriotic initiative.[99]

Various accounts indicate that these Jewish volunteers made their way to the front and served alongside Muslim soldiers. Salonican correspondents for the English *Jewish Chronicle* and the Italian *Vessillo Israelitico* offered eyewitness accounts of Jewish soldiers marching off to war carrying bags of *matsot*, as their departure coincided with Passover.[100] The British consul of the city wrote that some hundred Jewish volunteers from Salonica, Kavala, and other nearby towns had been accepted into local military units. He had seen a detachment of twenty of them proceeding through Salonica's streets, he added, armed like the other soldiers, and each wearing a white fez bearing a red crescent at its center.[101] The choice of the white fez was likely not coincidental: of the only other non-Muslims known to have volunteered for the empire during the war with Greece in 1897, most were Roman Catholic Albanians who had served in separate irregular units and wore a white fez to mark them off from the rest of Ottoman troops. In this way, Salonica's Jewish volunteers in the army appear to have been integrated into its fighting forces while also remaining apart.[102]

The city's Jewish workers, students, and middle-class housewives all reportedly did their part for the war effort as well. From Istanbul, the Ottoman-language newspaper *Sabah* told of how Salonica's famous Jewish porters and carriage-drivers spontaneously offered to transport war munitions for the army across the city, free of charge.[103] Charitable women from Salonica's Jewish community donated beds to temporary hospitals erected on the front by the Red Crescent Society.[104] At the city's train station, a group of young Jewish men organized a special reception for wounded Ottoman soldiers returning from battle, distributing packs of cigarettes and greeting the troops with silver-plated watches engraved with the words "from the Jews of Salonica."[105] The organizers of the initiative won praise from the Ottoman-language press and reportedly inspired their coreligionists in Istanbul to undertake similar actions.[106] The Ottoman journal *Malumat* of Istanbul even honored the group's leaders by featuring their photographs within its pages.[107] Etchings produced during the war may also have been modeled on the welcome reception orchestrated by the city's Jewish youths, as they portrayed "Jews and imperial soldiers" socializing together at Salonica's train station where the group had gathered (Figure 3.1).[108]

All of these various demonstrations of loyalty merged so well with the ideals of the Jewish journalists of the city that their job was made easy; they recounted the news immediately and triumphantly.[109] Yet, since their larger

Figure 3.1 Jews and soldiers at Salonica's train station, 1897—C. A. Fetzer, *Aus dem thessalischen Feldzug der Türkei: Frühjahr 1897: Berichte und Erinnerungen eines Kriegskorrespondenten* (Stuttgart: Deutsche Verlags Anstalt, 1898).

project aimed at shaping their readership's self-perception, collective memory, and even behavior, they were also willing to do what they deemed necessary to bury certain realities they believed would jeopardize the position of their community or peace in their city.

Despite their best efforts to manage the public image of their community, Ottoman Jews also sometimes expressed their sense of identification with the empire and with Muslims in a manner that concerned rather than pleased Ottoman Jewish elites. These acts of patriotism were often spontaneous and regularly appeared as a form of opposition to a third party that became an adversary and a foil for Ottomanness.[110] When one such chaotic moment threatened to turn violent within the city itself during the height of the conflict, the Salonican Jewish press faced a dilemma. The disturbance did not match its reports of inter-communal harmony in the midst of war, nor did it fit with its position that "the Salonican resident represents the ideal of the malleable and governable citizen."[111]

But were Salonica's denizens in fact such perfectly governable citizens? Clues about underlying patterns of sociability and conflict in Salonica suggest otherwise. One such development surfaced in Salonican Jewish newspapers some two months before war was declared, in early February. At that moment, the *Journal de Salonique* called for the serious attention of police concerning the "scandalous activities" taking place in an open space behind Hamidie Boulevard every Saturday. There, the article explained, numerous gangs of young Greek and Jewish ruffians gathered and arranged themselves "in the order of battle." At this point, they would begin throwing rocks, which at times rained down "with such fury that they leave the site of battle and injure innocent passers-by on the boulevard." Local Greek Orthodox and Jewish leaders had done all they could to discourage this behavior, but nothing had worked to combat the "instinct of aggressiveness reigning among these little scoundrels."[112] At this point, the article concluded, only the strong hand of the police could help.

An article that appeared the following day in the Ladino serial *La Epoka* suggested that the fighting was a kind of ritualized violence.[113] It had plagued Salonica for some time and, as such, was a "chronic sickness" that was taxing the nerves of those who cared about the community.[114] The Ladino article counseled parents to keep a watchful eye on their children. It also asked that Salonica's rabbis offer sermons in synagogues across the city condemning both the stone throwing and the profanation of the Jewish Sabbath that resulted from the boys' choice of Saturday for their rows. In following weeks, both *La Epoka* and *Le Journal de Salonique* suggested that their intervention in the matter had effectively resolved the issue, as they noted that twenty stone-throwing youths had been arrested and both newspapers thanked the police for bringing the situation under control.[115]

On April 28, 1897, some ten days after the declaration of war with Greece, an incident occurred in Salonica that posed entirely new problems for those in charge of the Jewish community of the city. While journalists ascribed the routine rock fights to a group of lower-class Jewish and Greek youths—thus suggesting that the unfortunate pattern might still be "corrected" with time and education—this new development had allegedly involved large numbers of grown Jewish men. What is more, it occurred in a central location in the town, under the eyes of many, including foreign observers.

That day, as a trainload of wounded Greek prisoners returning from the battlefield passed through Salonica, local Muslims and Jews reportedly gathered at the train station and began taunting the train's passengers. According to the Athenian paper *Akropolis*, the threats the Jews and Muslims hurled at the Greek prisoners continued for over an hour, as they followed the railcars across Salonica's streets to its famous White Tower, where the prisoners were to be held.[116] The Greek Minister of Foreign Affairs later reported to the French Embassy in Athens that the number of individuals who antagonized the prisoners had exceeded fifteen thousand.[117] While this number may well have been exaggerated, it nonetheless provides an indication of the significant figures involved and—at the very least—of the enormity with which the event came to be painted by some.

Although Jews and Muslims of Salonica came out together to confront the Greek soldiers who represented their "enemy" at this moment, certain consular and foreign reports suggested that Jews had been at the center of this outburst.[118] The Athenian *Akropolis* even accused the entire Salonican Jewish community of having participated.[119] The clear hyperbole of this last claim aside, the fact that Jews became especially visible in the coverage of the train station scandal posed a problem for the leaders of the Jewish community and for its journalists, who responded only with silence. In fact, throughout the following weeks, they did not mention the disturbance The inter-communal scuffles that had previously occurred offstage, so to speak, in peacetime, and away from their city's center, had been disturbing but manageable enough. Yet when war broke out, and tensions were suddenly cast in clearly political molds, their former methods—calls to the chief rabbi for sermons and to the police for action—no longer sufficed.

The silence of Salonica's Jewish press in this case cannot be reduced to the simple presence of a censorship regime.[120] Jewish journalists might have chosen to decry the acts of their coreligionists in order to distance themselves from those who perpetrated the aggression against the Greek prisoners of war, for example, as the Jewish community of Greece chose to do through the medium of the Athenian periodical *Embros*.[121] They might also have addressed such reports in order to deny their veracity, an approach often employed by Ottoman journalists who met with news they believed might soil the reputation of the empire.[122] The harassment of prisoners of war held in Ottoman custody clearly fell into this last category. Both approaches—distancing and denunciation—were tactics employed commonly in the Jewish press of the empire, and both would have likely passed by the imperial censors.

The total silence of the local Jewish press in the face of the disturbances reported at the train depot in late April 1897 suggests that its journalists had chosen self-censorship as a means of keeping the peace in their city. No less important, it speaks to their inability to handle and fully assimilate the more complex and sometimes uncomfortable aspects of the very patriotism they espoused and attempted to foster among their readers. In the case of the rock fights occurring each Saturday, local journalists interceded and, at least briefly, succeeded in halting much of the violence. This time, the story of the harassment of Greek prisoners in Salonica had been picked up abroad, in particular by the Athenian press, which blamed Salonica's Jews for the affair. While the incident may have been influenced by preexisting tensions between local Ottoman Greeks and Jews, once Jews and Muslims of the city clashed with Greek prisoners of war, the battles waged on Salonica's streets took on newly urgent and political layers of meaning for all involved.

Also striking was the total sense of confidence that Salonican Jews displayed during the incident, as they goaded the captured Greek soldiers passing through town. With the additional police surveillance of wartime and the new presence of Ottoman soldiers in the city, the Jews—who formed the single largest community in Ottoman Salonica—appear to have felt a bolstered sense of security, in contrast with local Christians, many of whom feared that they might become targets of anti-Greek and anti-Christian sentiments during the same period.[123] The applause with which Salonican Jews' patriotic campaigns had been met by Ottoman Muslim officials and journalists may have further emboldened them and contributed to the spontaneous manifestations of animosity they exhibited toward the empire's "enemy" in their midst.

Yet, these Jews' sense of ownership over the city's public spaces clearly clashed with the bourgeois mindset of the city's Jewish journalists, who complained about such attitudes a few months later, well after the fighting on the battlefront had ceased. In August, a writer for *La Epoka* bemoaned the fact that Salonican Jews had the unfortunate habit of praying on the streets and at the quay, in the path of passersby. Although the onlookers did not dare laugh out loud upon seeing this sight, the author wrote, he cringed to imagine what they might be thinking to themselves.[124] The fact that such scenes took place along the quay, an area understood by many as a showcase of Salonica's modernity, must have made the "backward" behavior of the Jews who prayed there particularly disturbing to Jewish reformers.[125]

The appeals Jewish journalists made to their readers about how to act in public expressed more than a simple concern for the maintenance of the public image of their particular community, however. As they entreated their coreligionists to behave with decorum they also expressed their ideal vision of an Ottoman public sphere. Their visions seemed to have been modeled more closely on the closed balls of the empire's high society—where participants, decorous and decked out in frock coat and fez, appeared equally as modern Ottoman citizens—than on the quotidian realities of their city's streets, where young Jewish and Greek Orthodox boys continued to throw stones at each other, where Jews announced their difference publicly by praying along the quay, and—worst of all—where grown Jewish and Muslim men broke international codes of conduct concerning the treatment of prisoners of war. These uncomfortable examples suggested to Jewish elites that their work in turning their coreligionists into obedient, patriotic citizens was far from complete.

When a representative of the Alliance in Salonica assessed the effects of the conflict a few months later, he worried that the events of recent months had disturbed the progress of civic Ottomanism and inter-communal harmony. In contrast to the official story of calm offered by the city's Jewish press, this observer wrote with concern about the excessive "zeal and noise" that had accompanied the Jews' public demonstrations of loyalty to the Ottoman Empire during the war. He feared that the Jews—having abandoned their usual reserve—had turned the local Greek Orthodox population against them.[126] Although the Jewish periodicals of the time were not inclined to mention it, various sources indicate that Greek-Jewish tensions deteriorated following the conflict.[127]

Indeed, throughout the war, Salonican Jews had found that taking part in patriotic projects was never a neutral act. Rather, the increasingly polarized politics of wartime in their city often forced them to take sides or identified them with one group of Ottomans as opposed to another, as had been the case for Istanbul's Jews in the wake of the massacres of Armenians in that city a year earlier. During the war, the Salonican Jewish press, like the Ottoman Jewish press as a whole, sent mixed messages. While it officially endorsed inter-communal cooperation and civic models of Ottoman belonging, it also often prioritized alliances with Muslims and called on Jews to prove that their patriotism knew no bounds. Yet disorganized and unplanned manifestations of any sort—even those of a patriotic character—greatly disturbed Jewish elites in Salonica, who hoped to erase either their practice or their memory, or both. Despite the claims of Jewish papers to the contrary, the war raging off in the distance had—in fact—found its way home, to the streets of Salonica.

Between Civic and Islamic Ottomanism: Negotiating the War in Izmir

Like the reports on the exemplary cooperation of all of Salonica's denizens during the war, the Ladino press in Izmir also boasted about the harmony that reigned among the different groups living in the city.[128] Early in 1897, the Ladino journal *El Meseret* published an article describing the cooperation and openness that abounded in Izmir. It told the story of a young man, who early one morning awakened his neighbors with alarming cries. As they soon realized, he was drowning at the nearby docks and calling for help. "It was early in the morning," the paper recounted, "most people were still asleep, some were already in the synagogue reciting their prayers . . . All those around responded rapidly and ran out . . . but he lost all his remaining strength and began to sink. If it had not been for a Jewish boy . . . who tied a rope around his body . . . "[129]

The story ended happily, and with a Jewish hero, although, for the time being, the drowning man remained unidentified. "No one knew to which religion this man belonged, or how he had fallen into the sea," but this did not stop them from saving him, the editorial continued. As it turned out, the man was a Greek Orthodox Christian. The paper proudly pointed to this fact in order to demonstrate the level of inter-communal respect and support present in the city: the denizens of Izmir risk their lives for the sake of their fellow man, readers learned, without noticing or inquiring after his religion.

A variant of this ideal vision of inter-ethnic "blinders" was echoed in the columns of the same paper a month later, when it reminded its audience that "our magnanimous sultan protects all of his citizens without distinction of race or religion." The paper introduced the image in the context of an article it published concerning the regular weekend outings the residents of Izmir were known to take in and around the city. Thankfully, the sultan took good care of all Ottomans, the article continued: "the surveillance of the police is not wanting, there is no reason to be afraid," and everyone found nothing but "safety and peace" during their excursions.

Yet, the same article, which had begun with discussions of the sultan, safety, and peace, continued with a warning. Despite these near-perfect conditions, it explained "we Jews take our outings in such a strange manner that we invite malicious gossip. And so it is that every year the non-Jewish periodicals of our city relate at least one or two unpleasant incidents . . . which, even if they do not shame our entire nation, clearly do not bring us any honor. And why is this? It is because . . . we go walking *a la Europea* [in European fashion], men and women together, hand in hand, with drinks and food. These good people believe themselves to be acting like Europeans without understanding the

European way. They go just to have fun and forget that they are not at home—they are in a public place . . . a place which is open to all eyes."[130]

The article further detailed how "alcohol, a poor counselor," was leading Jews of both sexes to get drunk, sing, prance around, and shout, which in turn spawned the laughter and ridicule of non-Jewish passersby. Consequently, brawls broke out, women tried to interfere, and in the end, the article explained, "Jewish men and women get entangled with non-Jews, the public attempts to intervene, and the blame is laid upon the Jew, or, better put, upon 'the Jews.'" The paper admonished its readership, noting that as a small, non-Muslim community they occupied a precarious position, and that they must maintain "serious caution in their actions and movements." In light of these comments, the paper's earlier insistence on the invisibility of communal boundaries appears more clearly for what it was—the excessive protestations of a newspaper intent upon shaping both its readers' behavior and the way they interpreted their reality.

While the context of inter-communal tensions was different in Izmir, where Jews were less numerous than in Salonica, the immediate solution proposed by the city's Ladino press coincided with the approach advocated by Salonica's Jewish papers in response to the weekly rock fights. The veteran Ladino periodical of the city, *La Buena Esperansa*, had dedicated various columns to the unsettling subject of these outings for a number of years already, *El Meseret* clarified. It now called upon the chief rabbi to denounce these activities in the city's synagogues once and for all. The author of the article further suggested that the Jewish spiritual leader also call in the force of the police, since only "they wield the power to prevent these people from getting drunk in public."[131]

The moral the article drew from these "scandalous activities" represents a drastic departure from the conclusions arrived at by Jewish elites in Salonica in response to the rock fights, however. There, journalists and representatives of the Alliance concluded that such exchanges were a sign of "backward" behavior that could be rectified through "modern," western-style education. The Izmir-based piece did not treat such clashes as vestiges of a disagreeable past, but rather as the result of embarrassing and mistaken attempts among local Jews to be both "modern" and "European." It explained: "We thank God that we live side by side with a people that shares our moral code almost entirely—the Turkish nation also does not tolerate the mixing of the sexes. Its decency is exemplary." "Rather than imitate the Europeans," the author continued, "many of whose customs do not suit us, we would be well-served to imitate the Turks, removing from our midst various European customs which we enact only awkwardly and which bring us great moral and material harm."[132] The newspaper thus used the occurrence of regular disturbances between Jews and their neighbors to offer its readership a moral and political lesson: Ottoman

Jews were to be made aware, if they were not already, of their special affinities with their Muslim neighbors and to consciously strengthen these connections as they read their morning papers.[133]

Expressing their gratitude to those responsible, subsequent reports indicated that the campaigns against the ill-advised drunken strolls were proving successful. By March, however, a new problem had arisen, "an even dirtier wound," the paper reported, "worse than the earlier-mentioned outings."[134] Apparently, the Sabbath excursions were being undertaken by "newly Europeanized Jewish youths" who rented boats and conducted themselves in such a manner that they almost invariably ended up overturned. The message was clear: those involved were told that they were lucky to have ended up with only a bath and were admonished for behaving irresponsibly, risking their own lives as well as those of the people who came to their aid.

In sharp contrast to the case of the drowning Greek man saved by a Jewish youth some months before, the news this time did not bring with it a message of a city blind to communal boundaries. With Jews in need of rescue from the city's waters, the paper's stance changed radically, as it acknowledged that communal divisions were important elements of the local landscape. When reporting on local news, the serial alternated between attempts to reinforce its ideal of inter-communal harmony and its sense of obligation to respond to the reality of Izmir's streets. Calls to halt embarrassing or disgraceful behavior among the city's Jewish population continued in the following months, evincing an underlying anxiety about the place of Izmir's Jewish minority.

As war approached, indications of Jewish leaders' concern about the behavior of their coreligionists in Izmir coincided with exuberant accounts of Jewish patriotism as well as identification with the Ottoman Empire. The Ladino weekly *El Meseret*, for its part, began a special subscription during the war, announcing that it would donate all income generated by new subscribers to the empire's military campaign during a three-month period.[135] Jews in Izmir and its outlying areas held special ceremonies for their military and prayed for its rapid and total victory. They gave public speeches in Ladino and Turkish emphasizing their dedication to the cause and to their state; many donated money, clothing, or supplies to funds created for the army.

Revelling in the Ottoman victory and, apparently, competing with one another, the Ladino newspapers *El Meseret* and *El Nuvelista* of Izmir both published poems entitled "Domokos," the scene of the war's final battle. One of these poems extolled the strength and courage of the "Ottoman race" as embodied by its soldiers.[136] The other foretold that the time had come for the enemies of the "Turks" to tremble in the face of men who fought like lions, a well-known trope in Ottoman literature.[137]

An article entitled "Patriotism and Religion" published by *El Meseret* shortly after war was announced similarly praised the bravery of the empire's soldiers, entreating its readers to think of their "Ottoman brothers" who left their homes, wives, and children to fight and serve the cause of their "offended *patria*." "Women, men, old and young, girls and boys, we must all do everything in our power to better the lives of our brothers the soldiers who bear the hardships of war with so much sufferance," the author exhorted his audience. "Money, flour, quilts, tents, clothes, shoes, fezzes and other items; all of these are good," he continued. Any of these items were worthy donations for their country's cause.[138]

The author's reference to the Jews' Ottoman brothers as soldiers in this instance made clear that those he had in mind were Muslims, despite the fact that Jews had now begun to volunteer in the army as well. Although scores of young Jewish men from Salonica, Kavala, Istanbul, Bursa, and Izmir's own Aydın province had enlisted during the war, the vast majority of Ottoman forces were still Muslims. *El Meseret* thus suggested to its Jewish readership that it was their Islamic compatriots who sacrificed everything for the empire.[139]

The article also reminded readers of their precarious position in larger imperial configurations. Its author cautioned them to remain moderate in their conduct and, "if at all possible," to "wear the fez as a permanent sign of patriotism." Outward signs of private loyalties were crucial, he explained, for it was "not enough to have only a heart full of patriotism." Jews obligations were instead "to show through our acts and our clothing that we are proud to be the faithful subjects of the great and powerful Ottoman Empire."[140] The author clearly considered donning the fez as evidence of patriotic zeal, but the fact that he had felt the need to make this plea suggests that he considered his ideal to be too far from reality in this moment of heightened visibility.

These prescriptions were part of a larger campaign *El Meseret* conducted during this period in order to dissuade Ottoman Jews from going the way of the West. Just a few months earlier the newspaper had warned its readers that attempting to ape European ways was unnatural for them. It now suggested that coming closer to the habits—and headgear—of Ottoman Muslims offered Jews a way of becoming more patriotic and morally upright at the same time. In this sense, the Hamidian state's discourse of Islamic morality influenced even its Jewish inhabitants' understandings of how to be proper Ottomans.[141]

A new report soon indicated that things had begun moving in the right direction. In nearly every city of the empire, readers learned, men who formerly wore hats were trading them in for the fez, the great marker of allegiance to the empire.[142] It was perhaps no coincidence that a Jewish charity group of Izmir chose to earmark the money it donated to the imperial army for the purchase of one thousand fezzes. Associating themselves with the empire's official headgear in this way was clearly a symbolic act that may have earned the society's members—and the city's Jewish community in general—more political capital than the donation of any other single item could.[143]

As *El Meseret*'s author had suggested, however, patriotic duties did not lay only with Ottoman men. Trying to ensure that women were also doing their part, another of the city's Ladino papers, *La Buena Esperansa*, publicly invoked the patriotic sentiments of a certain Madame Joselin, who it noted had, "during the time of the Russo-Turkish War . . . been president of a Jewish women's charitable society and at numerous times expressed her sympathy for the [empire's] soldiers."[144] The author of the article, explaining that he did not understand why Madame Joselin had failed to heed the call of duty this time, apparently compelled her into action. A subsequent issue of the same paper announced that she had managed to bring her society back together and that the group had already sewn one hundred shirts for Ottoman soldiers stationed in the region.[145]

Through its treatment of Madame Joselin, *La Buena Esperansa* exposed its desire to exert a coercive power over even the most respected members of his community. Madame Joselin had been publicly singled out and scolded—however gently—when her activities did not match up with those the editor had in mind for her and her one-time patriotic society.[146] While the irresponsible actions of Jewish youths in Salonica and Izmir had drawn severe criticism and elicited calls for harsh measures, this most recent story made clear that the elites of the community were to be no less immune from receiving public lessons in propriety, patriotism, or both, through the pages of the Ladino press.

What is perhaps most striking of all is that, as in Salonica, there came a moment for the Jewish community of Izmir when the patriotism of the local Jewish population appeared to have run amok. This moment posed a challenge for the leaders and journalists of the Jewish community, who until then had so glibly reported the spectacular shows of patriotism performed by local Jews during the war. It was no doubt a simple coincidence that this moment occurred just a few days after the disturbance in Salonica.

The first notices of trouble in Izmir came not from the local Jewish press, but rather from the pages of Ottoman-language journals in the empire. A representative of the Alliance based in Istanbul soon noted the occurrence in his reports back to Paris as well. The story sounded familiar enough when it began; it consisted of exuberant young Jewish men, caught up in a wave of patriotism, presenting themselves as volunteers in the imperial army. Yet what followed seemed to suggest that Ottoman Jewish patriotism had gone awry, at least in the estimation of those who believed themselves to be the guardians of the community and its future. These Jewish leaders and elites now confronted the unforeseen and—for them—clearly negative consequences of their community's sometimes overly exuberant patriotism. As Jewish youths across the empire presented themselves as volunteers for military service, a large group of Jewish men from Izmir reportedly came forward with a new interpretation of this request: in addition to proclaiming their desire to serve in the ranks of the Ottoman military, they also made it known to local officials that they intended to convert to Islam.

The numbers of those who underwent this process vary according to the source. Apparently, a few separate groups undertook the task over a period of about a week. The first notices of the phenomenon appeared in the Ottoman-language press. On May 5, 1897, İkdam and Tercüman-ı Hakikat told of three Jewish men from Izmir who converted to Islam, then applied to serve in the army.[147] The same day, Tercüman-ı Hakikat and Sabah wrote of a fourth Jewish man who had converted and taken the name Ali Abdullah before attempting to join the imperial forces in Izmir.[148] Three days later, Sabah reported that some sixty-five Jews had converted to Islam while voluntarily inscribing themselves into the army in a show of total dedication to their empire.[149] İkdam reported twenty-five convert volunteers on the same day.[150] By May 11, Sabah and İkdam registered another thirty-two conversions of Jewish men who had lodged requests to join the army.[151] İkdam soon reported that another eight Jewish individuals from the city had converted to Islam.[152] Over the course of just eight days, over a hundred Jewish men had reportedly changed their religion as they announced their intention to join the Ottoman army.[153]

Not surprisingly, this news, which showed up in private Jewish sources such as the correspondence of the Alliance, did not find its way as easily into the local Jewish press. Izmir's Jewish leaders were apparently at a loss. While conversions were known and in fact somewhat routine occurrences within the Jewish community, they usually occurred on a small scale and for seemingly more personal reasons, primarily economic ones.[154] Any sort of conversion en masse was so out of the ordinary as to lead to suspicions that foul play might have been involved, or perhaps large-scale disaffection with the community or some of its members. Yet, this was not the explanation offered by the sources of the time. They pointed only to the will of these Jewish youths to serve their country and to their great sense of Ottoman patriotism. The fact that no evidence of coercion has surfaced and that Jews elsewhere in the empire were being accepted as volunteers within the ranks of the Ottoman army without becoming Muslims makes the occurrence of such large-scale conversions appears all the more perplexing.[155]

Indeed, the leaders of the Jewish community in Izmir had great difficulty formulating either an explanation or a response to the news. Most local Jewish papers stayed silent on the subject, much as the Salonican Jewish press had done in the face of accusations of Jewish misconduct with Greek prisoners of war.[156] Only the oldest and most-established Ladino newspaper of the city, *La Buena Esperansa,* dedicated a short and well-hidden note without a subheading of its own to the recent chain of conversions. The editors did not hide their dismay or their thinly veiled criticism of the choice of these youths who had left their community: "It is being said by [various Ottoman] periodicals that all of these conversions have been animated by the patriotic sentiments of those who wanted to serve among the ranks of the Ottoman army as volunteers. In reality, we are unable to explain the motives that obliged these youths to abandon their religion, since they were perfectly able to serve their homeland without any obligation to convert."[157] As a testament to this, the paper offered the example set by young Jewish men elsewhere in the empire: "We are aware that in Salonica and in Bursa various Jewish youths have enlisted themselves as volunteers in the army while still holding fast to the religion of their forefathers."[158]

In the midst of the war, the young Jewish volunteer converts from Izmir and the crowds of Jewish onlookers who heckled Greek prisoners at Salonica's train station appear to have taken their communal leaders' visions of solidarity with "their Muslim brothers" to unprecedented extremes. Perhaps the Jews enacting this form of identification with their state felt they were simply pushing the patriotic project they had imbibed in their newspapers, schools, and synagogues to their logical conclusion as they put their love of country above all else. For the leading elites of these communities, however, the disturbance at the train depot in Salonica and the group conversions in Izmir represented the excesses of the very patriotism they had been trying to foster over the course of various decades. Finding their messages distorted and misread, they approached with silence the troubles that now cast such a long shadow at the height of the 1897 war with Greece. In the end, Ottoman patriotism and identification with local Muslims, both goals the Ottoman press had pursued vociferously throughout the conflict, seemed to have slipped just beyond the control—and even the comprehension—of the Jewish journalists who had perhaps done the most of all to advance these campaigns within their community.

Conclusion

The varied and ambivalent reactions of Jews in the empire to the massacres of Armenians in Istanbul in 1896 and the Ottoman war with Greece in 1897 taught those who considered themselves the custodians of their respective communities that they needed to find ways not only to foster patriotism among their

constituencies but also to manage it. The process of trying to shape the identity
and behavior of Ottoman Jews was in the end inextricably linked with their own
visions and values. In fact, it was not patriotism alone they desired, but patriotism in a particular packaging, wrapped up in middle-class notions of propriety,
moderation, and duty as well as modern civil and urban belonging. Even if all
of these other components had come in the form of unspoken or only partially
articulated expectations, Jewish elites in all three cities sought to create modern
Ottoman Jewish patriots who shared a certain set of values with them. Their
vision was similarly predicated on their own understandings of "proper" and
peaceful behavior in the urban public sphere, which was not to be confused with
the officially sanctioned and appropriate violence on the battlefield.

When acts of identification with the state, against its enemies or with
local Muslims and even Islam appeared in other guises (popular, spontaneous, and unrestrained) and in the wrong places (the city), these elites looked
on with dismay. Their project of promoting patriotic action within their
communities—which appears from an initial reading of their own press a successful venture—was in fact fraught with internal contradictions that they
themselves embodied and that were part of the larger project of Ottoman state
patriotism at that time.

Responding to the Hamidian regime's emphasis on the Islamic nature of
the empire, various Jewish individuals—ranging from young male army volunteers and journalists to rabbis and charitable women—found ways of announcing their imperial belonging by emphasizing their special alliance with
Ottoman Muslims. The different symbols and values associated with Islam in
late Ottoman public spheres also made their way into the patriotic repertoire
of Ottoman Jews, who repeatedly emphasized their identification with their
"Muslim brothers" in speeches and the press and attempted to make such links
concrete through their participation in projects clearly marked as Islamic.
Alignment with local and even distant Ottoman Muslims became an integral
way for Ottoman Jews to express their loyalty to the empire during the war.
While they continued to support an inclusive vision of harmony among all
religious groups of the empire, both in the midst of the 1896 massacres of Armenians and during the war, proclamations of this type receded, giving way
to other forms of allegiance. Yet, just as had been the case after the massacres,
once the war with Greece was over, the Ottoman chief rabbi and members of
his staff paid an official visit to the Orthodox Patriarch's headquarters in the
Fener district of Istanbul. There he was "received with every honor," while the
head of the Greek Orthodox Church reportedly assured him that he considered it his first duty to "aid in maintaining cordial relations between the two
peoples." A few days later, the Patriarch made his way to the residence of the
chief rabbi in Kuzguncuk.[159]

Exploring the varied responses of Ottoman Jews to the Armenian massacres of 1896 and to the Greco-Ottoman War of 1897 shows how Jews in the empire engaged—both wittingly and unwittingly—with two parallel discourses of what it meant to be Ottoman. One of these focused on the multi-ethnic and multi-religious make-up of the empire. It included Jewish communal leaders' attempts to distance themselves from attacks on Armenians in Istanbul and to emphasize the aid Jews had given to those fleeing the massacre, their conciliatory visits with Armenian and Greek Orthodox leaders, and the regular balls they attended alongside members of various Ottoman communities. The other version of Ottoman belonging, which emphasized the Islamic identity of the empire and its predominantly Muslim subjects, often excluded groups that appeared to fall on the wrong side of the dividing line demarcating imperial identity during times of heightened tensions.

Taking this position allowed Jews to attempt to create a place for themselves in the rapidly changing political landscape of the empire, but it also sometimes had negative consequences. Jews in Larissa—having openly celebrated the Ottoman entry into their city in 1897—suffered greatly when Greek forces reoccupied the town in 1898. At that time, Greek Larissans charged Jews and Muslims alike with wrongdoing during the war and the yearlong Ottoman occupation that followed.[160] Jewish merchants and communal leaders of that city were imprisoned, accused of insulting the Greek flag, questioning the bravery of Greek soldiers, and having "philo-Turkish" tendencies.[161] Many of the city's Jewish and Muslim families fled to Ottoman territory, never to return.[162] Even years later, observers suggested that the massacres of Armenians in Istanbul in 1896 had drawn a wedge between Armenians and Jews in the city and that Jews' enthusiastic demonstrations of support for the empire during the war with Greece soured relations between Jews and Greek Orthodox Christians in both Salonica and Izmir.[163] Some of these same observers counseled a more cautious approach to patriotic positions and attempted to repair Jews' relations with their Christian neighbors, thus returning to the civic Ottomanism that many members of their community had largely relegated to the sidelines during moments of violence.

Despite the challenges the Islamic version of Ottomanism posed to non-Muslims, the new options Jews found for imperial identification within an Islamic framework clearly suggest that the Hamidian turn toward Islamic politics did not categorically foreclose non-Muslim participation. As Ottoman historian Mustafa Aksakal writes, even discussions of jihad—potentially "hostile towards non-Muslims in the Ottoman Empire"—could sometimes "explicitly include non-Muslims in the Ottoman fold."[164] As an ideology of state patriotism, Abdülhamid II's Islamic politics were not simply the domain of Muslims, but also of those willing to express their allegiance to the state by engaging with Islamic symbols and rhetoric. Ottoman Jews told each other stories about the caliphate and the glory of Islamic martyrs because these were formal elements of the Islamic Ottomanism of their day. While their position within this new framework was not always clear, the actions they undertook at these moments shed light on their search for a place for themselves in imperial politics, even as the ground beneath their feet was shifting. The results themselves were only sometimes harmonious: they also exposed rifts between Jews of different classes, education, and worldviews; between different Ottoman communities; between committed Ottoman patriotism and local civic belonging; and between identifying as Jews and simultaneously identifying with Muslims and Islam.

4

Contest and Conflict

Jewish Ottomanism in a Constitutional Regime

The Second Constitutional period that came on the heels of the Young Turk revolution of 1908 reinstated the short-lived Ottoman constitution of 1876 and brought new freedoms to Ottoman citizens. It also witnessed an explosion of new publications, clubs, political parties, and—along with all of these new developments—new rivalries. The situation Ottoman Jewish leaders faced in the wake of such dizzying changes necessarily altered their approach to politics and patriotism. Swiftly, they realized that it was no longer enough to simply portray Ottoman Jews as the most loyal *millet*. In their rapidly shifting political landscape, various competing Jewish groups battled one another while striving to earn the attention and support of the new regime. Although they continued to invoke their special relationship to the state, under the new government, Jewish leaders found it increasingly difficult to speak of Ottoman Jewry as a single collective. Ottoman Jews were now Zionists and anti-Zionists, socialists and liberals, supporters of the new regime or members of the old guard.

While under the Hamidian regime (1876–1909) Jewish elites had often attempted to distance themselves and their communities from other Ottomans government authorities considered suspect, various Jewish elites now attempted to distance themselves from members of their own community whose politics they disavowed. The multiplication of different political affiliations among Ottoman Jews in the wake of the 1908 revolution brought to the fore new and conflicting definitions of Jewish Ottomanism.[1]

In contrast to the pre-revolutionary era, when Zionist activism had not officially (or, at least, publicly) been an option for Ottoman Jews, the explosion of political parties under the new regime allowed a local form of Zionism to emerge as a significant player on the political scene.[2] Almost immediately, the appearance of the new movement sent shock waves across Ottoman Jewish communities. Supporters of the integrationist platform of the Alliance Israélite Universelle went on the defensive, suggesting that Zionism's goal of securing a Jewish homeland in Ottoman Palestine worked against the interests of Ottoman unity. Fearing that the Jewish nationalist movement would compromise the position of Jews in the empire, numerous Ottoman Jewish leaders came out against Zionism, including the new chief rabbi, Haim Nahum, and various Jewish deputies in the reconvened Ottoman parliament.[3] Through the medium of his Ladino serial *El Tiempo*, the vocally anti-Zionist journalist David Fresco of Istanbul warned that supporting the fledgling movement would spell disaster for the Jews of the empire should it lead Ottoman Muslims to question the loyalty of their Jewish compatriots.[4]

Zionists responded by suggesting that their opponents misunderstood and misrepresented their movement, which was deeply patriotic and thoroughly Ottoman in nature.[5] Proponents of the movement judged their interest in the renaissance of Jewish culture and the Hebrew language to be in line both with the national aspirations of other Ottoman *millets* and with the promise of the new constitutional regime more generally.[6] Like their Zionist allies across the globe, Ottoman Zionists argued that Jewish immigrants to Palestine would be a boon to the empire and would promote new economic growth in the region.[7] They were also careful to articulate a vision in which Palestine would become a national center and place of refuge for persecuted Jews without becoming a separate state—a position the World Zionist Congress also adopted by 1911.[8] On one point Ottoman Zionists were perhaps more adamant than non-Ottoman Zionists, however: Jews residing in Palestine needed to Ottomanize.[9] Individuals who were not already citizens of the imperial state should quickly change their papers and their outlook, Ottoman Zionists insisted. Against those who claimed that Zionism was intent upon wresting Palestine from Ottoman control, the Salonican author, journalist, and Zionist activist David Florentin invoked the myth of the Jews' special relationship to the Ottoman government to Zionist ends, protesting that no group could be "more loyal to Turkey than those immigrants who, chased from their countries by oppressive restrictions, now enjoy complete religious liberty under the protection of the caliphs and the constitution."[10]

Beside the widening rifts that emerged between Zionists and their detractors, those who found themselves in new positions of leadership after 1908 had to contend with the disenfranchised partisans of the Ottoman old regime, including the supporters and former employees of the ex-chief rabbi of the empire, Moshe Halevi.[11] Amidst these confusing developments, increasing numbers of Ashkenazi Jews resident in Istanbul opposed what they saw as a Sephardi monopoly over Jewish communal politics in the capital.[12] In Salonica, these tendencies collided with a newly emerging group that—at least in theory—aimed to question the very validity of the concept of the Jewish community: These were the Jewish socialists, who came to compete with middle-class Jewish associations for the hearts and minds of their working-class coreligionists during this period.[13]

All of this occurred against the backdrop of a regime in turmoil. In the months immediately following the revolution, inflation spiked and workers' strikes spread across the empire.[14] By the spring of 1909, a counterrevolutionary coup orchestrated by an unlikely coalition of liberals, political Islamists, non-Turkish nationalists, and army units loyal to Abdülhamid II briefly took over the imperial capital. The leading party of the besieged constitutional regime, the Committee of Union and Progress (CUP), quickly organized an "Action Army" of soldiers and volunteers from Ottoman Macedonia and recaptured the capital. Among those who made the trip from Salonica to Istanbul to foil the coup was a Jewish unit, a development that reinforced the growing association of Jews with the new regime.[15] Once back in power, the government introduced a series of repressive measures in order to secure its rule, replacing Abdülhamid II with his more docile brother Mehmed V, imposing martial law, banning workers' strikes, and curtailing the short-lived freedom of press that had reigned in the empire during the early months of the constitutional regime.[16]

The enthusiasm of many who had supported the country's new rulers during the first days of the revolution was soon tested in other ways. Just months after successfully quelling the coup in Istanbul, the government introduced universal military conscription across the empire, a measure that met with mixed reactions among different Ottoman groups. While the new obligation to military duty provided Christian and Jewish men with new opportunities to express their patriotism through service, it also produced new frictions and challenges. On an official level, various non-Muslim communal elites expressed their cautious support of universal military service as a requirement of Ottoman citizenship but also voiced their concerns about the suddenness of the measure and the ability of the imperial army to offer the appropriate provisions for their coreligionists' continued religious observance. Yet, even as their leaders offered tepid support for the new laws, many non-Muslims began leaving the empire rather than serve.[17]

The new regime also faced threats from within. Two years after the revolution had brought the CUP to power, the party found itself split in two. Ministers were constantly threatening to quit, being warned to resign, or leaving their posts. As was true of various Ottoman publications, Jewish newspapers assiduously detailed the changing political fortunes of the government and its representatives.[18]

Equally unsettling was the fact that a number of revolts had broken out and various Ottoman territories had been lost even after the ascension of the CUP, which had fashioned itself the guarantor of the empire's territorial integrity.

Only months after the revolution, Austria-Hungary officially annexed Bosnia-Herzegovina, Bulgaria declared its independence from the Ottoman state, and the provisional government of Crete proclaimed its union with the Kingdom of Greece. This series of events spurred rearguard responses not only from imperial representatives but also different Ottoman interest groups, who began national boycotts—first, after the Habsburg annexation of Bosnia-Herzegovina, of Austrian goods and later, in response to the situation in Crete, of Greek wares.[19]

Following these developments, calls for the empire to put up its defenses moved beyond the realm of economic retaliation. Government representatives announced new initiatives meant to put an end to the alleged national free-for-all that promised to pull the empire apart from within. European Freemason lodges, which had recently sheltered opponents of the Hamidian regime due to their extraterritorial privileges under the Capitulations, were now nationalized.[20] Foreign headmasters and teachers were no longer allowed to offer instruction in the empire's schools, Turkish-language education was to be given higher priority, and non-Muslim nationalist societies closed.[21]

The Ottoman parliament also turned to the topic of Zionism at various points during the Second Constitutional period, with two major debates over the movement erupting in 1911 alone.[22] In the wake of these developments, Moïse Cohen—the Salonican Jewish lawyer, author, and activist who would later adopt the name Tekinalp in a gesture of Turkish nationalism—wrote privately of his disquiet at the new public debates, which he feared signaled the rise of anti-Jewish sentiment in the empire.[23] During this period Ebüziyya Tevfik, an influential Ottoman journalist in Istanbul, began an anti-Zionist campaign in the press of the capital, sparking what some scholars have identified as the first example of Ottoman antisemitism.[24]

While various opponents of the CUP categorically opposed Zionism, the new party's relationship with the movement remained ambivalent. Many government representatives expressed their wariness about Zionism's ultimate aims, yet, during uncertain financial times, state officials accepted loans from foreign investors with known Zionist sympathies. Although the new government maintained Abdülhamid II's restrictions on Jewish immigration to Palestine, in a conciliatory gesture (possibly intended to earn sympathy in European diplomatic circles), members of the regime also flirted with the idea of offering Ottoman Iraq as a potential site of Jewish settlement.[25] Inspired in part by such gestures of cooperation, conspiracy theories attributing the revolution to a Judeo-Masonic plot based in the heavily Jewish city of Salonica soon spread across Europe and the empire.[26] The fact that the ties Ottoman statesmen forged with Zionists during this period were largely strategic, limited, and noncommittal at best did little to sway those disenchanted with the CUP regime. For many, Zionists were crucial players in the secret cabal pulling the strings of the new Ottoman government.[27]

The question of Zionism thus became a thorn in the side of the empire's new leaders not only because they understood it as a potential threat to Ottoman territorial integrity but also because, much to their chagrin, they had become associated with the international Jewish nationalist movement.[28] Many detractors of the country's new leadership portrayed Zionism as a serious danger to the empire, pointing to the government's inability to curb its growth as a sign either of weakness, complicity, or both.[29] CUP deputies responded by announcing their opposition to the movement, while also suggesting that their adversaries had overblown the issue in order to critique those holding the reigns of power.[30] All of this put the government in a position of having to actively dismiss claims of ties to Zionism despite the fact that some within its ranks had expressed sympathies for the movement. Many of those who did could not survive the rising tide against Zionism in the empire: Talaat Bey and Mehmed Cavid Bey, two prominent CUP leaders who stood accused of having links to Zionists and Jews, were eventually forced to resign.[31] The grand vizier İbrahim Hakkı Pasha, for his part, cautioned that Zionism was a movement of a small number of madmen who had little in common with Ottoman Jews. The latter could hardly be "suspected of sharing the views and fantasies of a few witless Zionists," he proposed.[32] Hakkı Pasha and his allies reminded their audience that the Jews of the empire had always stood by their state; there was no reason to believe things should suddenly change.[33] Ottoman Jews, according to this interpretation, had nothing in common with foreign Jewish Zionists.[34] Others were not so sure.

In the pages that follow, Salonica takes shape as the meeting place of many of the battles being waged among Ottoman Jews across the empire during this period. By charting the contests that emerged between Zionist, anti-Zionist, and socialist Jewish factions during the new sultan Mehmed V's tour of Ottoman Macedonia in the summer of 1911, this chapter explores the increasingly fractured nature of Jewish politics in the empire under the new constitutional regime. It also reveals new aspects of the story of post-revolutionary Ottoman Jewish politics, and, in so doing, forces us to rethink regnant assumptions about the place of different Jewish groups in the new political terrains of the day. Indeed, even as government officials were forced to resign because of their perceived connections with Zionists and Jews, Ottoman Jews of various political stripes performed their sense of confidence about their place within local and imperial political configurations as they received their sovereign in Salonica.

As had been the case during the heady days following the revolution of 1908, when the new movement for a constitutional empire had emerged from the cafes and lodges of Salonica, and in 1909, when loyalists of the new regime had marched from the city's streets to Istanbul in order to halt the short-lived military coup, all eyes were again on Salonica in 1911 as the sultan—and an estimated eighty thousand visitors—came to town.[35] Although foreign correspondents and dignitaries were among the crowds that descended upon Salonica for the occasion, the majority were tourists from elsewhere in the empire, including members of delegations arriving from Kavala, Edirne, Izmir, and Trabzon.[36] Plans for the imperial tour had first surfaced in the drawing rooms of officials in the capital as a means of shoring up popular support for the new government and solidifying loyalty in a region beset by revolts in the Albanian countryside.[37] But those who received the sultan behaved in ways that only sometimes coincided with what the authorities might have originally envisioned or hoped for.[38]

The different Jewish participants in the imperial tour took an event that had been planned and—to some extent—even scripted for them by the new regime and managed to make it their own.[39] Studying this moment from the vantage of those who received their monarch in Salonica uncovers a range of sometimes complementary, sometimes competing definitions of loyalty that different Ottoman Jews expressed—to their community, to their city, and to the empire. The words and photographs they left behind during this moment speak to Ottoman Jews' careful negotiation of their political and urban landscapes as they struggled to define a place for themselves in the empire as well as to fashion themselves anew as imperial citizens under the auspices of a reforming regime.

The constant current of competition that pulsed throughout the weeks of the sultan's stay in the region propelled different Jewish parties to attempt to outdo one another in their patriotic displays.[40] It also sparked new rivalries and behind-the-scenes schemes. Conflicts led to rumors, scandals, coercion and, eventually, government intervention and international outcry. All of these tensions became the site of extensive deliberations over where the loyalties of the city's Jews should lie. The first part of this chapter examines Jews' participation in the staged events of the sultan's tour—the parties, decorations, and various festivities of the moment—while the second explores what occurred behind closed doors both before and during the sultan's stay, as well as the struggles that ensued once the sultan had left town.

An Unspoken Contest

As the day of the sultan's arrival approached in June 1911, Salonica was transformed. The Jews, along with other denizens of the city, both official and private groups, had been preparing for the sultan's stay for weeks.[41] Efforts to renovate the imperial residence as well as various urban works projects gave warning of the momentous nature of the event many months ahead of time.[42] Streets were widened, paved, and lined with trees, the local mosques renovated, and the walls surrounding the famous White Tower along the waterfront torn down.[43] By late May, the government building was fully furnished and decorated with items sent from the royal palace in the capital.[44] Participating groups thus had the opportunity to put a great deal of thought into the decorations and festivities planned for the occasion. That May, local papers had announced that a series of twenty temporary "triumphal arches" would be built and strategically placed throughout the city along the routes the sultan and his imperial entourage would travel.[45] The list of these arches, which included their projected sites and the organization responsible for covering their costs, was subsequently augmented. By the time the sultan was on his way to Salonica, an impressive twenty-six different arches decked the city's streets.[46]

Preceding the sultan himself, visitors from all over the empire disembarked in Salonica. Jewish elites in different locales had already begun to offer their coreligionists guidelines about how to properly participate in the upcoming patriotic celebrations.[47] Those who joined a delegation to the city from Izmir, for example, were prepared by the Ladino press back home about what to wear for the twelve-day excursion. Required clothing included a red fez, a black frock coat, and a tie.[48] (Women were apparently either not expected to join or were not to be similarly restricted in their attire, for no such instructions for a female dress code were supplied.)

As the sultan finally approached the city on June 7, the Jews of Salonica sent their sovereign their first clear message from offshore. Before he docked, while his ship and others belonging to the Ottoman fleet neared Salonica's port, four boats carrying several hundred passengers each came to greet the sultan. The first was filled with local officials; the second was hired out to the public. The remaining two were Jewish boats.[49]

The Jews—it appeared—were not getting along. One of their boats had been rented by the Club des Intimes, the other by the Nouveau Club, which had formed two years earlier when members of the old club had objected to what they qualified as the excessively "assimiliationist" program of the Club des Intimes. The Nouveau Club took on a similar role to that of its predecessor, which had acted for some time to protect Jewish guilds and economic interests within Salonica, in addition to sponsoring lectures and sustaining a sizeable library. The difference, however, was meant to be one of vision and political alignment; the Nouveau Club was a Zionist organization.[50]

Various observers have suggested that the Zionist movement gained ground in Ottoman Jewish communities primarily because of the local solutions it offered Jews. Among Ottoman Sephardim, Zionism soon became a form of locally rooted oppositional politics that offered an alternative to the entrenched interests of local notables in different Jewish communities.[51] Personal conflicts merged with ideological differences as well as social grievances to give the movement new life. The fact that the Nouveau Club had emerged from the older club captures the ways that local forms of Ottoman Zionism constituted a breakaway movement.

The people the Zionists opposed, in other words, were very familiar to them. Not only had they formerly been members of the same association but many were also likely to have been their teachers or classmates, worked in the same professions, or hailed from the same neighborhood. While the Zionists appealed to large segments of the Jewish population and called for a democratization of local politics, the leaders of that movement tended to have similar middle-class and educational backgrounds as their anti-Zionist opponents. Although they shared a past, they parted ways over their visions for the future. The Zionists believed their rivals were slaves to the mission of the Alliance Israélite Universelle and its narrow interpretation of the duties of citizenship. They also suggested that the Club des Intimes's members were willing to sacrifice their fellow Jews on the altar of their patriotic quest. Indeed, just a few months before the sultan arrived in town, a scandal that went down in the annals of Ottoman Jewish history as "the Epstein Affair" reinforced the Nouveau Club members' conviction in this regard.[52] That winter, Yitzhak Epstein, the Zionist schoolteacher at Salonica's *Talmud Torah* school, learned that he had been denounced for harboring "anti-patriotic" sentiments. Although the issue was never publicly resolved, the Nouveau Club's members were convinced that the Club des Intimes was behind the denunciations.[53]

The Club des Intimes' members were part of a larger network of well-to-do Ottoman Jewish professionals who saw themselves as progressive and patriotic reformers. Though they did not have a single name for themselves—beyond the names they adopted through their societal affiliations—these Jewish "assimilationists" (to use the label employed by their opponents) saw themselves primarily as committed citizens of the empire. For them, being modern and patriotic implied subscribing to a set of bourgeois values that were deeply influenced by their contacts with European culture and schooling and which, in turn, colored their visions of an ideal Ottoman public sphere.[54] Members of this camp, representatives of the Club des Intimes included, considered the emergence of Zionism on the local scene as a threat on various levels. In addition to their claims that Zionists' interests in Palestine endangered Ottoman Jews' relationship with their state, they were equally convinced that calls for cultural Hebraism closer to home set too particularist an agenda for Jews who—first and foremost—needed to join their Ottoman compatriots of other faiths in order to forge a common civil society.

The disagreements that divided the two sides were clearly too deep to bring them together by the time Sultan Mehmed V made his appearance in the city in early June. In fact, one Ladino journalist described the break as having split the Jewish community into two enemy camps.[55] It was during moments such as these, when all eyes were on the city, that Jewish leaders were most concerned with proving their unconditional devotion to the government *as Jews*. The contingents aboard the Jewish boats were therefore charged with a difficult task during the imperial tour: they had to strike a fine balance, to find a means to compete—and more importantly to win—without letting on that they were engaged in their own private war.

Throughout the early days of the imperial tour of their city, they managed this challenge quite well: as the two Jewish boats greeted the sultan, he would have been hard pressed to guess who was who. Whether "assimilationist" or "Zionist," they appeared before their ruler equally as Ottomans. Any difference in the language and symbols they employed was difficult to discern. Each attempted to outdo the other, erecting patriotic decorations, hosting local government officials in honorary ceremonies, creating special objects of art and editions of their newspapers, and pledging extraordinary sums to the Ottoman imperial army campaign undertaken for the occasion.

The indirect and unspoken contest between these two groups continued throughout the course of the sultan's stay in Salonica. They competed over who could most effectively and memorably appropriate what they saw as the shared symbols of the new regime. If "union" and "progress" were important ideals and mottos of the empire—as the name of the reigning Committee for Union and Progress indicated—then both Jewish groups appear to have adopted a strategy by which they could claim to be the most ardent supporters of each of these ideals. Both clubs publicly promoted the need for unity among all of the different "elements" within the Ottoman Empire.[56] Only with this first goal achieved, they claimed, could the second target of progress be fully possible.

Unlike their rather straightforward pronouncements in the name of union, what the two groups did in order to demonstrate their intimate links to "progress" reached another level. The first group to make a clear reference to its connection to progress was the Club des Intimes, whose members designed their arch with a display of an electric star emanating rays of light at its center (Figure 4.1).[57] Sam Lévy, then editor-in-chief of the Ladino paper *La Epoka* and the French *Journal de Salonique*, both of Salonica, described the club's arch as "dominated by a replica of the sun, which even at night radiates beams of light" in a photographic album he created of the event.[58] By calling the star on the arch a sun, Lévy attempted to make the symbolic valence of the ornamentation clear to his readers: the light it portrayed was not just one source of

Figure 4.1 Arch of the Club des Intimes, 1911—Private collection of the author.

brilliant light among many, but the only one. Lévy was, after all, on the side of
the Club des Intimes.[59]

The design the Club des Intimes's members had chosen for their *Arc de Triomphe* was remarkable in a number of respects. Their use of electric lighting
offered an impressive sight to the residents of Salonica, where electricity had
arrived only three years earlier. Indeed, at the time of the sultan's visit, most
Salonicans did not have electric lighting in their homes or on their streets and
fewer still would have been accustomed to such extensive light displays, even
in public places.[60] On a symbolic level, the club's choice of design signaled

the enlightened nature of the new constitutional government in place since the revolution: references to the new regime and to the sultan as purveyors of progress appeared regularly in reports from the period.[61] Yet the club's decision to project rays of light from its arch also spoke to its own role within the city as a leading force that enlightened its constituents, through the library, regular lectures, and journal it offered to the Jews of Salonica. Its ability to harness so much electricity was meant to be a testament to the club's own material progress, while the image of its beaming rays spoke to its moral progress and leadership among the city's Jewish population and, by extension, within the city as a whole.[62]

The Club des Intimes was not the only organization to attempt to advance a symbolic message to the sultan—and about itself—through the use of lights. Various local journalists reported with an almost obsessive fascination that one could "not tell night from day during these many days of the festivities," "drowned" as the city was in a "sea of light."[63] It was under these circumstances that the Club des Intimes's greatest rival, the Nouveau Club, brought together its own spectacular light display. Just a few days after the sultan disembarked in Salonica, the Zionist Nouveau Club prepared a special party in honor of the Ottoman fleet along the waterfront. The guest list included some fifty officers of the imperial fleet, the entire municipal council of Salonica, the Minister of Public Instruction, several Ottoman deputies, local members of the CUP, members of the Jewish communal council, the chief rabbis of Salonica, Edirne, and Kavala, and a representative sent by the Governor-General on his behalf.[64] Observers who described the moment were impressed not only by the decorations of the club's reception hall, which was filled with flowers, carpets, Ottoman flags, and photographs of the sultan for the occasion, but also by the level of enthusiasm and cordiality the event reportedly engendered among attendees. A commentator writing for Salonica's Ladino serial *El Imparsial* suggested that the atmosphere recalled the first days of the new constitutional regime, "when spirits were inflamed by the success of the revolution."[65]

The evening began with a series of speeches. After the obligatory references to the political discourse of the time—the need for unity, praise of the heroes who had returned the constitution of 1876 to the empire and brought freedom to the realm after the countercoup of 1909—the speakers turned their attention to the Jews of the empire. Many of the Ottoman officials present seized the opportunity to speak to the unprecedented loyalty of Ottoman Jews, their commitment to progress, the vital role they had played in the birth of industry in Salonica, and their early support for the movement that had orchestrated the revolution only three years before. In this way, from the privacy of the Nouveau Club's salon, CUP representatives reinvigorated the myth of the Jews' special relationship to the Ottoman state as they dressed it in the language of the new era. Talaat Bey, former Minister of the Interior and now deputy of Edirne, praised Jews for their "considerable role in the revolution," while Hacı Adil Bey, the general secretary of the CUP, suggested that the Jews in particular had inspired a social revolution in Salonica well before the political revolution reached the empire.[66] Only months after Grand Vizier Hakkı Pasha had rejected claims that Jews played an exceptional role in shaping the new regime during a parliamentary debate in Istanbul, government officials in a different corner of the empire gave their Jewish interlocutors another impression entirely.

None of the guests made any mention of the incongruity of the messages different CUP representatives sent in different contexts during this period. The fact that the Nouveau Club was not simply a Jewish society, but a Zionist one appears to have gone unmentioned by contemporary observers. Instead, those in attendance as well as those who reported on the moment suggested that the event might serve equally as a tribute to the new constitutional government and to the Jewish organization that hosted its representatives that summer evening. This seems to have been the message the Nouveau Club's members hoped to send when, after their secretary offered a speech paying homage to the CUP for saving the empire from despotism, a "sea of lights" suddenly blinded the room, exposing a much larger, elaborately decorated reception hall. The commentator writing for El Imparsial explained the meaning of this moment to his readers: perfectly timed, the display "was symbolic," as it replicated the manner in which the CUP had "brought light to an empire drowning in darkness."[67] That night, and in that locale, the Nouveau Club had taken upon itself a similar role. As it did so, it had also found an impressive way to outshine its rival.[68]

Contestation and competition permeated the Jews' responses to the sultan's visit. Those participating in the moment found various ways to use the already available conventions and shared discourses of the regime in order to advance their own particular stance and vision. In some cases, they also chose to employ a symbolic language that could serve to reinforce connections between Muslims and Jews in particular. This was the approach that Jacob Meir, the chief rabbi of Salonica, employed at a second event held by the Nouveau Club on its location along the quay during the sultan's visit. Addressing a crowd that included the Ottoman Grand Vizier Hakkı Pasha, Meir commenced his official remarks by reciting a prayer in Arabic, wishing for the prolongation of the life of the sultan and of the empire as well as its ever-increasing prosperity in the Muslims' holy tongue. The remarkable thing about Meir's prayer was not so much its message as the language he had chosen for it.[69] That his prayer was meant to recall the prayers of Muslims was clearly acknowledged that night by Hakkı Pasha, who congratulated Meir ("in perfect French," according to the local Ladino press) for having chosen to recite it in Arabic. "This language," he had explained, "is the language of our religion, and a sister to your mother tongue."[70]

Throughout the sultan's stay in their city, Salonica's Zionist and anti-Zionist factions engaged in a symbolic battle: whoever could most effectively employ the language of the new regime or entertain its official representatives might claim at least a temporary victory. Yet during the same period, different Jewish individuals and interests also found the space for more imaginative responses to the sultan's visit. The flexibility that decorative choices made available to participants allowed them to veer further off script. This was most notable in the individual designs of the arches erected in honor of the sultan's tour. The photographs and postcards that remain of the moment offer new layers of meaning that the recorded speech and writings of the participants, so often bound by formulas and conventions, fail to uncover.

One such example can be found in the photographs of the Allatini arch, con-structed by the important Jewish industrialist firm in Salonica well in advance of the sultan's visit (Figure 4.2). In a gesture of unabashed self-referentiality and self-promotion, this arch boasted two huge replica chimney columns and spoke to the great achievements of both the brickworks and the flour mill run by the Allatinis in that city, thus reminding onlookers and passersby, as well as the sultan, that thanks to the work of the Allatini brothers over decades, the city had become the "pride of the empire" and a site of notable industrial progress. The mill itself had become the stuff of modernizers' legends; apart from being a major source of employment and providing flour for much of the region, it was also a major landmark in Salonica. By the time of the sultan's tour, its façade had become a popular image for postcards, while the building itself had earned the felicitous title of "largest mill in the Orient."[71]

The arch erected in honor of the mill—like the postcards that depicted it as a model of Ottoman industrial advancement—offered a message of boundless confidence and pride. The photographic album Sam Lévy pub-lished as a souvenir of the event praised the arch's "reconciliation of Moorish architecture with modern industrial design." The resulting effect conveyed a "harmony of contrasts that skeptics would have considered impossible," it continued.[72] The focus had, at least temporarily, left the sultan. It was now fixed squarely on those who had funded the arch, the factories it represented, and its architects. While officially celebrating their sovereign, Jewish elites also celebrated themselves, their collaborators, and their own political and commercial pursuits.

In a distinct sense, the official arch of the Jewish community of Salonica, captured in various photographs and postcards as well as in Sam Lévy's album of the sultan's Salonican tour, also gives the impression of the confidence and

Figure 4.2 Arch of the Allatini Mill Company, 1911—Private collection of the author.

sense of security Salonican Jews projected through their choice of design (Figure 4.3). In order to decorate their arch, the community had taken Jewish ritual objects from the interiors of Salonican synagogues and placed them onto the communal arch in plain public view. They had, essentially, turned their synagogues inside out for the length of the sultan's stay. The fabrics they draped from the arch's columns were Torah scroll covers. Countless ornate silver *rimonim*, or Torah scroll finials, decorated the width of the arch.[73] Enlisting these articles of clear religious value, the community's leaders

Figure 4.3 Arch of the Jewish community of Salonica, June 1911—Courtesy of Yannis Megas.

signaled their comfort in offering public displays of their Jewishness before the city and the sultan.

In another photograph of the event, one finds the arch designed by the Zionist Nouveau Club in front of its new locale along the water (Figure 4.4). The Ottoman-language paper *Şehbal* praised the Nouveau Club's arch for its elegance, while Sam Lévy, in his photographic album, ventured that the Zionist club's arch had been prepared in "the gracious style of Turkish architecture," with columns built "in the form of minarets."[74] The arch's style was indeed

Figure 4.4 Arch of the Nouveau Club of Salonica, 1911—Private collection of
the author.

remarkable: in addition to its minaret-columns, it featured an Ottoman crescent and star at its center and a message in Ottoman reading "From the New
Jewish Club on the Occasion of the Arrival of His Highness the Sultan."[75] In
constructing the arch's columns in the form of the white minarets that pep-
pered Salonica's cityscape, the Nouveau Club offered the sultan a replica of
elements of the city he approached. That Jews could take pride in these holy
sites of a faith not their own sent a message that they considered the city as a
whole as their own.[76]

Like the arches of the Allatini firm and the Nouveau Club, the Jewish community's arch also referenced a local landmark. According to Sam Lévy, the onion-shaped "Byzantine" domes topping each of the Jewish community arch's columns were meant to mimic the form of the nearby Aya Sofya mosque's tower. Indeed, both structures sported three small arched windows near the upper section.[77] Like the minaret-columns of the Nouveau Club's arch, the Jewish community's chosen arch design referenced a contemporary Muslim site—in this case one that was historically also a Byzantine church— thus reinforcing the message that the city's important edifices could also be claimed by all of its residents.

Yet the Jewish community's arch may have also been designed to send another message as well. Given that the Aya Sofya mosque sat at the heart of a largely Jewish area of Salonica, those who came up with the community's arch design may well have intended to call attention to the fact that the landmark served as a daily reference point for all the Jews who lived in the neighborhood.[78] Thus, in addition to sending a message of general civic pride, the Jewish community emerged with its own particular expression of attachment to the local Aya Sofya—one that coexisted now with local Christians' special claim to the site as a historical church, and that of the Muslims, to the site as a mosque.

As various Jewish groups bid for attention during the sultan's stay in their city, they sought to reinforce their roles within the local power structure. During this moment of heightened visibility, different groups and individuals were forced to clarify and display their allegiances and political visions in concrete form. Their works, meant to speak to the sultan, were not meant to speak to him alone.

Signs of Anxiety

As they staged their processions and carefully orchestrated their displays, local elites attempted to keep any signs of anxiety hidden from view. Yet the utter confidence that Salonican Jews, as well as other Ottomans, projected throughout the festivities emerges in a different light when one considers the stage upon which it appeared.[79] As residents of the Ottoman port city read about the festivities in honor of their monarch in their papers, they also learned about skirmishes on the border with Montenegro, with Bulgaria, with Greece, and of the looming presence of Russia. The future of Salonica had been threatened before. In 1878, the short-lived Treaty of San Stefano had pushed the city very close to the Ottoman state's new border with Bulgaria. Although the map of southeastern Europe was soon redrawn with the Treaty of Berlin later that year, the memory of the one-time threat to Salonica's status remained with the city's residents. More recently, various nationalist and independence movements had announced their plans to turn Macedonia into an autonomous province or to wrest it from Ottoman control altogether. In 1903, the actions of a number of Bulgarian anarchists with ties to the Internal Macedonian Revolutionary Organization had brought their struggle directly to the streets of Salonica, as they set bombs off throughout the city.[80]

Translating news from official sources, Jewish journalists informed their readers that a group of Bulgarian revolutionaries preparing bombs in the nearby countryside had been discovered and arrested.[81] They cautioned that continued incursions of Montenegran "bandits" into Ottoman territory might be cause enough for war.[82] Reporting on the ongoing revolts in the nearby Albanian countryside, *El Imparsial* issued a warning to the Albanian leaders directing the rebellion, explaining that it was against the Albanians' interests to break off from the empire. Albania could "only survive as an Ottoman province," it announced: the sole alternative was foreign rule.[83] Yet the editor who printed these words in his Ladino paper could hardly have suspected that they would reach the rebellious leaders he purported to address. His message instead reminded his Jewish readers that—like their Albanian fellow citizens—it was in their best interests to continue to support the Ottoman state against those who threatened to tear it asunder.

Even during the sultan's visit itself hints of disquiet made their way to Ottoman readers. The Albanian revolts that had begun the year before continued to fill the columns of newspapers in Salonica that summer. Journals entering the empire from Europe suggested that the situation in the countryside was deteriorating even as official Ottoman sources attempted to calm the population. The Jewish newspapers of Salonica got their news from both ends. Closer to home, the fate of certain displays erected in honor of the sultan's arrival similarly led to unsettling questions. In Salonica, the massive wooden arch built by the Greek Orthodox community was reported to have blown over due to strong winds. Although it took down tramlines as it fell during the night, the press gave no indication of foul play.[84] After the arch of the Serbian community in Monastir burned, however, talk of sabotage arose. *El Imparsial* attempted to quiet its readers' imaginations: "Since Friday," it reported:

> rumors have circulated in our city that Ottoman Bulgarians destroyed certain *Arcs de Triomphe* built in the neighboring city of Monastir on the occasion of His Majesty the Sultan's arrival. According to our information, these rumors are absolutely false.[85]

However emphatically they denied these charges, anxiety clearly remained just beneath the surface and behind the scenes of the staged processions.

This sense of unease also came through in official announcements alerting readers in the city to the strictly supervised nature of the events slated to take place. In order to avoid "fear and disturbances," precautionary measures were being taken across the city. These included installations of fire hydrants at designated spots, as well as other measures of damage and crowd control.[86] To ensure the public's safety, various journals informed potential onlookers of the ways in which balconies could and could not be used. They counseled readers to drape flags and other patriotic paraphernalia from their balconies. When people failed to adorn the facades of their homes or business, journals announced that they had not mustered the adequate levels of patriotic fervor. Crowds, however, were banned from appearing on the city's many balconies throughout the course of the sultan's stay. Firecrackers and flowers were not to be thrown at any point during the festivities.

Although many of these directives patently originated from local municipal orders, it is clear that Jewish papers as well as local Jewish groups also engaged in various means of social control in response to the planned visit.[87] Jewish elites worked with the authorities to ensure that the event would be carefully scripted. This approach comes through, for example, in the instructions published by *La Tribuna Libera*, the organ of Salonica's Nouveau Club, in advance of the sultan's trip. The announcement not only explained how the public could acquire tickets to watch the royal procession from the club's location on the waterfront, it also warned that entrance without a ticket was to be categorically prohibited, as would anyone who tried to bring children along.[88]

The reports of the Spanish consul stationed in Salonica at the time make clear that tight controls were in place throughout the city during the visit. Writing to his country's embassy in Istanbul, he noted that the police had "exercised an overzealous caution at times, considering peaceful foreigners as though they were dangerous anarchists until they were able to prove otherwise."[89] He later noted that Spaniards who had arrived on important business had faced the threat of expulsion from the city and had only been allowed to remain once he assumed full responsibility for their actions.

During the sultan's sojourn in Salonica, Jewish newspapers challenged all indications that the otherwise festive and patriotic celebrations might have been disrupted. As one author writing for *El Avenir* put it, during such an "auspicious" moment, "no one should have any unpleasantness."[90] Turning such wishful thinking into news, Jewish journals dismissed various stories circulating at the time, such as one that told of how, during the sultan's passage through the city, certain individuals had attempted to grab the reins of his carriage in order to direct it themselves. They similarly rejected another rumor concerning a certain "Turkish woman" who had purportedly thrown herself at the sultan with a request for aid, only to have him rebuff her and toss her to the ground.[91] Although different Ladino reports described such stories as mere fabrications, they nonetheless exposed the fact that cynical and unofficial versions of the moment were in circulation during the sultan's stay in their city. Attempting to put their readers' minds at ease, these announcements inadvertently revealed a sense of insecurity as well. More disturbing still, the newspaper editors who published these reports gave hints that they too would be involved in the enforcement of the various policies they announced and that they would not be beyond using intimidation to ensure that all orders were observed.

Revisiting the Sultan's Visit

On June 7, after waiting in the line of officials gathered to welcome the sultan, Chief Rabbi Jacob Meir finally got his turn to speak. He began by addressing the special nature of Jewish loyalty to the empire, explaining first how the Jews were ordered by their holy law to love the country in which they lived. Nowhere were such religious injunctions better suited than in the Ottoman state, he suggested, since in the sultan's realms Jews found themselves living in complete freedom. Meir continued with a rather remarkable statement: "I am pleased to report that nowhere in your vast empire does there live one single Jew who does not love and venerate his beloved homeland."[92] In order to make good on this promise, not even one Jew anywhere in any corner of Ottoman territory could be permitted to get out of line. It was a tall order to fill.

Those who considered themselves responsible for the Jewish community of the city and who lauded Ottoman Jewry as the most loyal, orderly, and least troublesome of all the *millets* would enter into a quandary, as a result, when faced with activities or remarks that raised suspicions to the contrary. It was precisely this type of situation that arose in the summer of 1911 in Salonica, as the city's patricians and authorities were planning to receive their *padişah*. In fact, amidst the elaborate arches, galas, and rows of well-dressed schoolchildren convened in honor of the sultan's visit, another development was brewing behind closed doors.

By the time the city's chief rabbi addressed the sultan, government officials had decided that Salonica's Socialist Federation, made up primarily of local Ottoman Jewish workers, constituted a public menace.[93] Four of the Federation's representatives, three of whom were Jews, were arrested immediately before the visit. Their leader, a Jewish man by the name of Abraham Benaroya, was exiled to Serbia.[94] According to a report the governor of the Salonica *vilayet* sent to Istanbul during the period, Benaroya was guilty of encouraging the working classes of the city to boycott the festivities planned in the sultan's honor.[95] Although the Socialist Federation he led was not officially a Jewish organization, the high number and profile of Jews in the association was difficult to ignore. The implications of the charges against the society threatened to destabilize the Jewish community's claims of its unswerving Ottoman loyalty.

Almost immediately after the sultan arrived in Salonica, rumors began to circulate about the reasons for the socialists' arrests. Blame quickly shifted away from the authorities, as Jews in Salonica pointed fingers at members of their own community. The events that followed highlight the interrelatedness of state control and intra-communal Jewish politics in late Ottoman contexts. They led to extensive discussions about what the accusations, as well as the actions of local government and Jewish agents meant for the Jewish community as a whole, its loyalty to the empire, and the obligations of its leaders and press toward the maintenance both of the public face of their community and of urban order.

Accusations against the Club des Intimes appeared in print on June 9, some four days after the arrests. At that time, the local organ of the Socialist Federation, a Ladino paper entitled *La Solidaridad Ovradera* published the following notice: "Something worthy of the times of Hamid has occurred this week . . . certain functionaries went beyond their mandate and abused their power." The same article detailed how, on the occasion of the sultan's upcoming tour, the local press had published a warning that suspicious people should be removed from the city. "This seemed completely incomprehensible to us," its author remonstrated. "Despite the fact that the police have gone through with this action, we continue to insist that the constitution does not permit them to arrest citizens without . . . a written order from the Minister of the Interior." The Federation's newspaper cited Article Ten of the Ottoman Constitution, which, it explained, guaranteed individual liberties. Attempting to demonstrate that local officials had acted against their own laws, the article concluded that their comrades had been arrested without having committed any crime.[96]

The socialist serial went on to describe how members of the Federation had demanded to know on what grounds their fellow workers were being held, only to be informed by local officials that the arrests had been based on accusations made on the part of a local club. *La Solidaridad Ovradera* soon identified the club by name: it was the influential "bourgeois" Club des Intimes that had purportedly turned the Federation's comrades over to the police.[97] The Club des Intimes was now implicated in a second scandal reminiscent of the recent "Epstein Affair" of earlier that year. Just as the Zionists had accused the Club des Intimes' members of denouncing the local school director Yitzhak Epstein for "anti-patriotic" activities, the Socialist Federation's paper now publicly accused the club's associates of having a hand in the arrests of the city's socialist leaders.

At the time of the scandal surrounding Epstein's denunciation, the Zionist Nouveau Club had announced that its members had definitive proof that their rival had been engaged in acts of espionage, or *"hafiyelik."* They had even offered to share the damning evidence they had in their possession with anyone who desired to see it.[98] As a new conflict flared, representatives of the Nouveau Club reiterated their offer to provide this evidence to the public.[99] The Club des Intimes responded to these initial allegations with silence.[100]

Opponents of the Club des Intimes remained unmoved by the society's refusal to engage with its critics. The Ladino and French Jewish press of Salonica initiated a series of articles criticizing the club's actions in the wake of the arrests. Members of the Club des Intimes soon responded that French-language journals in particular were no place to publish such accusations. What right did the Jewish-run *Progrès de Salonique* have to publicize a conflict that should have remained an internal Jewish affair? Were its editors not aware that by doing so they were making the Club des Intimes, and, by extension, the entire Jewish community, repugnant in the eyes of others? Once the French Jewish press of the city had broached the subject, the squabbles and discord besetting the Salonican Jewish community remained exposed for all to see, they protested.[101]

El Imparsial responded that the Club des Intimes's objections were based on false reasoning and hypocrisy. "We ask who is truly guilty, the one who honors the system of spying or the one who does everything within his power to make it disappear? Who dishonors his nation more, the one who creates the problem or the one who condemns it?" The article continued:

> It is true that it is best to keep one's dirty laundry within the family—however, if for whatever reason this is not possible, must we simply leave it dirty? Is it not better that someone wash it in public as soon as possible, and in this way give proof to everyone that it is clean once again? . . . Or might it be that these sophists, these false patriots, would like our French journals to keep silent at any price . . . at the risk of allowing the institution of *hafiyelik* to continue? Perhaps this is what they want! To them, it is nothing to perform acts of espionage—what is important is not to discuss it in our French papers.[102]

Assuming that non-Jewish Salonicans were bound to learn of the scandal one way or another, was it not preferable that people should simultaneously learn of the outrage the affair had caused among Jews in the city? Only indignation remained to save the honor of their community, the same author announced.

The Ladino press from beyond Salonica soon found itself caught up in the polemic. David Fresco, the anti-Zionist editor of *El Tiempo*, intervened in the debate from Istanbul. Responding to the attacks being leveled against the Club des Intimes from all sides, he wrote an article defending the club as a "center of enlightenment and progress" in the community, explaining that its members deserved the respect of their coreligionists, whom they had served faithfully for so long. The rumors that emerged shortly after the sultan had begun his tour of the region were surely the work of Zionist saboteurs, Fresco concluded.[103]

El Imparsial of Salonica was quick to respond, explaining sardonically that either Fresco had misunderstood the situation or he was blatantly trying to obscure the truth: those who had most recently accused the Club des Intimes of espionage could in no way be confused with Zionists—they were the city's local socialists, entirely opposed to the project of Zionism and to nationalist programs in general.[104] Indeed, *El Imparsial*'s editors added, they too were squarely opposed to Zionism and had spoken on more than one occasion about the damage they believed Zionist agitation would cause the Ottoman Jewish community. Yet their own stance against the movement would not stop them from "protesting against those who use anti-Zionism as a mask, thereby attempting to denounce their adversaries as Zionists and enemies of the state." "Such people are despicable," *El Imparsial*'s author protested. "While it is necessary to fight against Zionism, this struggle cannot excuse . . . dirty spying tactics. It is clear to us that if we allow them to continue they will simply begin to denounce anyone who displeases them."[105]

Other Jewish newspapers based in the imperial capital soon entered the fray.[106] Lucien Sciuto, the editor of Istanbul's French-language Zionist serial *L'Aurore*, expressed his dismay at the claims that members of the Club des Intimes had been responsible for the socialists' arrest. Yet what troubled him most of all was the fact that "in such a delicate situation three of the four people suspected [of conspiring against the sultan] were Jews." The carefully woven myth that posited the unflagging loyalty of all of Ottoman Jewry—reinforced by Jewish communal leaders over decades—suddenly threatened to unravel. The only explanation was that the socialists had been falsely charged, Sciuto ventured, since there was "no Jew in any party" who was not "sincerely respectful of order."[107] In making this declaration, Sciuto shifted Jewish communal leaders' claims about Jews' inherent respect for their state and monarch to claims about their reverence for law and order. Yet the message itself resembled the one Chief Rabbi Meir had offered at the outset of the sultan's tour. Both men vouched for the behavior of all Jews anywhere, in the empire and beyond. Meanwhile, members of the Club des Intimes were not speaking at all, neither daring nor deigning (depending upon whom one asked) to attempt to defend themselves in the face of the accusations mounting against them. Nor did they give any indication as to whether or not they considered the socialists guilty of the charges of which they stood accused.

Then, after weeks of silence and evasion, the Club des Intimes finally issued a statement condemning the rumors that were sullying its good name. An extraordinary session of three hundred of the club's members had produced a unanimous vote of confidence by the meeting's end, it reported.[108] *La Nasion*, the official organ of the Club des Intimes, reproduced a speech given during that meeting, which suggested that the club's detractors employed "wild and violent" tactics with the aim of creating "disorder in their midst."[109] Opposing the image of a club that helped maintain peace and order in Salonica with the disruptive and chaotic approach of its enemies, the speaker continued with the rather outlandish suggestion that those who tried to disrupt the goodwill project of the Club des Intimes were conducting an antisemitic campaign, since "only the most terrible antisemites were capable of such a furious war against a Jewish philanthropic organization."[110]

Only after praising their own club and vilifying its opponents did the article begin to address the previously mentioned "incidents that had occurred with the labor syndicate."[111] The Club des Intimes's representatives revealed the details of the deliberations that had resulted in the arrests of Benaroya and the other socialist leaders: well before Mehmed V was scheduled to arrive in their city, members of the club had joined a municipal commission charged with organizing the festivities for the sultan. Having invited various workers and guild leaders to contribute ideas about how they might participate in the upcoming events, the committee had been dumbstruck when one of these guests announced that Salonica's workers did not plan to take part in the festivities, clarifying that his response represented the official position of the city's Socialist Federation.[112] According to reports issued by the Club des Intimes as well as local imperial officials, a group of workers associated with the Socialist Federation had then reportedly proclaimed for all to hear that they had no use for a sultan and that, indeed, they did not want a sultan at all![113]

Whether rumor or reality, the fact that such a dramatic claim had surfaced complicated the lives of the local authorities as well as Salonica's Jewish notables. Word of the socialists' plans to boycott, or possibly even disrupt, the sultan's retinue was directed to the Ottoman Ministry of the Interior in the capital.[114] Claims of the insubordination of Jewish socialists in Salonica thus reached the very center of imperial power. These charges against Jewish activists flew in the face of the Salonican chief rabbi's claim of the unwavering loyalty of every Jew across the empire as well as the position of *L'Aurore* in the capital, that there was no Jew who was not sincerely respectful of order.

Reporting on the encounter with local workers at their site, the Club des Intimes' representatives were careful to emphasize that two local Ottoman officials had been present at that time. Their presence made the question of whether the club's members had informed upon local workers moot, they explained. There had been no need to do so, since representatives of the local government had directly witnessed the socialists' challenge to the sultan. Although the Club des Intimes's members decried the attacks against their organization, suggesting they were disruptive and inappropriate in the most categorical terms, its representatives never directly contradicted the accusations that their members had a hand in denouncing the Jewish socialists.

Nor did the club's spokesmen indicate that they considered such actions shameful. The blame surely lay with those who had publicly voiced their dissent, not with any members of the Club des Intimes, whose only fault was to have been witness to such disagreeable statements. Through its response, the Club des Intimes also communicated its position that a unified and orderly image of the community had to be upheld above all else. For this reason there were certain things one was not to say in public, under the scrutiny of all eyes—at least not without repercussions. Claims by local Jewish workers that they had no use for a sultan clearly fell into this category.

What the members of the Club des Intimes were not saying showed up in the records of the Austro-Hungarian consul in Salonica as he reported on the visit. After the local government had been apprised that bombs might go off during the event, he wrote, a series of detectives had been placed throughout the city, based both in private homes and in hotels. Working closely with the police and with the municipal council, the Club des Intimes had offered up fifty of its members to join the ranks of those assigned the task.[115] While they never publicly acknowledged their involvement in denunciations, either of Epstein or the socialist leaders, members of the Club des Intimes were apparently in the detective business after all. Or was this merely a rumor? The different notables who made up the club's three hundred members seemed to make an art of eliding the topic in public and on paper. Perhaps in the intimacy of their own homes, or between the four walls of their association's meeting hall, the Club des Intimes' members provided an answer. As far as the Habsburg consul understood it, they had undertaken the task out of "patriotic zeal." They had, in other words, simply been doing their duty—as loyal imperial citizens and as patricians of their city.

Conclusion

It was precisely this interpretation of proper patriotic conduct that other members of the Jewish community of Salonica and beyond came to contest in the debates surrounding the sultan's visit in 1911. The picture that

emerges from the scandals of that year is one of conflicting visions of where
the loyalties of the Jewish community—and its leaders—belonged. Many
Jewish elites, including the members of the Club des Intimes, asserted that
working to save the public face of their community at all costs served the
common good. Others suggested that hiding behind closed doors and carefully formulated pronouncements did not serve the Jewish community at all.
The members of the Socialist Federation, as well as various Jewish journalists
from Salonica to Istanbul, announced their position that difference, discussion, and even dissent were healthy, and that by attempting to foster each
they paid tribute to their community (however defined). Those who found
themselves on this side of the scandal during the sultan's visit declared themselves unwilling to live with the fears of the "times of Hamid," including self-
censorship and the extreme restraint of the established Jewish communal
elite of their city.

While the Club des Intimes and the Nouveau Club had vied for public
recognition during the sultan's stay in their city, the Socialist Federation of
Salonica had been excluded from participating in—and, according to certain
accounts, had purposefully opted out of—the festivities altogether. Although
three of the four socialist leaders were allowed to return to Salonica once
the sultan left the city, Abraham Benaroya was forced to remain in exile for
many months.[116] Indeed, well after the sultan had left the region, the governor
of Salonica wrote the Ministry of the Interior that he considered Benaroya
an ongoing threat and counseled that he should not be allowed to return.[117]
Acts of repression and limitations on the Federation's ability to organize were
symptomatic not only of the heightened visibility and tensions engendered
by the sultan's visit, but also of the political conditions that obtained in the
regime more generally during this period. Word of the repression of the Socialist Federation in Salonica even made its way across Europe, to the offices
of the International Socialist Bureau, which reported in a communiqué dated
July 27, 1911, that a "great Labour demonstration convened to protest the
arrest of four Socialists on the occasion of the Sultan's visit to Salonica" had
been forbidden by the authorities.[118]

The rifts within Salonica's Jewish community were real. By late June, members
of the Zionist and "assimilationist" camps in Salonica came to blows over their
differences on their city's streets.[119] Yet, even as they clashed, members of each
faction exhibited a striking level of confidence regarding their rightful place in the
city, while simultaneously offering hints of their anxiety over the prospect of an
uncertain future if that place were to be challenged. The centrifugal forces of rebellion that promised to pull the empire apart were patently a cause for concern,
but one that lay beyond the control of Ottoman Jewish leaders. Signs of dissent
emanating from within the community, however, were seen in a different light,

as challenges to the carefully crafted image of the Jewish community that its leaders had worked so hard to uphold for decades.

Many who employed the new regime's slogans of "harmony," "peace," and "progress" apparently also felt compelled to respond to any potential disruption by engaging in the repression of members of their own community, acts that paralleled the tactics of the regime itself. Still, those Jewish elites who had hoped to suppress dissent and keep internal differences hidden were not entirely successful, nor were those who hoped to prove their community's unswerving love for the sultan and for "peace and order." Ottoman Jews' patriotic project had become increasingly fractured. The different Jewish individuals who erected elaborate monuments to their patriotism no longer did so in the name of the Jewish *millet* as a whole, but on behalf of their private enterprise or social club in the hopes of furthering their own personal and political causes.

Given the incessant competition of the moment, who had proven themselves the most loyal, the most patriotic, the most Ottoman of all? Representatives of the Club des Intimes could easily venture that they had emerged the victors. Having worked with local government agents to prevent agitators from disrupting the imperial tour, the club's members had strengthened their ties with the authorities, who had invited the association's leaders to help organize the imperial tour from the start. This alliance would appear to have been borne out by the fact that a local government official came out in support of the Club des Intimes during this period, categorically denying allegations that its members had denounced any of their coreligionists or fellow Salonicans.[120]

Then there were the socialists. Though their leaders were arrested in anticipation of the sultan's arrival, their official organ warned that history unequivocally demonstrated how rulers who tried to suppress socialism only made the movement grow stronger.[121] Indeed, their situation drew international attention and protest in response to the arrests of their leaders.[122] Expressing their demands through the medium of the federation's newspaper as well as official appeals to the Porte, Salonica's socialists called upon their government to live up to its own laws and the constitution it had reinstated. In a missive sent to the offices of the grand vizier, Jewish, Muslim, Bulgarian, and Greek Orthodox individuals concerned by Benaroya's exile appealed to the government to acknowledge that undertaking such arrests without trial violated Ottoman civil law.[123] A representative of the Socialist Federation similarly issued an official plea for an impartial governmental investigation into the matter, while another of the organization's leaders wrote that the CUP had to learn that a constitutional regime could not exist without freedom of press and expression.[124] The same author reminded CUP officials that Abraham Benaroya—the man they had exiled as a threat to the country and its ruler—was a national hero who had fought in the Action Army that had liberated Istanbul and brought the constitutional regime back to power in 1909.[125] As they made these and other appeals, the city's socialists also claimed to be Ottoman loyalists—if not royalists—to the end. In their view, it was government representatives who remained untrue to the requirements of their regime.[126]

While both the Club des Intimes' members and the socialists had reasons to claim victory, the Zionists did so in no uncertain terms. Despite the attempts of anti-Zionists in the city to undermine the position of the Zionist director of the *Talmud Torah* school in the city, Yitzhak Epstein remained in his post. During the sultan's tour, he had even earned the public praise of Ottoman officials, who thanked him for instilling the "most profound Ottoman spirit" in the city's Jewish children after he arranged to have his pupils perform patriotic songs for their monarch in both Hebrew and Turkish.[127] Similarly, Salonica's Chief Rabbi Meir, a well-known supporter of Zionism, had earned the sympathies of his Muslim compatriots by offering a prayer for the sultan in Arabic during the course of the sultan's visit. Most remarkably, the Ottoman head of state had responded by thanking the rabbi on behalf of the empire's Muslims for pronouncing the prayer in the "language of their religion," one that he noted was related to the "mother tongue" of the Jews.[128]

Had anyone noticed that the Zionists scored an enormous symbolic victory with that last utterance? Having found new ways of expressing their Ottoman identity through the use of Hebrew, Turkish, and even Arabic during different official ceremonies held in honor of the sultan's presence in their city, Ottoman Zionists received nothing less than the recognition of their national aspirations in return. Never mind that the grand vizier's statement was not wholly accurate—Ladino, not Hebrew, was in fact the mother tongue of the vast majority of Salonica's Jews—thanks to instructors like Epstein, local Zionists were raising new generations in Hebrew and hoped to eventually make their reality match that vision. Their Hebraist orientation did not stop Ottoman Zionists from supporting the study of Turkish among their coreligionists, however. They believed there was also room for that language in their community's linguistic repertoire: if Hebrew was to be their mother tongue, as Hakkı Pasha had noted, then Ottoman Turkish, the language of their *patria*, or fatherland, would be their "father tongue."[129]

The Zionists also delighted in the fact that some of the most prominent representatives of their state had graced the Nouveau Club with their presence. Dining and socializing alongside the city's Zionists, these officials had praised their works, thus apparently legitimizing Ottoman Zionism in the eyes of the world. What occurred in a rather unimposing locale perched just off the Salonican quay—and what had happened on the streets of Salonica in the summer of 1911 more generally—could not have appeared more different from the scenes being played out in the Ottoman parliament during the same period. There, in the capital, deputies debated the potential dangers of Zionism, Jews were warned not to join the growing movement, and Jewish deputies agreed that a commission should be formed to "look into the matter." Back in Salonica, local Zionists and Ottoman officials mingled, shared tables and speeches, and exchanged prayers and praise for each other and for their empire.

How was it that Hakkı Pasha ended up sitting down at the tables of Zionists? How did it happen that Salonica's Zionists—and not the long-established and promiment members of the Ottomanist Club des Intimes—persuaded none other than the Ottoman grand vizier to attend their celebration?[130] Although it may be impossible to definitively answer this question, its very formulation complicates the master narratives of late Ottoman politics.

The coup of the city's Zionists in gaining the attention of high-ranking state officials also challenges the notion that ideologies and social practices necessarily overlap.[131] An individual's political stance does not always determine the soirées he might attend, the networks with which he affiliates, or even the friends he makes. Hakkı Pasha, the Ottoman grand vizier who showed up as the guest of honor to the Salonican Zionist Nouveau Club's gala event in the summer of 1911, was, after all, the very same grand vizier who had called Zionism a movement of madmen when speaking before the Ottoman parliament just a few months earlier. Lest we take the Zionists entirely at their word, and conclude that this was proof that the Ottoman state had finally given their movement its blessing, another interpretation of the events might be that people who share worlds need not share visions. Surely this can be said of members of Salonica's Zionist club and those of another group with which they shared worlds, including many very intimate ones. This was the Club des Intimes—their bitterest foe and their fellow Ottoman Jewish patriotic association.

Conclusion

Imperial Citizens beyond the Empire

Hidden within the heart of what was once the financial district of the Ottoman capital sits an imposing two-story red brick building. Once known as the Zülfaris Synagogue, or Kal Kadoş Galata, the building remains open to the public today, albeit in a different form. It now houses the museum of the Quincentennial Foundation designed "to commemorate the amicable relations between Turks and Jews which began with the Ottoman conquest of Bursa . . . and were cemented when the Ottoman Turks offered a new homeland to the Sephardic Jews" in 1492.[1] The "Turk" stands in for the Muslim; the modern Turkish Republic inherits the legacy of the Ottoman Empire: the myth of the special Jewish relationship to the Ottoman state has found a permanent home in the twenty-first century.

Viewing the history of an empire that is no more from the vantage point of the present should caution us that the story of Ottoman-Jewish alliance is not the only one that might have been told. The events of the twentieth century, the undoing of the empire and the disentanglement of its "mixed but unmixable populations," paved the way for the nation-states that came in its place.[2] The violence that followed this transformation sealed the fate of millions of victims of war and ethnic cleansing in the formerly Ottoman regions alone. Not surprisingly, it also drowned out the stories of past loyalties that no longer made sense within the framework of the new national borders that appeared in its wake. Among the historical actors who have too often been silenced in the process we might include the Phanariots—Orthodox Christians deeply enmeshed in the mechanisms of Ottoman governance for a period that extended over many generations.[3] Also rendered illegible today is the loyalty of the empire's Armenians, who gained increasing prominence within Ottoman imperial ranks in the early decades of the nineteenth century, earning the title of the "loyal millet" (*millet-i sadıka*) for a good part of the century.[4]

The weight of the history of conflicts between the modern states of Turkey and Greece, the unresolved question of Cyprus, border issues between Turkey and Armenia, and the ongoing debates over the Armenian genocide have turned the likes of the Phanariots and the loyal Armenians into historical anomalies. They remain specters of the past with no home in the present. Not so Ottoman Jews. Their history—and that of the Judeo-Spanish communities from the imperial heartland in particular—has enjoyed a very different fate. The discourse of a special Ottoman-Jewish friendship has served as an effective counterweight in Turkey's attempts to conduct an image management campaign in response to objections to its treatment of its Kurdish population, as well as calls for the government to recognize the mass annihilation of Ottoman Armenians as a genocide. As one author recently put it, in an "ocean of negative perceptions, the narrative of the long harmony between Turks and Jews appears as a little island of light."[5]

Turkish Jews have also participated in the perpetuation of this narrative. After the 1992 Quincentennial Foundation celebrations in recognition of five hundred years of "Turkish-Jewish amity" came and went, those behind the initiative sought to create a lasting memory of the anniversary.[6] Thus was born the Turkish "Museum of Tolerance," located within the former Zülfaris Synagogue of Istanbul.[7] The Ottoman Jews who had first invented a similar holiday in 1892 would no doubt have been impressed. One among them even foresaw the possibility that the celebration he imagined in 1891 might be repeated. "Our children may have the chance to surpass us," he explained, "but before that time, much water will have passed under the bridge, as the saying goes."[8]

That writer's proverbial water under the bridge consisted of nothing less than the end of the empire he called home and—as fate would have it—of all the old land-based empires of Europe along with it. Despite his premonition that the same celebration undertaken one hundred years later might occur under very different circumstances, he likely could not have imagined that not only his colleagues, but also the empire they celebrated would be nothing more than a memory by the time of the next anniversary held in its honor. Although the Ottoman Empire had been threatened with collapse by enemies and skeptics alike for many decades by the time of his writing in 1891, Ottoman Jewish authors had come to resist the pessimistic projections about the future of their empire. This resistance was built into their patriotic project from its earliest stages: almost immediately after the constitution of 1876 declared all imperial inhabitants Ottomans in the eyes of the law, the Russo-Ottoman War of 1877–1878 had threatened to undo their empire. "The crescent will live forever and will never die," one Ottoman Jewish author retorted in the midst of claims to the contrary during the war that year. His claim resonated with the tradition among Ottoman officials of calling the empire the *devlet-i ebed-müddet*, or the "eternally lasting state."[9]

As the Balkan Wars of 1912–1913 engulfed the remaining European portions of the empire, Ottoman Jews once again offered public expressions of allegiance to their state. When Salonica was captured by Greek forces in 1912, local Jews—having draped Ottoman flags and erected arches during the sultan's visit just the year before—stayed at home as the invading troops entered the city, and as their Greek Orthodox neighbors raised flags of blue and white in public places.[10] It was now the local Christians' turn to display their "zeal and noise" for the victors, much as the Jewish population had done during the Greco-Ottoman War in 1897. The chief rabbi of the city, Jacob Meir, the Ottoman Zionist who had pronounced a prayer in Arabic for the sultan just a year earlier, claimed that he "would have taken up arms if that had not been an impossibility, in order to prevent the fate which befell the Turks."[11] Under Greek rule, Salonica's Jews—along with local Muslims and Bulgarians—faced physical violence as well as new pressures to Hellenize. It took a number of years, and concerted government campaigns, to convince the city's Jews to adopt Greek citizenship and abandon their fezzes in favor of new forms of headgear more compatible with the shifting political landscape.[12] In the wake of these changes, numerous Salonican Jews left their native city to settle in Istanbul.[13] Others joined the thousands of their coreligionists from the empire who had begun heading to Western Europe and the Americas.[14]

Although various accounts suggest that many Jews chose to emigrate rather than serve according to the newly instated universal conscription laws of the Second Constitutional regime, Ottoman Jewish journalists did not cease to call upon their coreligionists to fight for their empire and to praise those who did, as they had in earlier decades when Ottoman Jews had volunteered for the imperial army.[15] In 1912, the French-language periodical, *Le Trait d'Union*, issued by Jews in Izmir, printed a photograph of a group of Ottoman Jewish soldiers, just as a contributor to Salonica's Ladino serial *La Epoka* had suggested should have been done for those who had volunteered during the wars of 1877 and 1897.[16] Throughout the Balkans Wars, Jewish leaders and journalists across the empire celebrated the Jewish men who fell in battle and offered tales of new Jewish martyrs who had spontaneously risked their lives for the cause of their country.[17]

From afar, Ottoman Jews continued to observe events in the empire with great interest. Responding to the Ottoman state's war with Italy in 1911–1912 and the Balkan Wars that followed immediately in its wake, a Ladino newspaper entitled *La Amerika*—published in New York since 1910—offered its readers detailed updates on Ottoman troop movements and diplomatic negotiations back home.[18] When the borders of southeastern Europe were redrawn with the conclusion of the Second Balkan War in 1913, the same paper printed a map of the Balkans made to scale with its readers' new place of residence—the state of New York.[19]

Beyond expressing admiration for Jewish soldiers and concern over their country's seemingly endless wars, Ottoman Jews abroad also gave other indications of their continued attachment to their state in the years following their emigration. Just as they had done while still resident in Ottoman lands, many continued to refer to the empire as their "*patria*," or homeland, and to themselves as Ottomans.[20] Jewish émigrés from the empire also donated to the imperial Red Crescent Society from locations as diverse as New York, Los Angeles, Argentina, Vienna, Antwerp, and Salisbury, Rhodesia.[21]

A number of advertisements published in the Ladino press of New York during the 1910s offer additional evidence of the ways in which Jews from the empire imported their Ottoman identity to foreign soil. One remarkable example of this phenomenon can be found in an advertisement that first appeared in *La Amerika* in 1911 and ran for many years.[22] The product it announced was Turkish coffee, made—as the ad explained—especially for "*turkinos*," or the Ottoman community in the region.[23] The advertisement appealed to its readers by inducing them to "buy coffee where all *turkinos* shop." It also offered them a Turkish phrase in Hebrew characters, reading "*Sabahlar hayır olsun*," a greeting meaning "may your morning be auspicious." The expression was not translated, however, as had been the case of the expression that appeared in David Fresco's Ottoman-Ladino dictionary excerpt in Istanbul's *El Nasional* in 1877. Apparently, the Ottoman Jewish audience of 1911 was expected to know such a common Turkish expression by this time. Most impressive of all, the vendors of the coffee had integrated an image of the sultan, Mehmed V, also known as Mehmed Reşad, into their advertisement. In the image, the sultan, decked in frock coat and fez, is surrounded by two banners and a shield, all emblazoned with the imperial crescent and star (Figure 5.1). The coffee—sold by Jews in the United States to other Jews—had even taken the imperial sovereign's name as its own: this was "Sultan Rechad's Coffee," the ad informed its readers. Intended for those who had come to the United States from the Ottoman Levant, the sultan's coffee was meant to give them a little taste of home.

That the promoters of this product used imperial elements to attract Ladino readers well beyond the bounds of the empire indicates the extent to which Ottoman Jews had adopted the symbols of their state and claimed them as their own. Cobblers, restaurateurs, garment vendors, and even greengrocers publishing in New York's Ladino press similarly employed imperial images to speak to their readers and—presumably—to convince them to buy from their shops out of a sense of Ottoman solidarity. Such was the case of the shoe store that paired an image of a boot with the imperial

Figure 5.1 "Sultan Rechad's Coffee," *La Amerika*, 1913.

crescent and star in order to advertise its wares in the pages of *La Amerika* in 1913 (Figure 5.2).[24] A clothing shop on Chrystie Street, an area with a dense population of Levantine Jews living in New York's Lower East Side, similarly combined the crescent and star of the empire with the American flag in order to sell its products, as did an association of Ottoman Jewish produce vendors that emerged during the period (Figure 5.3–5.4).[25] The same paper also promoted an "Ottoman restaurant" that boasted Ottoman-language newspapers and sold tea, coffee, and yoghurts all prepared in a manner familiar to its readers, the same "Oriental" style that Ottoman Jews visiting the Chicago Fair in 1893 had praised and identified as their own two decades before (Figure 5.5). Unlike most of the other advertisements published in *La Amerika*, however, this last ad made clear that the restaurant it promoted was owned by an Ottoman Muslim, as indicated by his name: Mehmed Fadil.[26] That the Muslim restaurateur advertised in the Judeo-Spanish serial suggests that, by the early twentieth century, the civic Ottomanist project that imperial elites had begun to pursue so many decades earlier had found a home on new shores, as Ottomans of different religious backgrounds continued to display their commitment to forging bonds with each other half a world away from the empire they had left behind.

Taken together, the different advertisements printed in *La Amerika* during this period offer a striking example of the ways in which Jews from the empire

Figure 5.2 Cobbler's ad, *La Amerika*, 1913.

Figure 5.3 Clothing ad, *La Amerika*, 1912.

Figure 5.4 Greengrocer's ad, *La Amerika*, 1913.

Figure 5.5 Restaurant ad, *La Amerika*, 1913.

had come to construe Ottoman symbols and allegiance as an integral part of their public self-expression. Even in the years that followed, *La Amerika* issued statements similar to those published in the Ottoman Jewish press in previous decades as they rejected predictions of the impending collapse of the empire. Thus it was that in 1916, in the middle of the First World War, one writer for the American Ladino serial *La Bos del Puevlo* expressed his conviction that the Ottoman state "still exists and will exist for . . . a long time to come."[27]

These statements can be read in a number of ways. For the Ottoman Jews invested in turning their coreligionists into imperial citizens, such expressions served as incontrovertible proof of their steadfast patriotism during a period of intensive state reform and crisis. Even today, quotes strung together for an exhibit in an Istanbul museum continue to tell a story of timeless Jewish devotion to the empire; yet they remain out of context, bound together only by the curator's desire to tell the story of Turkish-Jewish amity. This book has aimed to offer a different interpretive frame, one that presents Ottoman Jewish expressions of dedication to the empire from another perspective entirely.

Understanding Jewish Ottomanism as a form of inherited loyalty that Jews passed down from one generation to the next assumes that Ottoman Jews remained unmoved by the world around them. This interpretation not only takes the historical sources at face value, it also treats modern Jews' expressions of allegiance to their empire within a pre-modern frame, thus bypassing the question of precisely what motivated the particular forms their allegiance took in different contexts and at different moments. Although examples of Jews who praised the Ottoman sultans as their saviors can be traced over the course of many centuries, this tradition captured Jews' attention in the modern period only because they continued to find it meaningful and useful.[28] Careful readings of Ottoman Jewish sources from Istanbul, Izmir, Salonica, and beyond indicate that Ottoman Jews of the nineteenth and early twentieth centuries were responding not only to the traditions and motifs they had in their communal arsenal but also—indeed, most immediately—to the requirements of their time. Inspired by the new obligations and promises of imperial citizenship, Ottoman Jews learned to harness the regnant discourses of official circles and use them to their own advantage. In this sense, they learned to "speak Ottomanism," even when they did not know Ottoman Turkish.[29] The paths through which they participated in patriotic discourses were many: the Jewish and non-Jewish press, schools, clubs, libraries, dance halls, the marketplace, coffee houses, world fairs, and public squares were all sites where Ottoman Jews, along with other Ottomans, negotiated the meaning of imperial citizenship.[30] Close analyses of the writings, images, and objects different Ottoman Jews left behind indicate that their identification with their state was hardly static or predetermined.

What Ottomanism meant changed over time and space, as did the ways that different Jewish individuals drew from it.[31] When Ottomanism appeared in the mid-nineteenth century as an ideal articulated in various imperial edicts, Jews across the empire announced their adherence to the reform decrees of the era to different ends—whether to prove their loyalty to imperial officials or to shake off the oppressive rule of their own communal leaders. When it represented a supranational project of uniting all Ottoman subjects regardless of their religion, Jews in the empire partook in conversations to this effect and promoted a vision of civic Ottomanism predicated on the bourgeois values of intercommunal cooperation, progress, and public propriety.[32]

Yet, framing Ottomanism in these terms did not prevent Jews, or other non-Muslims for that matter, from simultaneously engaging in other conversations about imperial belonging.[33] When attachment to the Ottoman state manifested itself as an identity centered around the Islamic nature of the empire, Jews also drew Islamic motifs into their writings, making reference to the importance of the Caliphate, to holy wars, religious martyrs, and to their "Muslim brothers."

Mobilizing a common image of the bravery of Ottoman soldiers who "fought like lions" to defend their country, Jewish journalists employed an expression from Ottoman Turkish used commonly in other Ottoman circles as a cliché of patriotic discourse. This was also true of Ottoman Jews' critiques of European intervention in the empire, as well as their resistance to the westernizing ways of some in their own communities. Such anti-colonial and anti-Westernist discourse was a crucial element of the language of Hamidian Ottomanism.[34] When Ottoman Jews praised their empire's "Oriental" displays in Chicago they participated in such discussions, signaling their identification with their empire by employing a rhetoric of Easternism that they shared with various Ottoman authors and politicians of the time.[35]

By the Second Constitutional period, Zionists adapted the language of "Eastern" origins to their own purposes. They were no longer simply Orientals because they were Ottomans, but rather—or also—because they were Jews with origins in the ancient Near East. Instead of alienating them from broader Ottoman discussions, their approach offered new opportunities in alliance building, such as the links they made between Hebrew and Arabic, the two Semitic languages employed by Jews and Muslims, respectively. The extent to which Ottoman Zionists felt comfortable using the symbolism and language of Easternism to advance their cause appear most strikingly in Rabbi Jacob Meir's Arabic-language prayer for the empire during the sultan's visit to Salonica in 1911 and in the arch the Zionist Nouveau Club erected in the form of minarets for the same occasion.

It was also during the Second Constitutional Era that various individuals employed references to popular themes of "union and progress" and the constitution as they attempted to ground their claims to belonging in the language of the new regime. Jewish socialists suggested they were the true custodians of Ottoman law while representatives of the new government had lost sight of their mandate. Even the socialists' unwillingness to celebrate the sultan resonated in the larger political milieu of their day. However radical, the position Salonica's Socialist Federation took during Mehmed V's tour of their city found echoes in the suggestion of the Ottoman satirical press of the period that a "traditional monarch . . . was an obsolete breed."[36] Meanwhile, using the image of espionage as a foil, different Ottoman Jews distanced themselves from the "times of Hamid" in order to disparage their opponents, while placing themselves squarely in the camp of the new regime.[37] As they did so, however, they obscured the fact that they had once spoken "Hamidian" as well. Ottoman Jewish patriotism was an evolving project. Responding to changing circumstances and political exigencies, different Jewish leaders from across the empire continued to invent their allegiance anew in each age.

There was one element of Sephardi Jews' patriotic discourse that changed little across the Tanzimat, Hamidian, and Second Constitutional eras, however. This was the narrative of the Ottoman state's reception of the Jews of Spain in 1492, when no one else would have them. Making continual reference to the empire's benevolent welcome of their ancestors served the aims of Ottoman Jewish leaders well: they used it when dealing with state representatives as proof of their patriotism and when speaking with their coreligionists, to explain why Jews—more than other groups in the empire—owed their full allegiance to their state. Indeed, in the words of different Ottoman Jewish authors, they owed a "double debt" to their state—both as newly emancipated citizens and as Jews. The empire's enemies—many of whom also figured in Ottoman Jewish discourse as the enemies of the Jews—thus appeared as a "double enemy," as various Jewish communal leaders suggested was the case during the Russo-Ottoman War of 1877–1878.

The trope of Ottoman welcome also merged with a broader Ottoman discourse of tolerance that had developed as a rebuttal to European claims of the empire's backwardness. Throughout the nineteenth and early twentieth centuries, numerous Ottoman statesmen and intellectuals suggested that their empire had practiced religious tolerance at a time when the various states of Europe were mired in religious wars and persecution. In the words of the Ottoman statesman and two-time grand vizier Midhat Pasha, in centuries past, "the nations of the East and of the North had not yet emerged from the state of barbarism in which they existed." For this reason, he posited, immigrants had come "from all directions" to settle in Ottoman lands.[38] The idea of the Ottoman state as a place of refuge from persecution and as a forerunner of tolerant and enlightened policies meant that the theme of the expulsion of the Jews from Iberia in 1492 served as an ideal foil.

Yet the logic of the continued references to 1492 as the justification for Ottoman Jews' allegiance to the state also meant that they were obliged to be eternally grateful to the Ottomans, who became their protectors rather than their peers in such formulations. By speaking about the double debt they owed the empire, Jews offered a particularist discourse about their Ottoman allegiance, such as when they invented a patriotic holiday in 1892 meant to mark the "Four-Hundredth Anniversary of the Arrival of the Jews of Spain in Ottoman Lands." Although the objective of those who planned and orchestrated this celebration was to demonstrate their active attachment to the empire in a way that matched the expectations of their day, their holiday was not an Ottoman holiday. It was not meant to be observed by or to resonate with all imperial citizens. It was, rather, an Ottoman Jewish holiday intended—in the words of the journalist who first dreamt up the idea—to "bring about great satisfaction at the imperial court and among the Ottoman nation," a term he employed to refer to the Muslims of the empire.[39]

As much as Jewish leaders and authors hoped to invoke the trope of 1492 in order to claim a special place for their community within the empire, the narrative could also be turned against them. This was the case in 1899 when a debate erupted between the Ottoman-language newspaper *Ahenk* and the Ladino serial *La Buena Esperansa*, both of Izmir. *Ahenk* fired the first shot by criticizing the young Jewish men of the city for replacing their fezzes with European-style hats, then quickly turned the discussion from the present to the past: "At the time when the Jews were expelled from Spain, the Ottoman state was the only one to take them in," he chided. "The Jews have now lived here for four hundred years in peace under the shadow of the empire. We are astonished to see that the [Jewish] youths act as if they have forgotten this history."[40]

Aron de Yosef Hazan, the editor of *La Buena Esperansa* and the original architect of the four-hundredth anniversary celebrations of Jews' arrival in Ottoman lands, attempted to defend the Jews of his city and the empire, writing that even though he counseled young Ottoman Jewish men to wear the fez, the simple act of wearing a hat did not mean they had forgotten the special recognition that all Jews owed the sultan's government. Hazan continued by expressing his discomfort with the direction the debate had taken, writing that his colleague from *Ahenk* "surely cannot mean to suggest that the Jews have failed even once in the long period [since they were received into the empire] to offer abundant proof of their ties of loyalty to our homeland and the sacred person of his Majesty the Sultan."[41] Yet the author of the article in *Ahenk* had done just that. Before the debate died down in the press of Izmir, it surfaced in editorials of Ottoman and Ladino papers in Salonica and Istanbul, reminding thousands of readers across the empire that the narrative of Ottoman tolerance could be used as a warning to Jews rather than simply serving their patriotic project.[42] It sent a message that they were permanent guests in the country in which they had been settled for centuries.

Ottoman Jews' choice to dwell on the year 1492 as a moment of Jewish redemption emphasized their status as symbolic immigrants, and thus had the effect of excluding Jews from discursive constructions of Ottoman identity. Although the idea of the Jews as guests became pronounced as racial definitions of Turkishness took root during the early Turkish Republican era, clearly, it was present already in the late Ottoman period.[43] Paradoxically, it was the product not simply of those who sought to exclude or chastise Jews but also of the attempts of Ottoman Jews themselves to become Ottomans, to study and teach each other the history of their state, and to ensure their belonging by claiming a special place for themselves in the empire. In this sense, Ottoman

Jews' continued insistence on their gratitude to the empire helped to distance them from the very imperial polity into which they sought integration. The paradoxical situation of Ottoman Jewry has persisted into the present. In 1991, when a Turkish Jewish reporter explained to the Turkish consul-general in Marseilles that Turkish Jews "feel a sense of gratitude" to Turkey, while also noting that they felt genuinely Turkish, the consul-general simply replied, "In order to feel gratitude, you cannot be one of us. If you actually feel that you are Turks, there is no need to feel gratitude."[44]

NOTES

Preface

1. W. E. B. Du Bois, *The Souls of Black Folk* (Chicago: A. C. McClurg & Co., 1903), 1–2.
2. Du Bois also made this link, writing that his travels to Eastern Europe during the first half of the twentieth century raised his awareness of the "Jewish problem of the modern world." Michael Rothberg, *Multidirectional Memory: Remembering the Holocaust in the Age of Decolonization* (Stanford, CA: Stanford University Press, 2009), 111.
3. "Siyonizm," *Yeni İkdam*, 6 Rebiülevvel 1329 (March 6, 1911), 1; Sam Lévy, Ladino diary (in *soletreo*), June 11, 1894, in the collection of Jean Carasso. I am grateful to Gaëlle Collin for providing me with her transcription. Claims about the absence of a Jewish question continued to find echoes under the modern Turkish Republic. "Il n'existe aucune question juive en Turquie: L'opinion officielle exprimée par le député turc Huseyn Djahid Yalcin," *Le Judaïsme Sephardi* 8, no. 68 (February 1939), 24. In late Ottoman politics, observers spoke more often of an Ottoman Armenian "Question" or "Problem." On this, see, for example: Nadir Özbek, "The Politics of Taxation and the 'Armenian Question' during the Late Ottoman Empire, 1876–1908," *Comparatives Studies in Society and History* 54, no. 4 (2012): 770–797; Masayuki Ueno, "'For the Fatherland and the State': Armenians Negotiate the Tanzimat Reforms," *International Journal of Middle East Studies* 45 (2013): 93–109, esp. 93. Louis Fishman has argued that the Second Constitutional Era in the Ottoman Empire witnessed the birth of a Jewish Question. See his "Understanding the 1911 Ottoman Parliament Debate on Zionism in Light of the Emergence of a "Jewish Question," in *Late Ottoman Palestine: The Period of Young Turk Rule*, ed. Yuval Ben-Bassat and Eyal Ginio (New York: I. B. Tauris, 2011), 103–123.
4. Vijay Prashad, *The Karma of Brown Folks* (Minneapolis: University of Minnesota Press, 2001), viii.
5. For related arguments about American Jews as a model minority: Karen Brodkin, *How Jews Became White Folks and What That Says About Race in America* (New Brunswick, NJ: Rutgers University Press, 1998); Jonathan Freedman, *Klezmer America: Jewishness, Ethnicity, Modernity* (New York: Columbia University Press, 2008).
6. I use the term "minority" advisedly here. For a critique of the use of the term in the Ottoman context, see: Aron Rodrigue, "Difference and Tolerance in the Ottoman Empire," interview by Nancy Reynolds, *Stanford Humanities Review* 5 (Fall 1995): 81–92; Rodrigue, "Reflections on Millets and Minorities: Ottoman Legacies," in *Turkey Between Nationalism and Globalization*, ed. Riva Kastoryano (New York: Routledge, 2013), 36–46.
7. Enver Ziya Karal, *Osmanlı Tarihi*, vol. 5, *Nizam-ı Cedit ve Tanzimat Devirleri (1789–1856)* (Ankara: Türk Tarih Kurumu Basımevi, 1947), 266–272.
8. See, for example, Bernard Lewis, *The Emergence of Modern Turkey* (New York: Oxford University Press, 2001), 344, which suggests that "Ottomanism had proved a failure."

9. Erik-Jan Zürcher, "The Ottoman Conscription System, 1844–1918," *International Review of Social History* 43, no. 3 (1998): 449.

10. Harvey E. Goldberg, ed., *Sephardi and Middle Eastern Jewries* (Bloomington: Indiana University Press, 1996), 20; Isa Blumi, "Teaching Loyalty in the Late Ottoman Balkans: Educational Reform in the Vilayets of Manastir and Yanya, 1878–1912," *Comparative Studies of South Asia, Africa and the Middle East* 21, nos. 1–2 (2001): 15–23; Blumi, *Reinstating the Ottomans: Alternative Balkan Modernities, 1800–1912* (New York: Palgrave Macmillan, 2011).

11. In recent years a growing body of works has come to challenge the assumption that Ottomanism held little sway over anyone outside of small elite and state circles, and that non-Muslims rarely participated in advancing Ottomanist programs. See, for example: Hasan Kayalı, *Arabs and Young Turks: Ottomanism, Arabism, and Islamism in the Second Constitutional Period of the Ottoman Empire, 1908–1918* (Berkeley: University of California Press, 1997); Elizabeth B. Frierson, "Mirrors Out, Mirrors In: Domestication and Rejection of the Foreign in Late-Ottoman Women's Magazines (1875–1908)," in *Women, Patronage and Self-Representation in Islamic Societies*, ed. D. Fairchild Ruggles (New York: State University of New York Press, 2000), 177–204; Frierson, "Gender, Consumption and Patriotism: The Emergence of an Ottoman Public Sphere," in *Public Islam and the Common Good*, ed. Armando Salvatore and Dale F. Eickelman (Leiden: Brill, 2004), 99–125; Ussama Makdisi, "After 1860: Debating Religion, Reform, and Nationalism in the Ottoman Empire," *International Journal of Middle East Studies* 34, no. 4 (November 2002): 601–617; Milen Petrov, "Everyday Forms of Compliance: Subaltern Commentaries on Ottoman Reform, 1864–1868," *Comparative Studies in Society and History* 46, no. 4 (2004): 730–759; Sia Anagnostopoulou and Matthias Kappler, "Zito Zito o Sultanos/Bin Yaşa Padişahımız: The *Millet-i Rum* Singing the Praises of the Sultan in the Framework of Helleno-Ottomanism," *Archivum Ottomanicum* 23 (2005/06): 47–78; Nadir Özbek, "Philanthropic Activity, Ottoman Patriotism and the Hamidian Regime, 1876–1909," *International Journal of Middle East Studies* 37 (2005): 59–81; Blumi, "Teaching Loyalty;" Blumi, *Reinstating the Ottomans*; Elke Hartmann, "The 'Loyal Nation' and its Deputies," in *The First Ottoman Parliament: Perception, Significance and Prosopography*, ed. Christoph Herzog and Malek Sharif (Würzburg: Ergon, 2010), 187–222; Orit Bashkin, "'Religious Hatred Shall Disappear from the Land': Iraqi Jews as Ottoman Subjects, 1864–1913," *International Journal of Contemporary Iraqi Studies* 4, no. 3 (December 2010): 305–323; Christine Philliou, *Biography of an Empire: Governing Ottomans in an Age of Revolution* (Berkeley: University of California Press, 2010); Lital Levy, "Partitioned Pasts: Arab Jewish Intellectuals and the Case of Esther Azhari Moyal (1873–1948)," in *The Making of the Arab Intellectual: Empire, Public Sphere and the Colonial Coordinates of Selfhood*, ed. Dyala Hamzah (New York: Routledge, 2012), 128–163, 140; Darin Stephanov, "Minorities, Majorities, and the Monarch: Nationalizing Effects of the Late Ottoman Royal Public Ceremonies, 1808–1908," (Ph.D. diss., University of Memphis, 2012); Abigail Jacobson, *From Empire to Empire: Jerusalem Between Ottoman and British Rule* (Syracuse, NY: Syracuse University Press, 2011); Masayuki Ueno, "'For the Fatherland and the State': Armenians Negotiate the Tanzimat Reforms," *International Journal of Middle East Studies* 45(2013): 93–109.

12. Elizabeth Thompson, *Colonial Citizens: Republican Rights, Paternal Privilege, and Gender in French Syria and Lebanon* (New York: Columbia University Press, 2000); Sukanya Banerjee, *Becoming Imperial Citizens: Indians in the Late-Victorian Empire* (Durham, NC: Duke University Press, 2010); Michelle Campos, *Ottoman Brothers: Muslims, Christians and Jews in Early Twentieth-Century Palestine* (Stanford, CA: Stanford University Press, 2010).

13. Or, in many cases, from what Christine Philliou has called "the edge of the center." Philliou, *Biography*, xvii.

14. Özbek, "Philanthropic Activity;" Özbek, "The Politics of Taxation;" Philliou, *Biography*; Thompson, *Colonial Citizens*.

15. Thompson, *Colonial Citizens*, 17.

Introduction

1. A flurry of publications have resulted from these efforts: *Turkish Jews: 500 Years of Harmony: Celebrating the 500th Anniversary of the Welcoming of the Jewish People to the Ottoman Empire in 1492* (Berkeley, CA: Judah L. Magnes Museum, 1991); Bernard Cooperman, "Turco-Jewish Relations in the Ottoman City of Salonica, 1889–1912: Two Communities in Support of the Ottoman Empire" (Ph.D. diss., New York University, 1991); *The Quincentennial Foundation Gala Celebration: April 27, 1992*, the Plaza Hotel, New York City (Istanbul: Quincentennial Foundation of Istanbul, 1992); Marc Silberman, *A Curriculum on Five Hundred Years of Turkish Jewish Experience,* sponsored by the Quincentennial Foundation of Istanbul, 1993; Avigdor Levy, ed., *The Jews of the Ottoman Empire* (Princeton, NJ, and Washington, DC: Darwin Press and Institute of Turkish Studies, 1994); David F. Altabé, Erhan Atay, and Israel J. Katz, eds., *Studies on Turkish-Jewish History: Political and Social Relations, Literature and Linguistics: The Quincentennial Papers* (New York: Sepher-Hermon Press for The American Society of Sephardic Studies, 1996); *The Quincentennial Foundation: A Retrospection* ([Istanbul]: The Foundation, 1997); Mehmet Tütüncü, ed., *Turkish-Jewish Encounters: Studies on Turkish-Jewish Relations through the Ages/Türk-Yahudi Buluşmaları: Tarihte Türk-Yahudi İlişkileri Araştırmaları* (Haarlem, Netherlands: SOTA, 2001); Avigdor Levy, ed., *Jews, Turks, Ottomans: A Shared History, Fifteenth through the Twentieth Century* (Syracuse, NY: Syracuse University Press, 2002), especially Halil İnalcık, "Foundations of Ottoman-Jewish Cooperation," 3–14 and Feroz Ahmad, "The Special Relationship: The Committee of Union and Progress and the Ottoman Jewish Political Elite, 1908–1918," 212–230; Naim A. Güleryüz, *500. Yıl Vakfı Türk Musevileri Müzesi/Quincentennial Foundation Museum of Turkish Jews* (Istanbul: Gözlem Gazetecilik Basın ve Yayın A. Ş., 2004).
2. Rıfat Bali, *Model Citizens of the State: The Jews of Turkey during the Multi-Party Period* (Lanham, MD: Fairleigh Dickinson University Press, 2012).
3. *The Quincentennial Foundation: A Retrospection.*
4. On the concept of the royal alliance, see Yosef Hayim Yerushalmi, "'Servants of Kings and Not Servants of Servants': Some Aspects of the Political History of the Jews," Tenenbaum Family Lecture Series in Judaic Studies delivered at Emory University, February 8, 2005 (Atlanta: The Tam Institute for Jewish Studies, n.d.); Yerushalmi, "'Serviteurs des rois et non serviteurs des serviteurs.' Sur quelques aspects de l'histoire politique des Juifs," *Raisons politiques* 7 (2002): 19–52; Yerushalmi, *The Lisbon Massacre of 1506 and the Royal Image in the Shebet Yehudah* (Cincinnati: Hebrew Union College, 1976).
5. Elijah Capsali (1483–1555), Samuel Usque (n.d.), Yosef Ha-Kohen (1496–ca. 1575) and Yosef Sambari (ca. 1640–1703), all praised the Ottoman Empire as a redemptive power that had saved the Jews while Christian Europe expelled them. One of Ha-Kohen's works, *Divre ha-Yamim le-Malkhe Tsarfat u-le-Malkhe Bet 'Otman ha-Togar,* which described history as a conflict between Islam and Christianity (as represented by the Ottoman Empire and France, respectively), was consequently banned in Russia in 1800 due to passages "disrespectful to Christians and the Christian religion." See "Censorship of Hebrew Books," *Jewish Encyclopedia* (New York: Funk and Wagnalls Co., 1902), 3:651; Eduard Neumann and Richard Gottheil, "Joseph ben Joshua ben Meïr ha-Kohen," *Jewish Encyclopedia* (1904), 7:266–267. See also Joseph R. Hacker, "Ottoman Policy toward the Jews and Jewish Attitudes toward the Ottoman during the Fifteenth Century," in *Christians and Jews in the Ottoman Empire*, ed. Benjamin Braude and Bernard Lewis (New York: Holmes & Meier Publishers, 1982), 1:117–126; Hacker, "The Sürgün System and Jewish Society in the Ottoman Empire during the Fifteenth to the Seventeenth Centuries," in *Ottoman and Turkish Jewry: Community and Leadership*, ed. Aron Rodrigue (Bloomington: Indiana University Press, 1992), 1–65.
6. Hacker, "The Sürgün System."
7. Hacker, "The Sürgün System," 23; Marc Baer, *Honored by the Glory of Islam* (New York: Oxford University Press, 2008), for similar initiatives taken by Mehmet IV.
8. Gershom Scholem, *Sabbatai Sevi: The Mystical Messiah 1626–76* (Princeton, NJ: Princeton University Press, 1973), 433.

9. Chevalier de la Croix, *Mémoire . . . contenant divers relations très curieuses de l'Empire Ottoman* (Paris, 1684), 2:296, as cited in Scholem, *Sabbatai Sevi*, 435.

10. Baer, *Honored by the Glory of Islam*, 123.

11. Scholem, *Sabbatai Sevi*, 344.

12. A different Jewish messianic pretender of the early modern era, David Reubeni, also reportedly sought to "conquer Palestine" from the "Turks." Moïse Franco, *Essai sur l'histoire des Israélites de l'Empire Ottoman depuis les origines jusqu'à nos jours* (1897, repr.: New York: Georg Olms Verlag, 1973), 52. In 1637, the Ottoman government reportedly had the Salonican rabbi Judah Covo executed for providing it with cloth of an "unacceptable" quality. Benjamin Braude, "The Rise and Fall of Salonica Woollens," *Mediterranean Historical Review* 6, no. 2 (1991): 233.

13. Examples include Jewish marriage contracts (*ketubot*), prayer shawls (*talitot*), Hanukah lamps and Torah scroll covers, shields, and finials: Esther Juhasz, *Sephardi Jews in the Ottoman Empire: Aspects of Material Culture* (Jerusalem: Israel Museum, 1990), 57, 58, 81, 83, 225; Vivian B. Mann, *A Tale of Two Cities: Jewish Life in Frankfurt and Istanbul 1750–1870* (New York: The Jewish Museum, 1982), 14, 157, 162–163; Mann, "Jewish-Muslim Acculturation in the Ottoman Empire," in Levy, *The Jews of the Ottoman Empire*, 561–562; *Turkish Jews: 500 Years of Harmony*, 5; *Embellished Lives: Customs and Costumes of the Jewish Communities of Turkey* (Berkeley: Judah L. Magnes Museum, 1989), 12, 14, 22; Güleryüz, 500. *Yıl Vakfı*, 9, 10, 17, 54; Peter Kelley, "A Family's Lost Story Found, and the Sephardic Studies Initiative," www.washington.edu/news/2013/01/16/a-familys-lost-story-found-and-the-sephardic-studies-initiative/, accessed January 27, 2013.

14. The cities and communities studied here made up part of the Judeo-Spanish heartland, or culture sphere, which was reconstituted in the eastern Mediterranean region after the expulsion of the Jews from Spain. For a comprehensive overview of these communities, see Esther Benbassa and Aron Rodrigue, *Sephardi Jewry: A History of the Judeo-Spanish Community, 14th–20th Centuries* (Berkeley: University of California Press, 2000).

15. James C. Scott, *Domination and the Arts of Resistance: Hidden Transcripts* (New Haven, CT: Yale University Press, 1992).

16. For the special niche Jews held as textile producers during the early modern period: Benjamin Braude, "International Competition and Domestic Cloth in the Ottoman Empire, 1500–1650: A Study in Underdevelopment," *Review (Fernand Braudel Center)* 2, no. 3 (Winter 1979): 437–451; Braude, "Rise and Fall of Salonica Woollens." For the decline of Ottoman Jewish commercial activity in the late seventeenth and eighteenth century: Karen Leal, "The Balat District of Istanbul: Multiethnicity on the Golden Horn" in *The Architecture and Memory of the Minority Quarter in the Muslim Mediterranean City*, ed. Susan G. Miller and Mauro Bertagnin (Cambridge, MA: Harvard University Press, 2010), 193; Fatma Müge Göçek, *Rise of the Bourgeoisie, Demise of Empire* (New York: Oxford, 1996), 89; Bernard Lewis, *The Muslim Discovery of Europe* (New York: Norton, 1982), 107–109. On the continued prosperity of particular Jewish individuals and communities amidst the overall decline in Ottoman Jews' economic fortunes: Jacob Barnai, "Kavim le-toldot kehilat Kushta ba-meah ha-18," *Mi-Kedem U-mi-Yam* 1 (1981): 64–65; Haim Gerber, "Yozmah u-Mishar Ben-Leumi ba-Pe'ilut ha-Kalkalit shel Yehude ha-Imperyah ha-'Otmanit ba-Meot 16–17," *Zion* 43 (1978): 36–67; Christopher Oscanyan, *The Sultan and His People* (New York: Derby and Jackson, 1857), 376–379.

17. Alison Games, *The Web of Empire: English Cosmopolitans in an Age of Expansion, 1560–1660* (New York: Oxford University Press, 2008), 56; Yaron Ben-Naeh, *Jews in the Realm of the Sultans* (Tübingen. Mohr Siebeck, 2008), 129; Cevdet Paşha, *Tezâkir*, vol. 1 (Ankara: Türk Tarih Kurumu, 1953), 67–68; Roderic Davison, *Reform in the Ottoman Empire 1856–76* (Princeton, NJ: Princeton University Press, 1963), 119; Ludwig August Frankl, *The Jews of the East*, trans. Rev. P. Beaton (London: First and Blackett Publishers, 1859), 1:189; Aron Rodrigue, *Jews and Muslims: Images of Sephardi and Middle Eastern Jewries in Modern Times* (Seattle: University of Washington Press, 2003), 138; Başbakanlık Osmanlı Arşivi (hereafter BOA), DH. MTV. 25/34, 6 Cemaziyelahir 1329 (June 4, 1911); Istoriko Archeio Makedonias. Archeio Ieras Mitropoleos Thessalonikis. Phakelos 121: Praktika tou Simvouliou tes Dimogerondias Thessalonikis [Historical

Archives of Macedonia. Archive of the Holy Eparchy of Thessaloniki. File 121: Minutes of the Elders' Council]. Meeting of March 24, 1911. I am grateful to Paris Papamichos Chronakis for this last reference.

18. A report from 1908 set the Ottoman Jewish population at 439,000: *L'Univers israélite*, August 21, 1908, 710, cited in Esther Benbassa, "Le Sionisme dans l'Empire Ottoman à l'aube du 20e siècle," *Vingtième Siècle* 24 (October–December 1989): 69–80, 70. Others have set the numbers lower, at approximately 250,000 around the turn of the twentieth century. Benbassa and Rodrigue, *Sephardi Jewry*, 70. For the cited Greek Orthodox and Armenian population statistics from the mid-nineteenth century: Aron Rodrigue, *French Jews, Turkish Jews: The Alliance Israélite Universelle and the Politics of Jewish Schooling in Turkey, 1860–1925* (Bloomington: Indiana University Press, 1990), 26.

19. Richard Davey, *The Sultan and His Subjects* (London: Chapman and Hall, 1897), 2:214, 2:216; Abdolonyme Ubicini, *Letters on Turkey* (London: J. Murray, 1856) 2:346; Rodrigue, *French Jews, Turkish Jews*, 43.

20. See, for example, the tale told of a man who rode past the imperial residence of Mahmud II without dismounting, only to be stopped by the guard on duty, who explained that the sultan's orders to dismount before the imperial residence applied "to all Christians and Turks equally." "I am not a Christian. I am a Jew," was allegedly the man's reply. As the legend had it, the man was allowed to pass. For the British author who recounted the story some decades later this anecdote was proof of the state's "indifference toward the Jews in the East." Samuel Sullivan Cox, *Diversions of a Diplomat in Turkey* (New York: Charles L. Webster, 1887), 193. See also the poem of the Ottoman statesman Ziya Pasha, which suggested that Jews lagged behind Christians in the wake of nineteenth-century state reforms: "If but the help of God assist in his purpose dear / Full soon will these gypsies sit on the couch of the Grand Vizier / *It is but the Jews alone that form the exception here* / For of Greeks and Armenians both doth he make Bey and Mushir." Emphasis mine. E. J. W. Gibb, *Ottoman Poetry* (London: Luzac & Co., 1907), 5:105–106.

21. Just a few years earlier, in 1819, an influential Jewish businessman of Acre by the name of Hayim Farhi was murdered by the local governor: Minna Rozen, *The Last Ottoman Century and Beyond: The Jews in Turkey and the Balkans, 1808–1945* (Ramat Aviv: Tel Aviv University, 2005), 1:55.

22. Rozen, *The Last Ottoman Century*, 1:57.

23. Ibid., 37, 48. Although Mahmud II's targeted destruction of the Janissary Corps was celebrated in official Ottoman histories as the *vaka-i hayriye*, or "Auspicious Event," many experienced the moment as one of great trauma and dislocation: not only did Mahmud II orchestrate the murder of thousands of Janissaries in the capital and beyond, his purge also upset the lives of untold others with links to the corps, including different communal elites, Ottoman artisans, and Bektaşi Sufis. On this, see Donald Quataert, "Clothing Laws, State, and Society in the Ottoman Empire, 1720–1829," *International Journal of Middle East Studies* 29, no. 3 (August 1997): 403–425; Frederick F. Anscombe, "Islam and the Age of Ottoman Reform," *Past and Present* 208, no. 1 (August 2010): 159–189.

24. Aron Rodrigue, *French Jews, Turkish Jews*, 28.

25. Rodrigue, *French Jews, Turkish Jews* 27; Benbassa and Rodrigue, *Sephardi Jewry*, 49; Abraham Galante, *Histoire des juifs de Turquie* (1940; repr., Isis: Istanbul, 1985–1986), 1:147.

26. Franco, *Essai*, 139; Avigdor Levy, "Millet Politics: The Appointment of a Chief Rabbi in 1835," in Levy, *The Jews of the Ottoman Empire* (Princeton, NJ, and Washington, DC: Darwin Press and Institute of Turkish Studies, 1994), 428; Aron Rodrigue, *French Jews, Turkish Jews*, 27; Caroline Finkel, *Osman's Dream* (New York: Basic Books, 2005), 438; Anscombe, "Islam," 169.

27. Galante, *Histoire des juifs de Turquie*, 1:144–145; Stanford Shaw, *The Jews of the Ottoman Empire*, 148–149.

28. Translations are mine. For the original Ladino (in transliteration), see Franco, *Essai*, 135–137.

29. Rozen, *The Last Ottoman Century* 1:385–386; 387.

30. Frankl, *The Jews of the East*, 159.

31. Salomon A. Rosanes, *Korot ha-Yehudim be-Turkiyah ve-artsot ha-kedem* (Jerusalem: Rabbi Kook Institute, 1945), 6:78, cited in Levy, "Millet Politics," 428. Bernard Lewis has repeated this view in his "The Ottoman Empire in the Mid-Nineteenth Century: A Review," *Middle Eastern Studies* 1, no. 3 (April 1965): 289.

32. On this, see also: "Der Orient: Konstantinopel (Zweiter Brief)," *Allgemeine Zeitung des Judenthums* 5, no. 8 (February 20, 1841): 97–98, whose author claims that after their leaders were murdered in the 1820s, Ottoman Jews remained "without influence or protection."

33. Abraham Galante, *Histoire des juifs de Turquie*, 1:143; Enver Ziya Karal, "Non-Muslim Representatives in the First Constitutional Assembly, 1876–1877," in Braude and Lewis, *Christians and Jews in the Ottoman Empire*, 1:388; Avigdor Levy, "Introduction" in *The Jews of the Ottoman Empire*, 103: *L'Univers israélite*, April 1856, 341; Davison, *Reform in the Ottoman Empire*, 31; Walter F. Weiker, *Ottomans, Turks, and the Jewish Polity* (Lanham, MD: University Press of America, 1992), 121.

34. Karal, "Non-Muslim Representatives;" Reşat Kaynar, *Mustafa Reşit Paşa ve Tanzimat* (Ankara: Türk Tarif Kurumu Basimevi, 1954), 99–100.

35. Donald Quataert, *The Ottoman Empire, 1700–1922* (Cambridge, UK: Cambridge University Press, 2001), 146–147; Quataert, "Clothing Laws," 416.

36. Niyazi Berkes, *The Development of Secularism in Turkey* (Montreal: McGill University Press, 1964), 125; Serafettin Turan, *Türk Kültür Tarihi* (Ankara: Bilgi Yayınevi, 1990), 216–222; Selçuk Esenbel, "The Anguish of Civilized Behavior: The Use of Western Cultural Forms in the Everyday Lives of the Meiji Japanese and the Ottoman Turks during the Nineteenth Century," *Japan Review* 5 (1994): 145–185, especially 169; Quataert, "Clothing Laws," 414; Bruce Masters, *Christians and Jews in the Ottoman Arab World: The Roots of Sectarianism* (Cambridge: Cambridge University Press, 2001), 137; Hayim Cohen, *Jews of the Middle East, 1860–1972* (New York: Wiley, 1973), 38.

37. Quataert, *The Ottoman Empire*, 148; Quataert, "Clothing Laws," 414, 416.

38. For the internal impetus for this reform decree: Butrus Abu-Manneh, "The Islamic Roots of the Gülhane Rescript," *Die Welt des Islams* 34 (1994): 173–203; Abu-Manneh, *Studies on Islam and the Ottoman Empire in the 19th Century (1826–1876)* (Istanbul: Isis, 2001).

39. For the above quote, see Ahmet Ersoy, "Mustafa Reşid Paşa: The Gülhane Edict," in *Discourses of Collective Identity in Central and Southeast Europe (1770–1945), Texts and Commentaries*, ed. Balázs Trencsényi and Michal Kopeček (Budapest: CEU Press, 2006), 1:332–339. For a modern Turkish transliteration: Enver Ziya Karal, *Osmanlı Tarihi*, vol. 5, *Nizam-ı Cedit ve Tanzimat Devirleri (1789–1856)* (Ankara: Türk Tarih Kurumu Basımevi, 1947), 263–266.

40. On the persistence of this duality: Masayuki Ueno, "'For the Fatherland and the State': Armenians Negotiate the Tanzimat Reforms," *International Journal of Middle East Studies* 45 (2013): 93–109.

41. For the effects of this decree on the Jews of the empire, see Rodrigue, *French Jews, Turkish Jews*, 39.

42. Davison, *Reform in the Ottoman Empire*, 52–53; Candan Badem, *The Ottoman Crimean War (1853–1856)* (Leiden: Brill, 2010), 344–346.

43. "The Members of the Consistoire Central," *Jewish Chronicle*, April 28, 1854, 255; "El kolel de Pariz," *Or Israel*, 29 Nisan 5614, 3–4; *Archives israélites* 17, no. 4 (April 1856): 234, 236; Rodrigue, *French Jews, Turkish Jews*, 40. Their concern was not entirely misplaced: early discussions of new emancipatory reforms in the empire only mentioned Christians: Badem, *The Ottoman Crimean War*, 337.

44. For this quote: J. C. Hurewitz, *Diplomacy in the Near and Middle East: A Documentary Record: 1535–1914* (Princeton, NJ: D. Van Nostrand, 1956), 1:149–153. The decree was also published in various official translations at the time. See, for example, "Hat-Houmayoum: Traduction Officielle," *Journal de Constantinople-Écho de l'Orient*, February 21, 1856, 1–2. For the Turkish text of the decree: Karal, *Nizam-ı Cedit*, 266–272.

45. For this quote: Norman Stillman, "The Khatt-ı Humayun (February 18, 1856)," in *The Jews of Arab Lands*, ed. Stillman (Philadelphia, PA: Jewish Publication Society of America, 1979), 357–360.

46. Erik-Jan Zürcher, "The Ottoman Conscription System in Theory and Practice, 1844–1918," in *Arming the State: Military Conscription in the Middle East and Central Asia, 1775–1925*, ed. Zürcher (New York: St. Martin's Press, 1999), 89; Ufuk Gülsoy, *Osmanlı Gayrimüslimlerinin Askerlik Serüveni* (Istanbul: Simurg, 2000), 97–127.

47. Kemal Karpat, *The Politicization of Islam: Reconstructing Identity, State, Faith and Community in the Late Ottoman State* (New York: Oxford University Press, 2001), 314. For an English translation of the 1869 law, see *British Parliamentary Papers*, Misc. No. 2 (1927), Cmd. 2852.

48. This was the Maarif-i Umumiye Nizamnamesi. For Ottoman educational reforms during the nineteenth century, see Selçuk Akşin Somel, *The Modernization of Public Education in the Ottoman Empire, 1839–1908* (Leiden: Brill, 2001); Benjamin Fortna, *Imperial Classroom: Islam, the State, and Education in the Late Ottoman Empire* (New York: Oxford University Press, 2002); Emine Ö. Evered, *Empire and Education under the Ottomans* (New York: I. B. Tauris, 2012).

49. Abigail Jacobson has suggested that this was true for Ottoman Jews in Palestine even "until a relatively late stage" of the First World War: Abigail Jacobson, *From Empire to Empire: Jerusalem Between Ottoman and British Rule* (Syracuse, NY: Syracuse University Press, 2011), 51. The collapse of Ottoman rule in Iraq also prompted a group of Jewish notables in Baghdad to request British citizenship: Stillman, *Jews of Arab Lands in Modern Times*, 256–258. Such examples are remarkable in that they appeared only when the empire was on the brink of collapse.

50. On the changes introduced into Ottoman Jewish society by the appearance of a new ethical (*musar*) literature in Ladino starting in the eighteenth century: Matthias Lehmann, *Ladino Rabbinic Literature and Ottoman Sephardic Culture* (Bloomington: Indiana University Press, 2005).

51. Cevdet Pasha, *Tezâkir*, 67–68.

52. Obligatory universal conscription finally came in 1909. On Ottoman state schools: Somel, *Modernization of Public Education*; Fortna, *Imperial Classroom*; Evered, *Empire and Education*.

53. Carter Findley, "The Acid Test of Ottomanism: The Acceptance of Non-Muslims in the Late Ottoman Bureaucracy," in Braude and Lewis, *Christians and Jews in the Ottoman Empire*, 1:339–368.

54. On Ottoman Jews' low proficiency levels in Ottoman Turkish: Alliance Israélite Universelle (hereafter AIU) Archives, Turquie I C 6.4c, April 6, 1877, Fernandez to Paris; "La lingua del pais," *El Nasional*, August 31, 1877, 3; "Universal Israelitish Alliance," *Jewish Chronicle*, February 2, 1877, 12; Albert Löwy, *The Jews of Constantinople: A Study of their Communal and Educational Status* (London: Wertheimer, Lea & Co., 1890), 8, 10; Franco, *Essai*, 249; David Fresco, *Le Sionisme* (Istanbul: Impr. Fresco, 1909), 65, 71. On their absence from civil service positions: Frankl, *The Jews in the East*, 1:189; Rodrigue, *Jews and Muslims*, 138; D. T[rietsch], "The Revolution in Turkey and Jewish Activities in Palestine," *The Jewish Review* 2, no. 7 (May 1911): 23.

55. AIU Archives, Turquie I C 6.4a, Brunswick, Istanbul, 1864 [?]; AIU Archives, Turquie I C 6.4 b, P. Baudin, Istanbul, August 27, 1876.

56. On Jews' efforts to propagate Ottoman Turkish among their coreligionists: BOA BEO. 1312/98364, 10 Muharrem 1317 (May 21, 1899); BOA BEO. 1551/116253, 23 Cemaziyelevvel 1318 (September 18, 1900); BOA. BEO. 1501/112507, 13 Safer 1318 (June 12, 1900); Nevres Sason, *Silabario en turko-espanyol* (Istanbul: Isaac Gabay, 1905); Abraham Galante, *Turcs et Juifs: étude historique, politique* (Istanbul: Haim, Rozio & Co., 1932), 143, 145–146; *Liga de Pas i Solidaridad: Fondada en 1909* (Izmir: Meşrutiyet Matbaası, [1931?]); Sam Lévy, *Salonique à la fin du XIXe siècle: Mémoires* (Istanbul: Isis, 2000).

57. Carter Findley, *Ottoman Civil Officialdom: A Social History* (Princeton, NJ: Princeton University Press, 1989); Findley, *Bureaucratic Reform in the Ottoman Empire: The Sublime Porte, 1789–1922* (Princeton, NJ: Princeton University Press, 1980).

58. Benbassa and Rodrigue, *Sephardi Jewry*, 71; Findley, *Ottoman Civil Officialdom*, 142.

59. BOA İ. HR. 41–1935, letter of 13 Şaban 1263 (July 27, 1847) to the Office of the Grand Vizier; BOA İ.DH 159–8269, letters of 18 Zilkade 1263 (October 28, 1847) and 20

Zilkade 1263 (October 30, 1847) to the Office of the Grand Vizier; See also Löwy, *The Jews of Constantinople*, 9; Onur Şar, trans., "A Kosher Kitchen in the Imperial Medical School," in *Sephardi Lives: A Documentary History, 1700–1950*, ed. Julia Phillips Cohen and Sarah Abrevaya Stein (Stanford, CA: Stanford University Press, 2014), forthcoming.

60. Gülsoy, *Osmanlı Gayrimüslimlerinin Askerlik Serüveni*, 107.

61. Levy, *The Sephardim*, 111, suggests that there were 99 Jews employed in governmental service in 1885; Gülsoy, *Osmanlı Gayrimüslimlerinin Askerlik Serüveni*, indicates that there were at least 29 Jews enrolled in military schools in the empire in 1886.

62. Rosanes, *Korot ha-Yehudim*, 78.

63. "Die Juden in Rhodus," *Der Orient* 32 (August 8, 1840): 245–248; Olga Borovaya, trans., "A Blood Libel in Rhodes," in Cohen and Stein, *Sephardi Lives*.

64. On the earliest attempt to establish a Ladino newspaper in the empire: Olga Borovaya, "La Buena Esperansa (Izmir), 1842," in *Encyclopedia of Jews in the Islamic World*.

65. "Viaje de su m[adjestad] el sultan," *Sha'are Mizrah*, August 23, 1846, 2. The original Ladino reads "La diferensia de relijion (emuna) no reguadra ke a la konosensia i no toka nada a los deretos de sivdadanos."

66. "Viaje de su madjestad imperial," *Sha'are Mizrah*, May 28, 1846, 2.

67. I. Raphael, ed., *Kitve haRav Yehuda Alkalai* (Jerusalem, 1974), 476, cited in K. E. Fleming, "South Balkan Rabbinic Readings of Ottoman Rise and Decline: Eliyahu Kapsali of Crete and Yehuda Alkalai of Zemlin," in *Greece and the Balkans: Identities, Perceptions and Cultural Encounters since the Enlightenment*, ed. Dimitris Tziovas (Aldershot: Ashgate, 2003), 106–107.

68. Ussama Makdisi, "Corrupting the Sublime Sultanate: The Revolt of Tanyus Shahin in Nineteenth-Century Ottoman Lebanon," *Comparative Studies in Society and History* 42, no. 1 (January 2000): 180–208, 182.

69. Dina Danon, trans., "Class Conflict amidst the Jews of Izmir: A Rebellion of the Jewish Poor," in Cohen and Stein, *Sephardi Lives*; Avner Levi, "Shavat Aniim: Social Cleavage, Class War and Leadership in the Sephardi Community—The Case of Izmir 1847," in *Ottoman and Turkish Jewry: Community and Leadership*, ed. Aron Rodrigue (Bloomington: Indiana University Press, 1992), 183–202.

70. For this quote: Makdisi, "Corrupting the Sublime Sultanate," 182. See also: Ariel Salzmann, "Citizens in Search of a State: The Limits of Political Participation in the Late Ottoman Empire, 1808–1913," in *Extending Citizenship, Reconfiguring States*, ed. Michael Hanagan and Charles Tilly (Lanham, MD: Rowman and Littlefield Publishers, 1999), 47; E. Atilla Aytekin, "Peasant Protest in the Late Ottoman Empire: Moral Economy, Revolt, and the *Tanzimat* Reforms," *International Review of Social History* 57 (2012): 191–227.

71. Frankl, *The Jews of the East*, 1:170–171.

72. Ibid., 184.

73. Abraham G. Duker, "Jewish Volunteers in the Ottoman-Polish Cossack Units during the Crimean War," *Jewish Social Studies* 16 (1954): 203–218 and 351–376, esp. 355, 361, 362, 367.

74. "Die jüdisch-orientalische Frage," *Allgemeine Zeitung des Judenthums*, July 16, 1855, 370; Duker, "Jewish Volunteers," 367.

75. Duker, "Jewish Volunteers," 362.

76. On the foreign Jews who came to fight "Turquie," *L'Univers israélite*, July 1853, 517; "Turkey: Patriotism of the Jews," *Jewish Chronicle*, July 8, 1853, 317; "Konstantinopel, im Juni," *Allgemeine Zeitung des Judenthums*, July 18, 1853, 373; *L'Univers israélite*, March 1854, 336; "Constantinople," *Jewish Chronicle*, November 14, 1856, 797; Duker, "Jewish Volunteers," 215. For Ottoman Jewish Donations to the War Effort: "Turquie," *L'Univers israélite*, July 1853, 517; "Turquie," *L'Univers israélite*, October 1853), 96; "Die jüdisch-orientalische Frage," *Allgemeine Zeitung des Judenthums*, April 3, 1854, 163–66; "Berlin, Anfang Mai," *Allgemeine Zeitung des Judenthums*, May 15, 1854, 247; Green, *Montefiore*, 240. A. Ubicini, *Letters on Turkey* (London: J. Murray, 1856), 1:365, also mentions an Ottoman Jew by the name of de Castro who served as a military doctor during the war, likely Jacques de Castro (1802–1876), head physician at Istanbul's military hospital during the

period. His surname also appears on Duker's list of Jewish volunteers for the Ottoman army during this period. Duker, "Jewish Volunteers," 353.

77. Ufuk Gülsoy, *Osmanlı Gayrimüslimlerinin Askerlik Serüveni;* Zürcher, "The Ottoman Conscription System." Resistance came from other quarters as well. Early into the war, Bulgarian, Armenian, and Greek Orthodox Ottomans reportedly volunteered to serve only to find their petitions denied: Badem, *The Ottoman Crimean War,* 50, 346. For Armenian elites who called upon their coreligionists to volunteer: Ueno, "For the Fatherland and the State."

78. "Konstantinople 16 r'h Heshvan 5614," *Or Israel,* [n.d.] 5614 (1853/1854), 1.

79. "Konstantinople hayom 11 r'h Nisan 5614," *Or Israel,* 29 Nisan 5614 (April 27, 1854), 1.

80. I am grateful to an anonymous reviewer for this formulation.

81. On this, see also Ilan Karmi, *The Jewish Community of Istanbul in the Nineteenth Century: Social, Legal, and Administrative Transformations* (Isis: Istanbul, 1996), 103; Gülsoy, *Osmanlı Gayrimüslimlerinin Askerlik Serüveni,* 115–122.

82. David Biale, *Power and Powerlessness in Jewish History* (New York: Schocken, 1986), 104 discusses the logic of a process that could eventually undo the authority of the very same Jewish communal leaders who attempted to guide the actions of their coreligionists. Ottoman Jews would experience their own version of this scenario only two decades later, a development discussed in chapter 3.

83. Benedict Anderson, *Imagined Communities: Reflections on the Origin and Spread of Nationalism* (London: Verso Editions, 1991), 86, also cited in Selim Deringil, "The Invention of Tradition as Public Image in the Late Ottoman Empire, 1808–1908," *Comparative Studies in Society and History* 35, no. 1 (January 1993): 5.

Chapter 1

1. His letter can be found in the archives of the Jewish community in Istanbul (Hahambaşılık), on microfilm at the Central Archives for the History of the Jewish People (CAHJP) in Jerusalem: CAHJP Tr/Is 162a—Hm2/8636, 2757, March 12, 1878—Rosenblit to Chief Rabbi Moshe Halevi in Istanbul. Rosenblit explained that he had first written the sultan and the minister of war on August 30, 1877. On this collection: Yaron Harel, "The Importance of the Archive of the Hakham Bashi in Istanbul for the History of Ottoman Jewry," in *Frontiers of Ottoman Studies: State, Province, and the West.* ed. Colin Imber and Keiko Kiyotaki (New York: I. B.Tauris, 2005), 1:251–264.

2. The Hebrew term Togarma is drawn from Genesis 10:3.

3. On the Muslim refugees: "Notes of the Day," *The Constantinople Messenger,* July 18, 1878, 14. Carter Findley, *Ottoman Civil Officialdom: A Social History* (Princeton, NJ: Princeton University Press, 1989), 34; Kemal Karpat, *Ottoman Population, 1830–1914* (Madison: University of Wisconsin Press, 1985), 75.

4. Abraham Galante, *Histoire des juifs de Turquie* (1940; repr., Istanbul: Isis, 1985–1986), 2:121–122.

5. Elsewhere Jews rallied for the Ottoman cause. In Britain, this led to accusations that Jews were Ottoman sympathizers: David Cesarani, "British Jews" in *The Emancipation of Catholics, Jews and Protestants: Minorities and the Nation State in Nineteenth-Century Europe,* ed. Rainer Liedtke and Stephan Wendehorst (Manchester: Manchester University Press, 1999), 50–53. The Hebrew periodical *Ha-Magid,* published in the Prussian town of Lyck, was also reportedly banned in Russia for exhibiting pro-Ottoman sentiments during the war. "Avizo importante," *El Nasional,* February 11, 1877, 4.

6. Greek Orthodox and Armenian individuals similarly proclaimed their pride in being Ottomans during this period: *Basiret,* 16 Ramazan 1292 (October 16, 1875), 2.

7. Robert Devereux, *The First Ottoman Constitutional Period: A Study of the Midhat Constitution and Parliament* (Baltimore, MD: Johns Hopkins University Press, 1963), 74; "Kompatriotos!" *La Epoka,* January 1, 1877, 1; "Novedades lokales," *La Esperansa,* January 4, 1877, 4.

8. Kemal Karpat, *The Politicization of Islam: Reconstructing Identity, State, Faith and Community in the Late Ottoman State* (New York: Oxford University Press, 2001), 314 writes

that before the citizenship laws of 1864 "no one outside the dynasty had legitimately been called *Osmanlı*."

9. In addition to state-led efforts to this effect, an oppositional group of Ottoman intellectuals known as the Young Ottomans also began promoting new forms of Ottoman patriotism in the 1860s. Şerif Mardin, *The Genesis of Young Ottoman Thought* (Princeton, NJ: Princeton University Press, 1962).

10. This was only true for half a year, as the Congress of Berlin convened later in 1878 and redrew the borders, creating a more sizeable hinterland for Salonica once again.

11. "El jurnal 'Zeman,'" *La Epoka*, November 13, 1876, 4, emphasis mine.

12. See, for example, "Los djidios i los turkos," *La Epoka*, November 13, 1877, 3.

13. Karpat, *Politicization of Islam*, 122.

14. "L'Alliance Israélite Universelle," *Le Levant Times*, March 27, 1874, 2. For an English translation of this source, see Julia Phillips Cohen, trans., "In Praise of Inter-communal Cooperation: A 'Rothschild of the East' on Progress and Tolerance," in Cohen and Stein, *Sephardi Lives*. See also "La Pâque en Orient," *Archives israélites* 35, no. 8 (April 15, 1874): 248–250. For more on the Camondos: Aron Rodrigue, "Abraham de Camondo of Istanbul: The Transformation of Jewish Philanthropy," in *From East and West: Jews in a Changing Europe 1750–1870*, ed. Frances Malino and David Sorkin (Oxford: Blackwell Publishers, 1990), 46–56; Nora Şeni, "The Camondos and their Imprint on 19th-Century Istanbul," *International Journal of Middle East Studies* 26, no. 4 (1994): 663–675; Nora Şeni and Sophie Le Tarnec, *Les Camondo ou l'éclipse d'une fortune* (Paris: Actes Sud, 1997).

15. "Novedades lokales," *La Esperansa*, April 19, 1877, 3.

16. Hazan's numbers correspond to a report the Alliance produced on the Jewish community of Izmir in 1873, which estimated that of the "approximately 3,500 families, numbering close to 20,000 souls," 1,000 families remain "without any means of subsistence and depended on public charity." Rodrigue, *French Jews, Turkish Jews*, 53–54; Rodrigue, *Jews and Muslims*, 136; *Bulletin de l'Alliance Israélite Universelle*, 1873, 141.

17. Henri Nahum, *Juifs de Smyrne, XIXe–XXe siècle* (Paris: Aubier, 1997), 122, notes that many of Izmir's Jews lived near "Ergat Bazar."

18. The Ladino used here is "*turko*," generally a synonym for Muslim during this period.

19. "Izmirna," *La Esperansa*, May 31, 1877, 3.

20. A similar case surfaced after a crowd of Jews reportedly bullied an Armenian barber who had given a Jewish man a shave on a Saturday. *La Esperansa* was quick to issue a protest, noting that it was the Jewish man who deserved opprobrium for desecrating his Sabbath, not the innocent Armenian to whom the same laws did not apply. "Novedades lokales," *La Esperansa*, September 14, 1876, 4.

21. "Sinyor redaktor," *La Epoka*, February 19, 1877, 4. The term "nation" (*nasion*) is used here to indicate a people, and can be considered synonymous with *millet* or religious community in the Ottoman context.

22. For further discussions of the incident: "Al sinyor redaktor jerente del jurnal 'La Epoka,'" *La Epoka*, February 26, 1877, 3; "Saloniko," *La Epoka*, March 5, 1877, 4.

23. See, for example, "Novedades lokales," *La Esperansa*, February 17, 1876, 3; "Novedades lokales," *La Esperansa*, February 8, 1877, 4; "Novedades lokales," *La Esperansa*, February 15, 1877, 4; "Balos de bienfezensia," *La Esperansa*, March 7, 1878, 3.

24. "Novedades lokales—el balo por el profito de nuestra eskola," *La Esperansa*, January 27, 1876, 3–4; *Archives israélites*, February 15, 1876, 104. See also "Balo masoniko," *La Esperansa*, February 1, 1877, 4.

25. "Avizo importante," *La Esperansa*, February 3, 1876, 3.

26. See also Meropi Anastassiadou, *Salonique, 1830–1912: Une ville Ottomane à l'âge des réformes* (New York: Brill, 1997), 368–370; Anastassiadou, "L'Hermis' de Salonique: Un journal ottoman de province," in *Presse und Öffentlichkeit im Nahen Osten*, ed. Christoph Herzog, Raoul Motika, and Anja Pistor-Hatam (Heidelberg: Heidelberger Orientverlag, 1995), 6; Rena Molho, "Le 'Cercle de Salonique' (1873–1958): Club des Saloniciens," in Molho, *Salonica and Istanbul: Social, Political and Cultural Aspects of Jewish Life* (Istanbul: Isis, 2005), 150–164.

27. The two men approached were Alexander Sidi and David Cazès. On Sidi, see Rodrigue, *French Jews, Turkish Jews*, 44, 53, 64. For Cazès: ibid., 53–54, 62, 63, 66, 100–101.

28. For more on Hazan, see Julia Phillips Cohen, "Aron de Yosef Hazan," in *The Encyclopedia of Jews in the Islamic World*, ed. Norman Stillman (Leiden: Brill, 2010), and chapter 2 of this volume.

29. On blood libels in the Ottoman Empire: Jonathan Frankel, *The Damascus Affair: "Ritual Murder," Politics and the Jews in 1840* (New York: Cambridge University Press, 1997). For other cases, see Jacob Barnai, "Blood Libels in the Ottoman Empire of the Fifteenth to Nineteenth Centuries," in *Antisemitism Through the Ages*, ed. Shmuel Almog (Oxford: Pergamon Press, 1988), 189–194; Esther Benbassa, "Kampana Çalanlar Davası: 1901'de İzmir'de Cereyan Etmiş Bir Kan İftirası Vakası," *Tarih ve Toplum* 30 (May 1986); Matt Goldish, "A Blood Libel Among the Sephardim (Ottoman Empire, Mid-Seventeenth Century)," in Goldish, *Jewish Questions: Responsa on Sephardic Life in the Early Modern Period* (Princeton, NJ: Princeton University Press, 2008), 13–14.

30. "El muzeo i la biblioteka elenika," *La Esperansa*, January 27, 1876, 1.

31. "Novedades lokales," *La Esperansa*, February 3, 1876, 3–4; "Novedades lokales," *La Esperansa*, March 23, 1876, 4; "Novedades lokales," *La Esperansa*, March 30, 1876, 4.

32. "Novedades lokales," *La Esperansa*, March 30, 1876, 4.

33. "Las reformas en Turkia i nuestra komunita," *El Tiempo*, September 3, 1876, 1–2.

34. "El progreso de los djudios en Turkia," *La Esperansa*, January 6, 1876, 1–2.

35. The Great Powers—and the program of Habsburg Count Andrássy in particular—had asked that the council be "half Moslem, half Christian." David Harris, "The Origin of the Andrássy Note of December, 1875," *Pacific Historical Review* 1, no. 2 (June 1932): 210.

36. For similar proposals, from Kuzguncuk (Istanbul) and Edirne: Rodrigue, *French Jews, Turkish Jews*, 51, 54.

37. This case received wide coverage in the Jewish press of the empire and Europe. See "Meldamos en el jurnal 'La Turki,'" *La Epoka*, September 4, 1876, 1; "Universal Israelitish Alliance," *Jewish Chronicle*, September 9, 1876, 335; "Saloniko," *La Epoka*, October 2, 1876, 1; "Constantinople," *Jewish Chronicle*, October 6, 1876, 428; "Relevamos del jurnal 'La Turki,'" *La Epoka*, October 16, 1876, 4; "Constantinople," *Jewish Chronicle*, October 13, 1876, 439; "Novedades israelitas," *La Esperansa*, October 26, 1876, 1–2; "Kostan," *La Esperansa* October 26, 1876, 4; "Novedades Israelitas—Los djidios i el konsilio de estado," *La Epoka*, November 6, 1876, 3; "El esfuenyo de un mes," *La Epoka*, November 6, 1876, 4; "The Jews of Turkey," *Jewish Chronicle*, November 10, 1877, 501; "The Israelites and the Turkish Council of State," *Jewish Chronicle*, November 17, 1876, 525; "Siempre la kuestion de los djudios en los konsilios de estado," *La Esperansa*, November 30, 1876, 1. See also Alliance Israélite Universelle, Turquie I C 6.4 b, P. Baudin, Istanbul, August 27, 1876.

38. "Saloniko," *La Epoka*, October 2, 1876, 1, emphasis mine.

39. As he put it, "the Sublime Porte has forgotten us." The *Levant Herald*, the British organ of the Ottoman capital, similarly called the failure of the government to appoint a Jewish councilmember "an oversight.": "The Israelites and the Turkish Council of State," *Jewish Chronicle*, November 17, 1876, 525.

40. *Sabah*, 2 Teşrinievvel 1292 (October 14, 1876), 3.

41. *İttihad*, 13 Teşrinisani 1292 (November 25, 1876), 2.

42. "Ashkenazi, or D'almeyda, Behor," in *Jewish Encyclopedia* (New York: Funk and Wagnalls Co., 1902), 1:194.

43. Cohen, "Aron de Yosef Hazan," in Stillman, *Encyclopedia of Jews in the Islamic World*.

44. Fresco is better known for his tenure as editor-in-chief of the capital's Ladino daily *El Tiempo*, a position he adopted shortly after the Russo-Ottoman War and held until shortly before his death in 1933. For more on Fresco, see Julia Phillips Cohen, "David Fresco," in Stillman, *Encyclopedia of Jews in the Islamic World*.

45. "La lingua del pais," *El Nasional*, August 31, 1877, 3. On the language politics of Ottoman Sephardim, see İlber Ortaylı, "Ottoman Jewry and the Turkish Language," in Ortaylı, *Ottoman Studies* (Istanbul: Bilgi University Press, 2004), 5–14; David M. Bunis, "Modernization and the Language Question among Judezmo-Speaking Sephardim in

the Ottoman Empire," in *Sephardi and Middle Eastern Jewries*, ed. Harvey E. Goldberg (Bloomington: Indiana University Press, 1996), 226–239.

46. "La lingua del pais," *El Nasional*, August 31, 1877, 3, emphasis mine.

47. Two decades later, another Jewish author in the Ottoman capital offered the same estimate, proposing that it was impossible to locate 1,000 Jews who spoke Turkish as well as they did French and none who spoke it better. See Franco, *Essai*, 249.

48. For useful comparative statistics on this point, see Rodrigue, *French Jews, Turkish Jews*, 45–46.

49. "La lingua del pais," *El Nasional*, August 31, 1877, 3.

50. Ibid.; "Diksionario turko-espanyol, espanyol-turko," *El Nasional*, September 5, 1877, 4; "Novedades lokales," *La Esperansa*, September 13, 1877, 4.

51. The Turkish and Ladino read, respectively: *Ayıpsız dost isteyen, dostsuz kalır/Ken kere tener un amigo sin falta restara solo (sin amigo)*.

52. Karpat, *Politicization of Islam*, 315. The unit is also mentioned in Ufuk Gülsoy, *Osmanlı Gayrimüslimlerinin Askerlik Serüveni* (Istanbul: Simurg, 2000), 116. The Ottoman-language press suggested that Greek Orthodox and Armenian Ottomans had taken the initiative and asked to be able to serve, also publishing the patriotic declarations of the Greek Orthodox volunteers: *Basiret*, 21 Cemaziyelahir 1293 (July 14, 1876), 1; *İttihad*, 29 Haziran 1292 (July 11, 1876), 2.

53. For a Ladino report on this special flag, see "Fatos diversos," *La Epoka*, July 31, 1876, 3.

54. "Novedades lokales," *La Epoka*, August 21, 1876, 3–4.

55. The unit reportedly trained in the Beşçınar gardens, on which: Anastassiadou, *Salonique, 1830–1912*, 165, 168, 195, 417.

56. "La guardia nasional," *El Koreo de Viena*, January 24, 1877, 5; "Turkey," *Jewish Messenger*, January 26, 1877, 3, and the notes below.

57. "Novedades lokales," *La Epoka*, August 28, 1876, 4; "Novedades lokales," *La Epoka*, September 4, 1876, 4.

58. This was presumably Sa'adi's eldest son, Haim Halevi. Little is known about Haim besides the fact that he operated the newspaper's printing press, and that he was excommunicated along with his father in 1874 for allegedly smoking on the Sabbath. *A Jewish Voice from Ottoman Salonica: The Ladino Memoir of Sa'adi Besalel a-Levi*, ed. Aron Rodrigue and Sarah Abrevaya Stein, trans. Isaac Jerusalmi (Stanford, CA: Stanford University Press, 2012).

59. "Novedades lokales," *La Epoka*, September 4, 1876, 4; "Novedades lokales," *La Epoka*, October 16, 1876, 4; "Novedades israelitas," *La Esperansa*, October 26, 1876, 2; "Turkey," *Jewish Chronicle*, August 3, 1877, 10. Isaac de Boton was promoted a second time the following year. "Novedades lokales," *La Epoka*, April 23, 1877, 4. De Boton was later known as an important businessman in the city and served on the municipal council. See *Zikhron Saloniki: Gedulatah ve-hurbanah shel Yerushalayim de-Balkan*, ed. David Recanati (Tel Aviv: Committee for the Publication of Books on the Salonica Community, 1972), 1:153. See also Isaac Gabay, *Yildiz i sus sekretos: el reino de Abdul Hamid* (Istanbul: Imp. Gabay, [1910?]), 300, which describes an exchange between de Boton and Memduh Pasha, commander of the Ottoman Third Army corps, wherein Memduh Pasha expressed his gratitude to Salonica's Jews for their patriotism during the 1897 war. On this see also "Patriotizmo delos israelitas de Saloniko," *El Tiempo*, June 24, 1897; "Selânik," *Asır*, 3 Safer 1315 (July 4, 1897), 3.

60. "Novedades israelitas," *La Esperansa*, October 26, 1876, 2.

61. "Novedades israelitas," *La Esperansa*, January 4, 1877, 2.

62. *Zaman*, 3 Zilkade 1293 (November 20, 1876), 1; *İttihad*, 15 Teşrinisani 1292 (November 27, 1876), 2.

63. "Novedades israelitas," *La Esperansa*, January 4, 1877, 2; "Universal Israelitish Alliance," *Jewish Chronicle*, February 2, 1877, 12.

64. "La konstitusion trae sus frutos," *La Epoka*, January 15, 1877, 2–3.

65. "Salonichi, 20. December," *Allgemeine Zeitung des Judenthums*, January 30, 1877, 77, reported that 108 Jews and three Greek Orthodox men were part of the Salonican guard.

"Turkey," *Jewish Chronicle,* January 5, 1877, 11, offered a higher number of 150 Jewish volunteers.

66. "La konstitusion trae sus frutos," *La Epoka,* January 15, 1877, 2–3.

67. "La verdad a luz," *La Epoka,* January 22, 1877, 4. For the Jewish presence in the Çorapçı Han neighborhod and the synagogue of the same name: Galante, *Histoire des juifs de Turquie,* 1:294.

68. "La verdad a luz," *La Epoka,* January 22, 1877, 4.

69. Hakan M. Yavuz and Peter Sluglett, eds., *War and Diplomacy: The Russo-Turkish War of 1877–1878 and the Treaty of Berlin* (Salt Lake City: University of Utah Press, 2011).

70. On the ceremony, see also "Abnegasion de la nasion judia por su governo," *El Nasional,* May 14, 1877, 2–3; "Orasion en favor de la armada imperial," *El Tiempo,* May 14, 1877, 2; "Seremonia relidjioza a Balat," *La Epoka,* May 21, 1877, 4; "Cérémonie religieuse à Balata," *La Turquie,* May 15, 1877, 2; "Les israélites de Constantinople priant dans la synagogue de Balata, pour le succès des armées ottomanes," *L'illustration: journal universel,* June 2, 1877, 345; "Konstantinopel, 10. Mai," *Allgemeine Zeitung des Judenthums,* June 5, 1877, 363–364; "Constantinople," *Jewish Chronicle,* June 15, 1877, 12; "Turkey," *Jewish Messenger,* July 6, 1877, 2–3; Naim Güleryüz, *İstanbul Sinagogları* (Istanbul: N. Güleryüz, 1992), 16–17.

71. That is, the *London Illustrated News, L'Illustration,* and an unidentified German source preserved in the University of Chicago's Harry and Branka Sondheim Jewish Heritage Collection.

72. Selim Deringil, *The Well-Protected Domains: Ideology and the Legitimation of Power in the Ottoman Empire, 1876–1909* (London: I.B. Tauris, 1998), 35–36, offers a related anecdote concerning Greek Orthodox officials who wore their imperial uniforms and decorations to Easter services during the same period.

73. "Orasion en favor de la armada imperial," *El Tiempo,* May 14, 1877. The Young Ottoman thinker Ali Suavi had issued a similar statement about Russia's sinister aims a decade earlier: "Will the Turkish people who once made the world tremble accept [the position of] serfs of the Russians?" he asked. Mardin, *Genesis of Young Ottoman Thought,* 370.

74. The reference to Russia as the Colossus of the North, common in the English-language literature of the day, also appears in Ladino publications of the empire. See, for example, "La kaida del kolozo del nord," *El Nasional,* October 17, 1877, 3. Other less flattering variants also made their way into the Ottoman Jewish press. See "Novetas politikas del interior: ungaros y turkos," *El Nasional,* July 2, 1877, 1, which refers to Russia as the "savage of the North" (*"el salvaje del nord"*); "Fideles djudios del imperio otomano," *El Nasional,* July 18, 1877, 2, referring to Russia as the "snake of the North" (*"kulevro del nord"*); "Los Jidios de Eski Zagra," *El Koreo de Viena,* September 8, 1877, 2, also referring to Russia as a "snake" (*"kulevro"*), and "Kon nuestra pendola," *La Epoka,* December 17, 1877, 1, which describes Russia as the "the terrible eagle of the North" (*"la terivle agila del nord"*). If Halevi's reference to the fear of entering into Russian "captivity" was anything more than a creative use of biblical imagery, it may been based on the stories of Jewish child recruits into the armies of Tsar Nicholas (r. 1825–1855) as part of the Cantonist system. Steven Zipperstein, *Imagining Russian Jewry: Memory, History, Identity* (Seattle: University of Washington Press, 1999), 25, 96, 119, and Olga Litvak, *Conscription and the Search for Modern Russian Jewry* (Bloomington: Indiana University Press, 2006) discuss the ways that the stories of forced conscription became powerful collective myths for Jews even beyond Russian borders and after the period in question.

75. For Halevi's prayer: "Abnegasion de la nasion judia por su governo," *El Nasional,* May 14, 1877, 2–3.

76. "3 Muharrem sene 94 tarihinde akd olunan meclis-i umumi zabtıdır," *İttihad,* 10 Kanunusani 1292 (January 22 , 1877), 1–3; *Zaman,* 21 Muharrem 1294 (February 5, 1877). Isidore Loeb, *La Situation des Israélites en Turquie en Serbie et en Roumanie* (Paris: Joseph Baer & Cie, 1877), 18, quotes Halevi as having declared that "Ottoman Jews were ready to sacrifice their possessions and their lives for their shared homeland."

77. For the decision to allow Armenian, Greek Orthodox (Rum), and Jewish citizens into the army during the war: BOA Y.A. RES. 1/18, January 3, 1877. For announcements of

a general call to arms in the press: "Segun el 'Vakit,'" *El Nasional*, May 16, 1877, 2; "La korua en Konstantinopole," *El Nasional*, May 21, 1877, 2; "Smyrna," *Archives israélites*, June 15, 1877, 374–374. For earlier calls for non-Muslim service among Young Ottoman thinkers: Gülsoy, *Osmanlı Gayrimüslimlerinin Askerlik Serüveni*, 104.

78. "Los soldados djudios," *La Esperansa*, May 24, 1877. For the discussion in the parliament: Enver Ziya Karal, "Non-Muslim Representatives in the First Constitutional Assembly, 1876–1877," in *Christians and Jews in the Ottoman Empire*, ed. Benjamin Braude and Bernard Lewis (New York: Holmes & Meier Publishers, 1982), 1: 387–400; Devereux, *The First Ottoman Constitutional Period*; Elke Hartmann, "The 'Loyal Nation' and its Deputies," in *The First Ottoman Parliament: Perception, Significance and Prosopography*, ed. Christoph Herzog and Malek Sharif (Würzburg: Ergon, 2010). On advocates for non-Muslim military service in Aleppo: Keith David Watenpaugh, *Being Modern in the Middle East: Revolution, Nationalism, Colonialism, and the Arab Middle Class*. (Princeton, NJ: Princeton University Press, 2006), 43.

79. "Los soldados djudios," *La Esperansa*, May 24, 1877, emphasis mine.

80. For Moses Mendelssohn's position on this issue: Michael K. Silber, "From Tolerated Aliens to Citizen-Soldiers: Jewish Military Service in the Era of Joseph II," in *Constructing Nationalities in East Central Europe*, ed. Pieter M. Judson and Marsha L. Rozenblit (Oxford: Berghahn, 2005), 19–36.

81. For such statements from Greek Orthodox and Armenian Ottomans respectively: *İttihad*, 29 Haziran 1292 (July 11, 1876), 2; *İttihad*, 15 Temmuz 1292 (July 27, 1876), 2.

82. "Tarihinde akd olunan meclis-i umumi zabtıdır," *İttihad*, 3 Muharrem 1294 (January 18, 1877), 1–3; *Zaman*, 21 Muharrem 1294 (February 5, 1877).

83. "Novedades israelitas," *La Epoka*, July 23, 1877, 3.

84. "Smyrna," *Archives israélites*, June 15, 1877, 374–374; "Smyrna, 25. Mai," *Allgemeine Zeitung des Judenthums*, June 26, 1877, 414.

85. "Novedades Lokales," *La Esperansa*, May 24, 1877, 4; "Kronika," *El Tiempo*, June 1, 1877.

86. For discussions of jihad during this period: *Zaman*, 25 Cemaziyelahir 1293 (July 18, 1876), 1; *İttihad*, 2 Temmuz 1292 (July 14, 1876), 1; Mehmet Emin Salmin, *Neyl ür-reşad fi emr il-cihad* (Istanbul: Ali Bey Matbaası, 1877); Karpat, *Politicization*, 86; Mustafa Aksakal, "'Holy War Made in Germany'? Ottoman Origins of the 1914 Jihad," *War in History* 18, no. 2 (2011): 190, 192. For a "jihad tax": *İttihad*, 3 Temmuz 1292 (July 15, 1876), 3; *İttihad*, 16 Teşrinisani 1292 (November 28, 1876), 2–3. While the Ottoman-language *Vakit* pronounced the war a jihad, others feared that using the term would further prejudice European public opinion against the empire: "Cihad ve gaza," *İttihad*, 2 Temmuz 1292 (July 14, 1876), 1; *Sabah*, 16 Eylül 1292 (September 28, 1876), 1.

87. "Prezentes patriotikos," *El Tiempo*, June 4, 1877, 3; "El mundo musulmano," *El Tiempo*, August 22, 1877, 3.

88. "La bandiera vedra," *El Koreo de Viena*, April 24, 1877, 1; "La santa gera," *El Koreo de Viena*, May 24, 1877, 1; *Levant Herald*, May 23, 1877, 164; "El estandarte de profeta," *El Nasional*, August 13, 1877, 1; "La opinion puvlika en Turkia," *La Epoka*, September 10, 1877, 3; "La bandiera vedre de la profeta," *El Koreo de Viena*, November 24, 1877, 2.

89. "La kamara de los diputados," *El Nasional*, December 28, 1877, 1.

90. Karpat, *Politicization of Islam*, 122.

91. On this community, see M. Papo, "The Sephardi Community of Vienna," in *The Jews of Austria: Essays on their Life, History and Destruction*, ed. Josef Fraenkel (London: Vallentine Mitchell, 1967), 327–346; N. M. Gelber, "Contribution à l'histoire des Juifs espagnols à Vienne: Début de la communauté sephardite et pièces justificatives," *Revue des études juives* 97, no. 191 (1934): 114–151 and 97, no. 192 (1934): 44–49; Adolf von Zemlinsky and Michael Menahem Papo, *Geschichte der türkisch-israelitischen Gemeinde zu Wien/Istoria de la komunidad israelit espanyola en Viena* (Vienna: M. Papo, 1888).

92. "Avizo importante," *El Koreo de Viena*, March 8, 1877, 4.

93. This is a reference to Deuteronomy 25:19. On Jewish references to other Christian groups—particularly Armenians—as Amalek, see Elliot Horowitz, *Reckless Rites: Purim and the Legacy of Jewish Violence* (Princeton, NJ: Princeton University Press, 2006).

94. "Ermanos suditos otoman!" *El Koreo de Viena*, June 24, 1877, 1.

95. Marc Saperstein, *Jewish Preaching in Times of War, 1800–2001* (Oxford: Littman Library of Jewish Civilization, 2008), 197, notes that the use of the image of Amalek would have evoked an "unprovoked attack against a defenseless civilian population."

96. Saperstein, *Jewish Preaching*, 198. See also "Ardor i patriotizmo de nuestra nasion," *El Nasional*, August 31, 1877, 2–3, which refers to the war as holy ("*santa*"). On the religious dimensions of this war, see also Roderic H. Davison, *Reform in the Ottoman Empire, 1856–1876* (New York: Gordian Press, 1973), 350.

97. "Aufruf an Juden," *Neue Freie Presse*, July 1, 1877, 5.

98. "Aus der Türkei, im Juni," *Allgemeine Zeitung des Judenthums*, July 17, 1877, 459.

99. "Novedades lokales," *La Esperansa*, July 26, 1877, 3.

100. BOA HR TO 519/10, June 24, 1877.

101. For a Ladino account of the great suffering inflicted on Jews in the war zone during this period, see *Istoria komfuesma* [sic] *de Yosef Haim b. Rey de Karnabat* (Plovdiv: Yosef Baruh Pardo, n.d.). I am grateful to Avner Perez for sharing this source with me.

102. See, for example, the report in *Basiret*, 6 Cemaziyelahir 1294 (June 18, 1877), 1 on Jews who fled Russian violence.

103. "With the Turks-Jewish Refugees at Rasgrad," *The Graphic*, August 18, 1877, 150, 165; "Novedades israelitas—Los djidios i la gera," *La Epoka*, September 10, 1877, 4.

104. William Gladstone, *Bulgarian Horrors and the Question of the East* (London: John Murray, 1876), 13.

105. *La Epoka*, March 5, 1877, 1.

106. "Comité de secours pour les émigrés," *Stamboul*, August 2, 1877, 2.

107. "Socheta otomana de ayudo a los soldado feridos," *La Epoka*, June 18, 1877, 4. See also Raphael Samuel Arditi, *Sefer Divre Shemuel* (Salonica: 'Ets ha-hayim, 1890/91), 50v–51v; *Zikhron Saloniki*, 1: 146, 149. For an English translation: Matt Goldish, trans., "When a Jew Can Work on the Sabbath: A Salonican Rabbi on War and Labor," in Cohen and Stein, *Sephardi Lives*.

108. "Turkey," *Jewish Messenger*, December 1, 1876, 4; "El patriotizmo de nuestros mansevos," *El Nasional*, November 21, 1877, 3.

109. "Novedades israelitas: los djidios i la gera," *La Epoka*, September 10, 1877, 4. Abraham Palache was decorated by the Ottoman government during this period. "Novedades lokales," *La Esperansa*, March 23, 1876, 4. Soon after, Aron de Yosef Hazan praised Rabbi Palache for encouraging Jews to participate in the imperial war fund, calling upon other rabbis to follow the example set by the "enlightened rabbi." "Novedades lokales," *La Esperansa*, July 27, 1876, 4.

110. "Novedades israelitas," *La Epoka*, October 22, 1877, 4.

111. On Jewish donations of tobacco to the army: *Basiret*, 15 Safer 1293 (March 12, 1876), 2–3; on the donations of clothing and bandages to the army by the Jewish women of Hasköy: "Havadis-i dahiliye," *İttihad*, 23 Teşrinievvel 1292 (November 4, 1876), 1.

112. "Ardor i patriotizmo de nuestra nasion," *El Nasional*, August 31, 1877, 2–3; "Una yamada ala nasion israelita," *El Nasional*, September 3, 1877, 2–3. They referred specifically to the silver finials (*rimonim*) used to decorate the scrolls of the law.

113. "Las platas de las kehilot," *El Nasional*, September 3, 1877, 2–3. Considerations of the rights and will of "the people ('*halk*')" had also begun to figure prominently in the writings of Young Ottoman reformers during this period. Mardin, *Genesis of Young Ottoman Thought*, 189, 266.

114. "Las platas de las kehilot," *El Nasional*, September 7, 1877, 3.

115. "Dons des israélites aux blessés ottomans," *Stamboul*, September 3, 1877, 2; "Las platas de las kehilot," *El Nasional*, September 11, 1877, 3.

116. "Las platas de las kehilot," *El Nasional*, October 3, 1877, 4. "El avizo nuevo i el dover de la patria," *El Tiempo*, September 7, 1877, 1, complained that Jews had fallen short of their patriotic duty.

117. "La kestion de las platas," *El Nasional*, October 10, 1877, 3.

118. The factory referred to here was presumably the one that made up part of the industrial complex on the outskirts of Istanbul. Donald Quataert, "The Age of Reforms," in *An Economic and Social History of the Ottoman Empire*, ed. Suraiya Faroqhi, Bruce McGowan,

Donald Quataert, and Şevket Pamuk (New York: Cambridge University Press, 1994), 2:899.

119. "Constantinople," *Jewish Chronicle*, September 21, 1877, 12.

120. A general consensus exists in late nineteenth-century reports that Ottoman Jews held a special position in the manufacture of arms during the war with Russia. Some link this to work in the arsenal: "Konstantinopel, 10. Mai," *Allgemeine Zeitung des Judenthums*, June 5, 1877, 364; "Turkey,"*Jewish Messenger*, October 20, 1876, 2; "Novedades israelitas," *La Epoka*, October 30, 1877, 3. Others write of their work in the gunpowder factory (*baruthane*): "El haham bashi de Konstantinopla," *El Koreo de Viena*, May 24, 1877, 1. "La fabrikasion de kartushes de los djudios," *El Nasional*, August 8, 1877, 3 and "Terrible Accident at Macrikeuy: Explosion of Powder Magazines," *Levant Herald*, October 10, 1877, 275. Before this time, the gunpowder factory had been run and staffed largely by Ottoman Armenians from the area: Archag Alboyadjian, *Les Dadian*, trans. Anna Naguib Boutros-Ghali (Cairo: n.p., 1965); Pars Tuğlacl, *Dadyan Ailesi'nin Osmanlı Toplum, Ekonomi ve Siyaset Hayatındaki Rolu* (Istanbul: Pars Yayın, 1993); Hagop Barsoumian, "The Dual Role of the Armenian *Amira* Class within the Ottoman Government and the Armenian *Millet* (1750-1850)," in Braude and Lewis, *Christians and Jews in the Ottoman Empire*, 1:174.

121. "La fabrikasion de kartushes de los djudios," *El Nasional*, August 8, 1877, 3.

122. The reference to Jews as the "most intimate friends" of the empire surfaced more than once. See, for example, "El invierno se aserka: pensemos nozotros por nuestros soldados," *El Nasional*, October 8, 1877, 1, which suggested that Jews were "the most intimate friends of the fatherland and of the government" (*"los mas intimos amigos de la patria i del governo"*), or "La simpatia de los djudios por la kavza turka," *El Nasional*, September 21, 1877, 2, which argued that Jews had proven that they were "the most intimate and loyal friends of the government of His Majesty the Sultan" ("los djudios . . . se mostran ser los mas intimos amigos i fideles del governo de su maestad el sultan").

Chapter 2

1. *La Epoka*, February 12, 1892, 8. For earlier calls to halt this practice, see "Los akompanyamientos funebres," *La Epoka*, November 27, 1891, 6; *La Epoka*, January 15, 1892, 8; "La muerte," *La Epoka*, January 29, 1892, 8. On the practice of hurriedly burying the dead, see also Michael Molho, *Traditions and Customs of the Sephardic Jews of Salonica*, ed. Robert Bedford, trans. Alfred A. Zara (1944/50; repr., New York: Foundation for the Advancement of Sephardic Studies and Culture, 2006), 168.

2. *El Tiempo*, February 18, 1892, 5; *La Epoka*, February 26, 1892, 6.

3. "Los akompanyamientos funebres," *La Epoka*, November 27, 1891, 6. Reports soon announced that Chief Rabbi Covo and the Salonican Jewish communal council had limited public mourning to daylight hours: *La Epoka*, December 4, 1891, 7. Later articles continued to complain about Salonican Jews' burial practices, however: "Kavod a los muertos," *El Luzero*, August 3, 1905, 2.

4. *La Epoka*, February 12, 1892, 8; "Los hazanim," *La Epoka*, February 19, 1892, 6. During the same period, other Jewish communities similarly attempted to keep their religious rituals out of public view. Susan G. Miller, "Apportioning Sacred Space in a Moroccan City: The Case of Tangier, 1860–1912," *City & Society*, 13:1 (2001): 57–83; esp. 67.

5. "Los hazanim," *La Epoka*, February 19, 1892, 6.

6. Ottoman communal elites elsewhere in the empire similarly attempted to enforce bourgeois norms among their constituents throughout the nineteenth century. See, for example, the call of the Maronite Patriach in 1858 to halt the "disgraceful" practice of wailing at funerals. Ussama Makdisi, "Corrupting the Sublime Sultanate: The Revolt of Tanyus Shahin in Nineteenth-Century Ottoman Lebanon," *Comparative Studies in Society and History* 42, no. 1 (January 2000): 199–200.

7. A year later, a Jewish author who penned a report on Jewish customs in Edirne expressed a similar sentiment about the "spectacle" Jews in that city made of themselves while

mourning publicly. "True pain should be hidden," he opined. Alliance Israélite Universelle, Turquie IC 1.4a, David Lévy of Edirne to Paris, March 29, 1893.

8. Selim Deringil, *The Well-Protected Domains: Ideology and the Legitimation of Power in the Ottoman Empire, 1876–1909* (London: I. B.Taurus, 1998).

9. Barbara Kirshenblatt-Gimblett, "A Place in the World: Jews and the Holy Land at World's Fairs," in *Encounters with the "Holy Land": Place, Past and Future in American Jewish Culture*, ed. Jeffrey Shandler and Beth S. Wenger (Hanover, NH: University Press of New England, 1997), 60–82; Shandler and Wenger, *Destination Culture: Tourism, Museums, and Heritage* (Berkeley: University of California Press, 1998), 79–105; "The Jew at the Centennial," *The Jewish Messenger*, September 1, 1876, 4; Alma Rachel Heckman and Frances Malino, "Packed in Twelve Cases: The Alliance Israélite Universelle and the 1893 Chicago World's Fair," *Jewish Social Studies* 19, no. 1 (Fall 2012), 53–69.

10. Eric Hobsbawm, *The Age of Empire, 1875–1914* (New York: Vintage Books, 1989), 13. See also Timothy Mitchell, *Colonising Egypt* (Cambridge: Cambridge University Press, 1988); Mitchell, "The World as Exhibition," *Comparative Studies in Society and History* 31, no. 2 (April 1989): 217–236.

11. Benjamin Mossé, *La révolution française et le rabbinat français* (Avignon: La Caravane, 1890), 11.

12. Mossé, *La révolution française*, 100.

13. Bernhard Traubenberg, "Zur 4. Säkularfeier der Vertreibung der Juden aus Spanien: Ein Appell an das jüdische Herz," *Der Israelit*, August 8, 1892, 1253–1255.

14. "Hag Leumi," *Ha-Magid*, August 14, 1891, 3 and "Le centenaire des israélites espagnols," *Stamboul*, August 4, 1891, 2, argue for the novelty of the holiday.

15. See, for example, Galante, *Histoire des juifs de Turquie*, 8: 8–15, which directly reproduces the celebratory language from 1892. Stanford Shaw, *The Jews of the Ottoman Empire and the Turkish Republic* (New York: New York University Press, 1991), 208, for his part, suggests that the 1892 celebrations represented "the high point of Levy's years as Grand Rabbi;" Avigdor Levy, *The Sephardim in the Ottoman Empire* (Princeton, NJ: Darwin Press, 1992), 1–3, 124, offers a more nuanced picture of the moment but nevertheless concludes that "[w]hatever the motives, the sentiments of gratitude were sincere." Paul Dumont, "Jewish Communities in Turkey during the Last Decades of the Nineteenth Century in the Light of the Archives of the Alliance Israélite Universelle," in *Christians and Jews in the Ottoman Empire*, ed. Benjamin Braude and Bernard Lewis (New York: Holmes & Meier Publishers, 1982), 1:225 writes that "[w]hen, in April, 1892, the Jews of Turkey celebrated the fourth centenary of the day when their ancestors . . . had found asylum in the lands of the sultan, it was with expressions of sincere gratitude that the regional committee of the Alliance thanked Abdülhamid for the protection which the Jews enjoyed in Turkish territory." Minna Rozen, "The Hamidian Era through the Jewish Looking Glass: A Study of the Istanbul Rabbinical Court Records," *Turcica* 37 (2005): 120 and, Rozen, *The Last Ottoman Century and Beyond: The Jews in Turkey and the Balkans, 1808–1945* (Ramat Aviv: Tel Aviv University, 2005), 1:97–98, offers an Istanbul-centered view of the event, writing that "there was no more appropriate year" for the celebration of the holiday, since it "served the interests of the members of the new Jewish Lay Council . . . [and] the Jewish community of Istanbul as a whole."

16. On Hazan: Abraham Galante, *Histoire des juifs de Turquie* (Isis: Istanbul, 1985–1986), 3:74–75; Henri Nahum, *Juifs de Smyrne, XIXe–XXe siècle* (Paris: Aubier, 1997), 146–147; *Liga de Pas i Solidaridad: Fondada en 1909* (Izmir: Meşrutiyet Matbaası, [1931]); Julia Phillips Cohen, "Aron de Yosef Hazan," in *The Encyclopedia of Jews in the Islamic World*, ed. Norman Stillman (Leiden: Brill, 2010), www.encquran.brill.nl/entries/encyclopedia-of-jews-in-the-islamic-world/hazan-aron-de-yosef-SIM_000256. Galante, *Histoire des juifs de Turquie* 2:266. Hazan, while from a family long resident in the empire, was among Izmir's *francos* (individuals with foreign protection in Ottoman lands). On Hazan's family links to the Italian consulate in his city: Laurence Abensur-Hazan, "La reconstitution de cinq générations à travers les archives du consulat d'Italie à Izmir," *Etsi: Revue de généalogie et d'histoire séfarades* 1, no. 1 (Spring 1998): 10–13.

17. For Ottoman Jewish reports on the 1891 centenary of the emancipation of French Jewry: "La revolusion franseza y los djudios," *La Buena Esperansa,* May 22, 1891, May 2 and 26, 1891, 1; "El sentenario de la emansipasion de los djudios de Fransia," *La Epoka*, October 2, 1891, 4–5, "Parte Israelita," October 9, 1891, 4–5; "Sentenario de la emansipasion de los djudios fransezes," *El Telegrafo*, October 15, 1891, 6; "El sentenario de la emansipasion de los djudios de Fransia," *El Tiempo*, October 6, 1891, 4–5 and "El sentenario de la emigrasion [*sic*] de los djudios de Fransia," October 13, 1891, 6–7.

18. Ottoman Jewish papers reported extensively on the fate of these immigrants, including those who entered Istanbul and other Ottoman cities, often alongside reports of Muslim refugees from the Balkans. See, for example, the notices of Jewish and Muslim refugees from Odessa and Bosnia in the same column of *Stamboul*, August 4, 1891, 2. For the influx of Corfiote Jews following the violence on the island in 1891, see Sakis Gekas, "The Port Jews of Corfu and the 'Blood Libel' of 1891: A Tale of Many Centuries and of One Event," in *Jews and Port Cities, 1590–1990: Commerce, Community and Cosmopolitanism,* ed. David Cesarani and Gemma Romain (London: Vallentine Mitchell, 2006), 171–196 and Joseph Nehama, *Histoire des Israélites de Salonique* (Salonica: Librairie Molho, 1935), 6/7:741. On the Jewish immigrants from Russia and Romania to Izmir, see Abraham Galante, *Histoire des juifs d'Anatolie* (Istanbul: M. Babok, 1937), 1:161. On their establishment in Salonica, see Nehama, *Israélites de Salonique*, 739; Rena Molho, "Jewish Working Class Neighborhoods Established in Salonica following the 1890 and 1917 Fires," in *The Last Ottoman Century*, ed. Minna Rozen (Ramat Aviv: Tel Aviv University, 2002), 2:173–194, reprinted in Rena Molho, *Salonica and Istanbul: Social, Political and Cultural Aspects of Jewish Life* (Istanbul: Isis, 2005), 107–126; Lévy, *Salonique à la fin du XIXe siècle*, 64; Paula Daccarett, "Jewish Social Services in Late Ottoman Salonica (1850–1912)" (Ph.D. diss., Brandeis University, 2008), 52–60. For the arrival of these Jewish refugees in Istanbul, see Cyrus Adler, *I Have Considered the Days* (Philadelphia: Jewish Publication Society of America, 1941), 91–92. Selim Deringil, "Jewish Immigration to the Ottoman Empire at the Time of the First Zionist Congresses: A Comment," in *The Last Ottoman Century*, ed. Rozen, 2:142–149, offers the perspective of the Ottoman Porte on the subject.

19. "La Fiesta Judia en 1892," *El Tiempo*, August 24, 1891, 3. "The Jews in Turkey," *Jewish Chronicle*, February 26, 1892, 14 mentions 2,150 Russian Jewish refugees who had recently found shelter in Istanbul, 1,300 of whom had since been sent to America by the Baron de Hirsch while the rest remained in the Ottoman capital.

20. "Le centenaire des israélites espagnols," *Stamboul*, August 4, 1891, 2.

21. "Un buketo de rozas," *El Tiempo*, July 23, 1891, 6.

22. For an analysis of difference in Ottoman society, see Aron Rodrigue, "Difference and Tolerance in the Ottoman Empire," interview by Nancy Reynolds, *Stanford Humanities Review* 5 (Fall 1995): 8–92, where he argues that before the Tanzimat period, difference was not so much tolerated as "vertically integrated into the political system." For what Ussama Makdisi terms "the common Tanzimat refrain that the Ottomans were the avatars of tolerance": Makdisi, "Ottoman Orientalism," *American Historical Review* 107, no. 3 (June 2002): 768–796

23. "La fiesta djudia en 1892," *El Tiempo*, August 24, 1891, 3. That their empire had been the sole place of refuge in 1492 was a commonly accepted view among Ottoman Jewish writers of the time, even though the historical record makes it clear that Iberian Jews had also fled to various other locations in the wake of the expulsion, including North Africa and Italy. In later centuries, European Jewish scholars returned to the use of this dichotomous view, though for new reasons. On the scholars of the *Wissenschafts des Judentums* and their representations of an Islamic "golden age," see Ismar Schorsch, "The Myth of Sephardi Supremacy," *Leo Baeck Institute Year Book* 34 (1989): 47–66, reprinted in Schorsch, *From Text to Context: The Turn to History in Modern Judaism* (Hanover, NH: University Press of New England, 1994). For other studies of "philo-Islamic" Jews in modern times, see *The Jewish Discovery of Islam: Studies in Honor of Bernard Lewis*, ed. Martin Kramer (Tel Aviv: Moshe Dayan Center for Middle Eastern and African Studies, Tel Aviv University, 1999).

24. See "El sirkulo israelita de Andrinopla," *El Tiempo*, July 23, 1891, 6, where the influential Ottoman Jewish enlightener Abraham Danon of Edirne is cited as praising the empire as "truly the most tolerant country that exists in the civilized world," and "La Fiesta Judia en 1892," *El Tiempo*, August 20, 1891, 5, where the monarchs of the Ottoman dynasty are blessed with the title of the "most tolerant rulers on earth." On Danon: Albert Navon, *Abraham Danon, 1857–1925* (Paris, Impr. H. Elias, 1925).

25. "La fiesta djudia en 1892," *El Tiempo*, August 24, 1891, 3. Emphasis mine.

26. "Ala onorivle redaktor del djurnal 'La Epoka' en sita," *La Epoka*, August 7, 1891, 4.

27. "El aniversario de su maestad el Sultan," *El Tiempo*, August 31, 1891, 1. For another example see "Aniversario imperial," *La Epoka*, August 24, 1900, 5, where the author claims that "more than other communities, we Jews have a sacred obligation to prove our recognition towards the government." The reference to "moral and material" forms of progress echoed the pronouncements of other Ottoman public figures of the time: Carter Vaughn Findley, "An Ottoman Occidentalist in Europe: Ahmed Midhat Meets Madame Gülnar, 1889," *American Historical Review* (February 1998): 15–49.

28. Deringil, "Jewish Immigration," 143.

29. Ibid., 144. Ottoman Jewish journalists claimed that large numbers of the refugees were legitimately Ottoman citizens long resident in the Russian empire. "Los israelitas rusos en Konstantinopla," *El Tiempo*, October 29, 1891, 2; *Habatselet*, January 1, 1892, 2–3.

30. "General," *Levant Herald and Eastern Express*, July 17, 1893, 357; "Le emigrasion djudia," *La Epoka*, February 5, 1892, 4. It was also during this period that the Ottoman government implemented new policies limiting Jews' ability to acquire land in Palestine: Neville J. Mandel, "Ottoman Policy and Restrictions on Jewish Settlement in Palestine: 1881–1908—Part 1," *Middle Eastern Studies* 10, no. 3 (October 1974): 312–332; Mandel, "Ottoman Policy as Regards Jewish Settlement in Palestine: 1881–1908," *Middle Eastern Studies* 11, no. 1 (January 1975): 33–46.

31. "Turkey and the Jews: Immigration Prohibited," *Jewish Chronicle*, October 30, 1891, 11; "Turkey and Jewish Immigration," *Jewish Chronicle*, November 6, 1891, 17.

32. Many of these aid societies were run by Ottoman Jewish women, including a committee formed for the refugees among the Ashkenazim of Istanbul in late 1891, and the "Société de Bienfaisance des Dames Israélites de Péra," founded in 1892. On the formation of the two societies, see "Los judios rusos en Konstantinopla," *El Tiempo*, January 7, 1892, 2; "Una sosiedad interesante," *El Tiempo*, March 10, 1892, 2–3; *Société de bienfaisance des Dames Israélites de Péra: Statuts* (Istanbul: Imprimerie de Castro, 1893). "Una fiesta en Salonika en favor de los emigrados rusos," *La Buena Esperansa*, September 29, 1892, 4, cites fundraising activities undertaken to help the immigrants in Izmir. The Salonican Jewish press also issued a call to form an aid society for these refugees: "Parte israelita," *La Epoka*, November 20, 1891, 5. These efforts coincided with a general explosion of Ottoman Jewish philanthropic societies during this period. "Rolo del rabino," *El Tiempo*, March 23, 1891, 4. "Parte israelita," *La Epoka*, August 7, 1891, 3, mentions the emergence of a Jewish charitable society in Monastir entitled "El Avenir," while "Sosieta 'La Karidad,'" *La Epoka*, November 27, 1891, 5, refers to a new Jewish women's society founded in Salonica in 1890, when a fire devastated the community in that city. The rapid increase of philanthropic activities in this case appears to confirm the claims of Nadir Özbek on the expansion of imperial philanthropic activities in the Hamidian period more broadly. On this, see Nadir Özbek, "The Politics of Poor Relief in the Late Ottoman Empire, 1876–1914," *New Perspectives on Turkey* 21 (Fall 1999): 1–33; Özbek, "Philanthropic Activity, Ottoman Patriotism and the Hamidian Regime, 1876–1909," *International Journal of Middle East Studies* 37 (2005): 59–81, and Özbek, *Osmanlı İmparatorluğu'nda Sosyal Devlet: Siyaset, İktidar ve Meşrutiyet, 1876–1914* (Istanbul: İletişim, 2002).

33. "Nuestra Propozision," *La Buena Esperansa*, July 10, 1891, 1. For a reference to the Jews' obligations toward the sultan and the "Turkish nation": "Un Buketo de Rozas," *El Tiempo*, July 23, 1891, 5. For the same message but in reference to the "Muslim nation": "El Kuarten Sentenario," *El Tiempo*, February 25, 1892, 4.

34. "Nuestra propozision," *La Buena Esperansa*, July 10, 1891, 1.

35. "La fiesta del 1892," *La Epoka*, August 14, 1891, 7. See also "El Kuarten Sentenario," *El Tiempo*, February 24, 1892, 4.

36. "Le centenaire des israélites espagnols," *Stamboul*, August 4, 1891, 2.

37. Ibid.

38. "De muestro kolaborador," *La Epoka*, March 4, 1892, 5. The author of this proposal may well have drawn inspiration for his plan from the many commemorative plaques Sultan Abdülhamid II erected at public sites during this period. Deringil, *The Well-Protected Domains*, 30.

39. The idea of building a hospital in honor of the centenary holiday echoed similar plans for the "anniversary of Jewish emancipation" in France. For Ladino press coverage of French Jews' plans for a hospital: *La Epoka*, October 16, 1891, 4.

40. "Le centenaire des israélites espagnols," *Stamboul*, August 4, 1891, 2. The author's reference to this emerging interest in sculpture may have been inspired by the recently established Academy of Fine Arts in Istanbul, which trained students in drawing and sculpture, among other subjects. Wendy K. Shaw, *Possessors and Possessed: Museums, Archaeology and the Visualization of History in the Late Ottoman Empire* (Berkeley: University of California Press, 2003).

41. "Una Djusta Propozision," *La Epoka*, July 17, 1891, 5.

42. Precedents certainly existed for non-Muslim processions to be accompanied by Ottoman guards: Sibel Zandi-Sayek, "Orchestrating Difference, Performing Identity: Urban Space and Public Rituals in Nineteenth-Century Izmir," in *Hybrid Urbanism*, ed. N. AlSayyad (New York: Praeger, 2001), 42–58.

43. "Ala onorivle redaktor," *La Epoka*, August 7, 1891, 4; "Le centenaire des israélites."

44. "Nuestra propozision," *La Buena Esperansa*, July 10, 1891, 1 and "Una Djusta Propozision," *La Epoka*, July 17, 1891, 5; both cite the need to decide upon a date.

45. "Smirne," *Il corriere israelitico* 30, no. 4, 86–87.

46. "La manifestasion del 1892," *La Epoka*, February 26, 1892, 4.

47. "Le centenaire des israélites espagnols," *Stamboul*, August 4, 1891, 2. The initials M.F. likely stand for Moïse Franco, the well-known historian of Ottoman Jewry cited in the introduction of this book and—in the early 1890s—an Alliance school teacher in Istanbul.

48. "La fiesta del 1892," *La Buena Esperansa*, July 31, 1891, 1; "Ala onorivle redaktor del djurnal 'La Epoka' en sita," *La Epoka*, August 7, 1891, 4.

49. "La fiesta del 1892," *La Buena Esperansa*, July 31, 1891, 1. Among the Ottoman-language newspapers that wrote about the event during the planning stages were *Sabah, Servet* and *Tarik*. On this see Mahir Aydın, "Musevilerin Osmanlı Topraklarına Kabulünün 400: Yıldönümü Kutlamaları," *Osmanlı Araştırmaları* 13 (1993): 29–28; "Le centenaire des israélites espagnols," *Stamboul*, August 4, 1891, 2.

50. "El kuarten sentenario," *La Buena Esperansa*, August 24, 1891, 4. "La fiesta del 1892," *La Buena Esperansa*, August 27, 1891, 3. The letter from Alexandria came from Hazan's brother, Eliyahu Hazan, who was chief rabbi of that city since 1888. See Galante, *Histoire des juifs de Turquie*, 3:29–30; Norman Stillman, *Sephardi Religious Responses to Modernity* (Luxembourg: Harwood Academic Publishers, 1995), 29–48; Zvi Zohar, "Elijah Bekhor Hazzan," in *Encyclopedia of Jews in the Islamic World*, ed. Stillman.

51. "La fiesta del 1892," *La Buena Esperansa*, August 24, 1891, 2.

52. "La fiest djudia en 1892," *El Tiempo*, August 20, 1891, 5. "La fiesta del 1892," *La Buena Esperansa*, August 31, 1891, 2 and "La Fiesta del 1892," *La Buena Esperansa*, September 3, 1891, 1.

53. "La fiesta djudia en 1892," *El Tiempo*, August 24, 1891, 3. The announcement was also cited in "Novedades lokales—la fiesta del 1892," *La Epoka*, August 28, 1891, 4.

54. "La fiesta djudia en 1892," *El Tiempo*, August 20, 1891, 4.

55. "La fiesta del 1892," *La Buena Esperansa*, August 27, 1891, 3; "El Kuarten Sentenario," *El Tiempo*, February 25, 1892, 4; "Una Djusta Propisizion," 17 *La Epoka*, July 1891, 5.

56. "Novedades lokales—la fiesta del 1892," *La Epoka*, August 28, 1891, 4–5.

57. Ibid., 5.

58. "La fiesta del 1892," *La Buena Esperansa*, August 31, 1891, 2. *La Epoka* later made a similar argument, warning that antisemites would use Jews' failure to celebrate the 1892 against them. "La manifestasion del 1892," *La Epoka*, January 15, 1892, 5. For foreign Jewish press coverage of the plans: "Smirne," *Il corriere israelitico* 30, no. 4, 86–87; "Hag Leumi," *Ha-Magid*, August 14, 1892, 2–3; an untitled notice in *Habatselet*, September 4, 1891, 4; and, in the same paper, "Yerushalayim," January 15, 1892, 1; "The Jews in Turkey," *Jewish Chronicle*, September 18, 1891, 9.

59. "La fiesta djudia del 1892," *El Tiempo*, August 20, 1891, 4–5.

60. "La fiesta del 1892," *La Buena Esperansa*, September 3, 1891, 1; "Novedades lokales—la fiesta del 1892," *La Epoka*, August 28, 1891, 5; "La fiesta del 1892," August 24, 1891, 3 and "La fiesta del 1892," *La Epoka*, August 14, 1891, 7 refer to the holiday as a "sacred an-niversary"; "La Fiesta Judia en 1892," *El Tiempo*, August 24, 1891, 4, "La Fiesta Nasional del 1892," *La Epoka*, September 11, 1891, 6 and "La fiesta nasionala de 1892," *La Buena Esperansa*, September 17, 1891, 1; "La manifestasion del 1892," *La Epoka*, January 15, 1892, 5, all refer to the observance of the holiday as a "sacred obligation."

61. "La fiesta del 1892," *La Buena Esperansa*, September 9, 1891, 1.

62. "La fiesta nasionala del 1892," *La Buena Esperansa*, September 28, 1891, 4.

63. "La manifestasion del 1892," *La Epoka*, December 18, 1891, 6. Already in October, Sam Lévy of Salonica suggested that there was talk of celebrating the holiday in late March although he did not give a specific date: Sam Lévy, "Turquie," *Archives Israélites*, October 22, 1891, 346.

64. "La fiesta del 1892," *La Buena Esperansa*, December 31, 1891, 1. See also "La fiesta djudia en 1892," *El Tiempo*, August 24, 1891, 4, for a similar warning.

65. "La manifestasion del 1892," *La Epoka*, December 18, 1891, 6.

66. The choice of this date, which the authors of the event no doubt took directly from the history books at their disposal, is an odd choice even as a symbolic approximation of the moment of the Jews' "arrival" in Ottoman lands, since the expulsion edict was not pub-licly announced for another month, at which time Spanish Jews were given three more months to leave their homes.

67. "Por la fiesta," *La Buena Esperansa*, February 25, 1892, 2.

68. "Kolelot 'ir Kushta—Gran Rabinato. Avizo," *El Tiempo*, February 25, 1892, 2–3.

69. *La Epoka*, February 12, 1892, 8. Compare to Hazan's compromise proposal that the holi-day transpire "without much noise."

70. BOA YA HUS 260/112, 27 Şevval 1309 (May 25, 1892); BOA Yıldız Mütenevvi Maruzat 61/51, 16 Ramazan 1309 (April 14, 1892); BOA HR. TO 44/48, 6 Ramazan 1309 (April 4, 1892).

71. "Intérieur," *Stamboul*, April 12, 1892, 1; *Sabah*, 21 Ramazan 1309 (April 19, 1892), 2; "Yevm-i Mahsus," *Tercüman-ı Hakikat*, 21 Ramazan 1309 (April 19, 1892). For foreign press reports on the event: "Israélites de Turquie," *Bulletin de l'Alliance Israélite Univer-selle*, no. 4 (April 1892), 27; "Turkey," *Jewish Chronicle*, May 6, 1892, 16; "Correspon-dance particulières," *Archives israélites*, June 9, 1892, 23, 180–181; "Turchia," *Il corriere israelitico* 30, no. 2, 280–281 and 30, no. 2, 41.

72. "De muestro kolaborador," *La Epoka*, March 4, 1892, 5–6.

73. Enver Ziya Karal, *Osmanlı Tarihi*, vol. 8, *Birinci Meşrutiyet ve İstibdat Devirleri (1876–1907)* (Ankara: Türk Tarih Kurumu, 1988), 264; Edwin Pears, *Life of Abdul Hamid* (London: Constable & Company, 1917), 200. This prohibition was enforced most strictly in the imperial capital, making the proposals to gather notables from communities across the empire in Istanbul for the occasion all the more daring.

74. That March 31 in the Julian calendar coincided with the first day of Passover that year was first mentioned in "De Muestro Kolaborador," *La Epoka*, March 4, 1892, 5. The chief rab-binate officially announced its choice to celebrate the holiday on Passover in "El Kuarten Sentenario," *El Tiempo*, April 7, 1892, 3.

75. "El kuarten sentenario dela venida de los djudios espanyoles en turkia," *La Buena Esper-ansa*, May 5, 1891, 2.

76. "Numero espesial a la okazion del aniversario del kuarten sentenario," *El Tiempo*, n.d. 1892, 16: Hazan was also honored for coming up with the idea in "Edision Espesial," *La*

Buena Esperansa, 1896, 31–32, a special issue the paper published in honor of the twenty-fifth anniversary of its existence.

77. M. Şükrü Hanioğlu, *The Young Turks in Opposition* (New York: Oxford University Press, 1995); Hanioğlu, *Preparation for a Revolution* (New York: Oxford University Press, 2001).

78. Mandel, "Ottoman Policy;" Mim Kemâl Öke, "The Ottoman Empire, Zionism, and the Question of Palestine (1880–1908)," *International Journal of Middle East Studies*, 14, no. 3 (August 1982): 329–341; Deringil, "Jewish Immigration."

79. Özbek, "Philanthropic Activity," 62.

80. Ibid., 64.

81. It had originally been slotted to open on October 21, 1892, a date meant to recall "the precise anniversary of Columbus's first sighting of the New World." *Fair America*, ed. Robert W. Rydell, John E. Findling, and Kimberly D. Pelle (Washington and London: Smithsonian Institution Press, 2000), 36.

82. "Evel Kavod: Elia Souhami," *El Tiempo* May 8, 1893, 1–2; "Nekrolojia: Elia Souhami," *La Buena Esperansa,* May 11, 1893, 3; "Nekrolojia: Elia Souhami," *La Epoka*, May 12, 1893, 7; "The Late Elia Souhami," *Levant Herald and Eastern Express*, May 15, 1893, 252; "M. Elia Souhami," *Jewish Chronicle*, May 19, 1893, 9.

83. For studies of Ottoman participation in the Chicago World's Fair: Zeynep Çelik, *Displaying the Orient: Architecture of Islam at Nineteenth-Century World's Fairs* (Berkeley: University of California Press, 1992); Çelik, "Speaking Back to Orientalist Discourse at the World's Columbian Exposition," in *Noble Dreams, Wicked Pleasures: Orientalism in America, 1870–1930*, ed. Holly Edwards (Princeton, NJ: Princeton University Press, 2000); Deringil, *The Well-Protected Domains*; Deringil, "The Hamidian State and the World's Fairs: 'The Whole World is Watching!' " in *Studien zu Wirtschaft und Gesellschaft im Osmanischen Reich*, ed. Raoul Motika, Christoph Herzog, and Micahel Ursinus (Heidelberg: Heidelberger Orientverlag, 1999), 191–207; Gülsen Sevinç and Ayşe Fazlioğlu, "1893 Şikago Sergisi'nde Osmanlılar," *Toplumsal Tarih* 6 (August 2001): 6–9; *Türk Fuarcılık Tarihi* (Istanbul: Fuar Merkezi, 2007); Öykü Potuoğlu-Cook, "Night Shifts: Moral, Economic, and Cultural Politics of Turkish Belly Dance Across the Fins-de-Siècle" (Ph.D. diss., Northwestern University, 2008), chapters 1–2.

84. "The Late Elia Souhami," *Levant Herald*, 252. On Abraham de Camondo's funeral, see Moïse Franco, "Count Abraham Camondo," *Jewish Encyclopedia*, 3:521; Franco, *Essai sur l'histoire des Israélites de l'Empire Ottoman depuis les origins jusqu'à nos jours* (1897; repr., New York: Georg Olms Verlag, 1973), 152.

85. "Evel Kavod," *El Tiempo*, 2. The fact that various communities honored Elia Souhami at his death made a lasting impression on members of his family. In an unpublished memoir written by his granddaughter, Frances Valensi Bishop (the daughter of Elia and Sultana Souhami's daughter, Esther), she recalled "My mother's favorite story was that when her father died, a funeral dirge rang out from all the mosques in the city, [and] all the church bells chimed." I am grateful to Randa Bishop for providing me with a copy of her mother's memoir.

86. The large number of Persian merchants present at Souhami's funeral can be explained in part by his dealings in Persian goods. See, for example, "Grand choix varié de tapis orientaux," *Le Moniteur oriental,* January 4, 1886, which advertises Persian rugs among the company's wares. That the Persian ambassador graced a benefit event decorated and endorsed by Elia Souhami's company may also speak to Souhami's personal connections with Persian officials in Istanbul. "Un bal masqué à Constantinople," *Archives israélites,* April 9, 1891, 118. Evidence of Souhami's connections with local Armenian merchants, particularly those of the well-known Gulbenkian family, also appeared regularly in the Ladino press of the period. See, for example: "Liberalidad dela familia Gulbenkian," *El Tiempo,* March 7, 1892, 2–3, which sings the praises of the Gulbenkians for sponsoring Istanbul's Jewish hospital for seven consecutive years. The patriarch of that family was also honored in the Ladino press upon his death in early 1893. "Sarkis Efendi Gulbenkian," *El Tiempo,* January 27, 1893, 3. On Souhami's Muslim partner, Sadullah Bey: John J. Wayne, "Constantinople to Chicago: In the Footsteps of Far-Away Moses," *Library of*

Congress Information Bulletin (January 13, 1992): 15; "Queer Sign Manuals," *Chicago Daily Tribune*, June 11, 1893, 11. Adler, *I Have Considered the Days*, 139; BBA Y. A. RES 95/24, 15 Cemaziyelevvel 1316 (October 1, 1898); "Sadullah Talib Bey," *Türkiye Teracimi Ahval Ansiklopedesi*, 498.

87. For Souhami's many philanthropic pursuits: "Evel Kavod," 1; "Nekrolojia," Galante, *Histoire des juifs de Turquie* 1: 331–332.

88. "Amerika'da kain Şikago Şehri'nden varid olan bir mektubdan iktibas olunmuştur," *Sabah*, 22 Rebiülevvel 1309 (October 26, 1891), 2; "El Sabah," *El Tiempo*, November 2, 1891, 2; "Turkey's Flag is First," *Chicago Daily Tribune*, September 21, 1891, 1; "World's Fair Notes," *Los Angeles Times*, October 12, 1891, 4; *El Tiempo*, November 2, 1891, 2; James Wilson Pierce, *Photographic History of the World's Fair and Sketch of the City of Chicago* (Baltimore: R. H. Woodward & Co., 1893), 315; Adler, *I Have Considered the Days*, 159.

89. The author of "Şikago sergisinde Kısm-ı Osmaninin Resm-i Küşadı Hakkında Malumat," *Servet-i Fünun*, 5 Ağustos 1309 (August 17, 1893), 365–366, wrote that the Turkish Village was built on the most honorable spot on the Midway. On the Ottoman government's interest in earning a proper symbolic place in the world through international expositions: Deringil, *The Well-Protected Domains*, 154–165; Deringil, "The Hamidian State and the World's Fairs: 'The Whole World is Watching!'" in *Studien zu Wirtschaft und Gesellschaft im Osmanischen Reich* ed. Raoul Motika, Christoph Herzog, and Micahel Ursinus (Heidelberg: Heidelberger Orientverlag, 1999), 191–207; Rıfat Önsoy, "Osmanlı İmparatorluğu'nun katıldığı ilk Uluslararası Sergiler ve Sergi-i Umumi-i Osmani," *Belleten* 47 (1983): 195–235; "Interest in the Fair: France and Turkey Eager to Make a Good Showing at Chicago," *New York Times*, June 23, 1892, 9. See "Dahiliye," *Sabah*, 19 Safer 1310 (September 12, 1892), 3, on the advantages of the Turkish Village's location on the Midway.

90. The Ottoman state had joined Great Britain, Germany, Austria, and Russia in boycotting the 1889 fair celebrating the 100th anniversary of the French Revolution because, in Abdülhamid II's words, it was an "insalubrious" event that challenged "the idea of monarchic sovereignty." Deringil, *The Well-Protected Domains*, 155; Zeynep Çelik, *Displaying the Orient*, 78, 107–108.

91. "Havadis-i Dahiliye-Şikago sergisi," *Tercüman-ı Hakikat*, 3 Muharrem 1309 (August 9, 1891), 1; "Dahiliye," *Sabah*, 19 Safer 1310 (September 12, 1892), 3. See also "The Chicago Exhibition," *The Oriental Advertiser*, January 9, 1892, 2; "La ekspozision de Shikago," *El Tiempo*, January 18, 1892, 2.

92. "Amerika'da kain Şikago Şehri'nden varid olan bir mektubdan iktibas olunmuştur," *Sabah*, 22 Rebiülevvel 1309 (October 26, 1891), 2; "El Sabah," *El Tiempo*, November 2, 1891, 2.

93. "Resimlerimiz: Midvey Plaza," *Servet-i Fünun*, 7 Teşrinievvel 1309 (October 19, 1893), 91; "Şikago sergisinde Kısm-ı Osmaninin Resm-i Küşadı Hakkında Malumat," *Servet-i Fünun*, 5 Ağustos, 1309 (August 17, 1893), 365–366.

94. For the text of the Ottoman government contract with Elia Souhami Sadulah & Co: BOA Y.A. Res 58/33, 25 Şevval 1309 (May 23, 1892). Ottoman Ministry of Trade and Public Works and Elia Suhami Saadullah & Co; "Malumat-ı Dahiliye-Şikago Sergisi," *Tercüman-ı Hakikat*, 2 Zilhicce 1309 (June 28, 1892), 3. On the signing of the contract, see: "Franco-American Treaty," *Washington Post*, February 1, 1892, 1; "Intérieur," *Stamboul* January 26, 1892, 1; "The Jews in Turkey," *Jewish Chronicle*, February 26, 1892, 14; Deringil, *The Well-Protected Domains*, 155.

95. "La ekspozision de Shikago," *El Tiempo*, January 11, 1892, 2; "Novedades del interior," *El Tiempo*, January 28, 1892, 2.

96. "La ekspozision de Shikago," *El Tiempo*, January 18, 1892, 2. Once in Chicago, various observers also commented on the Ottoman "bedchamber": Hubert Howe Bancroft, *The Book of the Fair* (Chicago: The Bancroft Co., 1893), 853; Pierce, *Photographic History*, 364, 366; "The Sultan's Realm," *Chicago Tribune*, April 4, 1893, 9.

97. "Turkey Holds the Key," *Chicago Daily Tribune*, September 13, 1891, 10.

98. Levy appears to have been agitated by the appearance in mid-1891 of two Russian "volunteer vessels bearing soldiers and weapons" in the Dardanelles, despite the fact that

Russian warships were prohibited from passing through the Dardanelles by the Treaty of Paris: "Russia and the Dardanelles," *Harper's Weekly*, September 19, 1891, 702.

99. Ibid.

100. Çelik, "Speaking Back," 77–79; "World's Fair Notes," *Chicago Daily Tribune*, July 8, 1893, 3.

101. For the stories Levy told to American audiences of "life in the land of the Sultan": "Never Ending Stream of People," *Chicago Daily Tribune*, December 9, 1892, 2.

102. "Orient at the Fair," *Chicago Daily Tribune*, April 12, 1893, 9.

103. "La ekspozision de Shikago," *El Tiempo*, May 18, 1893, 7.

104. "La ekspozision de Shikago," *El Tiempo*, July 31, 1893, 6. Reports in Ottoman-language papers offered similar observations. See, for example, an article suggesting that Americans were very favorably inclined to "the East" and to all things Islamic during the fair. "Şikago sergisinde Kısm-ı Osmaninin Resm-i Küşadı Hakkında Malumat," *Servet-i Fünun* 22 Muharrem 1311 (August 5, 1893), 365.

105. "La ekspozision de Shikago—seksion turka," *El Telegrafo*, July 5, 1894, 2.

106. Ibid., 1–2.

107. See, for example, the reference to "wily Turks" or the article claiming that the "Orientals" of the Turkish Village included "Arabs and Turks and other indolence-loving people." "Wily Turks Claim Poverty," *Chicago Daily Tribune*, November 1, 1893, 16; "Palanquin Bearers Frightened," *Chicago Daily Tribune*, May 5, 1893, 1.

108. "La ekspozision de Shikago," *El Tiempo*, May 18, 1893, 7. The Ottoman-language press offered similar reports of the imperial replicas to be found in Chicago: "Şikago sergisinde Kısm-ı Osmaninin Resm-i Küşadı Hakkında Malumat," *Servet-i Fünun* 22 Muharrem 1311 (August 5, 1893), 365–367, which praised the mosque erected in the Turkish Village on the Midway as a realistic reproduction in miniature of the Sülemaniye mosque of the imperial capital.

109. "La ekspozision de Shikago—seksion turka," *El Telegrafo*, July 5, 1894, 2.

110. "La seksion turka en la ekposzision de Shikago," *El Telegrafo*, April 7, 1894, 1. The same image appeared in *Servet-i Fünun*, 7 Teşrinievvel 1309 (October 19, 1893), 1.

111. "Resimlerimiz," *Servet-i Fünun*, 23 Şubat 1309 (March 7, 1894), 410.

112. "La Ekspozision de Shikago—La Seksion Otomana," *El Tiempo*, July 3, 1893, 6. In his quest to complete the "Oriental" atmosphere of his Turkish Village in Chicago, Robert Levy went so far as to ask American women he hired as cashiers and saleswomen to wear "Oriental" bloomers, a request they met with threats to strike. "Object to Bloomers," *Chicago Daily Tribune*, May 5, 1893, 1.

113. On Albert Souhami's participation in the Ottoman exhibit in San Francisco: BBA BEO 319/23865, 19 Cemaziyelevvel 1311 (October 28, 1893); Grace Cohen Grossman and Richard Eighme Ahlborn, *Judaica at the Smithsonian: Cultural Politics as Cultural Model* (Washington, DC: Smithsonian Institute Press, 1997), 52, 60, although the authors appear to confuse Albert with his father. Ship manifests preserved by the Statue of Liberty-Ellis Island Foundation record the voyage of Mr. and Mrs. A. Souhami, presumably Albert and his wife, who arrived in New York on March 10, 1893. A. Souhami was listed as a merchant on his way to Chicago and carrying ten pieces of luggage.

114. "San Fransisko muhbirimiz Urfalıyan Efendi tarafından varid olan mektubtur," *Sabah*, 23 Şaban 1311 (March 1, 1894), 2.

115. "La ekspozision de San Fransisko," *El Tiempo*, March 5, 1894, 7.

116. "San Fransisko muhbirimiz Urfalıyan Efendi;" "La ekspozision de San Fransisko."

117. For discussions of American racism and drunkenness, respectively, see: *Servet-i Fünun* 12 Mart 1308 (March 24, 1892), 8 and 19 Mart 1308 (March 31, 1892), 9.

118. "La ekspozision de Shikago—la seksion otomana," *El Tiempo*, July 3, 1893, 7.

119. The Ottoman-language press also published Ottoman travel accounts of journeys that followed a similar route, from Le Havre and New York to Chicago. See the series "Şikago'ya Azimet bir ruzname-i seyahatden muhrec sahifeler" in *Servet-i Fünun* that ran from 29 Nisan 1309 (May 11, 1893), 130 through 27 Mayıs 1309 (June 8, 1893), 194–195. For another Ottoman's account of his travels to the Chicago fair: Ahmet Turan Alkan, *Sıradışı Bir Jöntürk: Ubeydullah Efendi'nin Amerika Hatıraları* (Istanbul: İletişim, 1989).

120. Writers for the Ladino press of the time consistently used the term "*indijinos,*" to refer to white Americans, also employing the term "America" as a metonym for the United States. For a similar approach among other Ottoman journalists of their day: Elizabeth Frierson, "Mirrors Out, Mirrors In: Domestication and Rejection of the Foreign in Late-Ottoman Women's Magazines (1875–1908)," in *Women, Patronage and Self-Representation in Islamic Societies* (New York: State University of New York Press, 2000), 190.

121. "Vamos a Shikago!" *El Telegrafo,* April 19, 1894, 1.

122. "Nuestro arivo a Neu York," *El Telegrafo,* May 3, 1894, 2.

123. Muslim reformers Ahmed Midhat and Fatma Aliye both expressed their opposition to the veil during this period: Carter Findley, "Competing Autobiographical Novels: His and Hers," in *Many Ways of Speaking About the Self: Middle Eastern Ego-Documents in Arabic, Persia, and Turkish (14th–20th century)* (Wiesbaden: Harrassowtiz, 2010), 138; Elizabeth Paulson Marvel, "Ottoman Feminism and Republican Reform: Fatma Aliye's Nisvan-ı İslam" (master's thesis, Ohio State University, 2011), 54. The schools of the Alliance Israélite Universelle also sought to reform the lives of "Eastern" Jewish women by providing them with schooling for the first time. Aron Rodrigue, *French Jews, Turkish Jews: the Alliance Israélite Universelle and the Politics of Jewish Schooling in Turkey, 1860–1925* (Bloomington: Indiana University Press, 1990); Rodrigue, *Jews and Muslims: Images of Sephardi and Eastern Jewries in Modern Times* (Seattle: University of Washington Press, 2003); Rodrigue, "From Millet to Minority: Turkish Jewry," in *Paths of Emancipation: Jews, States, and Citizenship,* ed. Pierre Birnbaum and Ira Katznelson (Princeton, NJ: Princeton University Press, 1995), 238–261; Rodrigue and Esther Benbassa: *A Sephardi Life in Southeastern Europe* (Seattle: University of Washington Press, 1998) and *Sephardi Jewry* (Berkeley: University of California Press, 2000), 65–115. For an Ottoman Jewish journalist's ruminations on the value of praying with decorum, see: Olga Borovaya, "Shmuel Saadi Halévy/Sam Lévy Between Ladino and French: Reconstructing a Writer's Social Identity in a Polyglossic Situation," in Sheila Jelen, Michael Kramer, and L.Scott Lerner, eds. *Modern Jewish Literatures: Intersections and Boundaries* (Philadelphia: University of Pennsylvania, 2010), 87–88; Borovaya, *Modern Ladino Culture: Press, Belles Lettres, and Theater in the Late Ottoman Empire* (Bloomington: Indiana University Press, 2012), 115–116.

124. "Nuestro arivo a Neu York," *El Telegrafo,* May 3, 1894, 2.

125. "La ekspozision de Shikago—seksion turka," *El Telegrafo,* July 5, 1894, 2.

126. See, for example, *New York Times,* November 11, 1876, referring to the Philadelphia Exposition of that year: "The Exposition has had a good effect in keeping alive the patriotism of the people," also cited in Eric Davis, "Representations of the Middle East at American World Fairs, 1876–1904," in *The United States and the Middle East,* ed. Abbas Amanat and Magnus T. Bernhardsson (New Haven, CT: Yale Center for International and Area Studies, 2002), 380. For further discussion of this point: Robert Rydell, *All the World's a Fair: Visions of Empire at American International Expositions, 1876–1916* (Chicago: Chicago University Press, 1984) and Rydell, *World of Fairs: The Century-of-Progress Expositions* (Chicago: Chicago University Press, 1993).

127. "Le centenaire des israélites espagnols," *Stamboul,* August 4, 1891, 2.

128. Margaret Anderson has also pointed to the lasting power—and sometimes disturbing uses—of the myth of 1492 and Muslim tolerance: Anderson, "'Down in Turkey, Far Away': Human Rights, the Armenian Massacres, and Orientalism in Wilhemine Germany," *Journal of Modern History* 79, no. 1 (March 2007): 97–98.

129. "El 'Mizan' y la komunita ermena," *El Tiempo,* August 11, 1890, 2.

130. İbrahim Hakkı, "Is Turkey Progressing?" in *The Imperial and Asiatic Quarterly Review and Oriental and Colonial Record* (April 1892): 271. For the Ottoman Grand Vizier Ali Pasha's suggestion that "the law of Muslim conquerors obliges them to respect the religion of the conquered": Ali Pasha, "Mémoire transmis à Londres et à Paris par Aalı Pacha," May 1855, Archives du Ministère des Affaires Etrangères de France: Mémoires et Documents, Turquie, vol. 51, no. 9, 63. Other references to Ottoman Christians as the "conquered" and Ottoman Muslims as "conquerors" include: Devereux, *The First Ottoman Constitutional Period,* 40; Hanioğlu, *Preparation,* 402.

131. Atıf Hüseyin, TTK Library, Y-255, Defter 11, 4–7; 18–19, as cited in Engin Deniz Akarlı, "The Problems of External Pressures, Power Struggles, and Budgetary Deficits in Ottoman Politics under Abdulhamid II (1876–1909): Origins and Solutions" (Ph.D. diss., Princeton University, 1976), 39.

132. On Ottoman Jews being "mistaken" for Muslims or Turks at the fair: Kirshenblatt-Gimblett, "A Place in the World," 68; Kirshenblatt-Gimblett, *Destination Culture*, 100.

Chapter 3

1. Alliance Israélite Universelle (hereafter AIU) Archives, Série Turquie, IC 7.3h, V. Gerson to Paris, September 27, 1896.

2. Gerson's use of "Ottomans" here is ambiguous: it is unclear whether he meant to refer specifically to the Ottoman authorities or Ottoman Muslims more generally. Echoing Gerson's concerns, an author writing for London's *Jewish Chronicle* claimed to be "informed by those in a position to know" that public expressions of "pro-Armenian" sympathies by Jews anywhere in the world could have a deleterious effect on the position of Jews within Ottoman realms. "Jews and the Armenian Cause," *Jewish Chronicle*, January 24, 1896, 8.

3. "İlan-ı Resmi," *Tercüman-ı Hakikat*, 19 Rebiülevvel 1314, 1 (August 28, 1896); "Los ajitadores: ofisial," *El Tiempo*, September 1, 1896, 2–3.

4. Donald Quataert, "Clothing Laws, State, and Society in the Ottoman Empire, 1720–1829," *International Journal of Middle East Studies* 29, no. 3 (August 1997): 420; AIU Archives, Série Turquie, IC 7.3h, Gerson to Paris, September 27, 1896; Edhem Eldem, "26 Ağustos 1896 'Banka Vakası' ve 1896 'Ermeni Olayları,'" *Tarih ve Toplum* 5 (2007): 121, citing Osmanlı Bankası Arşivi (OBA), LA 23, 999, Sir Edgar Vincent to London Committee, August 28, 1896. Different authors have attributed Kurdish involvement in the massacres to Kurdish migrants as well as to a Hamidiye light cavalry unit composed of Kurds from southeastern Anatolia stationed in Istanbul at the time. For more on the Hamidiye institution: Janet Klein, *The Margins of Empire: Kurdish Militias in the Ottoman Tribal Zone* (Stanford, CA: Stanford University Press, 2011).

5. For the first quote, see Salahi Ramsdam Sonyel, *The Ottoman Armenians* (London: K. Rustem & Brother, 1987), 215. On uniform clubs and police involvement, see Herbert to Marquess of Salisbury, September 7, 1896 in Turkey No 1 (1897), *Correspondence Respecting the Disturbances at Constantinople in August 1896 presented to both Houses of Parliament by Command of Her Majesty January 1897*, 18, 27–29; Victor Bérard, *La politique du sultan* (Paris: Calmann Lévy, 1897), 11, 30; Loius Rambert, *Notes et impressions de Turquie* (Geneva: Atar, 1926), 18; Wilfrid Scawen Blunt, *My Diaries* (New York: Knopf, 1932), 186; and Christopher Walker, *Armenia: The Survival of a Nation* (Chatham, U.K.: Mackays of Chatham, 1991), 167. On this debate, and other aspects of the massacres, see Eldem, "26 Ağustos," 113–146.

6. Eldem, "26 Ağustos," 116.

7. Claims about the varied responses of Greek Orthodox Ottomans to the massacres of Armenians in the mid-1890s also surfaced during these years: J. K. Hassiotis, "The Greeks and the Armenian Massacres (1890–1896)," *Neo-Hellenika* 4 (1981): 69–109.

8. Albert Adatto, "Sephardim and the Seattle Sephardic Community" (master's thesis, University of Washington, 1939), 262.

9. "Our Ambassadors Abroad: The Legation Near the Sublime Porte," *Harper's Weekly*, February 24, 1900, 180. On Jews who aided Armenians, see also Adatto, "Sephardim," 259–262; Marie-Christine Bornes-Varol, "La vision de l'autre chez les juifs de Balat: Les arméniens," *Revue du monde arménien moderne et contemporain* 4 (1998): 42.

10. "False Accusations against the Jews of Crete and Constantinople," *Jewish Chronicle*, October 2, 1896, 5–6.

11. AIU, Série Turquie, IC 5, Fresco to Paris, September 4, 1896; "Jews and the Massacres in Constantinople," *Jewish Chronicle*, September 18, 1896, 8; "Die Woche," *Allgemeine Zeitung des Judenthums* 60, no. 44 (October 30, 1896): 519.

12. See Turkey No 1 (1897), 18, 34; Richard Davey, *The Sultan and His Subjects* (London: Chapman and Hall, 1897), 2:215; AIU Archives, Série Turquie, IC 5, Fresco

to aris, September 4, 1896; "Konstantinopel, 30. August," *Neue Freie Presse,* August 31, 1896, 5; "The Constantinople Massacre," *The Contemporary Review* 70 (1896): 462; *Documents diplomatiques: Affairs Arméniennes. Projets de Réformes dans l'Empire Ottoman 1893–1897* (Paris: Imprimerie Nationale, 1897), 276; Bérard, *La politique,* 14, 20; and, most recently, Yair Auron, *The Banality of Indifference: Zionism and the Armenian Genocide* (New Brunswick, NJ: Transaction Publishers, 2009), 150–152.

13. BOA İ HUS 49, 19 Rebiülevvel 1314 (August 28, 1896).

14. "Peace in Constantinople," *New York Times,* September 2, 1896. A similar claim appeared in "Wien, 1. September," *Neue Freie Presse,* September 2, 1896, 4.

15. Adatto, "Sephardim," 260.

16. Aaron Menahem, "Un skandal sin eshemplo," *El Amigo del Puevlo,* May 29, 1897, 645. On restrictions against discussing the Armenian massacres: Milena Methodieva, "The Debate on Parliamentarism in the Muslim Press of Bulgaria, 1895–1908," *The First Ottoman Experiment in Democracy,* ed. Christoph Herzog and Malek Sharif (Würzburg: Ergon, 2010), 111.

17. "Die Woche," *Allgemeine Zeitung des Judenthums,* September 11, 1896, 435; "Jews and the Massacres in Constantinople," *Jewish Chronicle,* September 18, 1896, 8.

18. "The Riots in Constantinople," *Jewish Chronicle,* September 4, 1896, 8.

19. Turkey No. 1 (1897), 18.

20. "Die Woche," *Allgemeine Zeitung des Judenthums,* September 25, 1896, 459.

21. "Die Woche," *Allgemeine Zeitung des Judenthums,* October 30, 1896, 519.

22. Gerson's view of Jews' structural vulnerability in this context is worth noting: although Muslims also helped protect Armenians during the Istanbul massacres, he feared that exposing the actions of the Jews who had done so might shift Ottoman perceptions of the loyalty of the Jewish community as a whole. This was a predicament peculiar to non-Muslims. On Muslims who sheltered Armenians in 1896, see "Havadis-i Dahiliye," *Tercüman-ı Hakikat,* 8 Rebiülahir 1314, 1 (September 16, 1896); Bérard, *La politique,* 25, 27; and Eldem, "26 Ağustos."

23. "Die Woche," *Allgemeine Zeitung des Judenthums,* October 30, 1896, 519.

24. "Jews and the Massacres in Constantinople," *Jewish Chronicle,* September 18, 1896, 8; "Echos de la ville," *Journal de Salonique,* January 25, 1897, 1.

25. "Monsinyor Ormanian en Haskoy," *El Tiempo,* January 14, 1897, 2. See also "Turkey," *Jewish Chronicle,* February 19, 1897, 27; and "News," *Jewish Missionary Intelligence: Monthly Record of the London Society for Promoting Christianity amongst the Jews* (May 1897): 79. On *El Tiempo,* see Sarah Abrevaya Stein, *Making Jews Modern: The Yiddish and Ladino Press in the Russian and Ottoman Empires* (Bloomington: Indiana University Press, 2004). Paul Fesch, *Constantinople aux derniers jours d'Abdul-Hamid* (Paris: Rivière,1907), 68, suggests it had a print run of 900 issues while its competitor, *El Telegrafo,* produced only 500. Since such papers were passed from hand to hand, read in cafes and libraries, and also read aloud to groups of listeners, their audience can be assumed to have been many times the number of paying subscribers. A Jewish journalist from late Ottoman Salonica suggested a figure of as many as eight to ten readers and listeners for every subscriber, a reckoning that would imply a reach of 7,200–9,000 for *El Tiempo:* Sam Lévy, *Salonique à la fin du XIXe siècle,* 101.

26. Children orphaned as a result of the massacres of Armenians in Istanbul and on a much greater scale in eastern Anatolia were flooding the Ottoman capital by 1897: Nazan Maksudyan, "'Being Saved to Serve': Armenian Orphans of 1894–1896 and Interested Relief in Missionary Orphanages," *Turcica,* 42 (2010): 47–88. Their resettlement was also mentioned in the Ladino press; see, for example, "Novedades del interior," *El Tiempo,* March 25, 1897, 1. On the massacres of Armenians in eastern Anatolia during this period, see: Ronald Grigor Suny, ed., special issue on the Hamidian massacres, *Armenian Review* 47, no. 1–2 (Summer 2002).

27. The chief rabbi soon visited the new Armenian patriarch as well. "Novedades del interior," *El Tiempo,* January 28, 1897, 2.

28. See *El Tiempo,* February 25, 1897, 4; *El Tiempo,* February 29, 1897, 3; *El Tiempo,* March 22, 1897, 3; *El Tiempo,* April 1, 1897, 3. Evidence that members of different communities

danced together at such events is confirmed by an article that railed against the phenomenon in a Jewish nationalist newspaper of Salonica just a few years later: "Los chikos balos," *El Avenir,* January 31, 1900, 3.

29. For one such case, concerning the marriage of Jacques Bey de Leon, a Jewish Council member of the capital, to an Ottoman Greek Orthodox woman: Minna Rozen, *The Last Ottoman Century and Beyond: The Jews in Turkey and the Balkans 1808–1945* (Ramat Aviv: Goldstein-Goren Diaspora Research Center, 2005), 1:102.

30. Noting that the overwhelming majority of the empire's Jewish population remained poor into the early twentieth century, Ottoman Jewish historians have suggested that Ottoman Jewry by and large lacked a middle class: Aron Rodrigue, *French Jews, Turkish Jews: The Alliance Israélite Universelle and the Politics of Jewish Schooling in Turkey, 1860–1925* (Bloomington, IN: Indiana University Press, 1990), 111–120; Stein, *Making Jews Modern,* 176. For a different interpretation, positing that what made someone bourgeois in late-Ottoman Istanbul was not simply a matter of wealth but rather whether his or her involvement was "perceived to be a capitalist type of investment and a western type of network:" Edhem Eldem, "Istanbul 1903–1918: A Quantitative Analysis of a Bourgeoisie," *Boğaziçi Üniversitesi dergisi: yöneticilik, ekonomi, ve sosyal bilimler* 11, no. 1–2(1997): 53–98, esp. 54–57 and Eldem, *A History of the Ottoman Bank* (Istanbul: Ottoman Bank Historical Research Center, 1999), 275–304. In any case, the ongoing economic misery of most of their coreligionists did not prevent Jewish journalists from inundating their readers with regular news of bourgeois balls or promotions of products they could not afford: Stein, *Making Jews Modern,* 123–149, 175–201.

31. Rumors that new violence was imminent continued to circulate in Istanbul throughout the fall of 1896: "Los ajitadores ermenos: komunikasion ofisial," *El Tiempo,* September 21, 1896, 2; "La trankilidad en la kapital," *El Tiempo,* November 5, 1896, 3; "Los ermenos: komunikasion ofisial," *El Tiempo,* November 12, 1896, 3. The breaking of a lamp or the ravings of a drunk man near a synagogue were enough to send Jewish worshippers running during Yom Kippur in 1896, just a month after the massacres. "La noche de Kipur," *El Tiempo,* September 21, 1896, 3.

32. Elizabeth Frierson, "Women in Late Ottoman Intellectual History," in *Late Ottoman Society: The Intellectual Legacy,* ed. Elisabeth Özdalga (New York: Routledge Curzon, 2005), 154.

33. Georgeon, *Abdulhamid II,* 197, suggests that Ottoman Muslims constituted 75 percent of the empire's total population by 1880, up from 66 percent in 1875.

34. Georgeon, *Abdulhamid,* 192–212. On Abdülhamid II's Islamic politics, see also Selim Deringil, *The Well-Protected Domains: Ideology and the Legitimization of Power in the Ottoman Empire, 1876–1909* (London: Tauris, 1998); and Kemal Karpat, *The Politicization of Islam* (New York: Oxford University Press, 2001).

35. Frierson, "Women," 144.

36. For Christians as "metaphorical foreigners" in Meiji Japan, see Carol Gluck, *Japan's Modern Myths* (Princeton, NJ: Princeton University Press, 1985), 135.

37. For negative portrayals of Armenian and Greek Orthodox communities in the Ottoman press and administration, see Elizabeth Frierson, "Mirrors Out, Mirrors In: Domestication and Rejection of the Foreign in Late-Ottoman Women's Magazines (1875–1908)," in *Women, Patronage and Self-Representation in Islamic Societies,* ed. D. Fairchild Ruggles (Albany, NY: State University of New York Press, 2000), 197; and Reşat Kasaba, "Izmir 1922: A Port City Unravels," in *Modernity and Culture: From the Mediterranean to the Indian Ocean,* ed. Leila Fawaz and C. A. Bayly (New York: Columbia University Press, 2002), 222.

38. For comparative thoughts about this case in the context of the late imperial politics of the Habsburg and Russian states, see Julia Phillips Cohen, "Between Civic and Islamic Otomanism: Jewish Imperial Citizenship in the Hamidian Era," *International Journal of Middle East Studies* 44, no. 2 (May 2012): 237–255.

39. Rodrigue, *French Jews, Turkish Jews.*

40. Throughout this period, the Ladino press launched various attacks against Theodor Herzl, the Zionist Congress, and Zionists in neighboring Bulgaria: "Israelitas de Bulgaria: la

gazeta 'Boz de Israel,'" *El Tiempo*, August 6, 1896, 5; "Ha-dokhim et ha-ketz," *El Tiempo*, August 17, 1896, 2; "La 'Boz de Israel,'" *El Tiempo*, September 21, 1896, 7; "Los israelitas de Bulgaria: el djurnal 'La Boz de Israel,'" *El Tiempo*, October 8, 1896, 5; "El djurnal 'La Boz de Israel,'" *El Tiempo*, October 19, 1896, 1; "Un interesante livrito kontra Doktor Hertzl," *El Tiempo*, November 5, 1896, 6; "Israelitas de Bulgaria: La 'Boz de Israel,'" *El Tiempo*, November 12, 1896, 5; "Israelitas de Bulgaria: la 'Boz de Israel,'" *El Tiempo*, December 3, 1896, 7; "El kongreso de la utopia," *El Tiempo*, July 19, 1897, 6. The fact that Zionism was making inroads among Jews in Bulgaria was a troubling prospect for the empire's Sephardi Jewish leaders, as the Jewish inhabitants of that principality (autonomous since 1878) maintained close contacts with their coreligionists in the empire. Esther Benbassa and Aron Rodrigue, *Sephardi Jewry: A History of the Judeo-Spanish Community, 14th–20th Centuries* (Berkeley: University of California Press, 2000), 116–117.

41. "Lettres de Salonique," *La Liberté*, April 5, 1897, 1.

42. On the Greco-Ottoman war of 1897, see Colmar Freiherr von der Goltz, *Osmanlı-Yunan Seferi (1313/1897)* (Dersaadet [Istanbul]: Mekteb-i Fünûn-i Harbiye Matbaası, 1326 [1910]); Pears, *Life of Abdul Hamid*, 205–213; Édouard Driault and Michel Lhéritier, *Histoire diplomatique de la Grèce de 1821 à nos jours*, (Paris: PUF, 1926), 4:301–456; Selim Sun, *1897 Osmanlı-Yunan Harbi* (Ankara: Genelkurmay Basımevi, 1965); T. G. Tatsios, *The Megali Idea and the Greek-Turkish War of 1897: The Impact of the Cretan Problem on Greek Irredentism 1866–1897* (New York: Columbia University Press, 1984); Bayram Kodaman, *1897 Türk-Yunan Savaşı* (Ankara: Türk Tarih Kurumu Basımevi, 1993); Metin Hülagü, *1897 Osmanlı-Yunan Savaşı* (Kayseri, Turkey: Erciyes Üniversitesi Matbaası, 2001); and Mehmet Uğur Ekinci, "The Origins of the 1897 Ottoman-Greek War: A Diplomatic History" (master's thesis, Bilkent University, 2006).

43. For tensions in Izmir, see Archives du ministère des Affaires étrangères de Nantes (hereafter AMAEF-Nantes), Ambassade Constantinople, E 241, April 4, 1897; Henri Nahum, *Juifs de Smyrne, XIXe—XXe siècle* (Paris: Aubier, 1997), 21; and Noémi Lévy, "Salonique et la Guerre Gréco-Turque de 1897: Le fragile équilibre d'une ville Ottomane" (Mémoire de maîtrise, Université Paris 1, 2002), 72–74, which additionally mentions conflicts in Ankara and Scutari. On Scutari (also Işkodra or Shkodër, Albania), see "Désordres a Scutari," *L'Indépendance belge* March 29, 1897, 1 and March 31, 1891, 1.

44. *Documents diplomatiques Affaires d'Orient: Affaire de Créte: Conflit gréco-turc: Situation de l'empire Ottoman, février-mai 1897* (Paris: Imprimerie nationale, 1897), 237; AMAEF-Nantes, Ambassade d'Athènes, A 218, May 11, 1897; Nicolas Politis, *La Guerre gréco-turque au point de vue du droit international* (Paris: A. Pedone, 1898), 49; Lévy, "Salonique et la Guerre," 72–73.

45. War was declared on April 18, 1897 and a peace treaty signed on December 18. The treaty is reproduced in Ekinci, "The Origins."

46. BOA, A.MKT.MHM., 612/10; BOA, Y.A.RES., 86/20; Ekinci, "Origins," 61, 69. European observers stationed in the empire at the time also suggested that the Ottoman government restricted the movements of its Greek Orthodox citizens near the border and prevented them from leaving their hometowns or from joining the Ottoman army on the front. National Archives, UK, Public Record Office (hereafter PRO) FO 195/1988, March 24, 1897; Henry W. Nevinson, *Scenes in the Thirty Days War* (London: J. M. Dent, 1898), 13.

47. Ottoman Greek Orthodox contributions to the imperial army in 1897 included donations made by the employees of the Istanbul Patriarchate, Jerusalem's Patriarch, and members of the Greek Orthodox communities of Salonica, Istanbul, and Izmir: "Havadis-i Dahiliye," *Tercüman-ı Hakikat*, 11 Şaban 1314 (January 15, 1897), 1; 8 Ramazan 1314 (February 10, 1897), 1; 24 Zilkade 1314 (April 26, 1897), 2; 25 Muharrem 1315 (June 26, 1897), 2; Nadir Özbek, "Philanthropic Activity, Ottoman Patriotism and the Hamidian Regime, 1876–1909," *International Journal of Middle East Studies* 37 (2005): 74; Lévy, "Salonique et la Guerre," 53. On volunteers for Greece: Richard Clogg, "The Greek *Millet* in the Ottoman Empire," in *Christians and Jews in the Ottoman Empire*, ed. Benjamin Braude and Bernard Lewis (New York: Holmes and Meier, 1982), 1:199; AMAEF-Nantes, Ambassade Constantinople, E 241, April 4, 1897; Sabri Sürgevil, "1897 Osmanlı-Yunan

Savaşı ve İzmir," in *Tarih Boyunca Türk-Yunan İlişkileri* (Ankara: Genelkurmay ATASE Başkanlığı, 1986), 303; Lévy, "Salonique et la Guerre," 78; Hülagü, *1897 Osmanlı-Yunan Savaşı*, 48; Ellis Ashmead Bartlett, *The Battlefields of Thessaly* (London: John Murray, 1897), 126, 299; BOA Y.PRK.HR., 23/68; BOA, Y.A.HUS., 369/4; Ekinci, "Origins," 52–53.

48. Vangelis Kechriotis, "The Greeks of Izmir at the End of the Empire: A Non-Muslim Ottoman Community between Autonomy and Patriotism" (Ph.D. diss., University of Leiden, 2005), 59–60, cites an announcement of this regulation published in Izmir's Greek-language periodical *Aktis*, but suggests that the regulation was designed less to make local Greeks flee than to "incorporate them into the tax system," an idea echoed in the correspondence of the British consul of Salonica at the time; see PRO FO 195/1989, May 12, 1897 and May 19, 1897. The measure is also mentioned in Süleyman Tevfik and Abdullah Zühdi, *Devlet-i Aliyye-i Osmaniye ve Yunan Muharebesi* (Istanbul: Mihran Matbaası, 1315 [1897/1898]); and Ekinci, "Origins," 74. Announcements calling for Greek citizens to take Ottoman citizenship or leave the empire were also posted in Ladino- and French-language Jewish newspapers of the empire: see *Journal de Salonique*, April 19, 1897, 1; *El Meseret*, April 30, 1897, 3; and *La Epoka*, May 7, 1897, 5. By late May, large numbers of Hellenic citizens in Izmir had reportedly applied for Ottoman nationality in order to stay in the empire. See *Tercüman-ı Hakikat*, 26 Zilhicce 1314 (May 28, 1897), 2; and "Havadis-i Dahiliye," *Hanımlara Mahsus Gazete*, 2 Muharrem 1315 (June 3, 1897), 7.

49. Kechriotis, "The Greeks of Izmir," 54. The majority of Izmir's Hellenic subjects were long-time residents of the city, many having come in search of a livelihood from the Aegean Islands in previous decades. Kemal Karpat, *Ottoman Population, 1830–1914* (Madison: University of Wisconsin Press, 1985), 46.

50. See, for example, BOA, A.MKT.MHM., 612/10; BOA, Y.A.RES., 86/20; and "Novedades del interior," *El Tiempo*, August 10, 1896, 2.

51. "Los echos de Kreta," *El Tiempo*, March 22, 1897, 3; "Politika i estranjer," *El Meseret*, April 2, 1897, 1; *El Telegrafo*, July 30, 1897, 2.

52. On the shared experience of flight between Jewish and Muslim refugees during this period, see Kemal Karpat, "Jewish Population Movements in the Ottoman Empire, 1862–1914," in Karpat, *Studies on Ottoman Social and Political History* (Leiden: Brill, 2002), 153.

53. On Indian Muslim support for the Ottoman cause, see "Los musulmanos delas indias i las viktorias delas armadas," *El Tiempo*, May 31, 1897, 1–2. On Viennese Jews' patriotic mobilization see the same issue, p. 3, and "Vitman ve Avrupa'dan Mecruhin-i Askeriyeye Muavenet," *Tercüman-ı Hakikat*, 1 Zilhicce 1314 (May 3, 1897), 2.

54. On the Bosnian Muslims who came to fight: "Novedades del interior," *El Tiempo*, July 26, 1897, 2. On Jewish volunteers from Vienna: "Los medicos israelitas enel kresiente kolorado," *El Tiempo*, July 1, 1897, 3. On young Jewish doctors arriving from Paris: *Journal de Salonique*, May 10, 1897, 1; "Medikos voluntarios israelitas," *El Tiempo*, June 14, 1897, 3.

55. "Ismirna," *El Tiempo*, May 6, 1897, 5.

56. According to Kechriotis, "The Greeks of Izmir," 54, there were 52,000 Ottoman Greeks and 25,000 Greek citizens living in Izmir in 1890, out of a total population of 200,000.

57. "Ofisiales judios en la flota ofisial," *El Meseret*, April 2, 1897, 4.

58. "La muerte de un bravo," *El Tiempo*, July 8, 1897, 5–6.

59. "El halifato," *El Tiempo*, August 16, 1897, 2–3.

60. For the first of this series, see "Patriotismo de los israelitas," *El Tiempo*, April 26, 1897, 3.

61. See "Patriotismo de los israelitas," *El Tiempo*, April 29, 1897, 3; and the series of articles that followed with the same title in *El Tiempo*, May 3, 1897, 4; May 6, 1897, 6; May 13, 1897, 3. News of Jewish volunteers to the army appeared in the series on 2, 5, and April 26, 1897, 3. For other reports on the Jewish army volunteers during the war, see *La Epoka*, April 30, 1897, 4–5; *Tercüman-ı Hakikat*, April 25, 1897 and May 5, 1897; *İkdam*, May 5, 1897, 2, and May 10, 1897, 3; *Sabah*, May 8, 1897, 2; May 10, 1897; May 11, 1897, 3.

62. "Unterredung mit Grumbckow Pascha über den Krieg," *Neue Freie Presse*, May 6, 1897, 2; *Jewish Chronicle*, May 7, 1897, 7.

63. "Un epizodo dela tomada de Larisa," *El Tiempo,* May 10, 1897, 4; "La fidelidad de un judio," *El Amigo del Puevlo,* May 21, 1897, 629–630, quoting Istanbul's Ladino serial *El Telegrafo;* "Hamiyetli bir Musevinin Fevkalade Sadakat ve Fedakârlığı ve Bunun Mükafat-ı Muhakkaka ve Mübeccelesi," *Sabah,* May 22, 1897, 2.

64. AIU Archives, Série Turquie IC 5. Eskenazi to Paris, May 17, 1897. See also Abraham Galante, *Appendice à l'ouvrage [Turcs et Juifs]: Documents officiels turcs concernant les juifs de Turquie* (Istanbul: Impr. Hüsnütabiat, 1941), 21–24.

65. "Musevi Vatandaşlarımız," *Sabah,* 20 Zilhicce 1314, 2; *El Meseret,* June 11, 1897, 3.

66. "El epizodo de Larisa," *El Tiempo,* June 17, 1897, 4–5.

67. Ibid., 5.

68. BOA BEO 1156/86693 22 Safer 1316 (July 12, 1898); BOA BEO 1156/86693 22 Safer 1316 (July 12, 1898).

69. *La Epoka,* May 28, 1897, 5; *El Meseret,* May 28, 1897, 6; Sam, "Turquie," *Archives israélites,* June 10, 1897, 183. The story resurfaced over a decade later. For this, see "Un judio salva una armada turka," in Isaac Gabay, *Yildiz y sus sekretos: el reino de Abdul Hamid* (Istanbul: Imp. Gabay, [1910?]), 300–302.

70. Katerina Lagos, "The Metaxas Dictatorship and Greek Jewry, 1936–1941" (Ph.D. diss., Oxford University, 2005), 82.

71. Galante, *Appendice à l'ouvrage,* 24; Galante, *Histoire des Juifs de Anatolie* (Istanbul: M. Babok, 1937), 1: 161. See also Joseph Jacobs, "The Jews of Europe," *American Jewish Yearbook* 1 (1899–1900): 26 and *Embros,* April 18, 1897, 2, which accused Jews of assisting the Ottomans in their attacks against the Greeks in the city. Many of the Jews fleeing Larissa (Tr. Yenişehir) after the 1897 war settled in Salonica, in the Vardar neighborhood, where they built a synagogue that came to be known locally as the "Kahal de los Yenişehirlis" (the Synagogue of those from Yenişehir). See *Zikhron Saloniki: Gedulatah ve-hurbanah shel Yerushalayim de-Balkan,* ed. David Recanati (Tel Aviv: Committee for the Publication of Books on the Salonica Community, 1972), 1:165. See also "Las famiyas israelitas emigradas de la Tesalia," *El Avenir,* June 1, 1898, 5 and the series entitled "Los djidios en Tesalia" in *El Avenir,* June 22, 1898, 6–7; June 19, 1898, 6; July 10, 1898, 6; July 20, 1898, 6; August 31, 1898, 4; December 21, 1898, 4, with the titles "Los djidios en Larisa," "En Tesalia," "Korespondensia-Volo," and "En Tesalia," on August 3, 1898, 6; October 12, 1898, 9, October 19, 1898, 6–7, and December 28, 1898, 6, respectively.

72. "La fiesta patriotika de alhad ultimo," *El Tiempo,* July 1, 1897, 4.

73. Projects supporting the needy Muslims of Crete were reported regularly in the Ottoman Jewish press and included Jewish names among the lists of donors. See "Novedades del interior," *El Tiempo,* April 1, 1897, 2; "Patriozmo," *La Buena Esperansa,* April 27, 1897, 1; the series entitled "Patriosmo de los israelitas" in *El Tiempo,* April 29, 1897, 3; May 3, 1897, 3; May 6, 1897, 2; May 13, 1897, 3; "Sokoros en favor delos feridos dela armada imperial," May 24, 1897, 4; "Novedades del imperio" *El Meseret,* March 26, 1897, 2; "Los nesesitozos de Kreta," *El Tiempo,* June 10, 1897, 4; "Echos de la ville," *Journal de Salonique,* April 8, 1897, 1. For an Ottoman booklet issued to raise money for Muslim refugees from the island, see *Girid Ahali-i İslamiyesi Muhtacini Menfaatine Mahsus Resimli Gazete Nüsha-i Fevka'l-adesi* (Istanbul: Mahmud Bey Matbaası 1315 [1897/1898]).

74. There were approximately 1,000 Jews living in Crete at this time, with the majority (some 800) concentrated in Hania, and the remaining 200 or so in Heraklion and Retimo. On the Cretan Jewish community during the period see: "Girit'te Museviler," *Sabah,* 4 Zilkade 1314 (April 6, 1897), 3; *Il vessillo israelitico* 45, no. 2 (1897): 69. On their flight: "The Jews in Crete," *Jewish Chronicle,* March 12, 1897, 10 and March 19, 1897, 10.

75. In Izmir, the Alliance director Gabriel Arié led many of the efforts directed at absorbing and caring for the Cretan Jews. "Los djidios de Kreta," *El Amigo del Puevlo,* February 26, 1897, 437; *El Meseret,* March 5, 1897, 4. In the capital, Fernandez initially attempted to care for the refugees alone, but soon wrote to Paris to ask for support. AIU Archives, Série Turquie, IC 5, Fernandez to Bigart, March 18, 1897.

76. For calls to reopen Jewish schools closed for lack of funds: "La eskuela de ijos dela Aliansa en Ortakoy," *El Tiempo,* June 21, 1897, 3. For a notice announcing the financial

troubles of the chief rabbinate, which remained unable to pay its employees for many months: "El gran rabinato de Konstantinopla," *El Tiempo,* June 24, 1897, 3.

77. For the conflation of the terms "Muslim" and "Ottoman" during this period, see Karpat, *Politicization,* 143, which suggests that after 1878, the term *milli,* or national, became "synonymous with the faith." Relatedly, Benjamin Fortna mentions an imperial decree of 1887 that referred to Ottoman state schools as "Muslim" schools: Fortna, "Islamic Morality in Late Ottoman 'Secular' Schools," *International Journal of Middle East Studies* 32 (August 2000): 376.

78. The society is identified as the Cemiyet-i İmdadiye by Serpil Çakır, "Fatma Aliye," in *Biographical Dictionary of Women's Movements and Feminisms: Central, Eastern, and South Eastern Europe, 19th and 20th Centuries,* ed. Francisca de Haan, Krassimira Daskalova, and Anna Loutfi (Budapest: Central European University Press, 2006), 23. Its activities are noted but no name provided in Nezihe Muhiddin, *Türk Kadını* (Istanbul: Numune Matbaası, 1931), 82. Contemporary Ottoman-language reports suggest other names may have been used, including Muhadderat-ı Osmaniye Cemiyeti, Nisvan-ı Osmaniye, and Cemiyet-i Muhtereme-i Muhadderat-ı İslamiye.

79. "Sokoros en favor delos feridos dela armada imperial," *El Tiempo,* May 10, 1897, 3; "Sokoros en favor delos feridos," *El Tiempo,* May 13, 1897, 4.

80. "Havadis-i Dahiliye," *Hanımlara Mahsus Gazete,* 18 Zilhicce 1314 (May 20, 1897), 7.

81. Madame Elias Pasha (Esther Cohen), decorated by the sultan for her philanthropy in the 1880s, was an active public figure in the Ottoman capital and president of a Jewish women's charitable society formed in Pera in 1892. "Sokoros en favor delos feridos," *El Tiempo,* May 17, 1897, 3; "Constantinople," *Jewish Chronicle,* August 29, 1884, 12; "Una sosiedad interesante," *El Tiempo,* March 10, 1892, 2–3; "Une fête de charité israélite à Constantinople," *Archives israélites,* April 20, 1894, 133–134; "The Jews in Constantinople," *Jewish Chronicle,* May 11, 1894, 9. For reports on her activities in 1897, see "Sokoros en favor delos feridos dela armada imperial," *El Tiempo,* May 24, 1897, 4; "Muhadderat-ı Osmaniye Cemiyet-i Hayriyesi," *Sabah,* 21 Zilhicce 1314 (May 23, 1897), 2; "Les blessés," *Le Moniteur oriental,* May 24, 1897, 3; "La guerre turco-hellène," *Le Moniteur oriental,* June 10, 1897, 3; "Décorations," *Le Moniteur oriental,* July 28, 1897, 3; "Elias Pasha," *El Telegrafo,* July 29, 1897, 563.

82. *El Tiempo* issued donors' lists on May 13, May 17, May 24, June 3, June 10, and June 24, 1897. For donors' lists including Jewish names in the Ottoman-language press see the series of articles entitled "Muhadderat-ı Osmaniye Cemiyet-i Hayriyesi ve Mecruhin Gazilerimize İane," in *Sabah,* 21 Zilhicce 1314 (May 23, 1897), 2; 3 Muharrem 1315 (June 4, 1897), 2; 5 Muharrem 1315 (June 6, 1897), 2; 7 Muharrem 1315 (June 8, 1897), 2; 12 Muharrem 1315 (June 13, 1897), 2. In *Le Moniteur oriental/Oriental Advertiser,* Jewish donations to the committee were mentioned on May 12, 1897, 3; May 21, 1897, 3; May 24, 1897, 3; May 28, 1897, 3; May 29, 1897, 3; June 1, 1897, 3; June 3, 1897, 3; June 5, 1897, 3; June 7, 1897, 3; June 10, 1897, 3; June 19, 1897, 3.

83. Fatma Aliye, "Yaralılara İmdad," *Tercüman-ı Hakikat,* 25 Zilkade 1314 (April 27, 1897), 2; "Muhadderat-ı Osmaniye Cemiyet-i Hayriyesi ve Mecruhin Gazilerimize İane," *Sabah,* 3 Muharrem 1315 (June 4, 1897), 2; "Comité des dames ottomanes," *Le Moniteur oriental,* May 21, 1897, 3; BOA BEO 958/71794, 29 Zilhicce 1314 (May 31, 1897); BOA Y. PRK. ASK 128/12, 24 Muharrem 1315 (June 25, 1897).

84. The names given to the society in other publications also varied. From Salonica one author referred to it as the "Ladies' Relief Committee," while the Istanbul correspondent for the London-based *Jewish Chronicle* simply called it a "Ladies' Committee." Sam, "Turquie," *Archives israélites,* June 10, 1897, 183; "Turkey," *Jewish Chronicle,* June 4, 1897, 26.

85. "Sokoros en favor delos feridos dela armada imperial," *El Tiempo,* 3, and June 10, 1897, 3. "Madame Şükrü" was married to Ibrahim Şükrü Pasha, and the eldest daughter of the grand vizier of the time, Halil Rıfat Pasha.

86. "Komite delas damas otomanas por los eridos," *El Tiempo,* June 24, 1897, 4. Reports in Ottoman, French, and English publications of the empire noted Christian women's donations to the committee much earlier than the Jewish press did. One such report even labeled the society a "Muslim and Christian Women's Committee," indicating that the

type of discursive erasure employed by Jewish journalists during the war could cut both ways: "Les blessés," *Le Moniteur oriental*, May 14, 1897, 3.

87. "Madam Elias Pasha," *El Tiempo*, July 1, 1897, 3.

88. "Gran rabinato de Turkia," *El Tiempo*, April 29, 1897, 3.

89. "La suskrision militar," *El Tiempo*, May 6, 1897, 3.

90. "La suskrision militar," *El Tiempo*, May 13, 1897, 5.

91. The situation remained unresolved for many months. See "La suskrision militar," *El Tiempo*, August 30, 1897, 3–4.

92. On Lena Navon's activities in the Hasköy Alliance Israélite Universelle school for girls, see the series of articles entitled "Patriotismo de los israelitas," in *El Tiempo*, April 29, 1897, 3; May 3, 1897, 4; May 6, 1897, 6; May 13, 1897, 3. In addition to her students, Navon enlisted local women to sew clothes for Ottoman soldiers. "Turkey," *Jewish Chronicle*, June 4, 1897, 26.

93. BOA İ TAL 60, 24 Safer 1315 (July 25, 1897); "Décorations," *Le Moniteur oriental*, July 28, 1897, 3; "Su ekselensia dr. Elias Pasha," *El Tiempo*, July 29, 1897, 3; "Novedades del imperio," *La Buena Esperansa*, July 30, 1897, 1; "Vice-Admiral Elias Pasha," *Jewish Chronicle*, November 30, 1900, 14; Anri Niyego, *Haydarpaşa'da Geçen 100 Yılımız* (Istanbul: Gözlem Gazetecilik Basın ve Yayın, 1999), 43.

94. *Le Journal de Salonique*, April 22, 1897, 1; *Il vessillo israelitico* 45, no. 4 (1897): 135; "La Guerre en Macédoine," *L'Indépendance Belge*, April 22, 1897, 2; "Lettres du théâtre de la guerre," *La Liberté*, April 22, 1897, 1, May 3, 1897, 2, and May 4, 1897, 2.

95. *Le Journal de Salonique*, April 19, 1897.

96. PRO FO 195/1988, April 24, 1897.

97. There were two Jewish-run papers in the city, the French *Journal de Salonique* and the Ladino *Epoka. El Avenir,* a second Ladino paper sympathetic to Jewish nationalism and Hebraist programs, appeared in Salonica towards the tail end of 1897, not long after the First World Zionist Congress convened in Basel.

98. *La Epoka*, April 30, 1897, 4–5.

99. "Selânik," *Asır*, 29 Zilkade 1314 (May 1, 1897), 3; "Malumat-ı Mahsusa," *İkdam*, 4 Mayıs 1897 (May 16, 1897), 2.

100. "Turkish Jews and the War," *Jewish Chronicle*, May 21, 1897, 16; "Turchia," *Il vessillo israelitico* 45, no. 5 (1897): 172. On the Jewish volunteers, see also Bartlett, *The Battlefields of Thessaly*, 75.

101. PRO FO 195/1989, May 3, 1897. See also Pierre Mille, "En Thessalie: Journal de champagne, première partie," *Revue des Deux Mondes* 67, no. 4 (October 1, 1897): 611.

102. Most authors appear to have missed the presence of non-Muslim volunteers during this war, including Ufuk Gülsoy, *Osmanlı Gayrimüslimlerinin Askerlik Serüveni* (Istanbul: Simurg, 2000). Özbek, "Philanthropic Activity," 74, writes that "no attempts appear to have been made to accept non-Muslim volunteers during the Ottoman-Greek war of 1897," noting that although Catholic Albanians fought for the empire at this moment, they were apparently "volunteered" en masse by Albanian notables rather than volunteering themselves as individual "citizen-soldiers"; Goltz, *Osmanlı-Yunan Seferi*; PRO FO 195/1989, May 20, 1897. Eyal Ginio, "Mobilizing the Ottoman Nation during the Balkan Wars (1912–1913): Awakening from the Ottoman Dream," *War In History* 12, no. 2 (April 2005): 172, mentions a Vlach war hero from 1897. Lévy, "Salonique et la Guerre," 36, is the only other source I have seen to mention Ottoman Jewish volunteers in 1897.

103. "Hamiyetli bir Musevi'nin Fevkalade Sadakat ve Fedakarlığı ve Bunun Mükafat-ı Muhakkaka ve Mübeccelesi," *Sabah*, 18 Zilhicce 1314 (May 21, 1897), 2. The report was later reproduced in Ladino newspapers of Istanbul and Izmir: "La prensa turka i el patriotismo de los israelitas," *El Tiempo*, May 24, 1897, 2; "El Sabah i los djudios," *El Meseret*, May 28, 1897, 6.

104. İkdam, 8 Zilhicce 1314 (May 10, 1897), 2; Gabay, *Yildiz y sus sekretos*, 298–299.

105. *La Epoka*, May 14, 1897; David Recanati, *Zikhron Saloniki: Gedulatah ve-hurbanah shel Yerushalayim de-Balkan* (Tel Aviv: Committee for the Publication of Books on the Salonica Community, 1972), 1: 165; Gabay, *Yildiz y sus sekretos,* 299; AIU Archives, Série Grèce, IC 40, June 25, 1897.

106. "Selânik," *Asır*, 10 Zilhicce 1314 (May 12, 1897), 3; "Havadis-i Dahiliye," *Tercüman-ı Hakikat*, 19 Zilhicce 1314 (May 21, 1897), 2; "Şefkat-i bi-payan Cenab-ı Şehriyari ve Mecruh Gazilerimizin Muvasaleti," *Sabah*, 18 Zilhicce 1314 (May 20, 1897); "Selânik," *Asır*, 5 Muharrem 1315 (June 6, 1897), 3; *Malumat*, 21 Safer 1315 (July 22, 1897), 1.

107. *Malumat*, 21 Safer 1315 (July 22, 1897), 4.

108. See also Walter B. Harris, "During the Armistice: Impressions of the War," *Blackwood's Edinburgh Magazine* (September 1897): 445.

109. For other attempts to create separate publications commemorating these events see *La Epoka*, June 25, 1897, 5 and *La Epoka*, July 2, 1897, 1.

110. This process is aptly captured in Benjamin Nelson's pithy conclusion that "brotherhood entails otherhood," quoted by Margaret Anderson, "Down in Turkey, far away: Human Rights, the Armenian Massacres, and Orientalism in Wilhelmine Germany," *Journal of Modern History* 79, no. 1 (March 2007): 82.

111. "Echos de la ville," *Le Journal de Salonique*, April 22, 1897, 1.

112. "Echos de la ville," *Le Journal de Salonique*, February 11, 1897, 1.

113. On ritualized violence see David Nirenberg, *Communities of Violence* (Princeton, NJ: Princeton University Press, 1998). The rock-throwing between Greek Orthodox and Jewish youths occurred on a cyclical basis, on Sabbaths and holidays, over the course of many years, see *Pharos tes Makedonias*, May 16, 1884, 1 and June 2, 1884, 1; *La Epoka*, December 27, 1889, 6; April 18, 1890, 6–7, April 25, 1890, 6–7; March 22, 1891, 7; February 17, 1893, 4; October 13, 1893, 6–7; March 27, 1896, 5–6. Thanks are due to Paris Papamichos Chronakis for providing me with the *Pharos* reference. A Salonican Jewish children's song recorded in the early twentieth century may speak to this pattern: it told of a young Jewish boy hitting a young Christian boy on the head with a stone ("*al-evantí una piedra y le dí en rosh kavesa*"). Michael Molho, *Traditions and Customs of the Sephardic Jews of Salonica*, ed. Robert Bedford, trans. Alfred A. Zara (1944/50; repr., New York: Foundation for the Advancement of Sephardic Studies and Culture, 2006), 223.

114. *La Epoka*, February 12, 1897, 6.

115. "Echos de la ville," *Journal de Salonique*, February 15, 1897, 1; *La Epoka*, February 19, 1897, 7.

116. *Akropolis*, May 2, 1897. Representatives of the Jewish community forwarded the question to the British consul in Salonica at the time, asking that he help calm the situation by acknowledging that most of Salonica's Jews were not to blame for the incident (which he did). See PRO FO 78/4828, June 9, 1897, J. E. Blunt to British Secretary of State for Foreign Affairs. See also AMAEF-Nantes, Ambassade d'Athènes, A 218, May 11, 1897; Rena Molho, "The Zionist Movement in Thessaloniki, 1899–1919," in *The Jewish Communities of Southeastern Europe: From the Fifteenth Century to the End of World War II*, ed. I. K. Hassiotis (Thessaloniki: Institute for Balkan Studies, 1997), 330; Lévy, "Salonique et la Guerre," 70; and K. E. Fleming, *Greece: A Jewish History* (Princeton, NJ: Princeton University Press, 2008), 57–58, citing French and British consular records on the matter, respectively.

117. MAE-Nantes, Minister of Foreign Affairs to royal legations, A 218, May 11, 1897.

118. *Embros*, May 18, 1897, 3.

119. Molho, "The Zionist Movement"; Lagos, "The Metaxas Dictatorship," 83.

120. For a discussion of censorship in Ladino during this period see Robyn Loewenthal, "Censorship and Judeo-Spanish Popular Literature in the Ottoman Empire," in *Studies on Turkish-Jewish History*, ed. David F. Altabé, Erhan Atay, Israel J. Katz (New York: Sepher Hermon Press, 1996), 181–191. For censorship in the Ottoman press, see the recent work of İpek K. Yosmaoğlu, "Ottoman Empire, 1831–1920," *International Encyclopedia of Censorship*, ed. Cindy C. Combs and Martin W. Slann (London: Fitzroy Dearborn, 2002), 1786 and Yosmaoğlu, "Chasing the Written Word: Press Censorship in the Ottoman Empire, 1876–1913," *The Turkish Studies Association Journal* 27, no. 1–2 (2003): 15–49.

121. *Embros*, May 5, 1897, 3.

122. My searches have yielded only one oblique reference to the disturbances at the train station, which came in the form of a denial and spoke of the need to disprove the "calumnies

being hurled" at the city's population "by the Greek press of Athens," without explaining what these calumnies had been. On this, see Julia Phillips Cohen, "'Zeal and Noise': Jewish Imperial Allegiance and the Greco-Ottoman War of 1897," Michael Laskier and Yaacov Lev, eds., *The Divergence of Judaism and Islam: Jews and Muslim in a Changing World* (Gainesville: University Press of Florida, 2011), 29–50.

123. Even before war was officially declared, the British foreign consul in Salonica wrote that, "In the absence of all reliable intelligence, rumours of an alarming nature are spread about, and the Greek community here apprehends a fanatical outbreak among the Mohammedans." PRO FO 195/1988, February 19, 1897. Also see C. A. Fetzer, *Aus dem thessalischen Feldzug der Türkei: Frühjahr 1897: Berichte und Erinnerungen eines Kriegskorrespondenten* (Stuttgart: Deutsche Verlags Anstalt, 1898), 30–32, who notes that his Armenian guide in Salonica asked him on a daily basis whether a massacre of Christians was afoot and begged to be warned in time if such violence appeared imminent.

124. "Orasion en la kaye," *La Epoka*, August 13, 1897, 1–2. A similar complaint appeared in Izmir's Ladino press the following year: "Las orasiones en Salonik," *El Meseret*, October 14, 1898, 4.

125. On the quay as the *"vitrine de la ville,"* or the showcase of modernizing Salonica, see Meropi Anastassiadou, *Salonique, 1830–1912: Une ville Ottomane à l'âge des réformes* (New York: Brill, 1997), 88; Brant Downes, "Constructing the Modern Ottoman Waterfront: Salonica and Beirut in the Late Nineteenth Century" (Ph.D. diss., Stanford University, 2008), 66–67.

126. AIU Archives, Série Grèce, IC 40, June 25, 1897.

127. According to Rena Molho in *Salonica and Istanbul: Social, Political and Cultural Aspects of Jewish Life* (Istanbul: Isis, 2005), 168, the Athenian newspaper *Akropolis* published various anti-Dreyfusard tracts around this time as a counter to Jews' vociferous identification with the empire during the 1897 war. Paul Dumont in "The Social Structure of the Jewish Community of Salonika at the End of the Nineteenth Century," *Southeastern Europe/L'Europe du Sud-Est* 5, no. 2 (1979): 65–68, similarly suggests that tensions between the two groups began to grow in the wake of mounting nationalist agitation and new economic pressures in the region throughout the 1890s. There is also evidence that the regular stone-throwing sessions between Jewish and Greek Orthodox boys in the city continued for many years: AIU Archives, Gr IC 41, May 13, 1897, Jewish community of Salonica to the Jewish community of Corfu; and a letter from January 10, 1900, Joseph Nehama to the Alliance in Paris. Nehama worried that street fighting between Greeks and Jews in the city was intractable, and lamented that the trend had not been corrected. On the stone-throwing battles see also Dumont, "The Social Structure," 66; Lévy, "Salonique et la Guerre"; Mark Mazower, *Salonica, City of Ghosts: Christians, Muslims and Jews, 1430–1950* (New York: Vintage, 2006), 157, 185.

128. These were *El Meseret*, founded that year, *La Buena Esperansa*, and *El Nuvelista/Le Nouvelliste*.

129. "Lokales," *El Meseret*, January 22, 1897, 2.

130. "Paseos de envierno," *El Meseret*, February 19, 1897, 6–7.

131. Ibid., 7.

132. Ibid. The Ladino term in question, *turkos*, was clearly intended to refer to the local Muslim population, which in Izmir would have been largely Turkish-speaking.

133. This message merged almost seamlessly with the journal's mission, announced in its first issue, to serve as an "interpreter between the Jewish community and the Ottoman authorities." "A los lektores," *El Meseret*, January 15, 1897, 1. The Ladino paper, which was owned by a Muslim (Mehmet Hulusi), later included a page in Ottoman Turkish as well.

134. "Lokales," *El Meseret*, March 12, 1897, 4.

135. "Ayudad la armada imperiala otomano mezo nuestro jurnal," *El Meseret*, April 30, 1897, 2.

136. "Alas gloriozas tropas otomanas," *El Meseret*, May 21, 1897, 2.

137. *El Nuvelista*, May 20, 1897, 1. For other contemporary references to Ottoman soldiers as lions: "Las negosiasiones de pas," *El Tiempo*, May 13, 1897, 2; "Una buena leksion," *El*

Amigo del Puevlo, May 14, 1897, 610; *Mütalaa,* 1 Muharrem 1315, 2 (June 2, 1897); Edhem Eldem, *Pride and Privilege: A History of Ottoman Orders, Medals and Decorations* (Istanbul: Ottoman Bank Archives and Research Center, 2004), 310.

138. "La gera: patriotismo i relidjion," *El Meseret,* April 30, 1897, 1–2. For an English translation of this article, see Julia Phillips Cohen, trans., "The Fez as a Sign of Patriotism: An Appeal for Imperial Allegiance during the Greco-Ottoman War," in Cohen and Stein, *Sephardi Lives.*

139. For Ottoman Jewish volunteers in 1897: "Havadis-i Dahiliye," *Tercüman-ı Hakikat,* April 25, 1897, 3; "Patriotismo de los israelitas," *El Tiempo,* April 26, 1897, 3; and the series of articles that followed with the same title in *El Tiempo,* April 29, 1897, 3; May 3, 1897, 4; May 6, 1897, 2, 5, 6; May 13, 1897, 3; "Lettre de Macédoine," *L'Indépendance Belge,* April 28, 1897, 2; *La Epoka,* April 30, 1897, 4–5; "Malumat-ı Mahsusa," *İkdam,* May 4, 1897, 2; *Jewish Chronicle,* May 21, 1897, 16; *Il vessillo israelitico* 45, no. 5 (1897): 172; "Selânik," *Asır,* May 1, 1897, 3; *Sabah,* May 8, 1897, 2; May 10, 1897; May 11, 1897, 3; "Malumat-ı Mahsusa," *İkdam,* May 10, 1897, 3; Juda Abastado, "Turquie," *Archives israélites* May 13, 1897, 149; AIU Archives, Série Turquie, IC 4 Eskenazi to Bigart, May 17, 1897; Adolf Friedemann, "Türken und Juden," *Allgemeine Zeitung des Judenthums,* May 21, 1897, 245–246; Pierre Mille, "En Thessalie," 611; Sam, "Turquie," *Archives israélites,* June 10, 1897, 182; "Echos d'Orient," *Univers Israélite,* June 18, 1897, 404–405; Gabay, *Yildiz y sus sekretos,* 298–300.

140. "La gera: patriotismo i relidjion," *El Meseret,* April 30, 1897, 1. Such pronouncements complicate the conclusions offered in Sarah Stein, *Making Jews Modern,* 185, 191, which suggests that Ottoman Jewish reformers and newspaper men counseled their readers away from wearing the fez due to their westernizing tendencies.

141. For attempts to reinforce an Islamic moral order during the Hamidian era: Benjamin C. Fortna, *Imperial Classroom: Islam, the State, and Education in the Late Ottoman Empire* (Oxford: Oxford University Press, 2002); Noémi Lévy-Aksu, *Ordre et désordres dans l'Istanbul ottomane (1879–1909): De l'État au quartier* (Paris: Karthala, 2012).

142. "Novedades del imperio," *El Meseret,* April 30, 1897, 3.

143. "Havadis-i Dahiliye," *Tercüman-ı Hakikat,* 8 Zilhicce 1314 (May 10, 1897), 2.

144. *La Buena Esperansa,* May 3, 1897, 3. Director of the AIU girls' school in Rusçuk during the Russo-Ottoman War of 1877–1878, Madame Joselin (Jousselin in the French sources) fled with her pupils to Varna in search of refuge: "Israélites de Turquie," *Bulletin de l'Alliance Israélite Universelle,* January 2, 1877, 9.

145. *La Buena Esperansa,* May 7, 1897, 1. On Madame Joselin, see also: "Patriotismo," *La Buena Esperansa,* May 11, 1897, 3; "Ismirna: en onor de Madam Joselin," *El Telegrafo,* September 24, 1897, 10. Greek women remained active during the war as well. On this, see Efi Avdela and Angelika Psarra, "Engendering 'Greekness:' Women's Emancipation and Irredentist Politics in Nineteenth-Century Greece," *Mediterranean Historical Review* 20, no. 1 (June 2005): 67–79.

146. Madame Joselin was the director of the Alliance's school for girls in Izmir during this period. See *Liga de Pas i Solidaridad: Fondada en el 1909* (Izmir: Meşrutiyet Matbaası, [1931?]), 24; "Los israelitas de Kreta," *El Tiempo,* March 22, 1897, 5; "Los jidios de Kreta," *El Amigo del Puevlo,* February 26, 1897, 437–438.

147. "Havadis-i Dahiliye," *Tercüman-ı Hakikat,* 3 Zilhicce 1314 (May 5, 1897), 3; *İkdam,* 3 Zilhicce 1314 (May 5, 1897), 2.

148. "İhtida ve gönüllü asker," *Sabah,* 3 Zilhicce 1314 (May 5, 1897), 2; "Havadis-i Dahiliye," *Tercüman-ı Hakikat,* 3 Zilhicce 1314 (May 5, 1897), 3.

149. "İhtida," *Sabah,* 6 Zilhicce 1314 (May 8, 1897), 2; AIU Archives, Série Turquie, IC 4, May 17, 1897.

150. *İkdam* 6 Zilhicce 1314 (May 8, 1897), 2. See also "Chronique," *Le Moniteur oriental,* May 8, 1897, 3.

151. "Yine İzmir Musevileri," *Sabah,* 8 Zilhicce 1314 (May 10, 1897), 3; "İhtida," *İkdam,* 8 Zilhicce 1314 (May 10, 1897), 3; "İzmir Musevileri," *Sabah,* 9 Zilhicce 1314 (May 11, 1897), 3; "İhtida," *İkdam,* 9 Zilhicce 1314 (May 11, 1897), 3.

152. *İkdam,* 11 Zilhicce 1314 (May 13, 1897), 2.

153. A Ladino newspaper of Sofia, Bulgaria, also suggested that the number of converts hovered around 100: Aaron Menahem, "Un skandal sin eshemplo," *El Amigo del Puevlo*, May 21, 1897, 631.

154. On this see Leah Bornstein-Makovetsky, "Jewish Converts to Islam and Christianity in the Ottoman Empire in the Nineteenth Century," in *The Last Ottoman Century and Beyond: The Jews in Turkey and the Balkans*, ed. Minna Rozen (Ramat Aviv: Tel Aviv University, 2002), 2:83–127. In contrast to Nahum, Bornstein-Makovetsky concludes conversion to Islam "was fairly prevalent among Jews of the Ottoman Empire" and was significantly more common and theologically less fraught for Jews than conversion to Christianity; see Nahum, *Juifs de Smyrne*, 85. For conversion in the late Ottoman period more generally see Selim Deringil, "'There is no Compulsion in Religion': On Conversion and Apostasy in the Late Ottoman Empire: 1839–1856," *Society for Comparative Study of Society and History* 42, no. 3 (July 2000): 547–575.

155. Avner Levi, "*Shavat Aniim*: Social Cleavage, Class War and Leadership in the Sephardi Community: The Case of Izmir 1847," in *Ottoman and Turkish Jewry: Community and Leadership*, ed. Aron Rodrigue (Bloomington: Indiana University Turkish Studies, 1992), 183–202; Bornstein-Makovetsky, "Jewish Converts," 106.

156. From the capital, *El Tiempo* reported on the conversions without comment: "La konversion de sesenta y sinko israelitas de Ismirna," *El Tiempo*, May 10, 1897, 4; "Konversion de israelitas en Ismirna," *El Tiempo*, May 13, 1897, 4.

157. *La Buena Esperansa*, May 7, 1897, 3. Indeed, everywhere else in the empire Jews appear to have been accepted into the army as volunteers without converting. On Ottoman Jewish volunteers in 1897: "Selânik," *Asır*, April 21, 1897, 3; "Havadis-i Dahiliye," *Tercüman-ı Hakikat*, April 25, 1897, 3; "Patriotismo de los israelitas," *El Tiempo*, April 26, 1897, 3; and the series of articles that followed with the same title in *El Tiempo*, April 29, 1897, 3; May 3, 1897, 4; May 6, 1897, 2, 5, 6; May 13, 1897, 3; "Lettre de Macédoine," *L'Indépendance Belge* April 28, 1897, 2; *La Epoka*, April 30, 1897, 4–5; "Malumat-ı Mahsusa," *İkdam*, May 4, 1897, 2; *Jewish Chronicle*, May 21, 1897, 16; *Il vessillo israelitico* 45, no. 5 (1897): 172; "Selânik," *Asır*, May 1, 1897, 3; *Sabah*, May 8, 1897, 2; May 10, 1897; May 11, 1897, 3; "Malumat-ı Mahsusa," *İkdam*, May 10, 1897, 3; Juda Abastado, "Turquie," *Archives israélites*, May 13, 1897, 149; AIU Archives, Série Turquie, IC 4 Eskenazi to Bigart, May 17, 1897; Adolf Friedemann, "Türken und Juden," *Allgemeine Zeitung des Judenthums*, May 21, 1897, 245–246; Pierre Mille, "En Thessalie," 611; Sam, "Turquie," *Archives israélites*, June 10, 1897, 182; "Echos d'Orient," *Univers Israélite*, June 18, 1897, 404–405; Gabay, *Yildiz y sus sekretos*, 298–300.

158. *La Buena Esperansa*, May 7, 1897, 3.

159. "Turkey," *Jewish Chronicle*, June 4, 1897, 26.

160. BOA Y. PRK. PT 13/58, 24 Zilhicce 1314 (26 May 1897).

161. "Los djidios en Larisa," *El Avenir*, August 3, 1898, 6; "En Tesalia," *El Avenir*, October 12, 1898, 9.

162. BOA İ.HUS 64, 22 Zilhicce 1315 (May 14, 1898); BOA BEO 1124/84240, 23 Zilhicce 1315 (May 15, 1898); BOA BEO 1133/84973, 11 Muharrem 1316 (June 1, 1898); "Emigrados," *El Meseret*, June 3, 1898, 7.

163. AIU, Série Turquie, IC 1, Nahum to Paris, May 15, 1908; AIU, Série Grèce, IC 40, June 25, 1897; Abraham Galante, *Histoire des juifs de Turquie* (1940; repr. Isis: Istanbul, 1985–1986), 3:171, 216. Others suggested that anti-Jewish feelings grew in Greece after the war: Jacobs, "The Jews of Europe," 26; *Embros*, May 5, 1897, 3; "Los djidios en Larisa," *El Avenir*, August 3, 1898, 6.

164. Mustafa Aksakal, "Holy War Made in Germany? Ottoman Origins of the 1914 Jihad," *War in History* 18, no. 2 (2011): 199.

Chapter 4

1. For other studies exploring intra-Jewish conflicts in the post-revolutionary era: Michelle Campos, *Ottoman Brothers: Muslims, Christians, and Jews in Early Twentieth-Century Palestine* (Stanford, CA: Stanford University Press, 2010); Abigail Jacobson, *From Empire to*

Empire: Jerusalem Between Ottoman and British Rule (Syracuse, NY: Syracuse University Press, 2011); Paris Papamichos Chronakis, "Middle-Class Sociability as Ethnic Hegemony: Jewish and Greek Merchants from the Ottoman Empire to the Greek Nation-State, 1880–1922," paper presented at the workshop "Crossing Borders: New Approaches to Modern Judeo-Spanish (Sephardic) Cultures," UCLA, April 2011; Papamichos Chronakis, "Class and Ethnic Conflict among the Merchants of Young Turk Salonica, 1908–1912," paper presented at the workshop "Ottomans/Turks in Conflict, 1800–2010: New Approaches," Columbia University, April 2011; Bedross Der Matossian, "Formation of Public Sphere(s) in the Aftermath of the 1908 Revolution among Armenians, Arabs, and Jews," in *L'ivresse de la liberté: La révolution de 1908 dans l'Empire ottoman*, ed. François Georgeon (Louvain: Peeters, 2012), 189–219.

2. Exceptions could be found in the ongoing efforts of "practical Zionists" to settle Jews in Palestine, and in Ottoman Jews' private affiliation with Zionism through their social gatherings and reading habits. For a report on Salonica's Hebraist Kadima Society, whose members were said to read Zionist serials and "sing Zionist songs in full chorus" during meetings: J. Nehama, Salonica, January 9, 1903, Alliance Israélite Universelle (hereafter AIU) Archives, Série Grèce, I.G.3, cited in Aron Rodrigue, *Jews and Muslims: Images of Sephardi and Eastern Jewries in Modern Times* (Seattle: University of Washington Press, 2003), 248–249.

3. *Haim Nahum: A Sephardic Chief Rabbi in Politics, 1892–1923*, ed. Esther Benbassa, trans. Miriam Kochan (Tuscaloosa: University of Alabama Press, 1995); Jacob Landau, "The 'Young Turks' and Zionism: Some Comments," in Landau, *Jews, Arabs, Turks: Selected Essays* (Jerusalem: Magnes Press, 1993), 169–177; Hasan Kayalı, "Jewish Representation in the Ottoman Parliaments," in *Jews of the Ottoman Empire*, ed. Avigdor Levy (Princeton, NJ: Darwin Press, 1994), 514. See also "Osmanlı Musevileri Ne Yapmalıdır," *Yeni İkdam*, 4 Rebiülevvel 1329 (March 5, 1911), 3; "Siyonizm Hakkında-İzmir'den Telegraf," *Yeni İkdam*, 11 Rebiülevvel 1329 (March 12, 1911), 3; "Siyonizm," *Servet-i Fünun* 27 Kanunusani 1326 (February 9, 1911), 284.

4. David Fresco, *Le sionisme* (Istanbul: Imp. Fresco, 1909).

5. "Zionismo i otomanizmo," *La Epoka*, February 13, 1911, 2.

6. Benbassa, *Une diaspora sépharade*; Campos, *Ottoman Brothers*, chapter 6.

7. David Florentin, *Nos devoirs comme Juifs et Ottomans* (Istanbul: M. Gorodichze, 1909); For an English translation of this source, see Julia Phillips Cohen, trans., "'Our Duties as Jews and as Ottomans': An Ottoman Zionist Vision for the Future," in Cohen and Stein, *Sephardi Lives*; D. T., "The Revolution in Turkey and Jewish Activities in Palestine," *The Jewish Review*, no. 7 (May 1911).

8. "El tzionismo delantre el tribunal supremo del puevlo otomano," *El Judio*, May 19, 1911, 1. For the related position of the Armenian Dashnak party, which proposed a federated system of autonomous regions within the empire, see Der Matossian, "Formation of Public Sphere(s)," 199.

9. Florentin, *Nos devoirs*, 8.

10. Florentin, *Nos devoirs*.

11. For one such perspective, see the response of the scribe of Istanbul's chief rabbinate to the 1908 revolution: Minna Rozen, "The Hamidian Era through the Jewish Looking Glass," *Turcica* 27 (2005): 150.

12. Ashkenazim in the Ottoman capital threatened repeatedly to boycott and withdraw from the Jewish communal elections on account of their under-representation: *Jewish Chronicle*, February 24, 1911, March 9 and 31, 1911, 16. On the Ashkenazim as a new interest group during this period: Esther Benbassa, "Zionism and the Politics of Coalitions in the Ottoman Jewish Communities in the Early Twentieth-Century," in *Ottoman and Turkish Jewry: Community and Leadership*, ed. Aron Rodrigue (Bloomington: Indiana University, 1992), 233.

13. For the battles waged between Jewish socialist and middle-class groups for the support of the Jewish lower classes in the post-1908 era, see Papamichos Chronakis, "Class and Ethnic Conflict," 13. For the Jewish socialists of Salonica more broadly, see Paul Dumont, "A Jewish, Socialist and Ottoman Organization: The Worker's Federation of

Thessaloniki," *Socialism and Nationalism in the Ottoman Empire, 1876–1923*, ed. Mete Tunçay and Erik-Jan Zürcher (London: British Academic Press, 1994), 49–76, and subsequent discussion and notes in chapter 4.

14. Yavuz Selim Karakışla, "The 1908 Strike Wave in the Ottoman Empire," *Turkish Studies Association Bulletin* 16, no. 2 (1992): 154.

15. David Farhi, "Yehude Salonika be-Mahpekhat ha-Turkim ha-Tse'irim," *Sefunot* 15 (1981): 135–152.

16. This description of events is largely based upon M. Şükrü Hanioğlu, *A Brief History of the Late Ottoman Empire* (Princeton, NJ: Princeton University Press, 2008), 154–155. On changing press regulation see: İpek Yosmaoğlu, "Chasing the Written Word: Press Censorship in the Ottoman Empire, 1876–1913," *Turkish Studies Association Journal* 27 (2003): 15–49. For an illuminating study of this period in the empire: Nader Sohrabi, *Revolution and Constitutionalism in the Ottoman Empire and Iran* (Cambridge: Cambridge University Press, 2011).

17. Erik-Jan Zürcher, "The Ottoman Conscription System in Theory and Practice, 1844–1918," in *Arming the State: Military Conscription in the Middle East and Central Asia, 1775–1925*, ed. Zürcher (New York: St. Martin's Press, 1999). For a call to delay the implementation of military conscription of non-Muslim Ottoman men, see Shemuel Sa'adi Halevy, "El servisio militar," *La Epoka*, February 23, 1911, 1.

18. See, for example: "La kriza del union i progreso," *El Avenir*, April 24, 1911, 1; "La kriza kontinua," *El Avenir*, April 26, 1911, 1; "Ahmed Riza Bey sovre la kriza," *El Avenir*, April 30, 1911, 1; "La kriz," *El Imparsial*, April 24, 1911, 1; "La grande kriz," *El Imparsial*, April 26, 1911, 1; "La kriz," *El Imparsial*, May 16, 1911, 1; "La kriz djoven turka," *El Imparsial*, June 21, 1911, 2; "La kriza en la union i progreso," *El Judio*, April 25, 1911, 1; "La situasion del kabineto-la kriza se alarga," *El Judio*, May 10, 1911, 1.

19. On the boycotts: Roderic Davison, "The Ottoman Boycott of Austrian Goods in 1908–9 as a Diplomatic Question," in *Nineteenth Century Ottoman Diplomacy and Reforms* (Istanbul: Isis Press, 1999), 281–308; Y. Doğan Çetinkaya, "Muslim Merchants and Working-Class in Action: Nationalism, Social Mobilization and Boycott Movement in the Ottoman Empire 1908–1914" (Ph.D. diss, Leiden, 2010); Campos, *Ottoman Brothers*, chapter 3.

20. Mim Kemâl Öke, "Young Turks, Freemasons, Jews and the Question of Zionism in the Ottoman Empire (1908–1913)," *Studies in Zionism* 7, no. 2 (1986): 209.

21. The contemporary Ladino press reported on the repercussions of these changes in the schools: the German-Jewish-run Hilfsverein school in Salonica was temporarily closed in 1911 when local officials noted that it had breached regulations by bearing a foreign name and employing a headmistress and teacher who were Russian subjects. "Novedades lokales," *La Epoka*, February 2, 1911, 1. Measures taken to have the school reopened included changing its name to *Talmud Torah* and employing Ottoman nationals as teachers. "Novedades lokales," *La Epoka*, February 3, 1911, 1. On the effect of the laws against nationalist societies on Jewish schools: AIU Archives, Série Grèce IC 1–52, January 27, 1910.

22. On these debates, see the Ottoman parliamentary proceedings: *Meclis-i Mebusan Zabıt Cerideleri*, 1327; "À la Chambre," *La Turquie*, March 2, 1911; AIU Archives, Turquie I. G 1a. 11, Letter of A. Brunswick to Paris, March 3, 1911; "Chambre des députés: une séance caractèristique," *Stamboul*, March 9, 1911; *Jewish Chronicle*, March 10, 1911, 2, 25; March 17, 1911, 28; "El tzionismo es un preteksto," *El Avenir*, May 21, 1911, 1; *Archives israélites*, June 1, 1911, 171, "Brief aus Konstantinopel: Nach der Kammerdebatte," *Die Welt*, June 6, 1911, 516; Fishman, "Understanding the 1911 Ottoman Parliament Debate," and notes below.

23. Moïse Kohen (later Tekinalp), diary entry, March 12, 1911, in Rıfat Bali, *Bir Günah Keçisi: Munis Tekinalp* (Istanbul: Libra, 2012), 2:45.

24. Özgür Turesay, "Antisionisme et antisémitisme dans la presse ottomane d'Istanbul à l'époque Jeune Turque (1909–1912): L'exemple d'Ebüzziya Tevfik," *Turcica* 41 (2009): 147–178. For other claims of Ottoman antisemitism: "L'antisemitisme à la chambre turque," *Le Siècle*, March 6, 1911.

25. Öke, "Young Turks," 204–205.

26. Elie Kedourie, "Young Turks, Freemasons and Jews," *Middle Eastern Studies* 7, no. 1 (January 1971): 89–104; Öke, "Young Turks," 199–218; M. Şükrü Hanioğlu, "Jews in the Young Turk Movement to the 1908 Revolution," in Avigdor Levy, ed., *The Jews of the Ottoman Empire* (Princeton, NJ: Darwin Press, 1994), 519.

27. Hanioğlu, "Jews in the Young Turk Movement," 519.

28. "El tzionismo delantre el tribunal supremo del puevlo otomano," *El Judio*, May 19, 1911, 1.

29. See, for example, "Filistin'de Siyonistler," *Servet-i Fünun* 15 Mart 1327, 470; "Les Sionistes et l'emprunt," *Le Moniteur oriental*, March 2, 1911, 2.

30. "Siyasiyat: Siyonizm," *Tanin*, 3 Rebiülevvel 1329 (March 4, 1911), 1; "L'Epouvantail du Sionisme," *Le Jeune-Turc*, March 5, 1911, 1.

31. Öke, "Young Turks," 213. Mehmed Cavid's position was further complicated by the fact that he hailed from a Dönme family whose ancestors had converted from Judaism to Islam in the seventeenth century and who, by the early twentieth century, increasingly faced racialist claims of biological Jewishness: Marc Baer, *The Dönme: Jewish Converts, Muslim Revolutionaries, and Secular Turks* (Stanford, CA: Stanford University Press, 2009).

32. For the parliamentary debate in which Hakkı Pasha made this pronouncement: "Meclis-i Mebusan Üçüncü Devre-i İçtimaiyye, Kırkdokuzuncu İctima-i Umumi," *Yeni İkdam*, 2 Rebiülevvel 1329 (March 2, 1911), 4; "Les Sionistes et l'emprunt," *Le Moniteur oriental*, March 2, 1911, 2; "À la Chambre," *La Turquie*, March 2, 1911. For the English quote provided here, see Kayalı, "Jewish Representation in the Ottoman Parliaments," in *The Jews of the Ottoman Empire*, ed. Avigdor Levy, 513.

33. See *Jewish Chronicle*, March 10, 1911, 25.

34. See also "Les Sionistes et l'emprunt," *Le Moniteur oriental*, March 2, 1911, 2; "Siyonizm," *Yeni İkdam*, 6 Rebiülevvel 1329 (March 6, 1911) 1; "Le Sionisme," *Stamboul*, March 18, 1911.

35. For this estimate: PRO FO 195/54, Salonica, June 11, 1911. For a contemporary paean to Salonica's role in shaping the new government: "14 Apriliou 1909–25 Maïou 1911," *Nea Alitheia*, May 26, 1911, 1.

36. "Seyahat-i Şahane," *Yeni İkdam*, 19 Rebiülevvel 1329 (March 20, 1911), 1 and 11 Cemazi-yelevvel 1329 (May 10, 1911), 2; "Şuunat," *Yeni İkdam*, 19 Cemaziyelevvel 1329 (May 18, 1911), 1; "Seyahat-i Şahane Tedarikatından," *Tanin*, 17 Cemaziyelevvel 1329 (May 16, 1911), 2; "Seyahat-i Padişahi ve Bulgaristan Müslümanları," *Tanin*, 23 Cemazi-yelevvel 1329 (May 22, 1911), 2; *Şehbal*, 41 15 Temmuz 1327 (July 28, 1911), 336; "Eis Proÿpantesin Tes A.M. Tou Soultanou Exo Tou Thermaïkou—Tou Apestalmenou Syn-taktou Mas," *Nea Alitheia*, May 27, 1911, 1; "El viaje imperial," *El Avenir*, June 5, 1911, 2; "Seyahat-i Padişahi," *Beyan-ül Hak*, 7 Cemaziyelahir 1329 (June 5, 1911), 2070; "Novedades del interior," *El Tiempo*, June 1, 1911, 4; "En Salonika: los aparejos por la resepsion del sultan," *El Tiempo*, June 5, 1911, 3–4; "El viaje del sultan," *El Judio*, June 12, 1911, 2; "El sultan en Makedonia-Albania," *El Judio*, June 14, 1911, 1; "El viaje del sultan," *El Tiempo*, June 14, 1911, 7; "El viaje del sultan," *El Judio*, June 16, 1911, 2; "El viaje del sultan en la yanura de Kosova," *El Judio*, June 19, 1911, 1; "El viaje del sultan," June 21, 1911, 2; "El retorno del sultan," June 28, 1911, 2; "El retorno de su maestad," *El Tiempo*, June 28, 1911, 7.

37. Erik-Jan Zürcher, "Kosovo Revisited: Sultan Reşad's Macedonian Journey of 1911," *Middle Eastern Studies* 35, no. 4 (October 1999): 26–39.

38. For official perceptions of the tour. ibid., Mevlüt Çelebi, *Sultan Reşad'ın Rumeli Seyahati* (Izmir: Akademi Kitabevi, 1999); Nadide Özge Serin, "Festivals of 'July 10' in the Young Turk Era (1908–1918)" (master's thesis, Boğaziçi University, 2000), 52–64; Lütfi Simavi, *Son Osmanlı Sarayında Gördüklerim: Sultan Mehmed Reşad Hanın ve Halifenin Sarayında Gördüklerim* (Istanbul: Örgün Yayınevi, [1924] 2004), 141–156.

39. Local officials announced a predetermined program for the sultan's visit: "Proklamasion de S' E' el governador djeneral," *El Avenir*, June 5, 1911, 2. For another example of the scripts onlookers were meant to follow: "Las eskolas al arivo del sultan," *El Imparsial*, June 6, 1911, 1.

40. On the competition the sultan's tour elicited among those attempting to gain imperial favor see "Seyahat-i Şahane: Muhabir-i Mahsusanın telegrafnamesi," *Yeni İkdam*, 10 Cemaziyelevvel 1329 (June 8, 1911), 2; "Yeni Musevi Kulübü'nün inşa ettirdiği tak," *Şehbal*, June 1911, 335; "To Taxidion Toy Anaktos," *Nea Alitheia*, May 25, 1911, 2.

41. "To Taxeidion Tou Anaktos," *Nea Alitheia*, May 25, 1911, 2.

42. News of the tour appeared for many months before the sultan set sail: "El sultan en Saloniko," *La Epoka*, February 23, 1911, 1; and the articles entitled "Seyahat-i Hümayun" and "Seyahat-i Şahane" in *Yeni İkdam*, 1 Rebiülevvel 1329 (March 2, 1911), 1; 2 Rebiülevvel 1329 (March 3, 1911), 1; 3 Rebiülevvel 1329 (March 4, 1911), 2; 5 Rebiülevvel 1329 (March 6, 1911), 1; 6 Rebiülevvel 1329 (March 6, 1911), 2; 8 Rebiülevvel 1329 (March 8, 1911), 2; 10 Rebiülevvel 1329 (March 11, 1911), 1; 15 Rebiülevvel 1329 (March 16, 1911), 1; 17 Rebiülevvel 1329 (March 18, 1911), 1; 4 Cemaziyelevvel 1329 (May 3, 1911). Members of the Salonica branch of the CUP also asked for the sultan's schedule well in advance: BOA DH. MTV 25/16 4 Cemaziyelevvel 1329 (May 3, 1911).

43. "Seyahat-i Hümayun," *Yeni İkdam*, 27 Cemaziyelevvel 1329 (May 26, 1911); "Seyahat-i Şahane," *Yeni İkdam*, 28 Cemaziyelevvel 1329 (May 27, 1911), 2; "Seyahat-i Padişahi," *Tanin*, 27 Rebiülevvel 1329 (May 28, 1911), 3. On the urban works the visit occasioned: "Le voyage du Sultan," *Le Moniteur oriental*, March 2, 1911, 2 "Seyahat-i Şahane," *Tanin*, 30 Rebiülevvel 1329 (March 31, 1911), 3; *Tanin*, 17 Cemaziyelevvel 1329 (May 16, 1911), 2; "Seyahat-i Şahane," *Tanin*, 5 Cemaziyelahir 1329 (June 3, 1911), 1; Meropi Anastassiadou, *Salonique, 1830–1912: Une ville ottomane à l'âge des Réformes* (New York: Brill, 1997), 415; MAE-Nantes 66/36 Consul of Salonica to Embassy in Constantinople, March 30, 1911.

44. Çelebi, *Sultan Reşad'ın Rumeli Seyahati*, 25.

45. "El viaje de su maestad el sultan en Makedonia," *La Nasion*, May 26, 1911, 2. See also "Seyahat-i Şahane Tedarikatından," *Tanin*, 9 Cemaziyelevvel 1329 (May 8, 1911).

46. This number is derived from a map of the arches provided by Sam Lévy, *Souvenir du voyage* (Salonica: 1911) and "Los arkos de triunfo," *La Epoka*, June 9, 1911, 2. The contemporary Ottoman Jewish press advertised Lévy's album, claiming that some 1,000 were being printed. *La Tribuna Libera*, June 23, 1911, 5; "Un album," *El Avenir*, June 21, 1911, 3; *La Buena Esperansa*, June 30, 1911, 1.

47. "El viaje imperial," *El Avenir*, June 5, 1911, 2; "The Sultan at Salonica: Jewish Celebrations," *Jewish Chronicle*, June 30, 1911, 8.

48. *La Buena Esperansa*, June 1, 1911, 1. Those who came to see the sultan before he departed the imperial capital were similarly instructed to wear a frock coat and tie: "Seyahat-i Hazret-i Padişahi Teşyi Merasimi," *Yeni İkdam*, 3 Cemaziyelahir 1329 (June 1, 1911), 2.

49. "S. M. el sultan en Saloniko," *El Avenir*, June 8, 1911, 1; "The Sultan at Salonica: Jewish Celebrations," *Jewish Chronicle*, June 30, 1911, 8. *El Avenir*'s report suggested that the boat rented out to the public had been engaged by a group of Muslim women.

50. AIU Archives, Série Grèce IG 3, June 28, 1911; Rena Molho, *Salonica and Istanbul*, 173–174.

51. Esther Benbassa, "Des Sionistes sans Sionisme," *Cahiers d'études sur le Méditerranée orientale et le monde turco-iranien* 28 (June–December 1999): 19–30; Benbassa, "Associational Strategies in Ottoman Jewish Society in the Nineteenth and Twentieth Centuries," in Levy, *The Jews of the Ottoman Empire*, 457–484; Benbassa, *Une diaspora sépharade en transition: Istanbul, XIXe-XXe siècle* (Paris: Cerf, 1993); Benbassa and Rodrigue, *Sephardi Jewry*; Rena Molho, *Salonica and Istanbul: Social, Political and Cultural Aspects of Jewish Life* (Istanbul: Isis, 2005); Minna Rozen, *The Last Ottoman Century and Beyond: The Jews in Turkey and the Balkans 1808–1945*, vol. 1 (Tel Aviv: Tel Aviv University, 2005); Devin Naar, "Jewish Salonica and the Making of the 'Jerusalem of the Balkans,' 1890–1943" (Ph.D. diss., Stanford University, 2011); Olga Borovaya, "Jews of Three Colors: The Path to Modernity in the Pages of the Ladino Press at the Turn of the Twentieth Century," *Jewish Social Studies* 15, no. 1 (Fall 2008): 110–130; Borovaya, *Modern Ladino Culture*.

52. "Basho las maskaras," *El Imparsial*, June 13, 1911, 2, refers to the events surrounding the denunciation as "*el fato Epstein*." Not surprisingly, the official publication of the Club

des Intimes referred to the club's alleged denunciation of Epstein merely as a "curious legend." "Asamblea djenerala," *La Nasion*, June 23, 1911, 5.

53. "A Turkish Official's Rebuke to an Anti-Zionist," *Jewish Chronicle*, January 13, 1911, 11; "Un akto de alta traizon," *El Judio*, 20 Tevet 5671 (January 20, 1911), 1; *La Epoka*, February 3, 1911; M. I. Cohen, "À Messieurs de la 'Nacion,'" *L'Aurore*, February 14, 1911, 1; "La vérité se fera," *L'Aurore*, February 14, 1911, 2; "A Turkish Official's Rebuke to an Anti-Zionist: A Denial," *Jewish Chronicle*, March 3, 1911, 30.

54. For more on the ways that middle-class values shaped Ottoman Jews' patriotism, see chapter 3. For a discussion of efforts to instill bourgeois values and consumption patterns among Ottoman Jews more generally, see Sarah Abrevaya Stein, *Making Jews Modern: The Yiddish and Ladino Press in the Russian and Ottoman Empires* (Bloomington: Indiana University Press, 2004).

55. "Abasho las maskas-dignita i koreksion," *El Imparsial*, June 14, 1911, 2.

56. Haim Bejerano, then chief rabbi of the Jewish community of Edirne, reportedly pronounced an entire speech on the occasion of the visit, exclusively dedicated to the need for "union and harmony" (*"union i konkordia"*). "En sivdad," *El Imparsial*, June 8, 1911, 2.

57. In 1909, the Club des Intimes had built an Arc de Triomphe in honor of the first anniversary of the revolution: Anastassiadou, *Salonique, 1830–1912*, 371. For an image of this arch: Michael Molho, *Traditions and Customs of the Sephardic Jews of Salonica*, ed. Robert Bedford, trans. Alfred A. Zara (1944/50; repr., New York: Foundation for the Advancement of Sephardic Studies and Culture, 2006).

58. Lévy, *Souvenir du voyage*, n.p. Unless otherwise noted, translations of the album are drawn from: Yannis Megas, *Souvenir: Images of the Jewish Community: Salonica 1897–1917* (Athens: Kapon editions, 1993), 172. For more on Sam Lévy see his memoir, *Salonique à la fin du XIXe siècle* and also Olga Borovaya, "Shmuel Saadi Halévy/Sam Lévy Between Ladino and French: Reconstructing a Writer's Social Identity in a Polyglossic Situation," in *Modern Jewish Literatures: Intersections and Boundaries*, ed. Sheila Jelen, Michael Kramer, and L. Scott Lerner (Philadelphia: University of Pennsylvania Press, 2010), 83–103; Borovaya, *Modern Ladino Culture*; Hélène Guillon, "Les ambitions d'un jeune journaliste séfarade: les *Carnets intimes* de Sam Lévy (1894), futur rédacteur en chef du *Journal de Salonique* (1895–1911)," *Yod: Revue des études hébraïques et juives* no. 11/12 (2006–2007): 271–287; Guillon, *Le Journal de Salonique: Un périodique juif dans l'Empire ottoman (1895–1911)* (Paris: Presses de l'Université Paris-Sorbonne, 2013). On the album see "El album prezentado al sultan," *La Epoka*, June 19, 1911, 1.

59. See, for example, his excoriating attack on those who targeted the Club des Intimes earlier in the year amidst the Epstein Affair; *La Epoka*, February 3, 1911.

60. Electricity, telephones, and electric tramways were all introduced into the city in 1908. See: Basil C. Gounaris, "Salonica," *Review (Ferdand Braudel Center)* 16, no. 4 (Fall 1993): 500.

61. "Priştine İttihad ve Terakki Kulubü Heyet-i İdaresi," *Tanin*, 1 Rebiülevvel 1329 (March 2, 1911), 1; "Seyahat-i Şahane," *Yeni İkdam*, 2 Rebiülevvel 1329 (March 3, 1911), 1. It is also reminiscent of the star with rays of light found on the gate of the Galatasaray Lycée in Istanbul: Carter Findley, *Ottoman Civil Officialdom* (Princeton, NJ: Princeton University Press, 1989), 156, reproduced from Sultan Abdülhamid II's Photograph Collection preserved at the Library of Congress.

62. Employing a different technology to patriotic ends, the Club des Intimes also reportedly projected "cinematographic images of Ottoman patriots" on its rooftop on a nightly basis during the sultan's visit. *La Tribuna Libera*, April [June?] 8, 1911, 6.

63. "Las iluminasiones," *El Imparsial*, June 8, 1911, 1; "El viaje del sultan," *El Judio*, June 9, 1911, 2. See also "Seyahat-i Şahane: Muhabir-i Mahsusanın telegrafnamesi," *Yeni İkdam*, 10 Cemaziyelevvel 1329 (June 8, 1911), 2, which wrote of the lights that made the night "seem like day" (*gündüz gibidir*).

64. "Fiesta grandioza al nuevo klub," *El Imparsial*, June 10, 1911, 2; "Al nuevo klub," *El Avenir*, June 12, 1911, 2; "Fiesta grandioza en onor dela flota enel nuevo klub de Saloniko," *El Judio*, June 16, 1911, 2; "Brief aus Saloniki," *Die Welt*, June 23, 1911, 586; *Archives*

israélites, June 29, 1911, 203; "The Sultan at Salonica," *Jewish Chronicle*, June 30, 1911, 8; *L'Univers israélite*, June 30, 1911, 503.

65. "Fiesta grandioza al nuevo klub," *El Imparsial*, June 10, 1911, 2.

66. "El nuevo klub," *El Avenir*, June 12, 1911, 2; "Onor alos djidios," *El Imparsial*, June 10, 1911, 2. On the grand vizier's rejection of Jewish influence over the government: Hasan Kayalı, "Jewish Representation in the Ottoman Parliaments," in Levy, *The Jews of the Ottoman Empire*, 513.

67. "Golpe de shena," *El Imparsial*, June 10, 1911, 2.

68. That the different Jewish groups involved were engaged in a competition, however subtle, permeated contemporary commentaries on the festivities. One paper lamented the fact the Jewish community had not managed to offer the best arch, suggesting that its "magisterial form . . . would have surely surpassed all the rest had it only been illuminated with electric lights." "S. M. el sultan en Saloniko," *El Avenir*, June 8, 1911, 1. See also "El nuevo klub," *El Avenir*, June 12, 1911, 2.

69. Meir's choice of Arabic may have been strategic in another sense as well since, according to more than one source, while he knew Arabic well, he did not know Turkish. "Sovre el tzionismo," *La Epoka*, January 18, 1911, 2; *Zikhron Saloniki*, 1: 198.

70. "En sivdad," *El Imparsial*, June 19, 1911, 2; "Una fiesta briante," *El Imparsial*, June 20, 1911, 2; "Novedades lokales," *La Epoka*, June 20, 1911, 1; "El gran vizir al nuevo klub," *El Avenir*, June 21, 1911, 1–2; "El viaje del sultan," *El Judio*, June 21, 1911, 2; "Brief aus Konstantinopel: Von der Sultanreise," *Die Welt*, July 7, 1911, 641; "Brief aus Saloniki," *Die Welt*, July 14, 1911, 667.

71. Megas, *Souvenir*, 81–83; Donald Quataert, "Premières fumes d'usines," in *Salonique 1850–1918: La "ville des Juifs" et le réveil des Balkans*, ed. Gilles Veinstein (Paris: Autrement, 1993), 191.

72. Ad. Beaune, "Les Arcs de Triomphe," in Lévy, *Souvenir du voyage*, 21; Megas, *Souvenir*, 173.

73. "The Sultan at Salonica: Jewish Celebrations," *Jewish Chronicle*, June 30, 1911, 8. The Jewish community of Monastir also placed Jewish ceremonial objects on the arch it erected during the sultan's visit to that city: Mark Cohen, *Last Century of a Sephardic Community: The Jews of Monastir, 1839–1943* (New York: Foundation for the Advancement of Sephardic Studies and Culture, 2003), 115–116; Esther Juhasz, *Sephardi Jews in the Ottoman Empire: Aspects of Material Culture* (Jerusalem: Israel Museum, 1990).

74. Beaune, "Les Arcs de Triomphe," 22.

75. "Arc de triomphe élevé par le Nouveau Club," in Lévy, *Souvenir du voyage*, 41.

76. For a related argument, see the incisive analysis offered in Papamichos Chronakis, "Middle-Class Sociality," 11–14, which suggests that the Jewish merchants of late Ottoman Salonica ultimately reinforced their own hegemony by announcing their investment in supra-communal cooperation in their city.

77. Beaune, "Les Arcs de Triomphe," 23. The translation here is mine.

78. For a contemporary reference to the mosque's location in the heavily Jewish quarter of Salonica: "The Sultan at Salonica: Jewish Celebrations," *Jewish Chronicle*, June 30, 1911, 9.

79. "El sultan en Makedonia-Albania," *El Judio*, June 14, 1911, 1.

80. Mark Mazower, *Salonica, City of Ghosts: Christians, Muslims, Jews* (New York: Vintage Books, 2006), 249–251.

81. "Novedades lokales," *La Epoka*, June 6, 1911, 1.

82. "Turkia i Montenegro," *El Imparsial*, May 31, 1911, 1; "Informasiones," *El Imparsial*, June 10, 1911, 1; "Informasiones," *El Imparsial*, June 20, 1911, 1.

83. "Fin dela revolta en Albania," *El Imparsial*, June 16, 1911, 1.

84. "En Saloniko," *El Avenir*, June 12, 1911, 3; "Abasho las maskaras," *El Imparsial*, June 13, 1911, 2.

85. "En sivdad," *El Imparsial*, June 5, 1911, 2. On the Monastir arch that burned, see also Zürcher, "Kosovo Revisited," 35.

86. "En kavso de insendio," *El Imparsial*, May 29, 1911, 1.

87. Suggesting that he was not beyond coercion, Salonica's chief rabbi Jacob Meir announced in a private note to the chief rabbi of neighboring Kavalla that attendance of the ceremony was not optional: Letter of the Salonican Chief Rabbi Meir to Chief Rabbi Abraham Molho of Kavalla, 3 Sivan 5671 (May 30, 1911), Central Archives for the History of the Jewish People (CAHJP) Gr/Kav 1. I am grateful to Devin Naar for bringing this correspondence to my attention.

88. *La Tribuna Libera*, May 21, 1911, 2.

89. *Archivo Central del Ministerio de Asuntos Exteriores* (AMAE), Madrid, H-2042, "Correspondencia con el consulado de Salónica, 1850–1932," June 21, 1911.

90. "Proklamasion de S' E' el governador djeneral," *El Avenir*, June 5, 1911, 2.

91. "Las manifestasiones de anoche," *El Avenir*, June 9, 1911, 1.

92. *La Tribuna Libera*, April 8, [June?] 1911, 3.

93. For concerns about a possible attempt on the sultan's life: Iakovos J. Aktsoglou, "The Emergence/Development of Social and Working Class Movement [*sic*] in the City of Thessaloniki," *Balkan Studies* 38, no. 2 (1997): 300. On the Federation, see Joshua Starr, "The Socialist Federation of Saloniki," *Jewish Social Studies* 7 (1945): 323–336.

94. On Benaroya's arrest and exile: BOA DH. SYS. 65/7–28, 9 Haziran 1327 (June 22, 1911); BOA DH. SYS. 65/7–23, 20 Temmuz 1327 (August 2, 1911); BOA DH. SYS. 65/7–22, 30 Temmuz 1327 (August 12, 1911); "En ke rejim bivimos?" *El Imparsial*, June 10, 1911, 1; "En Saloniko,"*El Avenir*, June 12, 1911, 3, *Osmanlı Imparatorluğunda Sosyalist Hareketler*, ed. Georges Haupt and Paul Dumont (Istanbul: Gözlem Yayınları, 1977), 116, 306; H. Şükrü Ilıcak, "Jewish Socialism in Ottoman Salonica," *Southeast European and Black Sea Studies* 2, no. 3 (September 2002): 139; and notes from the socialist Ladino organ, *La Solidaridad Ovradera*, below; Abraham Benaroya, "A Note on 'The Socialist Federation of Saloniki,'" *Jewish Social Studies* 11 (1949): 70. Emre Polat, *Osmanlı'nın İlk Yahudi Sosyalisti Avram Benaroya ve Faaliyetleri* (Istanbul: Truva Yayınları, 2004).

95. BOA DH. SYS. 65/7–28, 9 Haziran 1327 (June 22, 1911).

96. "Aktos arbitrarios," *La Solidaridad Ovradera*, June 9, 1911, 1.

97. "Arestasion non djustifikada," *La Solidaridad Ovradera*, June 9, 1911, 2.

98. In fact, they had named names, suggesting that the Club's secretary, Pepo Saul Modiano, an influential merchant in the city and head of Salonica's Jewish communal council, had denounced Epstein; *Jewish Chronicle*, March 3, 1911, 30.

99. "Abasho las maskaras," *El Imparsial*, June 13, 1911, 2.

100. One writer described their silence in the face of the accusations by suggesting that the club's members "did not descend from the heights of their three-storied building, nor did they depart from their habitual reserve." "Abasho las maskaras," *El Imparsial*, June 13, 1911, 2. The one exception to the official silence of the Club des Intimes during the period was its brief response issued in the Ladino paper of a sympathetic colleague. Even in this case, however, the club did not directly address the accusations that its members had been behind the denunciations: *La Epoka*, June 12, 1911, 1.

101. "Asamblea djenerala del serkle dezentimes," *La Nasion*, June 23, 1911, 2.

102. "Alos sophistas," *El Imparsial*, June 16, 1911, 1.

103. "El serkle delos intimos i la prensa tzionista," *El Tiempo*, June 14, 1911, 3–4. The original Ladino reads refers to the club as a *sentro de luz i de progreso*. See also "Mos eksplikamos," *El Imparsial*, June 20, 1911, 1; "Entre antisionistes," *L'Aurore*, June 27, 1911, 1.

104. The federation did indeed oppose Zionism. Among its critiques of the Jewish nationalist movement were the federation's position that it was a utopia that served as an opiate of the working classes and divided Jewish and non-Jewish workers: Sosialista, "El tzionizmo en Turkia," *La Solidaridad Ovradera*, May 26, 1911, 2.

105. "Mos eksplikamos," *El Imparsial*, June 20, 1911, 1.

106. See, for example: "El viaje del sultan," *El Judio*, June 12, 1911, 2.

107. "Inkreivle," *El Imparsial*, June 18, 1911, 1.

108. "Asamblea djenerala," *La Nasion*, June 23, 1911, 1.

109. Ibid., 2. The speaker also suggested that the opponents of his club "yell and shout and make all kinds of noise," a characterization that was echoed by another Ottoman Jewish liberal of the period, who claimed that Zionists mistook "noise for success," and

described Zionism as a movement of those who "act and shout." Rodrigue, *Jews and Muslims*, 251.

110. "Asamblea djenerala," *La Nasion*, June 23, 1911, 7.

111. Ibid., 2.

112. Ibid., 3.

113. Ibid., 4. The original Ladino reads: "*Responditesh ke no kieresh padishah.*"

114. BOA DH. SYS. 65/7–28, 9 Haziran 1327 (June 22, 1911).

115. HHStA PA VIII/Konsulat Thessaloniki, 414, no. 91, June 12, 1911. The private correspondence of Joseph Nehama, an Alliance schoolteacher and local intellectual, also describes the Club's tactics of denunciations of its political enemies to the authorities. See AIU Archives, Série Grèce IG 3, June 28, 1911.

116. S. Nahum, "Autour de Benaroya," *La Solidaridad Ovradera*, September 22, 1911, 1; Aktsoglou, "The Emergence/Development," 300–301.

117. BOA DH. SYS. 65/7–23, 20 Temmuz 1327 (August 2, 1911).

118. *Bureau socialiste international* 2, no. 7 (1911): 12.

119. AIU Archives, Série Grèce IG 3, Joseph Nehama to Paris, June 28, 1911.

120. "A propozito delas arestasiones," *La Solidaridad Ovradera*, June 16, 1911, 1.

121. "Politika de persekusion," *La Solidaridad Ovradera*, June 18, 1911, 1. The author of the article cited the cases of "Bismarck in Germany and Stambulov in Bulgaria" as proof of his argument.

122. *Bureau socialiste international* 2, no. 7 (1911): 12.

123. BOA DH. SYS. 65/7–9, 11 Şubat 1327 (February 24, 1911).

124. BOA DH. SYS. 65/7–22, 30 Temmuz 1327 (August 12, 1911).

125. S. Nahum, "Autour de Benaroya," *La Solidaridad Ovradera*, September 22, 1911, 1.

126. "Un procheso," *La Solidaridad Ovradera*, June 25, 1911, 1.

127. "Elevos del talmud torah al union i progreso," *El Avenir*, April 28, 1911, 3.

128. *Archives israélites*, June 29, 1911, 203; "Brief aus Saloniki" *Die Welt*, June 14, 1911, 667.

129. Florentin, *Nos devoirs comme Juifs et Ottomans*, 7.

130. The Club des Intimes's members were used to counting important Ottoman officials among their guests. On earlier visits by prominent Ottoman Muslims to the club: "Liga de otomanizasion," *La Epoka*, January 22, 1911, 2; "Por los djudios," *La Epoka*, January 30, 1911, 1.

131. Malte Fuhrmann, "Cosmopolitan Imperialists and the Ottoman Port Cities: Conflicting Logics in the Urban Social Fabric," *Cahiers de la Méditerranée* 67 (2003), cdlm. revues.org/document128.html, makes this point by focusing on the life-worlds of three different German-speaking "imperialists" resident in eastern Mediterranean Ottoman port cities. Fuhrmann shows quite persuasively that the politics of any of the given figures offered no clear formula for the way he ended up configuring his social life, and vice versa. İlber Ortaylı, "Ottomanism and Zionism During the Second Constitutional Period, 1908–1915," in Levy, *The Jews of the Ottoman Empire*, 534, offers another example of an Ottoman public figure (Ali Kemal) whose publication, *İkdam ve Peyam* was "considered an anti-Semitic publication," though Kemal himself "was apparently not so personally."

Conclusion

1. Naim Güleryüz, "Symbol of Turkish-Jewish Amity: The Zulfaris Synagogue," www. turkishjews.com/synagogues/zulfaris.asp.

2. I borrow this phrase from Margaret Anderson, "'Down in Turkey, Far Away:' Human Rights, the Armenian Massacres, and Orientalism in Wilhemine Germany," *Journal of Modern History* 79, no. 1 (March 2007): 110.

3. Christine Philliou, *Biography of an Empire: Governing Ottomans in an Age of Revolution* (Berkeley: University of California Press, 2010).

4. Carter Findley, *Ottoman Civil Officialdom: A Social History* (Princeton, NJ: Princeton University Press, 1989), 96; Ronald Grigor Suny, *Looking Towards Ararat: Armenia in Modern History* (Bloomington: Indiana University Press, 1993), 101. New work on the

subject explores Armenian ties to the Ottoman state in a new light. See Elke Hartmann, "The 'Loyal Nation' and its Deputies," in *The First Ottoman Parliament: Perception, Significance and Prosopography*, ed. Christoph Herzog and Malek Sharif (Würzburg: Ergon, 2010); Bedross Der Matossian, "Ethnic Politics in the Post-Revolutionary Ottoman Empire: Armenians, Arabs, and Jews in the Second Constitutional Period (1908–1909)" (Ph.D. diss., Columbia University, 2008).

5. Laurent-Olivier Mallet, *La Turquie, les turcs et les juifs: Histoire, représentations, discours et stratégies* (Istanbul: Isis, 2008), 7–8. On the recent uses of the Turkish-Jewish friendship narrative, see also: Rıfat Bali, *Model Citizens of the State: the Jews of Turkey during the Multi-Party Period* (Lanham, MD: Fairleigh Dickinson University Press, 2012); Marcy Brink-Danan, *Jewish Life in Twenty-First Century Turkey: The Other Side of Tolerance* (Bloomington: Indiana University Press, 2012).

6. Rıfat Bali, *Bir Türkleştirme Serüveni 1923–1945* (Istanbul: İletişim, 2000); Bali, *Musa'nın Evlatları Cumhuriyet'in Yurttaşları* (Istanbul: İletişim, 2001); Bali, *Les relations entre Turcs et Juifs dans la Turquie moderne* (Istanbul: Isis, 2001); Bali, *Cumhuriyet Yıllarında Türkiye Yahudileri Aliya* (Istanbul: İletişim, 2003); Bali, *Devlet'in Yahudileri ve "Öteki" Yahudi* (Istanbul: İletişim, 2004); Bali, *Model Citizens*; Brink-Danan, *Jewish Life*.

7. Marcy Brink-Danan, "Reference Points: Text, Context and Change in Definitions of Turkish-Jewish Identity" (Ph.D. diss., Stanford University, 2005), 150. A list of some of the publications printed by the foundation can be found in Mallet, *La Turquie, les turcs et les juifs*, 582–583.

8. "Le centenaire des israélites espagnols," *Stamboul*, August 4, 1891, 2.

9. For the Ladino statement, see "Lo ke aze la Evropa y lo ke deve azer," *La Epoka*, November 12, 1877, 2. In the original, the quotation reads "*la media luna bivira siempre y non morira.*" For the empire as eternally lasting, see Christoph Neumann, "Bad Times and Better Self: Definitions of Identity and Stategies for Development in Late Ottoman Historiography (1850–1900)," in *The Ottomans and the Balkans: A Discussion of Historiography*, ed. Fikret Adanir and Suraiya Faroqhi (Leiden: Brill, 2002), 60.

10. Aron Rodrigue, *Jews and Muslims: Images of Sephardi and Eastern Jewries in Modern Times* (Seattle: University of Washington Press, 2003), 236–237; Abraham Galante, *Histoire des juifs de Turquie* (1940; repr., Isis: Istanbul, 1985–1986), 1: 19.

11. From K. E. Fleming, "Becoming Greek: The Jews of Salonica, 1912–1917," paper presented at the International Conference on Religion, Identity, and Empire, Whitney Humanities Center, Yale University, April 16–17, 2005, and cited in Devin Naar, "From the 'Jerusalem of the Balkans' to the *Goldene Medina*: Jewish Immigration from Salonika to the United States," *American Jewish History* 93, no. 4 (2007): 435–473. Once Ottoman defeat became certain, Salonican Jews united to ask the Great Powers for diplomatic intervention in order to bring the city under international jurisdiction: N. M. Gelber, "An Attempt to Internationalize Salonika, 1912–1913," *Jewish Social Studies* 17 (1955): 105–120.

12. Mark Mazower, *Salonica, City of Ghosts* (New York: Vintage, 2006), 283; *Nea Alitheia*, March 18, 1915, 2; Thanks are due to Paris Papamichos Chronakis for the second reference.

13. Central Archives for the History of the Jewish People (CAHJP) Tr HM2/9072, Yomtov Baruch to the Istanbul Chief Rabbinite, August 25, 1914; Galante, *Histoire des juifs de Turquie*, 2: 121.

14. On these migrations, and the émigré communities they spurred: Marc D. Angel, *La America: The Sephardic Experience in the United States* (Philadelphia: Jewish Publication Society of America, 1982); Joseph M. Papo, *Sephardim in Twentieth Century America: In Search of Unity* (San Jose, CA: Pelé Yoetz Books, 1987); Corry Guttstadt, *Die Türkei, die Juden und der Holocaust* (Berlin: Assoziation A, 2008); Aviva Ben-Ur, *Sephardic Jews in America: A Diasporic History* (New York: New York University Press, 2009); Naar, "From the 'Jerusalem of the Balkans;'" *Contemporary Sephardic Identity in the Americas: An Interdisciplinary Approach*, ed. Margalit Bejarano and Edna Aizenberg (Syracuse, NY: Syracuse University Press, 2012); Devi Mays, "Transplanting Cosmopolitans: The Migrations of Sephardic Jews to Mexico, 1900–1934" (Ph.D. diss., Indiana University, 2013).

15. For accounts of Jews who emigrated to flee conscription, see Joseph Nehama, "The Jews of Salonika in the Ottoman Period," in *The Sephardi Heritage: Essays on the Historical and Cultural Contribution of the Jews of Spain and Portugal*, ed. Richard D. Barnett (Grendon: Gibralter Books, 1989), 240; Annie Benveniste, *Le Bosphore à la Roquette: la communauté judéo-espagnole à Paris, 1914–1940* (Paris: L'Hartmattan, 1989), passim; Mays, "Transplanting Cosmopolitans." For Ottoman Jews who praised their coreligionists in fighting units during the period, see "Acts of Bravery by Jewish Soldiers [From our Correspondent] Salonika," *Jewish Chronicle*, November 22, 1912, 15; Abigail Jacobson, *From Empire to Empire: Jerusalem Between Ottoman and British Rule* (Syracuse, NY: Syracuse University Press, 2011), 91; Eyal Ginio, "'Yehudim 'Otmanim! Hushu le-hatsel et moledatenu!': Yehudim 'Otmanim be-Milhemot ha-Balkan (1912–1913)," *Pe'amim* 105–106 (Autumn 2005/Winter 2006): 5–28; Ginio, "*El dovér el mas sànto*: The Mobilization of the Ottoman Jewish Population during the Balkan Wars (1912–1913)," in *Conflicting Loyalties in the Balkans: The Great Powers, the Ottoman Empire and Nation-Building*, ed. Hannes Grandits, Nathalie Clayer, and Robert Pichler (New York: I. B. Tauris, 2011), 157–181.

16. *Le Trait d'Union* was the organ of the Association of the former students of the Alliance Israélite Universelle of Izmir. For the earlier suggestion: *La Epoka*, June 25, 1897, 5.

17. Ginio, "*El dovér*," 170.

18. See, for example, "La gera turko-italiana: viktoria de la Turkia," *La Amerika*, December 22, 1911, 1; "La gera turko-italiana: la Italia roga por el pas," *La Amerika*, December 29, 1911, 1; "La gera turko-italiana," January 12, 1912, 1; "Novedades de la gera," *La Amerika*, April 4, 1913, 1; "Grave situasion en la Makedonia," *La Amerika*, June 27, 1913, 1.

19. "La nueva karta balkanika," *La Amerika*, August 15, 1913, 1.

20. Devin Naar, "Reformuler l'identité, réinventer la patrie: Juifs judéo-hispanophones en Amérique, entre Salonique et *Sefarad*," in *Itinéraires sépharades: Complexité et diversité des identités*, ed. Esther Benbassa (Paris: Presses de l'Université Paris-Sorbonne, 2010), 63–78. Not all Ottoman Jewish émigrés chose to emphasize their Ottomanness. Where continued identification with the Ottoman Empire directly threatened Jews' positions in their new homes, many readily renounced their ties to the empire. On this, see, for example: Benveniste, *Le Bosphore*, 57; Mays, "Transplanting;" "Enemy Aliens? Challenging a Wartime Classification in Britain," in Cohen and Stein, *Sephardi Lives*.

21. BOA HR. TO 542/146, 2 Teşrinisani 1328 (November 15, 1912); "Viyana'da Osmanlı Museviler," *Servet-i Fünun* 12 Şubat 1330 (February 25, 1915); Ginio," *El dovér*," 174; Galante, *Turcs et Juifs*, 64, 70.

22. For the advertisement's first appearance: "El mejor kafe toparesh onde Sal. Berkovich," *La Amerika*, December 22, 1911, 4. Interestingly, although the ads were always designed to appeal to Ottoman Sephardim, through 1912, the surnames of the vendors of the coffee indicate that they were of Ashkenazi origin. This changed by 1913, when Moïse Schinasi took over the business before passing it on to new co-owners with the surnames Israel and Castiel.

23. "Merkad kafe de ande merkan todos los turkinos," *La Amerika*, August 1, 1913, 3.

24. "D. Bensal i B. Cohen," *La Amerika*, March 7, 1913, 3.

25. "Sahon i Menashe," *La Amerika*, January 26, 1912, 4; "The Oriental American Produce Co.," *La Amerika*, April 4, 1913, 4.

26. "Restaurant Otoman," *La Amerika*, February 14, 1913, 4. The Ladino caption to the image read: "*Gazetas turkas de Turkia se resiven kada dia.*"

27. Shimon S. Nessim, "La Turkia de oy," *La Bos del Puevlo*, July 28, 1916, 3.

28. I take a cue here from David Nirenberg, *Communities of Violence* (Princeton, NJ: Princeton University Press, 1998), 6.

29. On this, see Milen V. Petrov, "Everyday Forms of Compliance: Subaltern Commentaries on Ottoman Reform, 1864–1868," *Comparative Studies in Society and History* 46, no. 4 (2004): 730–759, which speaks of the ways in which even Christian peasants living in an outlying Ottoman province learned to "speak Tanzimat." Petrov's discussion is, in turn, inspired by Stephen Kotkin, *Magnetic Mountain: Stalinism as Civilization* (Berkeley: University of California Press, 1995), which introduces the expression "speaking Bolshevik."

30. Cengiz Kırlı, "Coffeehouses: Public Opinion in the Nineteenth-Century Ottoman Empire," in *Public Islam and the Common Good*, eds., Armando Salvatore and Dale E. Eickelman (Leiden: Brill, 2004), 75–98.

31. For a similar observation, see Kayalı, *Arabs and Young Turks*, 207.

32. Noémi Lévy, "Salonique et la Guerre Gréco-Turque de 1897: Le fragile équilibre d'une ville Ottomane" (Mémoire de maîtrise, Université Paris I, 2002); Keith David Watenpaugh, *Being Modern in the Middle East: Revolution, Nationalism, Colonialism, and the Arab Middle Class* (Princeton, NJ: Princeton University Press, 2006); Noémi Lévy-Aksu, *Ordre et désordres dans l'Istanbul ottomane (1879–1909): De l'État au quartier* (Paris: Karthala, 2012); Vangelis Kechriotis, "Civilisation and Order: Middle-Class Morality Among the Greek-Orthodox in Smyrna/Izmir at the End of the Ottoman Empire," in *Social Transformation and Mass Mobilization in the Balkan and Eastern Mediterranean (1900–1923)*, eds. Christos Chatziosif and Andreas Lyberatos (Rethymnon: Crete University Press, 2013), 137–153.

33. Jews were not alone in incorporating elements of Islamic Ottomanism into their public pronouncements: see, for example, "Ermeni Patrik Kaimakamlığı tarafından Makam-ı sadaret-i azamiye takdim olunan tezkere," *Tercüman-ı Hakikat*, 19 Rebiülevvel 1314 (August 28, 1896), 1, where the Armenian Patriarch spoke of "our Muslim brothers" (*islam karındaşlarımız*).

34. Although this position is most often associated with the Muslims in the empire, the work of Harris Exertzoglou offers fascinating insights into the ways that Ottoman Greeks claimed their "Eastern" identity and railed against those in their community who tried to act—unnaturally in their view—like westerners: Exertzoglou, "The Cultural Uses of Consumption: Negotiating Class, Gender, and Nation in the Ottoman Urban Centers during the 19th Century," *International Journal of Middle East Studies* 35 (2003): 77–101; Exertzoglou, "Metaphors of Change: 'Tradition' and the East/West Discourse in the Late Ottoman Empire," in *Ways to Modernity in Greece and Turkey: Encounters with Europe, 1850–1950*, ed. Anna Frangoudaki and Çağlar Keyder (London: I. B. Tauris, 2007), 43–59.

35. For references to the "Easternist" option as it emerged both for and about Ottoman Jews in the Arab provinces during the same period: Lital Levy, "Partitioned Pasts: Arab Jewish Intellectuals and the Case of Esther Azhari Moyal (1873–1948)," in *The Making of the Arab Intellectual: Empire, Public Sphere and the Colonial Coordinates of Selfhood*, ed. Dyala Hamzah (New York: Routledge, 2012), 128–163; Jonathan Gribetz, "'Their Blood is Eastern': Shahin Makaryus and *Fin de Siècle* Arab Pride in the Jewish 'Race,'" *Middle Eastern Studies* 49, no. 2 (2013): 143–161.

36. Palmira Brummet, "Dogs, Women, Cholera, and Other Menaces in the Streets: Cartoon Satire in the Ottoman Revolutionary Press, 1908–1911," *International Journal of Middle East Studies* 27 (1995): 435. Other scholars have similarly commented upon the diminished role of the sultan after 1908. See, for example, Kayalı, *Arabs and Young Turks*; Campos, *Ottoman Brothers*.

37. This was a common slur of the Second Constitutional Era. See, for example, "Les Sionistes et l'emprunt," *Le Moniteur oriental*, March 2, 1911, 2, which notes that opposition members in parliament called a CUP party member a *curnalcı* and *hafiye* (informer or spy).

38. Midhat Pasha, "The Past, Present, and Future of Turkey," *Nineteenth Century* 16 (1878): 984, also cited in Makdisi, "Ottoman Orientalism," 789. Grand Vizier Ali Pasha similarly contrasted the European "Dark Ages" with Ottoman freedoms when he wrote that "during a time of obscurantism and intolerance . . . that encompassed all of Europe, it was not in the Ottoman realms that conquered minorities most regretted their situation." Ali Pasha, "Mémoire transmis à Londres et à Paris par Aali Pacha," May 1855, Archives du Ministère des Affaires Etrangères de France: Mémoires et Documents, Turquie, vol. 51, no. 9, 66b.

39. "Nuestra Propozision," *La Buena Esperansa*, July 10, 1891, 1.

40. *İkdam*, May 8, 1899, 3.

41. "Novedades lokales," *La Buena Esperansa*, May 5, 1899, 4.

42. "El Ahenk," *La Buena Esperansa*, May 12, 1899, 3; "Fes o chapeo," *El Avenir*, May 17, 1899, 1–2; *İkdam*, May 18, 1899, 3.
43. For the growing influence of exclusionary, racial forms of Turkish nationalism in the early twentieth century: Howard Eissenstat, "Metaphors of Race and Discourse of Nation: Racial Theory and State Nationalism in the First Decades of the Turkish Republic," in Paul Spickard ed., *Race and Nation: Ethnic Systems in the Modern World* (New York: Routledge, 2005), 239–256; On Jews as guests in the early Turkish Republic, see Esther Benbassa and Aron Rodrigue, *Sephardi Jewry: A History of the Judeo-Spanish Community, 14th–20th Centuries* (Berkeley: University of California Press, 2000), 103; Bali, *Bir Türkleſltirme Serüveni*, 513; Kader Konuk, "Eternal Guests, Mimics, and Dönme: The Place of German and Turkish Jews in Modern Turkey," *New Perspectives on Turkey* 37 (2007): 5–30. The idea that native Jews occupy "guest" status in Turkey remains prevalent still today. See the words of Muslim Turkish journalist Mehmet Gündem of the Gülen-affiliated newspaper *Zaman* in an interview with the Turkish Jewish paper *Şalom*: "I accept you in the sense [that you are] our guests. And I want to be hospitable in a way that is a credit to my culture." Teri Galimidi and Yusuf Altıntaş, "Husumete vakti olmayan muhabbet fedaisi: Mehmet Gündem," *Şalom*, March 12, 1997, cited in Bali, *Model Citizens*, 377.
44. Josephine Dayan, "Marsilya ziyaretleri," *Şalom*, July 24, 1991, cited in Bali, *Model Citizens*, 327.

BIBLIOGRAPHY

Archives

Archives of the Alliance Israélite Universelle, Paris
AIU Archives, Série Turquie
AIU Archives, Série Grèce

Archivo Central del Ministerio de Asuntos Exteriores (AMAE), Madrid

Archives du Ministère des Affaires Etrangères de France: Mémoires et Documents

Auswärtiges Amt, Politisches Archiv, Germany

Başbakanlık Osmanlı Arşivi, BOA
Bab-ı Ali Evrak Odası (BEO)
Dahiliye Siyasi Kısım (DH. SYS)
Hariciye Nezareti Tercüme Odası (HR. TO)
İrade Dahiliye (İ. DH)
İrade Hariciye (İ. HR)
İradeler Taltifat (İ. TAL)
Yıldız Hususi Maruzat (Y. A. HUS)
Yıldız Mütenevvi Maruzat (Y. MTV)
Yıldız Perakende (Y. PRK)
Yıldız Resmi Maruzat (Y. A. RES)

British Parliamentary Papers, Misc. No. 2 (1927)

Central Archives for the History of the Jewish People, CAHJP
CAHJP Tr/Is
CAHJP Gr/Kav

Centre des Archives diplomatiques de Nantes, MAE-Nantes

Haus-, Hof- und Staatsarchiv (HHStA), Vienna
HHStA PA VIII/Konsulat Thessaloniki

Istoriko Archeio Makedonias
Archeio Ieras Mitropoleos Thessalonikis

Meclis-i Mebusan Zabıt Cerideleri. 1327 [1911]

Private Collection of Randa Bishop.
  Frances Valensi Bishop, unpublished memoir.

Private collection of Jean Carasso.
  Sam Lévy, Ladino diary (in *soletreo*), 1894.

The National Archives, UK
  Public Record Office (PRO) FO (Foreign Office)

The University of Chicago Library, Special Collections
  Harry and Branka Sondheim Jewish Heritage Collection

Published Primary Sources

SERIALS

Akropolis
Allgemeine Zeitung des Judenthums
American Jewish Yearbook
La Amerika
El Amigo del Puevlo
Archives israélites
Asır
L'Aurore
El Avenir
Basiret
Habatselet
Beyan-ül Hak
Blackwood's Edinburgh Magazine
La Buena Esperansa (also *La Esperansa*)
Bulletin de l'Alliance Israélite Universelle
Bureau socialiste international
Chicago Daily Tribune
Constantinople Messenger
Il corriere israelitico
Embros
La Epoka
Harper's Weekly
İkdam
L'Illustration
El Imparsial
Der Israelit
İttihad
İzmir
Le Jeune-Turc
Jewish Chronicle
Jewish Messenger
Jewish Missionary Intelligence
Journal de Constantinople/Écho de l'Orient
Journal de Salonique
Le Judaïsme Sephardi
El Judio

Levant Herald and Eastern Express
Le Levant Times
La Liberté
London Illustrated News
Los Angeles Times
Ha-Magid
Malumat
Ha-Melits
El Meseret
Le Moniteur oriental
Mütalaa
La Nasion
El Nasional
Nea Alitheia
Neue Freie Presse
New York Times
El Nuvelista/Le Nouvelliste
Der Orient
Or Israel
Pharos tes Makedonias
Resimli Kitap
Revue des deux mondes
Sabah
Şehbal
Servet-i Fünün
Sha'are Mizrah/Puertas de Oriente
La Solidaridad Ovradera
Stamboul
Tanin
El Telegrafo
Tercüman-ı Hakikat
El Tiempo
Le Trait d'Union
La Tribuna Libera
La Turquie
L'Univers israélite
Il vessillo israelitico
Washington Post
Die Welt
World's Columbian Exposition Illustrated
Yeni İkdam
Zaman

BOOKS & PAMPHLETS

Adler, Cyrus. *I Have Considered the Days*. Philadelphia: Jewish Publication Society of America, 1941.

Alkan, Ahmet Turan. *Sıradışı Bir Jöntürk: Ubeydullah Efendi'nin Amerika Hatıraları*. Istanbul: İletişim, 1989.

Arditi, Raphael Samuel. *Sefer Divre Shemuel*. Salonica: 'Ets ha-hayim, 1890/91.

Bancroft, Hubert Howe. *The Book of the Fair*. Chicago: The Bancroft Co., 1893.

Bartlett, Ellis Ashmead. *The Battlefields of Thessaly*. London: John Murray, 1897.

Cevdet Pasha. *Tezâkir*, vol. 1. Ankara: Türk Tarih Kurumu, 1953.

Cox, Samuel S. *Diversions of a Diplomat in Turkey*. New York: C. L. Webster, 1887.

Davey, Richard. *The Sultan and His Subjects*, vol. 2. London: Chapman and Hall, 1897.

Du Bois, W. E. B. *The Souls of Black Folk*. Chicago: A. C. McClurg & Co., 1903.

Fetzer, C. A. *Aus dem thessalischen Feldzug der Türkei: Frühjahr 1897: Berichte und Erinnerungen eines Kriegskorrespondenten*. Stuttgart: Deutsche Verlags Anstalt, 1898.

Florentin, David. *Nos devoirs comme Juifs et Ottomans*. Istanbul: M. Gorodichze, 1909.

Franco, Moïse. *Essai sur l'histoire des Israélites de l'Empire Ottoman depuis les origines jusqu'à nos jours*. New York: Georg Olms Verlag, 1973. Reprint of the 1897 edition.

Frankl, Ludwig August. *The Jews of the East*, vol. 1. Translated by Rev. P. Beaton. London: First and Blackett Publishers, 1859.

Fresco, David. *Le sionisme*. Istanbul: Imp. Fresco, 1909.

Gabay, Isaac. *Yildiz y sus sekretos: el reino de Abdul Hamid*. Istanbul: Imp. Gabay, [1910?].

Gibb, E. J. W. *Ottoman Poetry*. London: Luzac & Co., 1907.

Goltz, Colmar Freiherr von der. *Osmanlı-Yunan Seferi (1313/1897)*. Istanbul: Mekteb-i Fünûn-i Harbiye Matbaası, 1326 [1910].

Istoria komfuesma [sic] *de Yosef Haim b. Rey de Karnabat*. Plovdiv: Yosef Baruh Pardo, n.d.

Korany, Hanna K. "The Glory of Womanhood." In *The Congress of Women: Held in the Woman's Building, World's Columbian Exposition, Chicago, U.S.A., 1893*, edited by Mary Kavanaugh Oldham, 359–360. Chicago: Monarch Book Company, 1894.

Lévy, Sam. *Souvenir du voyage*. Salonica: 1911.

Liga de Pas i Solidaridad: Fondada en 1909. Izmir: Meşrutiyet Matbaası, [1931?].

Löwy, Albert. *The Jews of Constantinople: A Study of their Communal and Educational Status*. London: Wertheimer, Lea & Co., 1890.

Midhat, Pasha. "The Past, Present, and Future of Turkey." *Nineteenth Century* 16 (1878): 981–1000.

Molho, Michael. *Traditions and Customs of the Sephardic Jews of Salonica*, ed. Robert Bedford. Translated by Alfred A. Zara. New York: Foundation for the Advancement of Sephardic Studies and Culture, 2006. Reprint from 1944/50.

Mossé, Benjamin. *La révolution française et le rabbinat français*. Avignon: La Caravane, 1890.

Muhiddin, Nezihe. *Türk Kadını*. Istanbul: Numune Matbaası, 1931.

Papo, Michael Menahem, and Adolf von Zemlinsky. *Geschichte der türkisch-israelitischen Gemeinde zu Wien/Istoria de la komunidad israelit espanyola en Viena*. Vienna: M. Papo, 1888.

Pears, Edwin. *Life of Abdul Hamid*. London: Constable & Co., 1917.

Pierce, James Wilson. *Photographic History of the World's Fair and Sketch of the City of Chicago*. Baltimore, MD: R. H. Woodward & Co., 1893.

Sason, Nevres. *Silabario en turko-espanyol*. Istanbul: Isaac Gabay, 1905.

Simavi, Lütfi. *Son Osmanlı Sarayında Gördüklerim: Sultan Mehmed Reşad Hanın ve Halifenin Sarayında Gördüklerim*. Istanbul: Örgün Yayınevi, [1924] 2004.

Société de bienfaisance des Dames Israélites de Péra: Statuts. Istanbul: Imprimerie de Castro, 1893.

Ubicini, Abdolonyme. *Letters on Turkey*, vol. 2. London: J. Murray, 1856.

Secondary Literature

Abensur-Hazan, Laurence. "Généalogie des Juifs de Smyrne (Izmir, Turquie): principales sources de recherche." *Etsi* 6, no. 21 (June 2003).

Abu-Manneh, Butrus. "The Islamic Roots of the Gülhane Rescript." *Die Welt des Islams* 34 (1994): 173–203.

Abu-Manneh, Butrus. *Studies on Islam and the Ottoman Empire in the 19th Century (1826–1876)*. Istanbul: Isis, 2001.

Adatto, Albert. "Sephardim and the Seattle Sephardic Community." Master's thesis, University of Washington, 1939.

Aksakal, Mustafa. "'Holy War Made in Germany'? Ottoman Origins of the 1914 Jihad," *War in History* 18, no. 2 (2011): 184–199.

Aktsoglou, Iakovos J. "The Emergence/Development of Social and Working Class Movement in the City of Thessaloniki," *Balkan Studies* 38, no. 2 (1997): 285–306.

Alboyadjian, Archag. *Les Dadian*. Trans. Anna Naguib Boutros-Ghali. Cairo: n.p., 1965.

Altabé, David F., Erhan Atay, and Israel J. Katz, eds. *Studies on Turkish-Jewish History: Political and Social Relations, Literature, and Linguistics: The Quincentennial Papers*. New York: Sepher-Hermon Press for The American Society of Sephardic Studies, 1996.

Anagnostopoulou, Sia, and Matthias Kappler. "*Zito Zito o Sultanos/Bin Yaşa Padişahımız:* The Millet-i Rum Singing the Praises of the Sultan in the Framework of Helleno-Ottomanism." *Archivum Ottomanicum* 23 (2005/06): 47–78.

Anastassiadou, Meropi. "L'Hermis' de Salonique: Un journal ottoman de province." In *Presse und Öffentlichkeit im Nahen Osten*, edited by Christoph Herzog, Raoul Motika and Anja Pistor-Hatam, 3–13. Heidelberg: Heidelberger Orientverlag, 1995.

Anastassiadou, Meropi. *Salonique, 1830–1912: Une ville Ottomane à l'âge des réformes*. New York: Brill, 1997.

Anderson, Benedict. *Imagined Communities: Reflections on the Origin and Spread of Nationalism*. London: Verso Editions, 1983.

Anderson, Margaret. "'Down in Turkey, Far Away:' Human Rights, the Armenian Massacres, and Orientalism in Wilhemine Germany." *Journal of Modern History* 79, no. 1 (March 2007): 80–111.

Angel, Marc. D. *La America: The Sephardic Experience in the United States*. Philadelphia: Jewish Publication Society of America, 1982.

Anscombe, Frederik. "Islam and the Age of Ottoman Reform." *Past and Present* 208 (August 2010): 159–189.

Avdela, Efi, and Angelika Psarra. "Engendering 'Greekness:' Women's Emancipation and Irredentist Politics in Nineteenth-Century Greece." *Mediterranean Historical Review* 20, no. 1 (June 2005): 67–79.

Aydın, Mahir. "Musevilerin Osmanlı Topraklarına Kabulünün 400: Yıldönümü Kutlamaları." *Osmanlı Araştırmaları* 13 (1993): 33–35.

Aytekin, E. Atilla. "Peasant Protest in the Late Ottoman Empire: Moral Economy Revolt, and the Tanzimat Reforms." *International Review of Social History* 57 (2012): 191–227.

Badem, Candan. *The Ottoman Crimean War (1853–1856)*. Leiden: Brill, 2010.

Baer, Marc. *Honored by the Glory of Islam*. New York: Oxford University Press, 2008.

Baer, Marc. *The Dönme: Jewish Converts, Muslim Revolutionaries, and Secular Turks*. Stanford, CA: Stanford University Press, 2009.

Bali, Rıfat. *Bir Türkleştirme Serüveni 1923–1945*. Istanbul: İletişim, 2000.

Bali, Rıfat. *Les relations entre Turcs et Juifs dans la Turquie moderne*. Istanbul: Isis, 2001.

Bali, Rıfat. *Musa'nın Evlatları Cumhuriyet'in Yurttaşları*. Istanbul: İletişim, 2001.

Bali, Rıfat. *Cumhuriyet Yıllarında Türkiye Yahudileri Aliya*. Istanbul: İletişim, 2003.

Bali, Rıfat. *Devlet'in Yahudileri ve 'Öteki' Yahudi*. Istanbul: İletişim, 2004.

Bali, Rıfat. *Model Citizens of the State: the Jews of Turkey during the Multi-Party Period*. Lanham, MD: Fairleigh Dickinson University Press, 2012.

Bali, Rıfat. *Bir Günah Keçisi: Munis Tekinalp*, vol. 2. Istanbul: Libra, 2012.

Banerjee, Sukanya. *Becoming Imperial Citizens: Indians in the Late-Victorian Empire*. Durham, NC: Duke University Press, 2010.

Barnai, Jacob. "Blood Libels in the Ottoman Empire of the Fifteenth to Nineteenth Centuries." In *Antisemitism Through the Ages*, edited by Shmuel Almog, 189–194. Oxford: Pergamon Press, 1988.

Barnai, Jacob. "Kavim le-toldot kehilat Kushta ba-meah ha-18." *Mi-Kedem U-mi-Yam* 1 (1981): 64–65.

Barsoumian, Hagop. "The Dual Role of the Armenian *Amira* Class within the Ottoman Government and the Armenian *Millet* (1750–1850)." In Braude and Lewis, *Christians and Jews in the Ottoman Empire*, 1: 171–184.

Bashkin, Orit. "'Religious Hatred Shall Disappear from the Land': Iraqi Jews as Ottoman Subjects, 1864–1913." *International Journal of Contemporary Iraqi Studies* 4, no. 3 (December 2010): 305–323.

Bejerano, Margalit, and Edna Aizenberg, eds. *Contemporary Sephardic Identity in the Americas: An Interdisciplinary Approach.* Syracuse, NY: Syracuse University Press, 2012.

Benaroya, Abraham. "A Note on 'The Socialist Federation of Saloniki.'" *Jewish Social Studies* 11 (1949): 69–72.

Benbassa, Esther. "Kampana Çalanlar Davası: 1901'de İzmir'de Cereyan Etmiş Bir Kan İftirası Vak'ası." *Tarih ve Toplum* 30 (May 1986): 364–370.

Benbassa, Esther. "Le Sionisme dans l'Empire Ottoman à l'aube du 20e siècle." *Vingtième Siècle* 24 (October–December 1989): 69–80.

Benbassa, Esther. "Associational Strategies in Ottoman Jewish Society in the Nineteenth and Twentieth Centuries." In Levy, *Jews of the Ottoman Empire,* 457–484.

Benbassa, Esther. *Une diaspora sépharade en transition: Istanbul, XIXe-XXe siècle.* Paris: Cerf, 1993.

Benbassa, Esther, ed. *Haim Nahum: A Sephardic Chief Rabbi in Politics, 1892–1923.* Trans. Miriam Kochan. Tuscaloosa: University of Alabama Press, 1995.

Benbassa, Esther. "Des Sionistes sans Sionisme." *Cahiers d'études sur le Méditerranée orientale et le monde turco-iranien* 28 (June-December 1999): 19–30.

Benbassa, Esther. "Zionism and the Politics of Coalitions in the Ottoman Jewish Communities in the Early Twentieth Century." In Rodrigue, *Ottoman and Turkish Jewry,* 225–251.

Benbassa, Esther, ed. *Itinéraires sépharades: Complexité et diversité des identities.* Paris: Presse de l'Université Paris-Sorbonne, 2010.

Benbassa, Esther, and Aron Rodrigue. *Sephardi Jewry: A History of the Judeo-Spanish Community, 14th-20th Centuries.* Berkeley: University of California Press, 2000.

Ben-Naeh, Yaron. *Jews in the Realm of the Sultans.* Tübingen: Mohr Siebeck, 2008.

Ben-Ur, Aviva. *Sephardic Jews in America: A Diasporic History.* New York: New York University Press, 2009.

Benveniste, Annie. *Le Bosphore à la Roquette: la communauté judéo-espagnole à Paris, 1914–1940.* Paris: L'Hartmattan, 1989.

Berkes, Niyazi. *The Development of Secularism in Turkey.* Montreal: McGill University Press, 1964.

Biale, David. *Power and Powerlessness in Jewish History.* New York: Schocken, 1986.

Birnbaum, Pierre. *Prier pour l'État: Les Juifs, l'Alliance royale et la démocratie.* Paris: Calmann-Levy, 2005.

Blumi, Isa. "Teaching Loyalty in the Late Ottoman Balkans: Educational Reform in the Vilayets of Manastir and Yanya, 1878–1912." *Comparative Studies of South Asia, Africa and the Middle East* 21: 1–2 (2001): 15–23.

Blumi, Isa. *Reinstating the Ottomans: Alternative Balkan Modernities, 1800–1912.* New York: Palgrave Macmillan, 2011.

Bornes-Varol, Marie-Christine. "La vision de l'autre chez les juifs de Balat: Les arméniens." *Revue du monde arménien moderne et contemporain* 4 (1998): 35–42.

Bornstein-Makovetsky, Leah. "Jewish Converts to Islam and Christianity in the Ottoman Empire in the Nineteenth Century." In Rozen, *Last Ottoman Century,* 2:83–127.

Borovaya, Olga. "Jews of Three Colors: The Path to Modernity in the Pages of the Ladino Press at the Turn of the Twentieth Century." *Jewish Social Studies* 15, no. 1 (Fall 2008).

Borovaya, Olga. "New Forms of Ladino Cultural Production in the Late Ottoman Period: Sephardi Theater as a Tool of Indoctrination." *European Journal for Jewish Studies* 2, no. 1 (2008): 63–86.

Borovaya, Olga. "Shmuel Saadi Halévy/Sam Lévy Between Ladino and French: Reconstructing a Writer's Social Identity in a Polyglossic Situation." In *Modern Jewish Literatures: Intersections and Boundaries,* edited by Sheila Jelen, Michael Kramer, and L. Scott Lerner, 83–103. Philadelphia: University of Pennsylvania, 2010.

Borovaya, Olga. *Modern Ladino Culture: Press, Belles Lettres, and Theater in the Late Ottoman Empire*. Bloomington: Indiana University Press, 2012.

Braude, Benjamin. "International Competition and Domestic Cloth in the Ottoman Emipre, 1500–1650: A Study in Underdevelopment." *Review* 2, no. 3 (Winter 1979): 437–451.

Braude, Benjamin. "Foundation Myths of the Millet System." In Braude and Lewis, *Christians and Jews in the Ottoman Empire*. New York: Holmes & Meier Publishers, 1982, 1: 69–88.

Braude, Benjamin. "The Rise and Fall of Salonica Woollens, 1500–1650. Technology Transfer and Western Competition." *Mediterranean Historical Review* 6, no. 2 (1991): 216–236.

Braude, Benjamin, and Bernard Lewis, ed. *Christians and Jews in the Ottoman Empire*. New York: Holmes & Meier Publishers, 1982.

Brink-Danan, Marcy. "Reference Points: Text, Context and Change in Definitions of Turkish-Jewish Identity." Ph.D. diss., Stanford University, 2005.

Brink-Danan, Marcy. *Jewish Life in Twenty-First Century Turkey: The Other Side of Tolerance*. Bloomington: Indiana University Press, 2012.

Brodkin, Karen. *How Jews Became White Folks and What That Says About Race in America*. New Brunswick, NJ: Rutgers University Press, 1998.

Brummet, Palmira. "Dogs, Women, Cholera, and Other Meances in the Streets: Cartoon Satire in the Ottoman Revolutionary Press, 1908–1911." *International Journal of Middle East Studies* 27 (1995): 433–460.

Bunis, David M. "Modernization and the Language Question among Judezmo-Speaking Sephardim in the Ottoman Empire." In *Sephardi and Middle Eastern Jewries*, edited by Harvey E. Goldberg, 226–239. Bloomington: Indiana University Press, 1996.

Campos, Michelle U. "Between 'Beloved *Ottomania*' and 'The Land of Israel': The Struggle Over Ottomanism and Zionism Among Palestine's Sephardi Jews, 1908–13." *International Journal of Middle East Studies* 37 (2005): 461–483.

Campos, Michelle U. *Ottoman Brothers: Muslims, Christians, and Jews in Early Twentieth-Century Palestine*. Stanford, CA: Stanford University Press, 2010.

Çelebi, Mevlüt. *Sultan Reşad'ın Rumeli Seyahati*. Izmir: Akademi Kitabevi, 1999.

Çelik, Zeynep. *Displaying the Orient. Architecture of Islam at Nineteenth-Century World's Fairs*. Berkeley: University of California Press, 1992.

Çelik, Zeynep. "Speaking Back to Orientalist Discourse at the World's Columbian Exposition." In *Noble Dreams, Wicked Pleasures. Orientalism in America, 1870–1930*, edited by Holly Edwards, 77–97. Princeton, NJ: Princeton University Press, 2000.

Cesarani, David. "British Jews." In *The Emancipation of Catholics, Jews and Protestants: Minorities and the Nation State in Nineteenth-Century Europe*, edited by Rainer Liedtke and Stephan Wendehorst, 50–53. Manchester, UK: Manchester University Press, 1999.

Çetinkaya, Y. Doğan. "Muslim Merchants and Working-Class in Action: Nationalism, Social Mobilization and Boycott Movement in the Ottoman Empire 1908–1914." Ph.D. diss, Leiden, 2010.

Clogg, Richard. "The Greek *Millet* in the Ottoman Empire." In Braude and Lewis, *Christians and Jews in the Ottoman Empire*, 1: 185–208.

Cohen, Hayim. *Jews of the Middle East, 1860–1972*. New York: Wiley, 1973.

Cohen, Julia Phillips. "'Zeal and Noise': Jewish Imperial Allegiance and the Greco-Ottoman War of 1897." In *The Divergence of Judaism and Islam: Jews and Muslim in a Changing World*, edited by Michael Laskier and Yaacov Lev, 29–50. Gainesville: University Press of Florida, 2011.

Cohen, Julia Phillips. "Between Civic and Islamic Otomanism: Jewish Imperial Citizenship in the Hamidian Era." *International Journal of Middle East Studies* 44, no. 2 (May 2012): 237–255.

Cohen, Julia Phillips, and Sarah Abrevaya Stein, eds. *Sephardi Lives: A Documentary History, 1700–1950*. Stanford, CA: Stanford University Press, 2014, forthcoming.

Cohen, Mark. *Last Century of a Sephardic Community: The Jews of Monastir, 1839–1943*. New York: Foundation for the Advancement of Sephardic Studies and Culture, 2003.

Combs, Cindy C., and Martin W. Slann, eds. *International Encyclopedia of Censorship*. London: Fitzroy Dearborn, 2002.

Cooperman, Bernard. "Turco-Jewish Relations in the Ottoman City of Salonica, 1889–1912: Two Communities in Support of the Ottoman Empire." Ph.D. diss., New York University, 1991.

Daccarett, Paula. "Jewish Social Services in Late Ottoman Salonica (1850–1912)." Ph.D. diss., Brandeis University, 2008.

Davis, Eric. "Representations of the Middle East at American World Fairs, 1876–1904." In *The United States and the Middle East*, edited by Abbas Amanat and Magnus T. Bernhardsson, 342–385. New Haven, CT: Yale Center for International and Area Studies, 2002.

Davison, Roderic. *Reform in the Ottoman Empire 1856–76*. Princeton, NJ: Princeton University Press, 1963.

Davison, Roderic. *Nineteenth Century Ottoman Diplomacy and Reforms*. Istanbul: Isis, 1999.

De Haan, Francisca, Krassimira Daskalova, and Anna Loutfi, eds. *Biographical Dictionary of Women's Movements and Feminisms: Central, Eastern, and South Eastern Europe, 19th and 20th Centuries*. Budapest: Central European University Press, 2006.

Der Matossian, Bedross. "Ethnic Politics in the Post-Revolutionary Ottoman Empire: Armenians, Arabs, and Jews in the Second Constitutional Period (1908–1909)." Ph.D. diss., Columbia University, 2008.

Der Matossian, Bedross. "Formation of Public Sphere(s) in the Aftermath of the 1908 Revolution among Armenians, Arabs, and Jews." In *L'ivresse de la liberté: La révolution de 1908 dans l'Empire ottoman*, edited by François Georgeon, 189–219. Louvain: Peeters, 2012.

Deringil, Selim. "Jewish Immigration to the Ottoman Empire at the Time of the First Zionist Congresses: A Comment." In Rozen, *Last Ottoman Century*, 2:141–49.

Deringil, Selim. "The Invention of Tradition as Public Image in the Late Ottoman Empire, 1808–1908." *Comparative Studies in Society and History* 35, no. 1 (Jan 1993): 3–29.

Deringil, Selim. *The Well-Protected Domains: Ideology and the Legitimation of Power in the Ottoman Empire, 1876–1909*. London: I. B. Tauris, 1998.

Deringil, Selim. "The Hamidian State and the World's Fairs: 'The Whole World is Watching!'" In *Studien zu Wirtschaft und Gesellschaft im Osmanischen Reich*, edited by Raoul Motika, Christoph Herzog and Micahel Ursinus, 191–207. Heidelberg: Heidelberger Orientverlag, 1999.

Deringil, Selim. "'There is no Compulsion in Religion': On Conversion and Apostasy in the Late Ottoman Empire: 1839–1856." *Society for Comparative Study of Society and History* 42, no. 3 (July 2000): 547–575.

Devereux, Robert. *The First Ottoman Constitutional Period: A Study of the Midhat Constitution and Parliament*. Baltimore, MD: Johns Hopkins University Press, 1963.

Downes, Brant. "Constructing the Modern Ottoman Waterfront: Salonica and Beirut in the Late Nineteenth Century." Ph.D. diss., Stanford University, 2008.

Duker, Abraham G. "Jewish Volunteers in the Ottoman-Polish Cossack Units during the Crimean War." *Jewish Social Studies* 16 (1954): 203–218, 351–376.

Dumont, Paul. "The Social Structure of the Jewish Community of Salonika at the End of the Nineteenth Century." *Southeastern Europe/L'Europe du Sud-Est* 5, no. 2 (1979): 33–72.

Dumont, Paul. "Jewish Communities in Turkey during the Last Decades of the Nineteenth Century in the Light of the Archives of the Alliance Israélite Universelle." In Braude and Lewis, *Christians and Jews in the Ottoman Empire*, 1: 209–242.

Dumont, Paul. "A Jewish, Socialist and Ottoman Organization: the Worker's Federation of Thessaloniki." In *Socialism and Nationalism in the Ottoman Empire, 1876–1923*, edited by Mete Tunçay and Erik-Jan Zürcher, 49–76. London: British Academic Press, 1994.

Eissenstat, Howard. "Metaphors of Race and Discourse of Nation: Racial Theory and State Nationalism in the First Decades of the Turkish Republic." In *Race and Nation: Ethnic Systems in the Modern World*, edited by Paul Spickard, 239–256. New York: Routledge, 2005.

Ekinci, Mehmet Uğur. "The Origins of the 1897 Ottoman-Greek War: A Diplomatic History." Master's thesis, Bilkent University, 2006.

Eldem, Edhem. "26 Ağustos 1896 'Banka Vak'ası' ve 1896 'Ermeni Olayları.'" *Tarih ve Toplum* 5 (2007): 113–146.

Eldem, Edhem. "Istanbul 1903–1918: A Quantitative Analysis of a Bourgeoisie." *Boğaziçi Üniversitesi dergisi: yöneticilik, ekonomi, ve sosyal bilimler* 11, no. 1–2 (1997): 53–98.

Eldem, Edhem. *A History of the Ottoman Bank.* Istanbul: Ottoman Bank Historical Research Center, 1999.

Eldem, Edhem. *Pride and Privilege: A History of Ottoman Orders, Medals and Decorations.* Istanbul: Ottoman Bank Archives and Research Center, 2004.

Embellished Lives: Customs and Costumes of the Jewish Communities of Turkey. Berkeley: Judah L. Magnes Museum, 1989.

Encyclopaedia Judaica, edited by Michael Berenbaum and Fred Skolnik. 2nd ed. Detroit: Macmillan Reference USA, 2007.

Ersoy, Ahmet. "Mustafa Reşid Paşa: The Gülhane Edict." In Balázs Trencsényi and Michal Kopeček, eds., *Discourses of Collective Identity in Central and Southeast Europe (1770–1945), Texts and Commentaries,* vol. 1. Budapest: CEU Press, 2006, 332–339.

Esenbel, Selçuk. "The Anguish of Civilized Behavior: The Use of Western Cultural Forms in the Everyday Lives of the Meiji Japanese and the Ottoman Turks during the Nineteenth Century." *Japan Review* 5 (1994): 145–185.

Evered, Emine Ö. *Empire and Education under the Ottomans.* New York: I. B. Tauris, 2012.

Exertzoglou, Harris. "The Cultural Uses of Consumption: Negotiation Class, Gender, and Nation in the Ottoman Urban Centers during the 19th Century." *International Journal of Middle East Studies* 35 (2003): 77–101.

Exertzoglou, Harris. "Metaphors of Change: 'Tradition' and the East/West Discourse in the Late Ottoman Empire." In *Ways to Modernity in Greece and Turkey: Encounters with Europe, 1850–1950,* 43–59, edited by Anna Frangoudaki and Çağlar Keyder. London: I. B. Tauris, 2007.

Farhi, David. "Yehude Salonika be-Mahpekhat ha-Turkim ha-Tse'irim." *Sefunot* 15 (1981).

Findley, Carter. "The Acid Test of Ottomanism: The Acceptance of Non-Muslims in the Late Ottoman Bureaucracy." In Braude and Lewis, *Christians and Jews in the Ottoman Empire,* 1:339–368.

Findley, Carter. *Bureaucratic Reform in the Ottoman Empire: The Sublime Porte, 1789–1922.* Princeton, NJ: Princeton University Press, 1980.

Findley, Carter. *Ottoman Civil Officialdom: A Social History.* Princeton, NJ: Princeton University Press, 1989.

Findley, Carter. "An Ottoman Occidentalist in Europe: Ahmed Midhat Meets Madame Gülnar, 1889." *American Historical Review* (February 1998): 15–49.

Findley, Carter. "Competing Autobiographical Novels: His and Hers." In *Many Ways of Speaking About the Self: Middle Eastern Ego-Documents in Arabic, Persia, and Turkish (14th-20th century).* Wiesbaden: Harrassowtiz, 2010.

Finkel, Caroline. *Osman's Dream.* New York: Basic Books, 2005.

Fishman, Louis. "Understanding the 1911 Ottoman Parliament Debate on Zionism in Light of the Emergence of a 'Jewish Question.'" In *Late Ottoman Palestine: The Period of Young Turk Rule,* edited by Yuval Ben-Bassat and Eyal Ginio, 103–123. New York: I. B. Tauris, 2011.

Fleming, K. E. "South Balkan Rabbinic Readings of Ottoman Rise and Decline: Eliyahu Kapsali of Crete and Yehuda Alkalai of Zemlin." In Tziovas, *Greece and the Balkans,* 101–113. Aldershot, UK: Ashgate, 2003.

Fleming, K. E. *Greece: A Jewish History.* Princeton, NJ: Princeton University Press, 2008.

Fortna, Benjamin C. *Imperial Classroom: Islam, the State, and Education in the Late Ottoman Empire.* Oxford: Oxford University Press, 2002.

Franco, Moïse. *Essai sur l'histoire des Israélites de l'Empire Ottoman depuis les origines jusqu'à nos jours.* New York: Georg Olms Verlag, 1973. Reprint of the 1897 edition.

Frankel, Jonathan. *The Damascus Affair: "Ritual Murder," Politics and the Jews in 1840.* New York: Cambridge University Press, 1997.

Freedman, Jonathan. *Klezmer America: Jewishness, Ethnicity, Modernity.* New York: Columbia University Press, 2008.

Frierson, Elizabeth B. "Unimagined Communities: Women and Education in the late-Ottoman Empire, 1876–1909." *Critical Matrix* 9, no. 2 (1995): 55–90.

Frierson, Elizabeth B. "Mirrors Out, Mirrors In: Domestication and Rejection of the Foreign in Late-Ottoman Women's Magazines (1875–1908)." In *Women, Patronage and Self-Representation in Islamic Societies,* edited by D. Fairchild Ruggles, 177–204. New York: State University of New York Press, 2000.

Frierson, Elizabeth B. "Gender, Consumption and Patriotism: The Emergence of an Ottoman Public Sphere." In *Public Islam and the Common Good,* edited by Armando Salvatore and Dale F. Eickelman, 99–125. Leiden: Brill, 2004.

Frierson, Elizabeth B. "Women in Late Ottoman Intellectual History." In *Late Ottoman Society: The Intellectual Legacy,* edited by Elisabeth Özdalga, 135–161. New York: Routledge Curzon, 2005.

Fuhrmann, Malte. "Cosmopolitan Imperialists and the Ottoman Port Cities: Conflicting Logics in the Urban Social Fabric." *Cahiers de la Méditerranée* 67 (2003), http://cdlm.revues.org/document128.html.

Galante, Abraham. *Appendice à l'ouvrage [Turcs et Juifs]: Documents officiels turcs concernant les juifs de Turquie.* Istanbul: Impr. Hüsnütabiat, 1941.

Galante, Abraham. *Turcs et Juifs: étude historique, politique.* Istanbul: Haim, Rozio & Co., 1932.

Galante, Abraham. *Histoire des juifs d'Anatolie.* Istanbul: M. Babok, 1937–1939.

Galante, Abraham. *Histoire des juifs de Turquie.* Istanbul: Isis, 1985–1986. 9 volumes.

Games, Alison. *The Web of Empire: English Cosmopolitans in an Age of Expansion, 1560–1660.* New York: Oxford University Press, 2008.

Gekas, Sakis. "The Port Jews of Corfu and the 'Blood Libel' of 1891: A Tale of Many Centuries and of One Event." In *Jews and Port Cities, 1590–1990. Commerce, Community and Cosmopolitanism,* edited by David Cesarani and Gemma Romain, 171–196. London: Vallentine Mitchell, 2006.

Gelber, N. M. "Contribution à l'histoire des Juifs espagnols à Vienne: Début de la communauté sephardite et pièces justificatives."*Revue des études juives* 97, no. 191 (1934): 114–151 and no. 192 (1934): 44–49.

Gelber, N. M. "An Attempt to Internationalize Salonika, 1912–1913." *Jewish Social Studies* 17 (1955): 105–120.

Gerber, Haim. "Yozmah u-Mishar Ben-Leumi ba-Pe'ilut ha-Kalkalit shel Yehude ha-Imperyah ha-'Otmanit ba-Meot 16–17." *Zion* 43 (1978): 36–67.

Ginio, Eyal. "Mobilizing the Ottoman Nation during the Balkan Wars (1912–1913): Awakening from the Ottoman Dream." *War In History* 12, no. 2 (April 2005): 156–177.

Ginio, Eyal. "'Yehudim 'Otmanim! Hushu le-hatsel et moledatenu!': Yehudim 'Otmanim be-Milhemot ha-Balkan (1912–1913)." *Pe'amim* 105–106 (Autumn 2005/Winter 2006): 5–28.

Ginio, Eyal. "*El dovér el mas sànto:* The Mobilization of the Ottoman Jewish Population during the Balkan Wars (1912–1913)." In *Conflicting Loyalties in the Balkans: The Great Powers, the Ottoman Empire and Nation-Building,* edited by Hannes Grandits, Nathalie Clayer, and Robert Pichler, 157–181. New York: I. B. Tauris, 2011.

Göçek, Fatma Müge. *Rise of the Bourgeoisie, Demise of Empire.* New York: Oxford University Press, 1996.

Goldberg, Harvey E. ed., *Sephardi and Middle Eastern Jewries* (Bloomington, IN: Indiana University Press, 1996).

Goldish, Matt. *Jewish Questions: Responsa on Sephardic Life in the Early Modern Period.* Princeton, NJ: Princeton University Press, 2008.

Gounaris, Basil C. "Salonica." *Review: Ferdand Braudel Center* 16, no. 4 (Fall 1993): 499–518.

Gribetz, Jonathan. "'Their Blood is Eastern': Shahin Makaryus and Fin de Siecle Arab Pride in the Jewish 'Race.'" *Middle Eastern Studies* 49: 2 (2013): 143–161.

Grossman, Grace Cohen, and Richard Eighme Ahlborn. *Judaica at the Smithsonian: Cultural Politics as Cultural Model*. Washington, DC: Smithsonian Institute Press, 1997.

Guillon, Hélène. "Les ambitions d'un jeune journaliste séfarade: les *Carnets intimes* de Sam Lévy (1894), futur rédacteur en chef du *Journal de Salonique* (1895–1911)." *Yod: Revue des études hébraïques et juives* 11/12 (2006–2007): 271–287.

Guillon, Hélène. *Le Journal de Salonique: Un périodique juif dans l'Empire ottoman (1895–1911)*. Paris: Presses de l'Université Paris-Sorbonne, 2013.

Güleryüz, Naim. *500. Yıl Vakfı Türk Musevileri Müzesi/Quincentennial Foundation Museum of Turkish Jews*. Istanbul: Gözlem Gazetecilik Basın ve Yayın A. Ş., 2004.

Güleryüz, Naim. "Symbol of Turkish-Jewish Amity: The Zulfaris Synagogue." http://www.turkishjews.com/synagogues/zulfaris.asp

Gülsoy, Ufuk. *Osmanlı Gayrimüslimlerinin Askerlik Serüveni*. Istanbul: Simurg, 2000.

Guttstadt, Corry. *Die Türkei, die Juden und der Holocaust*. Berlin: Assoziation A, 2008.

Hacker, Joseph R. "Ottoman Policy toward the Jews and Jewish Attitudes toward the Ottoman during the Fifteenth Century." In Braude and Lewis, *Christians and Jews in the Ottoman Empire*, 1:117–126 New York: Holmes & Meier Publishers, 1982.

Hacker, Joseph R. "The *Sürgün* System and Jewish Society in the Ottoman Empire during the Fifteenth to the Seventeenth Centuries." In Rodrigue, *Ottoman and Turkish Jewry*, 1–65.

Hanagan, Michael and Charles Tilly, eds. *Extending Citizenship, Reconfiguring States*. Lanham, MD: Rowman and Littlefield Publishers, 1999.

Hanioğlu, M. Şükrü. "Jews in the Young Turk Movement to the 1908 Revolution." In *The Jews of the Ottoman Empire*, edited by Avigdor Levy. Princeton, NJ: Darwin Press, 1994.

Hanioğlu, M. Şükrü. *The Young Turks in Opposition*. New York: Oxford University Press, 1995.

Hanioğlu, M. Şükrü. *Preparation for a Revolution* (New York: Oxford University Press, 2001).

Hanioğlu, M. Şükrü. *A Brief History of the Late Ottoman Empire*. Princeton, NJ: Princeton University Press, 2008.

Harel, Yaron. "The Importance of the Archive of the Hakham Bashi in Istanbul for the History of Ottoman Jewry." In *Frontiers of Ottoman Studies: State, Province, and the West*, edited by Colin Imber and Keiko Kiyotaki, vol. 1, 251–264. New York: I. B. Tauris, 2005.

Hartmann, Elke. "The 'Loyal Nation' and its Deputies." In *The First Ottoman Parliament: Perception, Significance and Prosopography*, edited by Christoph Herzog and Malek Sharif, 187–222. Würzburg: Ergon, 2010.

Hassiotis, J. K. "The Greeks and the Armenian Massacres (1890–1896)," *Neo-Hellenika* 4 (1981): 69–109.

Hassiotis, I. K., ed. *The Jewish Communities of Southeastern Europe: From the Fifteenth Century to the End of World War II*. Thessaloniki: Institute for Balkan Studies, 1997.

Haupt, Georges, and Paul Dumont, eds. *Osmanlı Imparatorluğunda Sosyalist Hareketler*. Istanbul: Gözlem Yayinları, 1977.

Heckman, Alma Rachel and Frances Malino. "Packed in Twelve Cases: The Alliance Israélite Universelle and the 1893 Chicago World's Fair," *Jewish Social Studies* 19, no. 1 (Fall 2012): 53–69.

Hobsbawm, Eric. *The Age of Empire, 1875–1914*. New York: Vintage Books, 1989.

Horowitz, Elliot. *Reckless Rites: Purim and the Legacy of Jewish Violence*. Princeton, NJ: Princeton University Press, 2006.

Hurewitz, J. C. *Diplomacy in the Near and Middle East: A Documentary Record: 1535–1914*. Princeton, NJ: D. Van Nostrand, 1956.

Ilıcak, H. Şükrü. "Jewish Socialism in Ottoman Salonica." *Southeast European and Black Sea Studies* 2, no. 3 (September 2002): 115–146.

Jacobson, Abigail. *From Empire to Empire: Jerusalem Between Ottoman and British Rule*. Syracuse, NY: Syracuse University Press, 2011.

Jewish Encyclopedia, edited by Isidore Singer. New York: Funk and Wagnalls, 1901–1906.

Judson, Pieter M., and Marsha L. Rozenblit. *Constructing Nationalities in East Central Europe.* Oxford: Berghahn, 2005.

Juhasz, Esther. *Sephardi Jews in the Ottoman Empire: Aspects of Material Culture.* Jerusalem: Israel Museum, 1990.

Karakışla, Yavuz Seilm. "The 1908 Strike Wave in the Ottoman Empire." *Turkish Studies Association Bulletin,* 16 (1992): 153–177.

Karal, Enver Ziya. "Non-Muslim Representatives in the First Constitutional Assembly, 1876–1877." In Braude and Lewis, *Christians and Jews in the Ottoman Empire,* 1: 387–400.

Karal, Enver Ziya. *Osmanlı Tarihi,* vol. 5 *Nizam-ı Cedit ve Tanzimat Devirleri.* Ankara: Türk Tarih Kurumu Basımevi, 1947.

Karal, Enver Ziya. *Osmanlı Tarihi,* vol. 8. *Birinci Meşrutiyet ve İstibdat Devirleri (1876–1907).* Ankara: Türk Tarih Kurumu, 1988.

Karateke, Haken T. *Padişahım Çok Yaşa! Osmanlı Devletinin Son Yüz Yılında Merasimler.* Istanbul: Kitap Yayınevi, 2004.

Karmi, Ilan. *The Jewish Community of Istanbul in the Nineteenth Century: Social, Legal, and Administrative Transformations.* Istanbul: Isis, 1996.

Karpat, Kemal H. *Ottoman Population, 1830–1914.* Madison: University of Wisconsin Press, 1985.

Karpat, Kemal H. *The Politicization of Islam: Reconstructing Identity, State, Faith and Community in the Late Ottoman State.* New York: Oxford University Press, 2001.

Karpat, Kemal H. *Studies on Ottoman Social and Political History Selected Articles and Essays.* Leiden: Brill, 2002.

Kayalı, Hasan. *Arabs and Young Turks: Ottomanism, Arabism and Islamism in the Ottoman Empire, 1908–1918.* Berkeley: University of California Press, 1997.

Kayalı, Hasan. "Jewish Representation in the Ottoman Parliaments." In Levy, *The Jews of the Ottoman Empire,* 507–517.

Kaynar, Resat. *Mustafa Reşit Paşa ve Tanzimat.* Ankara: Türk Tarif Kurumu Basimevi, 1954.

Kechriotis, Vangelis. "The Greeks of Izmir at the End of the Empire: A Non-Muslim Ottoman Community Between Autonomy and Patriotism." Ph.D. diss., University of Leiden, 2005.

Kechriotis, Vangelis. "Civilisation and Order: Middle-Class Morality Among the Greek-Orthodox in Smyrna/Izmir at the End of the Ottoman Empire." In *Social Transformation and Mass Mobilization in the Balkan and Eastern Mediterranean (1900-1923),* edited by Christos Chatziosif and Andreas Lyberatos, 137–153. Rethymnon: Crete University Press, 2013.

Kedourie, Elie. "Young Turks, Freemasons and Jews," *Middle Eastern Studies* 7 (January 1971).

Kelley, Peter. "A Family's Lost Story Found, and the Sephardic Studies Initiative," http://www.washington.edu/news/2013/01/16/a-familys-lost-story-found-and-the-sephardic-studies-initiative, accessed January 27, 2013.

Kırlı, Cengiz. "Coffeehouses: Public Opinion in the Nineteenth-Century Ottoman Empire." In *Public Islam and the Common Good,* edited by Armando Salvatore and Dale E.Eickelman, 75–98. Leiden: Brill, 2004.

Kirshenblatt-Gimblett, Barbara. "A Place in the World: Jews and the Holy Land at World's Fairs," in *Encounters with the 'Holy Land': Place, Past and Future in American Jewish Culture,* edited by Jeffrey Shandler and Beth S.Wenger, 60–82. Hanover, NH: University Press of New England, 1997.

Kirshenblatt-Gimblett, Barbara. *Destination Culture: Tourism, Museums, and Heritage.* Berkeley: University of California Press, 1998.

Kodaman, Bayram. *1897 Türk-Yunan Savaşı.* Ankara: Türk Tarih Kurumu Basımevi, 1993.

Konuk, Kader. "Eternal Guests, Mimics, and Dönme: The Place of German and Turkish Jews in Modern Turkey." *New Perspectives on Turkey* 37 (2007): 5–30.

Kramer, Martin, ed. *The Jewish Discovery of Islam: Studies in Honor of Bernard Lewis.* Tel Aviv: Moshe Dayan Center for Middle Eastern and African Studies, Tel Aviv University, 1999.

Lagos, Katerina. "The Metaxas Dictatorship and Greek Jewry, 1936–1941." Ph.D. diss., Oxford University, 2005.

Landau, Jacob. *Jews, Arabs, Turks: Selected Essays.* Jerusalem: Magnes Press, 1993.

Leal, Karen. "The Balat District of Istanbul: Multiethnicity on the Golden Horn." In *The Architecture and Memory of the Minority Quarter in the Muslim Mediterranean City*, edited by Susan G. Miller and Mauro Bertagnin. Cambridge, MA: Harvard University Press, 2010.

Lehmann, Matthias. *Ladino Rabbinic Literature and Ottoman Sephardic Culture.* Bloomington: Indiana University Press, 2005.

Levi, Avner. "*Shavat Aniim*: Social Cleavage, Class War and Leadership in the Sephardi Community—The Case of Izmir 1847." In Rodrigue, *Ottoman and Turkish Jewry*, 183–202.

Levy, Avigdor. *The Sephardim in the Ottoman Empire.* Princeton, NJ: Darwin Press, 1992.

Levy, Avigdor. "*Millet* Politics: The Appointment of a Chief Rabbi in 1835." In Levy, *The Jews of the Ottoman Empire*, 425–38. Princeton, NJ: Darwin Press, 1994.

Levy, Avigdor, ed. *The Jews of the Ottoman Empire.* Princeton, NJ, and Washington, DC: Darwin Press and Institute of Turkish Studies, 1994.

Levy, Avigdor, ed. *Jews, Turks, Ottomans: A Shared History, Fifteenth through the Twentieth Century.* Syracuse, NY: Syracuse University Press, 2002.

Levy, Lital. "Partitioned Pasts: Arab Jewish Intellectuals and the Case of Esther Azhari Moyal (1873–1948)." In *The Making of the Arab Intellectual: Empire, Public Sphere and the Colonial Coordinates of Selfhood*, edited by Dyala Hamzah, 128–163. New York: Routledge, 2012.

Lévy, Noémi. "Salonique et la Guerre Gréco-Turque de 1897: Le fragile équilibre d'une ville Ottomane." Mémoire de maîtrise, Université Paris I, 2002.

Lévy-Aksu, Noémi. *Ordre et désordres dans l'Istanbul ottomane (1879–1909): De l'État au quartier.* Paris: Karthala, 2012.

Lévy, Sam. *Salonique à la fin du XIXe siècle: Mémoires.* Istanbul: Isis, 2000.

Lewis, Bernard. "The Ottoman Empire in the Mid-Nineteenth Century: A Review." *Middle Eastern Studies* 1, no. 3 (April 1965): 283–295.

Lewis, Bernard. *The Muslim Discovery of Europe.* New York: Norton, 1982.

Lewis, Bernard. *The Emergence of Modern Turkey.* New York: Oxford University Press, 2001.

Litvak, Olga. *Conscription and the Search for Modern Russian Jewry.* Bloomington: Indiana University Press, 2006

Loewenthal, Robyn. "Censorship and Judeo-Spanish Popular Literature in the Ottoman Empire." In *Studies on Turkish-Jewish History*, edited by David F. Altabé, Erhan Atay, Israel J. Katz, 181–191. New York: Sepher-Hermon Press, 1996.

Makdisi, Ussama. "Corrupting the Sublime Sultanate: The Revolt of Tanyus Shahin in Nineteenth-Century Ottoman Lebanon." *Comparative Studies in Society and History* 42, no. 1 (January 2000): 180–208.

Makdisi, Ussama. "After 1860: Debating Religion, Reform, and Nationalism in the Ottoman Empire." *International Journal of Middle East Studies* 34:4 (November 2002): 601–617.

Makdisi, Ussama. "Ottoman Orientalism." *American Historical Review* 107, no. 3 (June 2002): 768–796.

Maksudyan, Nazan. "'Being Saved to Serve': Armenian Orphans of 1894–1896 and Interested Relief in Missionary Orphanages." *Turcica* , 42 (2010): 47–88.

Mallet, Laurent-Olivier. *La Turquie, les turcs et les juifs: Histoire, représentations, discours et stratégies.* Istanbul: Isis, 2008.

Mandel, Neville J. "Ottoman Policy and Restrictions on Jewish Settlement in Palestine: 1881–1908—Part 1." *Middle Eastern Studies* 10, no. 3 (October 1974): 312–332.

Mandel, Neville J. "Ottoman Policy as Regards Jewish Settlement in Palestine: 1881–1908." *Middle Eastern Studies* 11, no. 1 (January 1975): 33–46.

Mann, Vivian B. *A Tale of Two Cities: Jewish Life in Frankfurt and Istanbul 1750–1870.* New York: The Jewish Museum, 1982.

Mardin, Şerif. *The Genesis of Young Ottoman Thought.* Princeton, NJ: Princeton University Press, 1962.

Marvel, Elizabeth Paulson E. "Ottoman Feminism and Republican Reform: Fatma Aliye's Nisvan-ı İslam." Master's thesis, Ohio State University, 2011.

Masters, Bruce. *Christians and Jews in the Ottoman Arab World: The Roots of Sectarianism*. Cambridge: Cambridge University Press, 2001.

Mays, Devi. "Transplanting Cosmopolitans: The Migrations of Sephardic Jews to Mexico, 1900–1934." Ph.D. diss., Indiana University, 2013.

Mazower, Mark. *Salonica, City of Ghosts: Christians, Muslims and Jews, 1430–1950*. New York: Vintage, 2006.

Megas, Yannis. *Souvenir: Images of the Jewish Community: Salonica 1897–1917*. Athens: Kapon editions, 1993.

Methodieva, Milena. "The Debate on Parliamentarism in the Muslim Press of Bulgaria, 1895–1908." In *The First Ottoman Experiment in Democracy*, edited by Christoph Herzog and Malek Sharif. Würzburg: Ergon, 2010.

Mitchell, Timothy. *Colonising Egypt*. Cambridge: Cambridge University Press, 1988.

Mitchell, Timothy. "The World as Exhibition." *Comparative Studies in Society and History* 31, no. 2 (April 1989): 217–36.

Molho, Rena. "Jewish Working Class Neighborhoods Established in Salonica following the 1890 and 1917 Fires." In Rozen, *Last Ottoman Century*, 2 (2002): 173–94.

Molho, Rena. *Salonica and Istanbul: Social, Political and Cultural Aspects of Jewish Life*. Istanbul: Isis, 2005.

Molho, Rena. "The Zionist Movement in Thessaloniki, 1899–1919." In Hassiotis, *The Jewish Communities of Southeastern Europe*, 327–350.

Naar, Devin. "From the 'Jerusalem of the Balkans' to the *Goldene Medina*: Jewish Immigration from Salonika to the United States." *American Jewish History* 93, no. 4 (2007): 435–473.

Naar, Devin. "Reformuler l'identité, réinventer la patrie: Juifs judéo-hispanophones en Amérique, entre Salonique et *Sefarad*." In *Itinéraires sépharades: Complexité et diversité des identities*, 63–78, edited by Esther Benbassa. Paris: Presse de l'Université Paris-Sorbonne, 2010.

Naar, Devin. "Jewish Salonica and the Making of the 'Jerusalem of the Balkans,' 1890–1943." Ph.D. diss., Stanford University, 2011.

Nahum, Henri. *Juifs de Smyrne, XIXe – XXe siècle*. Paris: Aubier, 1997.

Navon, Albert. *Abraham Danon, 1857–1925*. Paris: Impr. H. Elias, 1925.

Nehama, Joseph. *Histoire des Israélites de Salonique*. Salonica: Librairie Molho, 1935.

Nehama, Joseph. "The Jews of Salonika in the Ottoman Period." In *The Sephardi Heritage: Essays on the Historical and Cultural Contribution of the Jews of Spain and Portugal*, 203–242, edited by Richard D. Barnett. Grendon: Gibralter Books, 1989.

Neumann, Christoph. "Bad Times and Better Self: Definitions of Identity and Stategies for Development in Late Ottoman Historiography (1850–1900)." In *The Ottomans and the Balkans: A Discussion of Historiography*, edited by Fikret Adanir and Suraiya Faroqhi, 57–78. Leiden: Brill, 2002.

Nirenberg, David. *Communities of Violence*. Princeton, NJ: Princeton University Press, 1998.

Niyego, Anri. *Haydarpaşa'da Geçen 100 Yılımız*. Istanbul: Gözlem Gazetecilik Basın ve Yayın, 1999.

Öke, Mim Kemâl. "The Ottoman Empire, Zionism, and the Question of Palestine (1880–1908)," *International Journal of Middle East Studies*. 14, no. 3 (August 1982): 329–341.

Öke, Mım Kemâl. "Young Turks, Freemasons, Jews and the Question of Zionism in the Ottoman Empire (1908–1913)." *Studies in Zionism* 7, no. 2 (1986): 119–218.

Önsoy, Rıfat. "Osmanlı İmparatorluğu'nun katıldığı ilk Uluslararası Sergiler ve Sergi-i Umumi-i Osmani." *Belleten* 47 (1983): 195–235.

Ortaylı, İlber. "Ottomanism and Zionism During the Second Constitutional Period, 1908–1915." In *The Jews of the Ottoman Empire*, edited by Avigdor Levy, 527–537. Princeton, NJ: Darwin Press, 1994.

Ortaylı, İlber. *Ottoman Studies*. Istanbul: Bilgi University Press, 2004.

Oscanyan, Christopher. *The Sultan and His People*. New York: Derby and Jackson, 1857.

Özbek, Nadir. "The Politics of Poor Relief in the Late Ottoman Empire, 1876–1914." *New Perspectives on Turkey* 21 (Fall 1999): 1–33.

Özbek, Nadir. *Osmanlı İmparatorluğu'nda Sosyal Devlet: Siyaset, İktidar ve Meşrutiyet, 1876–1914*. Istanbul: İletişim, 2002.

Özbek, Nadir. "Philanthropic Activity, Ottoman Patriotism and the Hamidian Regime, 1876–1909." *International Journal of Middle East Studies* 37 (2005): 59–81.

Papamichos Chronakis, Paris. "Middle-Class Sociability as Ethnic Hegemony: Jewish and Greek Merchants from the Ottoman Empire to the Greek Nation-State, 1880–1922." Paper presented at the workshop "Crossing Borders: New Approaches to Modern Judeo-Spanish (Sephardic) Cultures," UCLA, April 2011.

Papamichos Chronakis, Paris. "Class and Ethnic Conflict among the Merchants of Young Turk Salonica, 1908–1912." Paper presented at the workshop "Ottomans/Turks in Conflict, 1800–2010: New Approaches," Columbia University, April 2011.

Papo, M. "The Sephardi Community of Vienna." In *The Jews of Austria: Essays on their Life, History and Destruction*, edited by Josef Fraenkel, 327–46. London: Vallentine Mitchell, 1967.

Papo, Joseph M. *Sephardim in Twentieth Century America: In Search of Unity*. San Jose, CA: Pelé Yoetz Books, 1987.

Petrov, Milen V. "Everyday Forms of Compliance: Subaltern Commentaries on Ottoman Reform, 1864–1868." *Comparative Studies in Society and History* 46, no. 4 (2004): 730–759.

Philliou, Christine. *Biography of an Empire: Governing Ottomans in an Age of Revolution*. Berkeley: University of California Press, 2010.

Polat, Emre. *Osmanlı'nın İlk Yahudi Sosyalisti Avram Benaroya ve Faaliyetleri*. Istanbul: Truva Yayınları, 2004.

Prashad, Vijay. *The Karma of Brown Folks*. Minneapolis: University of Minnesota Press, 2001.

Quataert, Donald. "The Age of Reforms." In *An Economic and Social History of the Ottoman Empire*, edited by Suraiya Faroqhi, Bruce McGowan, Donald Quataert and Şevket Pamuk, 749–943. New York: Cambridge University Press, 1994.

Quataert, Donald. "Clothing Laws, State, and Society in the Ottoman Empire, 1720–1829." *International Journal of Middle East Studies* 29, no. 3 (August 1997): 403–425.

Quataert, Donald. *The Ottoman Empire, 1700–1922*. Cambridge, UK: Cambridge University Press, 2001.

The Quincentennial Foundation Gala Celebration: April 27, 1992, the Plaza Hotel, New York City. Istanbul: Quincentennial Foundation of Istanbul, 1992.

The Quincentennial Foundation: A Retrospection. [Istanbul]: The Foundation, 1997.

Recanati, David, ed. *Zikhron Saloniki: Gedulatah ve-Hurbanah shel Yerushalayim de-Balkan*, vol. 1. Tel Aviv: Committee for the Publication of Books on the Salonica Community, 1972.

Rodrigue, Aron. "Abraham de Camondo of Istanbul: The Transformation of Jewish Philanthropy." In *From East and West: Jews in a Changing Europe 1750–1870*, edited by Frances Malino and David Sorkin, 46–56. Oxford: Blackwell Publishers, 1990.

Rodrigue, Aron. *French Jews, Turkish Jews: The Alliance Israélite Universelle and the Politics of Jewish Schooling in Turkey, 1860–1925*. Bloomington: Indiana University Press, 1990.

Rodrigue, Aron, ed. *Ottoman and Turkish Jewry: Community and Leadership*. Bloomington: Indiana University, 1992.

Rodrigue, Aron. "Difference and Tolerance in the Ottoman Empire." Interview by Nancy Reynolds. *Stanford Humanities Review* 5 (Fall 1995): 81–92.

Rodrigue, Aron. "From Millet to Minority: Turkish Jewry." In *Paths of Emancipation: Jews, States, and Citizenship*, edited by Pierre Birnbaum and Ira Katznelson, 238–261. Princeton, NJ: Princeton University Press, 1995.

Rodrigue, Aron. *Jews and Muslims: Images of Sephardi and Eastern Jewries in Modern Times*. Seattle: University of Washington Press, 2003.

Rodrigue, Aron, and Sarah Abrevaya Stein, eds. *A Jewish Voice from Ottoman Salonica: The Ladino Memoir of Sa'adi Besalel a-Levi*. Trans. by Isaac Jerusalmi. Stanford, CA: Stanford University Press, 2012.

Rodrigue, Aron. "Reflections on Millets and Minorities: Ottoman Legacies." In *Turkey Between Nationalism and Globalization*, edited by Riva Kastoryano, 36–46. New York: Routledge, 2013.

Rosanes, Solomon A. *Korot ha-Yehudim be-Turkiyah ve-artsot ha-kedem*. Jerusalem: Rabbi Kook Institute, 1945.

Rothberg, Michael. *Multidirectional Memory: Remembering the Holocaust in the Age of Decolonization*. Stanford, CA: Stanford University Press, 2009.

Rozen, Minna, ed. *The Last Ottoman Century and Beyond: The Jews in Turkey and the Balkans, 1808–1945: Proceedings of the International Conference on "The Jewish Communities in the Balkans and Turkey in the 19th and 20th Centuries through the End of World War II," the Goldstein-Goren Diaspora Research Center, Tel Aviv University, June 5–8, 1995*, vol. 2. Ramat Aviv: Tel Aviv University, 2002.

Rozen, Minna. "The Hamidian Era through the Jewish Looking Glass: A Study of the Istanbul Rabbinical Court Records." *Turcica* 37 (2005): 113–154.

Rozen, Minna. *The Last Ottoman Century and Beyond: The Jews in Turkey and the Balkans, 1808–1945*, vol. 1. Ramat Aviv: Tel Aviv University, 2005.

Rydell, Robert. *All the World's a Fair: Visions of Empire at American International Expositions, 1876–1916*. Chicago: University of Chicago Press, 1984.

Rydell, Robert. *World of Fairs: The Century-of-Progress Expositions*. Chicago: University of Chicago Press, 1993.

Salzmann, Ariel. "Citizens in Search of a State: The Limits of Political Participation in the Late Ottoman Empire, 1808–1913." In Hanagan and Tilly, *Extending Citizenship, Reconfiguring States*, 37–66.

Saperstein, Marc. *Jewish Preaching in Times of War, 1800–2001*. Oxford: The Littman Library of Jewish Civilization, 2008.

Seni, Nora. "The Camondos and their Imprint on 19th-Century Istanbul." *International Journal of Middle East Studies* 26, no. 4 (1994): 663–675.

Şeni, Nora, and Sophie Le Tarnec. *Les Camondo ou l'éclipse d'une fortune*. Paris: Actes Sud, 1997.

Serin, Nadide Özge. "Festivals of 'July 10' in the Young Turk Era (1908–1918)." Master's thesis, Boğaziçi University, 2000.

Scholem, Gershom. *Sabbatai Sevi: The Mystical Messiah*. Princeton, NJ: Princeton University Press, 1973.

Schorsch, Ismar. "The Myth of Sephardi Supremacy." *Leo Baeck Institute Year Book* 34 (1989): 47–66.

Schorsch, Ismar. *From Text to Context: The Turn to History in Modern Judaism*. Hanover, NH: University Press of New England, 1994.

Scott, James C. *Domination and the Arts of Resistance: Hidden Transcripts*. New Haven, CT: Yale University Press, 1992.

Sevinç, Gülsen and Ayşe Fazlioğlu. "1893 Şikago Sergisi'nde Osmanlılar," *Toplumsal Tarih* 92, no. 6 (August 2001): 6–9.

Shaw, Stanford. *The Jews of the Ottoman Empire and the Turkish Republic*. New York: New York University Press, 1991.

Shaw, Wendy K. *Possessors and Possessed: Museums, Archaeology and the Visualization of History in the Late Ottoman Empire*. Berkeley: University of California Press, 2003.

Silber, Michael K. "From Tolerated Aliens to Citizen-Soldiers: Jewish Military Service in the Era of Joseph II." In *Constructing Nationalities in East Central Europe*, edited by Pieter M. Judson and Marsha L. Rozenblit, 19–36. Oxford: Berghahn, 2005.

Silberman, Marc. *A Curriculum on Five Hundred Years of Turkish Jewish Experience*. Sponsored by the Quincentennial Foundation of Istanbul, 1993.

Sluglett, Peter, and Hakan M. Yavuz, eds., *War and Diplomacy: The Russo-Turkish War of 1877–1878 and the Treaty of Berlin*. Salt Lake City: University of Utah Press, 2011.

Sohrabi, Nader. *Revolution and Constitutionalism in the Ottoman Empire and Iran*. Cambridge: Cambridge University Press, 2011.

Somel, Selçuk Akşin. *The Modernization of Public Education in the Ottoman Empire, 1839–1908: Islamization, Autocracy and Discipline*. Leiden: Brill, 2001.

Stanislawski, Michael. *Psalms for the Tsar: A Minute-Book of a Psalms-Society in the Russian Army, 1864–1867*. New York: Ktav Publishers, 1988.

Starr, Joshua. "The Socialist Federation of Saloniki." *Jewish Social Studies* 7 (1945): 323–336.

Stein, Sarah Abrevaya. *Making Jews Modern: The Yiddish and Ladino Press in the Russian and Ottoman Empires*. Bloomington: Indiana University Press, 2004.

Stephanov, Darin. "Minorities, Majorities, and the Monarch: Nationalizing Effects of the Late Ottoman Royal Public Ceremonies, 1808-1908." Ph.D. diss., University of Memphis, 2012.

Stillman, Norman, ed. *The Encyclopedia of Jews in the Islamic World*. Leiden: Brill, 2010

Stillman, Norman, ed. *The Jews of Arab Lands*. Philadelphia: Jewish Publication Society of America, 1979.

Stillman, Norman, ed. *Sephardi Religious Responses to Modernity*. Luxembourg: Harwood Academic Publishers, 1995.

Stillman, Norman, ed. *The Jews of Arab Lands in Modern Times*. Philadelphia: Jewish Publication Society of America, 2003.

Suny, Ronald Grigor. *Looking Towards Ararat: Armenia in Modern History*. Bloomington: Indiana University Press, 1993.

Suny, Ronald Grigor, ed. Special issue on the Hamidian massacres, *Armenian Review* 47, no. 1-2 (Summer 2002).

Tatsios, T. G. *The Megali Idea and the Greek-Turkish War of 1897: The Impact of the Cretan Problem on Greek Irredentism 1866–1897*. New York: Columbia University Press, 1984.

Thompson, Elizabeth. *Colonial Citizens: Republican Rights, Paternal Privilege, and Gender in French Syria and Lebanon*. New York: Columbia University Press, 2000.

Tuğlacl, Pars. *Dadyan Ailesi'nin Osmanlı Toplum, Ekonomi ve Siyaset Hayatındaki Rolu*. Istanbul: Pars Yayın, 1993. [Partly bilingual English-Turkish text; documents are in Turkish].

Turan, Serafettin. *Türk Kültür Tarihi*. Ankara: Bilgi Yayınevi, 1990.

Turkish Jews: 500 Years of Harmony: Celebrating the 500th Anniversary of the Welcoming of the Jewish People to the Ottoman Empire in 1492. Berkeley, CA: Judah L. Magnes Museum, 1991.

Tütüncü, Mehmet, ed. *Turkish-Jewish Encounters: Studies on Turkish-Jewish Relations through the Ages/Türk-Yahudi Buluşmaları: Tarihte Türk-Yahudi İlişkileri Araştırmaları*. Haarlem, Netherlands: SOTA, 2001.

Tziovas, Dimitris, ed. *Greece and the Balkans: Identities, Perceptions and Cultural Encounters since the Enlightenment*. Aldershot: Ashgate, 2003.

Ueno, Masayuki. "'For the Fatherland and the State': Armenians Negotiate the Tanzimat Reforms." *International Journal of Middle East Studies* 45 (2013): 93–109.

Veinstein, Gilles, ed. *Salonique 1850–1918: La 'ville des Juifs' et le réveil des Balkans*. Paris: Autrement, 1993.

Watenpaugh, Keith David. *Being Modern in the Middle East: Revolution, Nationalism, Colonialism, and the Arab Middle Class*. Princeton, NJ: Princeton University Press, 2006.

Wayne, John J. "Constantinople to Chicago: In the Footsteps of Far-Away Moses." *Library of Congress Information Bulletin* 3 (January 13, 1992): 14–16; 18–21.

Weiker, Walter F. *Ottomans, Turks, and the Jewish Polity*. Lanham, MD: University Press of America, 1992.

Yerushalmi, Yosef Hayim. *The Lisbon Massacre of 1506 and the Royal Image in the Shebet Yehudah*. Cincinnati, OH: Hebrew Union College, 1976.

Yerushalmi, Yosef Hayim. "'Servants of Kings and Not Servants of Servants': Some Aspects of the Political History of the Jews." Tenenbaum Family Lecture Series in Judaic Studies delivered at Emory University, February 8, 2005. Atlanta: The Tam Institute for Jewish Studies, n.d.

Yerushalmi, Yosef Hayim. "'Serviteurs des rois et non serviteurs des serviteurs.' Sur quelques aspects de l'histoire politique des Juifs." *Raisons politiques* 7 (2002): 19–52.

Yosmaoğlu, İpek K. "Chasing the Written Word: Press Censorship in the Ottoman Empire, 1876–1913." *The Turkish Studies Association Journal* 27, no. 1–2 (2003): 15–49.

Zandi-Sayek, Sibel. "Orchestrating Difference, Performing Identity: Urban Space and Public Rituals in Nineteenth-Century Izmir." In *Hybrid Urbanism*, edited by N. AlSayyad, 42–66. New York: Praeger, 2001.

Zipperstein, Steven. *Imagining Russian Jewry: Memory, History, Identity*. Seattle: University of Washington Press, 1999.

Zürcher, Erik-Jan. "The Ottoman Conscription System in Theory and Practice, 1844–1918." In *Arming the State: Military Conscription in the Middle East and Central Asia, 1775–1925*, edited by Erik-Jan Zürcher, 79–94. New York: St. Martin's Press, 1999.

Zürcher, Erik-Jan. "Kosovo Revisited: Sultan Reşad's Macedonian Journey of 1911." *Middle Eastern Studies* 35, no. 4 (October 1999): 26–39.

INDEX

Note: Page numbers in italics indicate figures.

Abdülaziz, 27, 28
Abdülhamid II, 17, 19, 27–28, 39, 84, 101, 105, 106,
 123, 128, 139, 159n.15, 162n.38, 165n.90
 1892 centenary celebrations and, 49, 52, 57,
  60–62, 71–72
 restrictions of Jewish immigration to
  Palestine, 106
 as spiritual leader (caliph), 78–79
 discourse of Islamic morality, 94, 96, 178n141
 Islamic politics of, 78–79, 98, 100, 101–2
Abdülmecid, xii, 9, 11–12, 13
Aboab, 75
Abraham, Isaac, 83
"Action Army," 105, 129–30
Adjiman, 7
advertisements, 135, 136–37, *136, 137*
Ahenk, 141
Ahrida Synagogue, 34–35, *35*
Akropolis, 90, 177n127
Aksakal, Mustafa, 101
Albania, 108, 120
Albanians, 82, 87, 120, 175n102
Aleppo, 37
Alexandria, 53, 162n50
Alkalai, Yehudah, 12
Allatini brothers, 115, *116*
Allatini Company, 77, 115, *116*, 119
allegiance. *See* loyalty
Allgemeine Zeitung des Judenthums, 40
Alliance Israélite Universelle, 26, 37, 74, 79, 82,
 84, 92, 94, 97, 110, 152n16, 173n75
 integrationist platform of, 103–4
 schools of, 10–11, 25, 86, 167n123, 175n92
Amalek, 39–40, 156n93, 157n95
La Amerika, 134–35, 136–37, *136, 137*
El Amigo del Puevlo, 76

anarchists, 74, 120, 121
Anglo-Jewish Association, *58*
Ankara, 80
Antalya, 6
anti-colonialism, 139
antisemitism, 54, 76, 106, 126, 163n58
anti-Westernist discourse, 139
anti-Zionism, 15, 103–4, 106–7, 110, 111, 115,
 125, 130, 186n104
Antwerp, 135
Arabic language, 2, 37, 82, 114–15, 130, 134,
 139, 185n69
arches, 109, 115–19, *116, 117, 118*, 120, 122
 of the Club des Intimes, 112–13, *112*, 184n57
 of the Allatini Mill Company, 115, *116*
 of the Jewish community of Salonica, 115–17,
  117
 of the Nouveau Club, 117–19, *118*, 139
Argentina, 135
Arié, Gabriel, 173n75
Armenia, 133
Armenians, 6–7, 10, 15–16, 21, 24–25, 30, 62,
 63, 64, 71–72, 79, 101, 133, 143n3, 152n20
 Armenian-Jewish relations, 74–78
 loyalty of, 132
 massacres of, 16, 74–77, 92, 99, 100–101,
  168n4, 168n7, 169n22, 169n26
Armenian genocide, 133
Armenian Patriarch, 76, 77
Armenian Revolutionary Federation (Hai
 Heghapokhakan Dashnaktsutiun), 75
arms manufacturing, 43, 158n120
Artin, Kazaz, 6
Ashkenazi, Behor Efendi, 28
Ashkenazi Jews, 104, 161n32, 180n12, 189n22
Asır, 87

Made in the USA
Monee, IL
23 February 2020

22218158R00146